WHY THE
BEST-LAID INVESTMENT PLANS
USUALLY GO WRONG

OTHER BOOKS BY HARRY BROWNE:

How You Can Profit from the Coming Devaluation (1970)
How I Found Freedom in an Unfree World (1973)
You Can Profit from a Monetary Crisis (1974)
The Complete Guide to Swiss Banks (1976)
New Profits from the Monetary Crisis (1978)
Inflation-Proofing Your Investments (with Terry Coxon, 1981)
Investment Rule #1 (published privately, 1985)

WHY THE BEST-LAID INVESTMENT PLANS USUALLY GO WRONG

&
HOW YOU CAN FIND SAFETY & PROFIT IN AN UNCERTAIN WORLD

Harry Browne

WILLIAM MORROW AND COMPANY, INC.
New York

Library of Congress Cataloging-in-Publication Data

Browne, Harry, 1933–
   Why the best-laid investment plans usually go wrong: & how you
can find safety & profit in an uncertain world / Harry Browne.
      p. cm.
   Includes index.
   ISBN 0-688-05995-3
   1. Finance, Personal.   2. Investments.   I. Title.
HG179.B748   1987
332.024—dc19   87-16593
                                                             CIP

Printed in the United States of America

First Edition

1 2 3 4 5 6 7 8 9 10

BOOK DESIGN BY RICHARD ORIOLO

TO
PLW Browne

CONTENTS

Part III—Investment Vehicles

Part IV—Making Investment Decisions

Epilogue

Appendices

Index

WHY THE
BEST-LAID INVESTMENT PLANS
USUALLY GO WRONG

Prologue

1

The Best-Kept Secret
in the
Investment World

The best-kept secret in the investment world is this:

Almost nothing turns out as expected.

Forecasts rarely come true, trading systems never produce the results advertised for them, investment advisors with records of phenomenal success fail to deliver when your money is on the line, the best investment analysis is contradicted by reality.

In short, the best-laid investment plans usually go wrong. Not sometimes, not occasionally—but *usually*.

A few investors take this for granted. They know that the world is full of surprises.

But most investors never discover the secret; it isn't what they're hoping to find. They're searching for certainty and reliability—a system, or an advisor, or a market indicator they can count on to tell them what to do. And any disappointment merely intensifies the desire to find a way to remove uncertainty from investing.

The experience of almost every investor includes example after example of one thing after another that didn't turn out as planned. But investors continue to hope that success and certainty are just around the corner.

There's no way for me to know what *your* experience has been. But a basic pattern could describe the careers of many, if not most, investors. So let me tell you the story of a typical investor. And let's make it *your* story, because some of the experiences may remind you of things that have happened to you.

The story begins as you first become interested in investing. Your interest is aroused by someone you know who seems to do very well with his money. While he doesn't dwell on the subject, from time to time he refers to investments in which he's made a profit. And he never mentions any losses.

When you ask him about it, he tells you that he invests in stocks or commodities or gold or currencies—whatever's hot. "I have a system that's never failed me," he explains.

From then on, he becomes a little more talkative, telling you here and there of his investment successes—a stock he just sold at a 60% profit, a big gain selling pork bellies short, or a windfall from a currency devaluation.

He always speaks knowledgeably, and he must be telling the truth. How else could he live so well with the type of job he has?

Finally, you can stand it no longer, and you summon the nerve to ask him to let you invest with him when he buys and sells. He agrees, and you begin dreaming of how rich you will be in a year.

Investing with a Champ

Your first trade shows a small profit, but not as much as you had expected. The second one pays off big—an option purchase that doubles your investment in three weeks. Now you're dreaming of how rich you'll be in just six months.

But the third trade is a disaster, and the fourth isn't much better. Your dream has been postponed indefinitely.

When you ask the investment genius what's wrong, he says it's just a brief slump—such things happen from time to time. But the slump continues, and finally you have to throw in the towel before your savings are wiped out.

He goes on with his investments, and somehow he still lives as well as he ever did.[1]

---

[1] A year later you find out about his rich aunt.

On Your Own

Despite your losses, you've tasted success. You know it's possible to make big profits—it just isn't easy.

So you start investing more methodically. You subscribe to investment newsletters, read brokerage reports, and watch the financial programs on television. Pretty soon, you're thinking about investments all the time—even when you should be thinking about something else.

Investing on your own, you do better than you did with your friend, but you know you have a lot to learn. So you're receptive when the mail brings a brochure advertising an investment seminar.

One speaker at the seminar explains how to identify major turning points in the markets. He tells how he made big money in precious metals in the 1970s, getting out at the top in 1980—and how he switched his customers into stocks in August 1982, on the first day of the big bull market. His track record is, as they say, incredible.

He promises that another once-in-a-lifetime opportunity is coming along soon—something as wonderful as buying gold in 1976 or stocks in 1982. So you ante up $295 to subscribe to his newsletter, and you start acting on his advice. Now you'll be working with a professional —someone who has a proven, documented track record.

He tells you to buy a little of this and a little of that. Some of the investments you don't understand, but you make them anyway because you don't want to miss out on anything. Many of the advisor's trades work nicely—well enough to offset the losers, and well enough to sustain your confidence in him.

Then comes the big day. He says, "This is it: the once-in-a-lifetime opportunity! This is our last chance to buy at today's historic low price—like buying gold at $35 or stocks when the Dow was 800. Commit everything you have—and do it now!"

This is what you've been waiting for. You sell every investment you own, borrow money from the bank, and buy in before it's too late. But the price goes down—not up.

He says, "Wonderful! Just what I'd hoped for—an opportunity to buy more at bargain prices!"

Buy more? With what? You've already invested everything and then some.

The price continues downward. The bank wants its money. You sell the investment, pay off the loan, and wonder what to do with the little that's left.

You know you're not the most sophisticated investor in the world;

perhaps you've misunderstood the advisor's instructions. He must know what he's doing; every issue of his newsletter talks about the profits his readers are making. Maybe he's just too advanced for you. So you look elsewhere.

To become more astute, you read a book on investing by an author who's billed as a "modern J. Paul Getty." Then you read another investment book and another and another. Finally you read one that explains that most investors lose money because they invest without a system—jumping from one investment to another without a careful plan for buying and selling.

Of course! *That's* been your problem.

So you start using a system that has worked for 23 years in a row, and has produced an average annual profit of 26%. You couldn't possibly go wrong with a system like that.

But you do. Somehow it suffers its first losing year—just as you begin using it.

Hooked

Still you persist. Millions of dollars are made in the markets every day, and you only want a few of them. You're sure there's an answer out there, if you only can find it.

You try buying new stock issues and then penny stocks—following insider trading statistics and the activities of stock-exchange specialists—playing the "TED" spread and the gold-silver ratio—using confirmed indicators, telephone switch systems, and contrary opinion.

You're very selective, of course—employing only systems with documented track records going back several years, and acting only on advice that's plausible and backed up with research. Sometimes these things actually show a profit—just often enough to keep you going, but not often enough to make real money for you.

Then you come across an advisor who seems to have the answers. Not only does he have an excellent track record, he's down-to-earth and realistic. He explains how much of each thing to buy, what to sell in order to buy something else, how and where to execute each trade. Everything is planned down to the last detail.

For the first time, your investments are being handled carefully and thoughtfully.

They just aren't showing a profit.

Enough!

Finally you decide that track records, research, and indicators are mostly shams. There's no point in trying to separate the fraudulent and incompetent advisors from the honest and talented—or in trying to separate the sensible ideas from the foolish.

Besides, you're beginning to suspect that you aren't cut out to be a speculator.

But you have to put your savings somewhere, and you want the money to grow. So it dawns on you that what you need is a good mutual fund—one with proven success. Newsletters and investment advisors might fudge their records, but a mutual fund's record is an open book.

You study the published ratings for mutual funds, and you find a fund that's produced a profit every year since 1975. A $10,000 investment in 1975 would have grown to $87,432.57 by 1987. If only you'd made *that* investment in 1975—instead of spending so much time and money for so little return.

So you put your money into the mutual fund—content to set worry aside and let the fund's experienced, professional management do the thinking for you. Unfortunately, the economy turns weak, the stock market sags, and the fund suffers a setback— its first losing year in over a decade. Then the stock market perks up and the fund comes to life, but it still trails behind most other stock funds.

So you find yourself recalled to active duty as an investor. Now you have to study mutual funds and switch from one to another to make sure your money is always in a "hot hand."

And on and on it goes.

At every step in your odyssey through the investment world, you've been careful to plan meticulously, to listen only to the best forecasters, to work only with proven systems, to employ the best and brightest minds—in short, to use only the best-laid plans.

But still, for some reason, nothing works out as it's supposed to.

THE BEST-LAID PLANS

Welcome to the world of investments—where almost nothing turns out as expected.

Wherever you turn, you find forecasts for the economy, forecasts for interest rates, the stock market, gold, foreign currencies, and com-modities—but rarely does any forecast turn out to have been correct.

Newsletter writers boast of sensational track records, even though only a small minority of their readers choose to renew their subscrip-tions.

Investors and their advisors swear by their latest trading systems—always armed with good reasons that the newest system is better than the predecessors that failed.

Economists and investment advisors appear at seminars and on tel-evision and radio to explain sensibly and convincingly why some event is inevitable. But the event never comes to pass, or it occurs much later than anticipated, or it arrives in a shape so unexpected that the forewarning was useless.

Despite the plausible ideas, the computer-tested systems, the eco-nomic wisdom, the refined techniques, the documented track records, and the common-sense approaches, the simple truth is that practically nothing in the economic or investment world works out as we were assured it would.

It isn't that no one ever makes money on his investments. In fact, some investors do quite well—and fairly consistently—over long periods of time. But even those profits are made, somehow, in spite of events that don't unfold as promised.

Checking for Yourself

If you disagree with me, if you think that events do unfold about as expected, it's easy enough to determine whether I'm right.

Dig out last year's forecast issue of your favorite investment news-letter. Read what the writer said was going to happen last year. Ask yourself how valuable those forecasts were. (Don't use this year's review of last year's forecasts; the retelling may differ considerably from the original.)

Then dig up a few issues of newsletters from two or five years ago. Or go to the library and ask for old copies of *Barron's, The Wall Street Journal, Futures, Business Week, Financial World, Money*—any financial publication. Read how the experts explained the events of the day, and see what they said was coming.

You may be amazed at how naïve yesterday's comments and fore-casts seem today. And you'll probably agree that there was very little money to be made by acting on them—and perhaps a good deal of money to be saved by ignoring them.

You may occasionally come across a gem—a prediction of something that actually came to pass. Very likely, the writer is still advertising that home run today. He doesn't want anyone to forget his uncanny forecast, his shrewd insight, his winning call.

But when you read the gem as it originally appeared, you find that it was hedged and qualified—and that it was buried among dozens of ideas that didn't prove out. You can't help but wonder whether you would have acted on the prediction if you'd encountered it at the time.

Certainties

Sensational predictions rarely make money for investors. But even more dangerous may be the less-sensational certainties of the day— the things we take for granted because everyone knows they're true.

The investment literature of the past tells of so many certainties— ideas that were so clear, so sensible, so obvious that they weren't even controversial. And yet time has proven them false.

In the early 1980s, it was easy to believe that huge federal deficits were about to send interest rates through the roof. Oil prices would soar to new highs again as soon as the economy picked up. Money-supply growth well above the Federal Reserve's own target was provoking an imminent resurgence of inflation. The way to beat inflation was to buy real estate and gold with borrowed money and pay off the loans later with cheaper dollars.

If these ideas seem quaint today—like Nehru jackets or hula hoops—try to remember how widely accepted they were just a few short years ago. Think how many well-laid plans—maybe even some of your own—were founded on them.

It should be humbling to recall these certainties. It should demonstrate to us how little we know about how the markets work—and how little we understand of what's going on in the world at any time.

If you remember the sure things of the past, you might be a little more skeptical of today's certainties—such "truths" as: federal deficits have to keep growing, a worldwide debt crisis is just around the corner, the Federal Reserve won't let any large bank fail, earnings in your IRA will always be tax-exempt.

Understanding the Present & the Past

It's not only the future that's mysterious. Experts rarely agree on what's happening in the present.

Remember the high interest rates of the early 1980s—rates that were abnormally higher than the rate of inflation? At the time, it was obvious to many people that the high rates were caused by the large federal deficits. No, said other people, it was because of the fear that inflation would come back. No, no, said others, it was because the Federal Reserve's monetary policy was too tight. No, no, no, it was because banking deregulation had given the banks the power to charge whatever interest rates they wanted.

Then came the arguments over what caused the 1980s bull market in stocks. It was obvious that the market went up because inflation was finally beaten. Or was it because interest rates declined? Neither; the stock market was just catching up after years of trailing other investments—or it was the Reagan tax cuts—or the flood of cash coming out of money market funds. Or was it all that money going into stock-market IRAs?

If even the present isn't obvious, how can we hope to read the future?

Nor is the past a closed book. Those in the know still argue about the causes of the oil shortage of the 1970s, the soaring silver prices of 1979–1980, the Great Depression, the Spanish-American War, and who killed Cock Robin.

Sharing the Secret

The secret, that things rarely work out as expected, is shared unwittingly by investors, brokers, advisors, newsletter writers, and financial journalists—each of whom has a reason to keep from acknowledging the truth.

Each tries to appear to be in command of the situation, on top of the markets, aware of what's happening and what's going to happen —and to appear as though everything that *has* happened was anticipated.

A professional strikes this pose because he thinks his business requires it. After all, every competitor acts as though he knows everything that matters, forecasts the future with "uncanny" accuracy, and has an "incredible" track record. So each advisor feels pressured to appear to know everything; if he seems unsure of anything, his customers will pass him over for someone who looks better.

An investor has his own reasons for keeping the secret. Most people risk their self-esteem along with their money when they invest. No one wants to appear to be the only loser, and everyone else seems to be doing so well.

And so everyone plays his part in protecting the secret. Forecasts are made and forgotten. Track records are displayed and never examined. Infallible systems lose money but are never questioned out loud. Investment advisors continue to practice what really are superstitions, but no one calls them that. Financial experts keep explaining the present and the future, even though very little of what they said last year would sound reasonable now—if we could even remember it.

Most investors go on expecting the future to evolve in a predictable fashion, positive that there's a reliable system that other people have found. They keep searching for the Holy Grail, but they never find it.

A BETTER WAY

The beginning of investment wisdom is to accept that we live in an uncertain world, that we don't fully understand what makes markets move, that we don't know a great deal about the present—much less about the future.

No one can tell you when the stock market will peak, how far it will fall, or which market group will lead the way back up. Human beings aren't able to predict the future in any reliable way. For every example you can cite of an investment forecast that came true, I can point to five that didn't—some of which may have come from the same forecaster you've cited.

When you give up the hope that some advisor, some system, some source of inside tips is going to give you a shortcut to wealth, you'll finally begin to gain control over your financial future.

When you give up the search for certainty, an enormous burden will be lifted from your shoulders—and then you can begin to invest realistically.

Purpose of the Book

In this book, I hope to show how you can find safety and profit in the uncertain world in which we live—without needing the right forecaster or system, without taking risks you shouldn't be taking, and without having to eat *The Wall Street Journal* for breakfast every morning.

I can't guarantee that you'll make a fortune using the ideas in this book—although that's possible. But I believe I can help you get the fullest return from your talent, your ambition, and your interest in investing.

And it should make your life easier. I think you can best achieve safety and profit by discarding your investment worries—not by accepting new pressures and concerns.

You probably question my assertion that almost nothing turns out as expected. So Part I of this book examines many of the ways in which investors search for the truth about tomorrow, execute the best-laid plans, and then count their losses.

Those ways include:

—looking for the fortune-teller with the perfect record;
—relying on advisors whose motivations conflict with yours;
—trying to find a scientific system that will signal every turn in the market;
—accepting superstitions that come with good credentials;
—wading in over your head trying to use sophisticated tactics;
—getting carried away with fundamental or technical analysis;
—accepting slogans or other one-liners as explanations of complicated economic matters;
—betting money you can't afford to lose; and
—many other ways that interfere with realistic investment planning.

If you're an experienced investor, some of these topics will strike a familiar chord—and I'm hoping that their meanings will be clearer now that we've acknowledged the secret. If you're new to investing, some of the things I'll describe may seem strange or remote—but they're normal practices in the investment world, and you need to be forewarned.

Strategy

The principal cause of investment failure is the lack of a strategy that fits the world as it is—a strategy that accepts your nature, your objectives, and your way of doing things. And so Part II of this book will provide a strategy that accepts the existence of an uncertain world—a strategy you can adapt to fit your own needs and style.

One of the many virtues of a reasonable strategy is that it takes you as you are—without asking you to devote more time, talent, or capital to your investments than you can give them. Another virtue is that it permits you to be as speculative as you want to be—without letting you risk a penny of what's precious. Still another virtue is that it permits you to avoid speculation entirely if you would rather do that.

The size of your capital will dictate some details of your investment program, but it doesn't determine what's realistic and what isn't. However much or little you have to work with, the principles of good investing can help you get the most from what you have.

Part III will discuss the investments available to use in carrying out your strategy—evaluating each to see how it might add safety to your portfolio or provide an opportunity for profit.

Part IV deals with tax implications and special situations, and with finding any help you might need to employ your strategy.

The Glossary on page 491 defines any word I use that might be unfamiliar to you. And if you forget where you saw something you want to recheck, there's a very detailed index to help you find it.

The Beginning

We live in an uncertain world. But that doesn't mean you can't create a sound investment program.

In every other area of your life, you deal easily with uncertainty. You don't rely on a fortune-teller to tell you how your business will do next year, how you'll get along with your spouse, or whom your daughter is going to marry. You know these things are unpredictable, and you approach them in ways that don't demand predictability.

No one guarantees that you'll have a job forever. But that doesn't stop you from working and earning a good living.

No one guarantees that your loved one will be with you always. But that doesn't keep you from enjoying each other today, tomorrow, next month, next year.

The investment world is no different. No one can foresee the future here either, but that doesn't mean you can't find safety and profit.

When you enter the investment markets, you aren't entering a fairyland in which the rules of life are suspended. There are no mystical secrets hiding behind the curtain, no alien logic to be learned, no infallible systems to be mastered.

The markets are part of the same world in which you've made successful decisions all your life. If you apply to your investments the same intelligence you use elsewhere, you can do well here, too.

Safety and profit can be yours—but only after you quit wishing you could find a perfect system, and instead devise a strategy that allows for human error, for uncertainty, and for the endless surprises that make the best-laid plans go wrong.

So let's get started.

PART I

How the Best-Laid Plans Go Wrong

2

Track Records
That Go Wrong

There was something strange in Mr. Jones' mail on Monday.

It was an envelope, with no return address, that contained a single sheet of paper—which was blank except for one sentence:

The stock market will go up on Tuesday.

Mr. Jones checked the stock market's close on Tuesday and was amused to find that, indeed, the stock market had gone up.

On Thursday he received a second note, saying simply:

The stock market will go down on Friday.

He watched the market with more interest on Friday, and felt a twinge of excitement when he saw it drop.

On the following Monday, Mr. Jones received a third letter. He tore open the envelope and read:

The stock market will go up on Tuesday.

He called his broker immediately. He placed an order to buy a stock index option (which would profit from any general rise in the market) just before the market's close that day. He gave a second instruction, to sell the option just before the close the next day, Tuesday.

On Tuesday, Mr. Jones left work early and spent the rest of the day at his broker's office, watching stock prices pass across a video screen. The market was up, and Mr. Jones made a profit of over $500.

On Thursday the fourth letter came:

The stock market will go up on Friday.

He called his broker again, and this time he bought six options. As promised, the market rose on Friday, although not as much as it had on Tuesday. Still, Mr. Jones showed a gain of $1,300 on his six options. For the week, he had a profit of over $1,800.

Mr. Jones didn't go to work the following Monday or Tuesday. Instead, he stayed home to wait for the mail.

He had no idea how someone could forecast the market so well. How did he do it? Did he use a computer? Did he have inside information? Did he eat a fortune cookie every day?

But what difference did it make *how* it worked? The important thing was that it *did* work.

On Tuesday another letter came, but this one was different. It said:

Now you know that I can forecast the market perfectly. To learn what the market will do next Monday, send $500 in cash to Mr. John Smith, c/o General Delivery at the downtown post office.

Mr. Jones went immediately to his bank to get the cash. He put the money in an envelope as instructed, and took it directly to the downtown post office for mailing. On Friday he received the fifth forecast:

The stock market will go down on Monday.

He called his broker and arranged to buy ten stock index put options—an investment that would profit if the market went down. And the market did drop on Monday, giving Mr. Jones a one-day profit of over $4,000.

The next letter asked for a $1,000 fee, which Mr. Jones gladly paid. He received the sixth forecast and won another $4,500.

The following letter asked for $2,000. Mr. Jones paid, received the seventh forecast, doubled his bet, and won over $6,000.

The mysterious forecaster had correctly called the direction of the market seven times in a row.

What a genius!

EXCITING PROSPECTS

Mr. Jones had stumbled on to a good thing—the kind of good thing that most investors spend their lives looking for. Imagine how much money you could make if you could find such a reliable forecaster.

We'll come back to Mr. Jones' story shortly—to see how it was possible for him to receive such good advice. But first, let's look at some other examples of investment success.

By reading investment publications, I've uncovered mutual funds and investment advisors that managed to show a profit seven years in a row—in up markets and in down markets. Seven straight winning years can't be dismissed as good luck.

And we find outstanding records elsewhere. There's a technical indicator that signaled the major turns in interest rates seven times in a row. A string of successes this long could hardly be coincidence. No wonder many advisors call it a "confirmed, reliable indicator."

And there's a moving average that has identified the start of major trends in gold seven times running. Such consistency seems too strong to be accidental.

Lastly, I've heard of a student in a college finance course who picked seven winning investments in a row. It appears that an investment genius has been discovered.

In each case, the long string of successes should be enough to convince even a skeptic that the results didn't come from coincidence, luck, or circumstance.

Genius at Work

Before we get carried away, however, let's look more closely at one of the examples.

It turns out that the college student's investment success grew out of a classroom experiment. Each student was asked to make his "investment" by flipping a coin. If the coin came up "heads," the investment was considered to be a success. Flipping "tails" meant that the investment was a loser.

The student genius achieved his success by flipping "heads" seven times in a row—not by picking stocks. But even flipping seven "heads" in seven tries is noteworthy. The odds against it must be extremely high.

Let's look at how the experiment was conducted. There were 128 students in the class. Each one flipped a coin to determine the outcome of his "investment"—with "heads" signifying a win and "tails" a loss. The experiment was conducted in seven steps:

1. Each of the 128 students flipped his coin. The results were: 66 "heads" and 62 "tails." The losers withdrew from the experiment.
2. The remaining 66 flipped again. When they did, 31 flipped "heads." The 35 who flipped "tails" withdrew.
3. On the next test, 17 of the remaining 31 flipped "heads."
4. Of these 17 winners, 8 flipped "heads" on the next test.
5. Of these 8, 4 flipped "heads" again.
6. Of the 4, 3 flipped "heads" on the next test.
7. Of the remaining 3, only one—the newly found investment genius—flipped "heads" on the seventh test.

Taken by itself, the student's accomplishment seemed remarkable. But it's not surprising to find that, at each stage of the experiment, approximately half the coin-flippers produced "heads." So if you start with enough people (128 in this case), the odds favor coming up with at least one participant who flips "heads" seven times in a row.

Advisory Records

Coin-flipping may seem far removed from investing, but the laws of chance don't care how serious or silly your purpose is. No matter what the goal, the purpose, or the method, if enough people try to accomplish something that's at all possible, some of them will succeed—even if none of them has any particular skill.

For example, suppose that, at the beginning of every year, 128 investment advisors forecast whether gold is going up or down for the year—each making his own, independent decision. At the end of seven years, there probably will be at least one advisor who was right every year (and at least one who was wrong every year).

Even if none of them had the slightest understanding of the gold market, a handful still would have terrific track records. Mere chance dictates that at least one out of every 128 investment advisors should wind up with a perfect record for seven years.

And I mean *mere* chance. If you took the annual forecasts of 128 gold experts, crossed out the word "gold" and replaced it with "cocoa," you probably would find at the end of seven years that at least one gold expert had a perfect record of forecasting cocoa prices.

Since there are *thousands* of investment advisors in the world, it's not surprising that on any day a few of them are on remarkable winning streaks. The very size of the crowd assures the emergence of at least a few apparently consistent winners.

And since the winners make the most noise, it's easy to gain the impression that you should be able to find an advisor who can make large gains for you every year.

It isn't that every advisor's results come from a coin toss. But unless you know *why* an advisor has been successful, you have no way to know that his success didn't result from mere chance. If he isn't very good at what he does, he still has a roughly even chance at a profit every year—and could easily stumble into several good years in a row.

Evaluating Advisors

The knowledge that chance has a lot to do with performance helps to clear up a few mysteries of the investment world. It explains why a mutual fund that's at the top of the class one year seldom finishes near the top the next year, and why an investment advisor who turns in a spectacular performance one year rarely does better than average the following year.

You shouldn't disregard the record of a mutual fund or an investment advisor, but you need to find out how that record was achieved (and whether the record you're shown is accurate). If you find that the advisor's investment philosophy makes sense to you, that he steers clear of the kinds of risk that worry you, and that his way of looking at things fits the world as you know it, then you may have found someone who can help you with your investments.

"Proven" Indicators

The same principles apply to indicators or systems that are supposed to tell you whether the market is going up or down. Even if the assumptions behind all of them are foolish, there are bound to be some indicators that have amazing records.

One example is the Super Bowl Indicator. It says that if the winner of the Super Bowl game (played in January) is a team that was a member of the old American Football League, then the stock market will have a losing year. Otherwise, the market will show a gain for the year. If the New York Stock Exchange Composite Index is used to measure the market's performance, the indicator performed perfectly from 1967 through 1983—17 years in a row.

Amazing, isn't it? Football and stocks may seem unrelated, but there must be *some* connection. Otherwise, how could the Super Bowl Indicator be right 17 times in a row? That's asking too much of coincidence.

However, the record of the Super Bowl Indicator is amazing only if you look at it by itself. Given the thousands of annual big games, playoffs, and championships, it's not surprising that one of them happens to have a pattern coinciding with the stock market for 17 years in a row—even though there's no more than a 50% chance it will do so again next year.

Have you heard about the World Series Barometer? It says that if the winner of the World Series is from the National League, the price of gold will rise during November. And the Ground Hog Indicator says that if the ground hog sees his shadow, interest rates will fall. There are several thousand more, but I won't burden you.

The reason you haven't heard of them is that they don't have very good records. If you *have* heard of the Super Bowl Indicator, it's because—out of the thousands of possibilities—it has been blessed by chance.

Persuasive Indicators

Of course, no one takes the Super Bowl Indicator seriously. It's a curiosity that investors kid about in January.

But other indicators, with no more power to reveal the future, *are* taken seriously—usually because of some apparent tie to the events they're supposed to forecast, or because people are willing to believe there's a reason for its success that hasn't yet been recognized.

Such is the case when someone presents a "moving average" that has consistently signaled the major turning points in an investment market. Because a moving average is computed from an investment's price history, its record is taken seriously—unlike the Super Bowl Indicator.

And yet the moving average's track record can be just as irrelevant as that of the Super Bowl Indicator. If a computer sifts through the daily record of prices for the past 20 years, testing several hundred different moving averages, it's bound to find a few that confirmed— quickly and accurately—each turning point in the market. But there's no reason they have to work the next time.[1]

This is how "confirmed, reliable" indicators are created—by pouring history through a strainer to catch the patterns that have persisted. But until they are explained by economic logic, such patterns are only descriptions of the past—and in most cases descriptions of coincidence and trivia.

Even if no indicator had the power to forecast the future, we still would be confronted by many that seem to have done so for long periods—simply because there are an infinity of possible indicators to choose from. On any day, if you look back, you're sure to find indicators with amazing track records.

But that doesn't mean they will work when you risk your money.

Testing an Indicator

To rely on an indicator, you need to know whether there's some connection, other than past success, between the indicator and the event it's trying to signal—a connection arising from what we know about the way the world works.

How, for example, does the outcome of the Super Bowl affect the economy so as to influence the stock market's direction? The answer is obvious: It doesn't.

Other indicators, based on economic or investment data, can seem more reasonable but still be just as meaningless. Why, for example, should the stock market's result for January foretell the result for the entire year, as many investors believe? Why should a price crossing a trendline on a graph signal a change in trend, as many technical analysts believe? Why should the stock market do better in years ending in 5, as many superstitious people believe?

Any indicator or system should be put to the test of economic logic—not just to the test of past performance.

---

[1]Moving averages, and how investors use them to detect market turning points, are explained in Chapter 11.

There are many economic relationships that you can use for guidance in making investment decisions. While not certainties, there's good reason to expect them to hold up. For example: lower interest rates encourage higher stock prices; greater inflation leads to higher gold prices; an increase in bank failures should widen the difference between yields on Treasury bills and bank CDs, and so on.

For each of these notions, there's a reason—based on what we know about the way human beings act—for it to be true. You may disagree with the explanation, you may want to qualify it, the relationship may even change in time—but there *is* an explanation that separates it from coincidence.

Not So Certain After All

Many investors and advisors like to feel that, because they spend a great deal of time on research, they're approaching their investments scientifically.

But if the research is simply a hunt for patterns that have repeated, it isn't science at all. In fact, it's no more scientific than betting on the number 5 at the roulette table whenever number 12 has come up —simply because twice before you saw 5 follow 12.

If a relationship has held 2 times, 5 times, or even 20 times in the past, that fact isn't—of itself—sufficient reason to expect the relationship to hold even one more time. The past is full of meaningless coincidences that are waiting to be discovered by investors and advisors.

Many of the best-laid plans go wrong because they assume that some past pattern will continue into the future. I've dwelt at length on this point because it's so tempting, and seemingly so reasonable, to rely on the track record of a trading system, an advisor, or an indicator. Too often, the track record begins to fall apart as soon as you risk your money—which might cause you to wonder whether you're a jinx.

You're not. Out of millions of potential possibilities, chance allowed something to look good long enough to catch your eye—just as chance allowed a particular student out of 128 to appear to have a talent for flipping coins.

When someone offers you an investment tool, system, or track record, ask why it works. The answer, "See, it *does* work," isn't good enough. Even a graph claiming to show a strict relationship between an indicator and a particular result is nothing more than a curiosity. A graph of the coin-flipper's results would be just as impressive.

If you're given a reason that you don't understand, treat it as a poor reason. Don't assume it's over your head; it may in fact be beneath you.

Investing isn't child's play. Don't believe that someone can reduce it to the simple task of following an indicator or relying on a perfect track record.

BACK TO MR. JONES

I almost forgot. What about Mr. Jones?

When we left him, he had received seven correct forecasts in a row from Mr. Smith.

The next letter he received asked for $3,000. He paid the money and received the eighth forecast, which said the market would go up on Wednesday. But the market went down. He lost $4,000 on his options.

Even after the loss, Mr. Jones was still $5,800 ahead. He was ready, even eager, to pay for the next forecast. After all, the mysterious John Smith had been right seven times out of eight—which was far better than Mr. Jones had ever done on his own.

But Mr. Jones never received another letter.

Forecaster at Work

On the day Mr. Jones took his loss, John Smith entered into his computer the news that the market had gone down. The computer, for the eighth time, deleted half the remaining names from Mr. Smith's mailing list.

The list was very short now. Three weeks before, it had contained 65,536 names and addresses; now there were only 92 left. Soon the scheme would be over.

For the first mailing, the computer had addressed envelopes to 65,536 people. The envelopes were stuffed with notes: 32,768 saying, "The stock market will go up on Tuesday," and 32,768 saying, "The stock market will go down on Tuesday."

When the market rose on Tuesday, the computer deleted the names of the people who had received the "down" letter. A similar routine was repeated after the second, third, and fourth letters, with the computer deleting half the names each time—the names of the people who had received the losing forecast.

After the fourth letter, the list was down to 4,096 names. To them, the computer addressed envelopes stuffed with the "Send $500" letter. Surprisingly, 1,481 people responded by sending Mr. Smith $500 to pay for the forecast.

Of course, only half those people (740) received a correct forecast. Those winners were asked to send $1,000 for the next forecast—and 739 of them did.

Of these, 370 received a correct forecast and were kept on the mailing list. After the "Send $2,000" letter and its forecast, the list was down to 185 names. Mr. Jones was dropped from the list when his $3,000 forecast happened to be on the wrong side of the market. Even then, there still were 92 people who had received eight correct forecasts.

The ninth forecast reduced the list to 46 winners, and the tenth forecast cut it to 23. By then, Mr. Smith had received over $3 million from grateful and admiring investors.

After thinking it over, he decided to end the scheme there. He had become so fascinated with the stock market and with mail-order advertising that he decided to publish an investment newsletter instead.

He contacted the 23 people who had received ten consecutive winning forecasts. Each of them was delighted to write an endorsement praising Mr. Smith's "incredible track record."[2]

---

[2]The story of Mr. Jones and Mr. Smith was adapted from an episode of *Alfred Hitchcock Presents* that my colleague Terry Coxon remembers seeing on television years ago. The coin-flipping example has been a staple of college finance courses for many years. The examples of seven-year successes early in the chapter were hypothetical proxies for the claims that you and I read frequently.

The Super Bowl Indicator was right 17 years in a row, 1967 through 1983. It failed in 1984, but was right again in 1985 and 1986. Since the New York Giants won the Super Bowl in January 1987, the stock market should have risen in 1987. Did it?

3

Forecasts
That Go Wrong

In the summer of 1981, a widely read and respected investment advisor published ten predictions. Here they are, exactly as written except for my comments in brackets:

1. While deflation and depression dominate the concerns of most Americans, inflation will begin soaring to a rate of 35% by 1983.
2. Within 24 months [meaning by mid-1983], the prime rate will hit 30%.
3. During the first quarter of 1982, several of the nation's top savings and loan institutions will collapse.
4. The Social Security system, despite President Reagan's best efforts, will face an increasingly desperate situation. The system *will* be saved, but in the only politically feasible way: by massive infusions of new paper money.
5. Defense spending, now $200 billion, will rise to $500 billion by 1984 and $650 billion by 1985.
6. Within 36 months [meaning by mid-1984], a revolution will break out in Saudi Arabia. Decisive action by President Reagan will prevent pro-Soviet revolutionaries from overthrowing the monarchy.

39

7. In 1982, Europe will be seized by the worst social and economic chaos in modern history. Expect riots, strikes, bank collapses and business failures in every Western European nation.
8. In 1982, Australia—and the entire Pacific basin—will experience an economic boom of unprecedented proportions. The Australian dollar will become the Swiss franc of the 1980s.
9. Within 18 months [meaning by early 1983], silver will be $20 an ounce, and platinum $750 an ounce.
10. We stand by our earlier prediction that 1981 will be remembered as "the last chance to buy gold at historic lows." By the end of 1982, gold will be $700–800 an ounce. By 1983, $1,500 to $2,000.

Not one of the ten predictions came to pass. The one that came closest to redeeming the forecaster was #4. But while Social Security's chronic problems received more than the usual attention in 1984 and 1985, the situation never became desperate; the government didn't have to print new money to pay off the beneficiaries.

As for the other nine predictions:

1. The inflation rate for 1983 was 3.8%.
2. The highest prime rate in 1983 was 11½%.
3. Not a single large or prominent savings & loan association collapsed during 1982. The largest association to fail in 1982 had barely $1 billion in assets, and it was taken over immediately by another institution.
5. Defense spending was only $227.4 billion in fiscal year 1984 and $252.7 billion in 1985.
6. Three years after the mid-1984 deadline, there has been no revolution in Saudi Arabia.
7. No Western European nation suffered from an unusual level of riots, strikes, bank collapses, or business failures in 1982.
8. Regarding Australia's economic boom, real (inflation-adjusted) Gross Domestic Product in Australia rose 0.9% in 1982 and 0.8% in 1983—a substantial reduction from the 3.4% average annual growth in the preceding three years. And it's safe to say that the Australian dollar hasn't become the Swiss franc of the 1980s. Between June 1981 and December 1986, the Australian dollar *fell* 40.6% against the U.S. dollar, and fell 32.8% against an average of the currencies of Australia's primary trading partners.
9. For 1982–1983, silver's highest price was $14.74; platinum's high was $502.00.

10. Gold's highest price in 1982–1983 was $511. Throughout 1984, the price was lower than it had been at any time during 1981.[1]

Typical Results

The newsletter that published these predictions isn't some rag that's mimeographed in a different garage every month. It's a large-circulation journal written by one of the most respected people in the precious metals field—a man who is neither a charlatan nor a dumb bunny.

Even so, it may seem that I've chosen a straw man—an extraordinary case in which ten predictions somehow all turned out to be wrong. Believe me, I haven't.

If the example strikes you as exceptional, it's probably because this is the first time you've looked at a set of six-year-old predictions, in their entirety, exactly as they were first published.

The forecasts may seem sensationalistic now, but remember that in 1981 the U.S. was in a recession, the inflation rate was 10%, and the future looked bleak. Had you seen these forecasts then, you might have been impressed. They did exactly what good predictions are supposed to do: they extended the present into the future in an original but plausible way. It is only now, after all the deadlines have passed, that the predictions seem naïve and simplistic.

You also may wonder whether I picked a particularly bad forecaster for my example. After all, you frequently read of advisors who made accurate forecasts that alerted their customers to important trends in advance.

You might even come across an advisor who is reputed to have warned his readers in 1981 of 1983's rise in interest rates, of the 1985 concern over Social Security, of the 1980s' rise in defense spending, of the 1982 rallies in gold, silver, and platinum. But, in fact, the reputation would belong to the same forecaster whose ten predictions you just read.

[1]Sources: (#1,#2) *Federal Reserve Bulletin* (February 1984) pages A24 and A49. (#3) *Federal Home Loan Bank Board Annual Report* (April 1983), pages 17–18. (#5) *Economic Indicators* (U.S. Government Printing Office, May 1986), page 33. (#7) Various publications of the Organization for Economic Cooperation and Development. (#8) *International Financial Statistics*, International Monetary Fund (IMF), January 1985, page 89, and February 1987, page 131. (Gross Domestic Product is similar to Gross National Product, and is the only figure reported for Australia by the IMF.) (#9, #10) *Green's Commodity Market Comments*, January 11, 1984, and *CRB Futures Chart Service*, December 6, 1985.

Standards aren't high in the forecasting business. If the smallest part of a forecast happens to resemble the eventual outcome in any way, the forecaster will say he told you so.

Don't Shoot the Messenger

Throughout Part I, I'll provide examples like this without mentioning the names of the people involved. It is the message, and the willingness to accept it, that I'm criticizing—not the messenger. Nothing would be gained by naming the advisors who made the bad forecasts.

Many of the advisors whose work I cite provide valuable services to their customers. Some of them are even my friends—when they're not upset with me for questioning their clairvoyance.

I hope you're willing to accept my word that the examples are true and that they come from prominent advisors.

BELIEF IN FORTUNE-TELLING

Predictions are only parlor games—a form of entertainment.

The average person wouldn't consult a fortune-teller to learn what the future holds for his career, his love life, or his health. He might read the astrology column in the morning paper, but by noon he's forgotten what it said.

He takes for granted that he lives in an uncertain world. He has seen surprises before and he knows he will see them again. It never occurs to him that he couldn't function without a soothsayer to tell him what the future holds.

But when he approaches the investment markets, the first thing he looks for is a fortune-teller—someone who can tell him what next year's inflation rate or Dow Jones average will be.

The Lure & the Lore

Why is it so easy to believe that forecasting can be fruitful? I can think of three reasons.

First, at some time or other, something in the investment world did happen pretty much as you thought it would—encouraging the idea that the future is predictable. However, if this successful prediction stands out in your memory, it's because it's the exception, not the rule. You may have forgotten many other forecasts, because there's no reason to remember the ones that didn't come true.

A second reason for believing in forecasting can be that you have found no other basis for making investment decisions; either you bet on a forecast or you leave your money in a savings account. In Part II, I'll offer alternatives that I think are safer and more profitable.

The third and most important reason is the mastery with which forecasters practice their art—not the art of foreseeing next year's events, but the art of making you believe that they foresaw last year's events.

Some very talented professionals have convinced their fans that they've been right again and again. And this apparent success nourishes the general idea that reliable forecasting is possible and necessary.

The top forecasters have developed some clever tricks—a few of which we'll examine now. If you can see that a lot of forecasting magic is only sleight of hand, you might be moved to depend on something else for safety and profit.

I hope you do, because plans that are laid on forecasts almost always go wrong.

Humble Pie with Whipped Cream

One of the best performers turns out 40 or 50 predictions each year in the January issue of his newsletter.

As a preface, he reviews the success of last year's forecasts and totals up the score. Amazingly, he almost always seems to have been around 87% right. Can you imagine how much money you could make if you had access to forecasts that were correct 87% of the time?

His January review doesn't actually reproduce last year's forecasts—probably because of space limitations. Instead, the writer provides a scorecard: so many right, so many wrong, so many that were inconclusive. He refers specifically to only a few of the predictions.

He usually cites one or two forecasts that seem now to have been especially shrewd. But, of course, you expect him to do that.

It's when he cites some that turned out to be wrong that you're won over. You can see that he's being more than open and honest. By treating a near-miss as "wrong," he demonstrates that his talent and even his standards tower far above yours and mine.

For example, reporting in January 1985 on his 1984 forecasts, he said:

Among the losers: I was a bit too optimistic about the high in gold (said 450 and was only 406); Ditto silver: I said 11.50 high, but was only 10.85.

Any man who's wrong only 13% of the time, and who's *that close* when he's wrong, must be a genius. At the time of the review, gold was at $300; so to have missed a top $106 away by only 10% seems—well, awesome.

The subject of fortune-telling fascinates me. So each year I dig out this advisor's forecasts for the previous year (as I do with other advisors' forecasts). I check the predictions against the events that actually happened, and I check the original forecast against the way it's described in the year-later review.

I've never found him to be even 40% right—let alone 87%. And he almost never repeats last year's forecasts accurately.

For example, that not-so-bad gold forecast that he humbly scored as a near-miss was not, in the original, quite as he described it a year later ("said 450 and was only 406"). The original actually said, "Gold forecast: probable high: $450–$500." When he made the forecast, gold was *already* at its $406 high for the year. So he missed the high by 10% to 19%—and failed to foresee that gold would spend the rest of the year heading downward.

The same was true for silver ("I said 11.50 high, but was only 10.85"). He originally said, "Silver forecast: probable high: $11.50–$12.00." And the actual high was $10.18, not $10.85. So he missed the high by $1.32 to $1.82, not by the 65 cents he implied a year later.

Heads I Win, Tails I Win

Another trick is to build up the score by including a few throwaways that can be judged to be correct no matter what happens.

The same forecaster regularly includes a few like "Europe, after a year of navel-examination, may begin to find its way in 1985." He can score this one right so long as Europe doesn't fall off the edge of the earth.

Another of his 1985 forecasts was more relevant and seemed more definite:

The Dow Jones Industrial Average chart says, in my opinion, that when DJIA breaks out from its 5-month line formation, it will move at least 100 points. Thus a DJIA close under 1160 would target a fall to 1060. A DJIA close over 1250 would target a rise to 1350. BOTH 1400 and 1000 are outside possibilities in 1985.

When the forecast was issued, it appeared to be alerting you to something—a pent-up energy in the market that was about to explode in one direction or the other. Even after the fact, it appears to have been perceptive, since the Dow Jones average confirmed the forecast by ending 1985 at 1546.[2]

But if you examine the prediction closely, you find that it didn't really say much of anything. The Dow needed to move only 150 points, or 12½%, *in either direction* within 12 months to make the forecast come true. In 26 of the previous 31 years, the Dow had moved 12½% or more. So the forecaster clearly had big odds on his side.

When you realize that many of this forecaster's predictions foresee what is nearly unavoidable, and that—even so—less than half his predictions turn out to be right, you have to wonder why you should pay attention to any of his forecasts.

His actual forecasting record could be equaled by a child, or by the legendary monkey throwing darts at a list of stocks. But he has what no child or monkey has—a large bag of tricks that help him create the illusion of second sight.

And there are many forecasters like him in the investment world. They encourage you to believe that—through fundamental analysis, technical analysis, a superior understanding of economics, a pipeline to inside information, a special mystical insight, or whatever—they can divine the future for you.

Plea Bargaining

Another trick that forecasters use to build your confidence in them is to admit their mistakes but point out that they were right about the really important things. In criminal proceedings, this is known as pleading guilty to a lesser charge.

---

[2]Needless to say, this was one of the forecasts highlighted in his review a year later. He let you know that he had said 1400 was a possibility, but he forgot to mention that he'd said that 1000 was equally possible.

An example of the I-candidly-tell-you-all-my-(harmless)-mistakes approach was provided in January 1985 when another advisor reviewed his 1984 predictions. He acknowledged forecasting mistakes for stocks, gold, and inflation, but implied that those lapses were unimportant alongside his all-important prediction for interest rates:

> I said all year that by January 1985 we would see a big drop in interest rates. I advised holding on to bonds and utility stocks until interest rates bottomed.
>
> We got a terrific fall in interest rates, even though we almost got scared out by a midyear rise. We hung in there tenaciously, and our patience was rewarded. . . .
>
> Forecasting interest rates may be the most valuable thing a financial advisor can do for you. . . . If I'm willing to rub my nose in the messes I make, you've got to forgive me for whooping it up when I do it right. On interest rates, I was impeccable.

At the time he wrote this, interest rates had been falling for six months—which seemed to prove the value of his earlier forecast.

Readers, especially new readers, who hadn't acted on the forecast, probably weren't aware of how events had unfolded. They may have wished they *had* acted on the advisor's forecast, and they may have resolved to follow his advice the next time.

In truth, however, the interest-rate drop in the second half of 1984 only undid the rise that had occurred in the first half. At the time of the forecast for 1984, the yield on long-term Treasury bonds was 11.4%. At the end of 1984, it was 11.3%.[3]

Readers who did act on the forecast of lower rates by buying (or holding) bonds or utility stocks at the beginning of 1984 had been in a loss position for *almost the entire year*. Their "patience was rewarded" at year-end by finally breaking even. Obviously, they didn't feel much like whooping it up.

The Power of Suggestion

Any investment advisor worth his salt will sprinkle into his regular commentary phrases like "as expected," "right on schedule," and "as we warned." To give some hypothetical examples:

---

[3]*Selected Interest Rates*, Federal Reserve Statistical Release H.15(519) January 16, 1984, and January 7, 1985. The date of the forecast was January 9, 1984.

As expected, interest rates began moving upward this month.

Right on schedule, the market took off last week.

As we warned in our last issue, the market was overbought and due for a correction.

Used artfully, these phrases build the impression that whatever has happened had been anticipated in the writer's forecast.

As you read his low-key hints of omniscience, you may feel a little foolish for somehow having ignored the forecasts and warnings when they appeared—because you certainly didn't act on them.

But if you were to get out the original writings, you'd see why you didn't: the events weren't so precisely described, nor so firmly expected, nor so definitely scheduled. In fact, the warnings were a little vague, as in:

At some point soon, the market may become more selective, with some industry groups rising while others lag behind.

HOW SOON WE FORGET

I'm one of those people who can't throw anything away. I still have every investment newsletter I've received since 1970—several file cabinets full of them. And there are all those years of *Barron's, The Wall Street Journal, Futures* magazine, and countless other financial publications stacked up in my garage.

When someone sends me his "15 Startling Predictions for 1988," I go to the file and pull out his "15 Startling Predictions for 1987." And when someone uses the "As expected" ploy, I often dig out previous issues to find out *how* expected today's events were.

If you believe there's someone who can usefully forecast the future, keep everything he writes. Whenever he mentions a successful prediction he made, dig it out and see what it looked like in the original.

And see what other forecasts he made at the same time—predictions he isn't bragging about now. Ask yourself what would have happened if you'd acted on *all* his forecasts.

A quicker test is to watch a financial television station for a few days. You'll see market experts saying that the current rally will peak at 11:00 a.m. on Friday, or that the market will bottom next Wednesday—or in other ways providing a timetable for the immediate future.

Jot down these forecasts, because you might distrust your memory.

See whether the peak really comes on Friday at 11:00 a.m., and whether the bottom arrives "on schedule" on Wednesday. Most likely, less than one forecast in four will prove to have come even close.

Sometimes a forecast can fill you with anxiety. You fear that ignoring it would leave you vulnerable to some danger or cause you to miss a golden opportunity. The best tranquilizer in such a case is to reread last year's forecasts. Seeing how rarely forecasts come true ought to settle you down quickly.

GETTING OFF THE HOOK

You may wonder how advisors can continue in business while making forecasts that almost never come true.

The answer is that while few people keep track of the predictions, most people want to keep hearing them. It's as simple as that.

Even when an investor loses money acting on a forecast, he may wonder whether he used the forecast properly—especially when the forecaster claims that the outcome is another victory for his forecasting record. And having lost money on one forecast, the investor can feel an even greater need to find another one that will help recoup his loss.

Even if a prediction was clearly awful and you confront the forecaster with it, he doesn't have to apologize. Forecasting means never having to say you're wrong, since there are so many ways to slip off the hook.

We should look at a few of those ways, so that you'll understand the nature of the talent underlying most "uncanny" forecasting records.

Didn't You See It?

When a forecast goes wrong, one way out is to say that the predicted event did occur, but that it's been concealed by other things.

Did your prediction of higher inflation by 1985 go wrong? Just say that the economy *is* permeated by intense inflationary pressure, but it's hidden by the exceptional fall in oil prices and the strong dollar in foreign exchange markets.

Were you the one whose cycle theory targeted 1986 for a stock-market crash? Tell them that the downside of the cycle arrived right on schedule—preventing the Dow Jones from reaching 3000 in 1986.

Timing

When the deadline passes without the predicted event occurring, another out is to adjust the timing. And then adjust it again, and again, and again.

On August 27, 1982, one famous investment advisor made it clear that inflation (then at 6.5%) was on the way up:

> Then look for gradually rekindling inflation, a recovery from recession, and eventually 25% to 30% inflation within four years.

By the middle of 1983, the inflation rate had dropped by over half—to 2.4%. So he said:

> The Commodity Research Bureau Index has jumped 24% from its September 1982 low, and is saying in no uncertain terms, *price inflation is coming*. It will take a while to work its way into the Consumer Price Index, but it is inevitable.

In January 1984, the latest inflation rate was a lethargic 3.2%—a letdown from the resurgence he had anticipated. He said, "The reasons for it are fairly simple," and explained that high interest rates and the severity of the last recession had caused the interlude before the next round of inflation to be longer than in previous monetary cycles. He said it so matter-of-factly that one couldn't help but wonder why he hadn't bothered to tell us this *before* we had bet our money on imminent inflation. But no matter:

> This has had a dampening effect on inflation but has only postponed the inevitable. . . . I don't expect much of anything on the inflation front until the second half of the year [1984].

By January 1985, the inflation rate had inched up to 4.0%. He said:

> This year (probably in the first six months), we'll see higher inflation, higher metals, cheaper stocks, and an end to the interest rate decline.

As it turned out, 1985 brought level inflation, level metals prices, much higher stocks, and a continuation of the interest-rate decline. Otherwise, he was right on target.

Then came January 1986 and inflation was back down to 3.6%. He explained:

Last year, I said inflation would probably start up early in the year. I got the year wrong . . . because the Fed maintained a strong dollar and high real interest rates much longer than I thought they could, delaying inflation way beyond our expectations. But that's now history. *That forecast for 1985 will happen in 1986*, and people who bought inflation hedges and held on will have their judgment vindicated. . . .

Right on schedule, our year-to-year inflation indicator has shown its first small upturn in a long time. I think it is significant, and *rising inflation should be the biggest surprise of 1986*.

At the time he wrote that, the inflation rate was 3.6%. By the end of 1986, the rate had dropped to 1.3%. I guess inflation *was* "the biggest surprise of 1986"—to the advisor.

In January 1987 there was no forecast issue.

Interestingly, this man often suggests that his most important asset as an investment advisor is his understanding of where we are in the business cycle at any given time.

Creative Redefinition

Another way to slip out of a prediction is to say that you meant something different from what some people seem to think you meant.

In the early 1980s, a number of advisors predicted a resurgence of inflation by 1983. When inflation hadn't returned by 1983 or 1984, or even by 1985 or 1986, some of them still insisted they'd been right —because the original, 19th-century, definition of "inflation" is an increase in the supply of money, which had in fact occurred. However, their readers who had acted on the forecast may be wondering why, in that case, they bought so much gold and real estate.

Those who have forecast deflation also know how to redefine words. One prominent investment advisor predicted over and over that there would be a full-scale deflation "in the early 1980s." What we got instead was disinflation—just as we'd had in the late 1950s, the late 1960s, and the mid-1970s. Undaunted, the forecaster said that we were going through a deflation, but that people who didn't want to admit he was right had renamed it disinflation.[4]

The world's record for audacious redefinition may have been set in 1975. After having predicted an imminent deflationary collapse for

---

[4]"Deflation" means a fall in prices. "Disinflation" (which is not a new word) means a slowing of the rate at which prices are rising.

several years, a prominent newsletter writer vindicated his prediction by describing the high prices he'd encountered on a recent trip— summing it all up, "If that isn't a deflation in the value of money, I don't know what is."

This astounding escape has been an inspiration to investment advisors ever since. We know that, whatever happens, there's a way to come out smelling like a rose.

Pay No Attention

Another way to slide out from under a bad prediction is simply to ignore it. No matter how much fanfare accompanied its birth, let it die quietly.

As far as I know, the advisor who made the ten forecasts that began this chapter never again referred to them. In fact, even the topics have been largely forgotten; of the ten covered in the list, only three have been discussed in his newsletter since he made his 1981 forecasts.

BEWARE OF SUCCESS

I'm not saying that predictions never come true.

With so many experts making so many predictions, it's inevitable that almost everyone will be right now and then—and that a few lucky forecasters will have a pile of correct predictions to stand on.

I mentioned in the preceding chapter that some advisors (and systems and indicators) are bound to compile impressive records over the years, even if only by luck. The same principle is at work when a crowd of people try to forecast a single event.

As an example, investment advisors in January routinely forecast the course of a market for the coming year. Each advisor's forecast will be somewhat like one of these 11 possibilities:

1. The market will go straight up from here;
2. It will rise after a mild correction;
3. It will rise after a large correction;
4. It will rise in a choppy, labored fashion;
5. It will trend upward for part of the year and then downward for the rest of the year;
6. It will head straight down in a crash;
7. It will fall after a mild rally;

8. It will fall after a big rally;

9. It will trend downward in a choppy fashion;

10. It will trend downward for part of the year and then upward for the rest of the year;

11. It will trade in a narrow range with no basic trend upward or downward.

Unless a year turns out to be very unusual, one of the 11 forecasts will prove to have been correct. And that will make heroes of a few hundred of the thousands of experts who made forecasts. The winners not only will have called the general direction of the market (which is a mere coin flip), but they will have described with "uncanny accuracy" the precise way in which the year would unfold.

The same principle applies when many forecasters predict the exact Dow Jones average or gold price for some day in the future—such as the end of the year. Out of all the forecasters, the odds favor there being at least a few who pick something very close to the right number.

In any of these cases, if we look closely at the winners, we'll find that each had his own reasons for forecasting as he did. Some used fundamental analysis, others technical analysis, and others cycle theory; some used good economic theory, some used bad economic theory; some relied on numerology, others on hunches, and others on tips from their brothers-in-law. There may even be an astrologer among them.

By your standards, some of these people had good reasons for their forecasts, but others were right for the wrong reasons. How could those with wrong reasons have been correct?

Easily. If we look at one incompetent forecaster, we expect him to guess wrong about the future. But if thousands of inept forecasters guess about something for which there are perhaps only a dozen possible outcomes, chance alone guarantees that many of them will come up with the right answer. There just aren't enough losing tickets to go around.

That doesn't mean all forecasters use foolish methods. It does mean that mere success isn't sufficient to assure you that a forecaster knows what he's doing.

The Cost of Victory

One of the worst things that can happen to you is to witness a prediction coming true. Having personally observed a genuine seer, you resolve to bet on his forecasts from now on—and you suffer through a string of losses before you realize that the one correct prediction was a fluke.

Several forecasters predicted higher prices for silver during the 1970s. The prediction came true, and as silver rose from $2 to $5 to $10, $20, $30, and then over $40, their followers piled up enormous profits.

But the investors never sold, because these forecasters—so right so far—just kept raising their predictions for the eventual top. Rather than sell, the investors bought more—right up to the day silver crashed—at prices considerably higher than we've seen since. For them, a successful prediction was the bait for a large loss.[5]

Failure of this kind isn't rare. Every speculation requires two steps: a purchase and a sale. Very often a forecaster who wins your confidence by getting the first step right will get the second step expensively wrong.

Another example occurred in November 1981, when the price of gold was $403. A seminar speaker told 3,500 investors that gold's two-year bear market would end between March and July 1982 at $300–$325, and that gold then would rise to around $4,000 by 1986.

Gold bottomed on schedule on June 21, 1982, at $296.75 (London afternoon fixing)—as close to $300 as you could want. But as it turned out, gold didn't quite make it to $4,000 by 1986. It rose to $511 in February 1983, ran out of gas, and slid back down to $285 in February 1985. In mid-1987, it was still in the $400s. And those who had bet on the second prediction because of the success of the first were still waiting.

The original prediction that gold would bottom in June 1982 was wonderfully and dramatically accurate. Considering the long odds involved, it was sad that the investors who bet on the right forecaster didn't win anything.

Such, too often, is the fate of the best-laid investment plans.

FORECASTING & STRATEGY

Some investment advisors and mutual fund managers have compiled impressive, verifiable records—and not by luck alone. In most cases, however, this success isn't testimony to their forecasting powers.

Rather, success has been earned with methods that help the advisor recognize investment values, enter markets when the risk is low, cut losses when investments turn bad, and let profits grow when the market

---

[5]Silver was still under $10 in mid-1987.

is kind. These methods don't involve forecasting; they are part of good strategy.

Nevertheless, many of these successful advisors insist that their greatest virtue is an ability to forecast the future. Like most investors, they assume that success comes from forecasting. And like most advisors, they believe their customers expect them to be good at it.

VALUE IN FORECASTS

Even though forecasts can't be relied upon, I don't think they should be ignored. You should be thankful for any forecast that makes you look seriously at a possibility you hadn't considered before.

If a prediction is persuasive enough to goad you into making your portfolio safer and more balanced, it doesn't matter whether the prediction actually proves out. You'll be glad that you heard it, and glad that you hedged a little, during those periods when your principal investment is doing poorly.

Forecasting would be genuinely useful if investment advisors titled their January pronouncements "Possibilities We Should Take Seriously," rather than "Ten Startling Forecasts."

Unfortunately, few advisors see it that way. Most are convinced that their forecasts will be proven correct, and that everyone should rearrange his life right now to allow for the latest urgent discovery.

During the early 1980s, "The Great Inflation-Deflation Debate" was a standard part of most big investment seminars. (That was before professional wrestling caught on.) Four or six advisors would argue whether the U.S. was about to plunge into a 1930s-style deflation or was about to be carried away by high inflation rates.

Every speaker argued his case with great urgency—maintaining that you could be ruined if you didn't bet everything in the direction he favored. As it turned out, both sides were wrong, the U.S. had low inflation without deflation, and somehow everyone survived without losing too much money.

FORECASTING THE FUTURE

Investing would be so simple and easy if a wizard could tell us what the future holds. So it's understandable that most people are reluctant to check a forecaster's record closely, and are so willing to give him the benefit of the doubt.

It's also understandable that you might refuse to accept what I say about forecasting—no matter how many examples of bad forecasting I trot out, or how many arguments against forecasting I assert.

And even if you do agree with me in principle, tomorrow you may come across a forecaster who seems to be truly different. I wouldn't be surprised; it's his trade, his craft, to seem different.

You might choose to believe in him because he's discovered a reliable new indicator, or because he has a wonderful track record, or because he builds his forecast from assumptions you share. And you may welcome him because you're not sure how you could invest without a forecaster to guide you.

To know the future is a perennial hope. And there is no end to the promises that the hope will be fulfilled.

But I'm going to keep working on you. As Part I continues, we'll look at other ways in which the best-laid investment plans go wrong. Many of these involve forecasting—directly or by implication. Maybe somewhere along the way you'll decide that your financial future would be brighter without fortune-telling.

I hope so, because then we can get down to the serious business of investing in the real world—the uncertain world in which we both live.

Then we can work out a strategy that will give you safety no matter what the future holds, while letting you profit handsomely when your expectations prove to be correct.

Then you can make investment plans that don't get turned upside down when a forecast goes awry or an advisor fails to deliver on his promises.

Then you'll no longer have to worry whether your well-laid plans might go wrong.

4

Going Wrong
Looking for Mr. Right

Investors receive advice from brokers, newsletters, financial newspapers and magazines, books, and personal advisors. And they receive the benefit of investment advice when they buy shares in a mutual fund or put money into a managed account.

More than once you may have found that a source of investment advice is profitable for a while, but then seems to go sour. So you turn to another advisor—perhaps one who's known to have produced big profits for his customers. But, even if you're satisfied with him at first, you find eventually that the results aren't as good as you'd hoped for.

Despite this experience, it's hard to stop hoping that somewhere in the world there's a Mr. Right—an advisor with the wisdom and sophistication to know exactly what you should do.

The truth is that Mr. Right doesn't exist. There is no one person who always knows what's best for everyone. And your investment plans are sure to fail if ever you believe you've found Mr. Right and can stop thinking for yourself.

No advisor should be allowed to make the basic decisions for you. Since you alone understand what you need, only you will always put your interests first. And you alone will live with the consequences of your decisions.

Fortunately, an investment advisor doesn't have to be the all-knowing Mr. Right to be useful to you. In Chapter 34, I'll describe the services a good advisor can perform, and I'll suggest ways to find one who can provide what you need. If you know what to look for, you probably won't pick Mr. Wrong. And if you know what to expect from an advisor, you won't be hurt badly even if you do pick Mr. Wrong.

However, I can understand that you may want to keep looking for Mr. Right. With so many advisors claiming to be Mr. Right, they encourage the idea that he exists—even when a particular candidate fails to persuade you that he's the one.

And the candidates don't always fail. Advisors have found many ways to make their claims plausible—claims that raise your expectations and allow you to believe that someone can take care of everything for you.

You'll be able to look at those claims more realistically if you understand what's behind them. Then maybe you can put aside your search for Mr. Right, focus on the kind of help that's actually available, and find someone to provide it for you.

So this chapter will look at three of the most common ways an advisor attempts to convince you he's Mr. Right—with a track record, with credentials, and with grand impressions.

TRACK RECORDS

The most frequent question an advisor gets is about his track record. The most common answer is "Terrific."

If your name is on any investor mailing list, you probably receive a lot of advertising for newsletters, brokers, mutual funds, money managers, and other financial services—all with terrific track records.

The advertising tells you of advisors and newsletters whose customers have reaped annual gains of 30% to 50% for the past five years, newsletters that put their readers into stocks that doubled in only four months, and advisors who have called every top and bottom in some market for the past ten years.

When you read how successful the top-of-the-line newsletters have been, you may wish you'd been following *them*, instead of the mediocrities you've been reading. Think how rich you would be.

But the mediocre newsletters you've been reading may be boasting right now of the very success you dream of. You don't see their claims because newsletter publishers go out of their way to avoid mailing ads to people who already subscribe.

If you saw their ads, you might discover that *you* were supposed to have made 30% to 50% annually for the past five years, *you* were tipped off to stocks that doubled in only four months, you were warned of every top and bottom in some market for the past ten years.

Advertising isn't the only medium proclaiming fabulous track records. Newspaper and magazine articles refer to the great records of "savvy" advisors. And you can hear the masters themselves on radio and television—relating how they moved investors into and out of markets at just the right times.

You can't help but imagine the profits such a pro could generate for you. But when you sign up for his advice and counsel, you may run into the first rule of investment advice:

> *The advisor with the perfect record up to now will lose his touch the moment you start using his advice.*

For many reasons, stories of past performance are no assurance of future success. The performance may be fictitious, the description of it may be selective, or the advisor may be on the last day of a lucky streak. And, as we'll see, the advisor may not even know what's being claimed for him.

You might think that an advisor's track record is a simple, straightforward matter—like his Social Security number or his Zip Code. But it isn't, and we'll look now at some of the reasons that a track record is no indication of what you can expect.

Incomplete

Very often, what an advisor tells you is less than the whole story.

When an advisor brags that he urged people to buy silver at $1.29, he may be neglecting to tell you that he also urged people to buy at $5, $10, $20, even $40 an ounce—and never got around to telling them to sell.[1]

An advisor may be right when he says that he called the start of the

---

[1]Silver rose from $1.29 in 1971 to $48 in 1980; it was back under $10 in 1987.

bull market in stocks two weeks before it occurred in August 1982. But the story would be more complete if he'd mention that he had called the start of the same bull market six times before getting it right.

The secret of success in the forecasting business is to keep forecasting. Sooner or later you'll get something right, and you can dine out on that for years.

Plain False

Some track records aren't incomplete or misleading. They're just plain false—created out of thin air.

Very few newsletter writers compose their own advertising. The presentation of the track record often is prepared by the company that publishes the newsletter or by an outside ad agency. Even if the advisor is honest and conscientious, his track record may be embellished by someone who isn't so fussy about the truth.

For example, one hard-money newsletter advertised that it had called every major top and bottom in the platinum market in the past decade—even though the newsletter had never even *tried* to call a top or bottom in the platinum market.

Ignorance

Not all false advertising is intentionally false. Sometimes an advisor makes a claim that he simply doesn't understand.

For example, in 1984 a money manager advertised that the stock-market accounts he handled had averaged a "24% compound annual rate of return" for the preceding seven years. Very impressive—especially since many of those years were difficult for the stock market.

After the claim had been publicized for several months, it turned out that neither the advisor, his advertising writer, nor even his accountant knew how to compute a compound annual rate of return.

The true figure was only 15% per year—not very far above the 10.4% average Treasury-bill yield during the 7-year period. Since his managed stock-market accounts entailed much greater risk than T-bills do, the advisor's record wasn't so remarkable after all.[2]

---

[2] The compound annual rate of return is explained in the Glossary on page 496.

Improbability

Some track records have to be rejected out of hand simply because they're so improbable.

For example, throughout 1981, in early 1982, and again through most of 1984, there was a downtrend in every major market—stocks, bonds, gold, commodities, currencies. Even then, some advisors kept on talking about current profits of 30%, 50%, or more—without mentioning the weak markets.

How did an advisor produce such profits when investment prices were falling? Either he recommended a steady diet of short sales, or the profits were made in Cambodian noodle futures.

Neither seems likely. And since the advisor doesn't explain how he conquered the bear markets, it's reasonable to assume that he didn't.

One-Decision Heroes

Even a track record that's accurate can be misleading.

An advisor might advertise a series of winning calls—such as six profitable stock recommendations in a row. But the six victories may have flowed from just one correct decision—the judgment that stocks in general were in a bull market. Given a strong bull market, a buy recommendation on any stock is a probable winner.

And, too, the advisor might boast of, say, three profitable years in a row—simply because the bull market lasts three years. One correct judgment leads to three years of success.

This isn't to say that the judgment as to whether a bull market has started is easy to make or that it isn't valuable. But it is a single judgment.

And many an advisor *always* forecasts a bull market in his specialty—stocks, gold, whatever—maybe because he doesn't do very well at other times, or perhaps because he knows a bull market is bound to show up sooner or later. His eventual, inevitable victory may be due more to stubbornness than to skill.

In the 1970s, a number of advisors made only one fundamental decision—that inflation had come to stay. This led them to recommend precious metals again and again, which made them right most of the time.

With such a record, an advisor would call himself "the world's #1 silver expert'' or award himself "the best track record in the gold market.'' In fact, his expertise was nothing more than a commitment to precious metals that he stuck with for 5 or 10 years.

When the bull market in precious metals peaked in 1980, these advisors peaked too. Writers who seemed always to be right in the 1970s now seem usually to be wrong.

The same thing probably will happen to many other advisors when the 1980s' bull market in stocks comes to an end. When stocks were weak in the 1970s, many of today's hottest advisors had poor records—or weren't even in business. They are heroes so long as the bull continues to roar, but they may not be much help when the roar gives way to a gasp.

Bull markets rescue every bullish advisor. So long as prices are rising, an advisor can make a lot of mistakes and still come out with a decent record. That was true for hard-money advisors in the 1970s, as it has been for stock-market advisors so far in the 1980s.

There probably are only a handful of advisors with impressive records for both the 1970s and the 1980s. And there's no guarantee that those few will extend their success into the 1990s.

Advisors and financial writers enjoy talking about the gains of 20% to 30% per year they've earned in the stock market during the 1980s—which is understandable. But they use these rates of return to show how the "magic of compounding" will build fabulous fortunes in only 10 or 20 years.

Unfortunately, bull markets don't last forever—usually not even for 10 years. And annual returns of 20% to 30% aren't available during the bear markets that follow.

Hidden Risk

A track record that tells how much you would have made over the years can mask a degree of volatility that you may not want to live with.

For example, suppose an advisor showed a gain of 184% over a 7-year period—a compound rate of growth of 16% per year. That sounds attractive—better than average, but perhaps not high enough to make you wonder how risky his program might be.

But you probably would feel differently if you learned that the yearly results were:

1977: + 23%	1981: − 32%
1978: + 36%	1982: + 14%
1979: +130%	1983: − 17%
1980: + 14%	

The overall result obscures the fact that most of the gain was earned in one wonderful year—and that the last three years show a net loss of 35%.

A summary can make a track record seem attractive, but what it took to achieve the final result might be too hair-raising for many people.[3]

Documented

"Documented" is a popular word among writers of investment advertising. And when you hear "documented," you know that "track record" can't be far behind.

A "documented track record" usually means one of four things:

1. The advisor has published a "complete" record of his advice—which may or may not be the truth, the whole truth, and nothing but the truth;

2. Another advisor has mentioned the track record admiringly—even though the other advisor hasn't checked it;

3. The advisor has filed a copy of the track record with some investment association—even though no association verifies the accuracy of track records; or

4. An accountant has certified the track record—which may mean that the accountant is also a notary public, but doesn't mean that the accountant has verified all the claims, transactions, and prices.

The only reliable track record is the one *you* reconstruct by checking everything the advisor has published and verifying the investment prices on which the gains and losses have been computed.

Verifying the prices is important. For example, the jacket of a book claimed for its author: "In 1973 his second investment book recommended the purchase of silver at $1.40 an ounce." But no price history

---

[3]The 7 years of results shown happen to be the results for gold. An advisor who had suggested putting all your money into gold in early 1977, and had never suggested taking it out, would still have been able to claim a 16% growth rate as late as 1983.

I've found indicates that silver sold for less than $1.96 in any market at any time during 1973.[4]

Detailed Track Records

Some advertisements for investment advice purport to list all of the advisor's past recommendations and compare them with subsequent market movements. The abundance of detail in such a presentation enourages you to feel that the track record is being verified for you.

Of course, you have no way of knowing how accurate or complete such a presentation is. And how would you check it?

William Baldwin made the effort for an article in *Forbes* magazine in 1984. He tried to verify the advertised track records of some highly rated market timers—advisors who tell you when to get into or out of the stock market. He found some track records that were—literally—incredible.[5]

One firm had advertised that its buy and sell signals produced a ten-year compound annual gain of 30.2%. (A 30.2% compound annual gain will turn $1 into $100 in only 18 years.)

One of the firm's partners said, "We have a problem with the record because it's almost too good to be true." The *Forbes* writer had to agree after trying to verify the record:

> [The firm] registered with the SEC only in 1981. Before that, [the owners] worked for a succession of brokerage firms, publishing a timing newsletter. . . . How, then, do they have a performance record going back to August 1971?
>
> That was when some foreigners, hearing tales of [one of the partners'] prowess as a technician, hired the pair for timing advice. . . .
>
> Could we see copies of the telexes [transmitting the advice to the foreign customers]? "I telephoned," says [the partner]. How about some contemporaneous work papers? [He] exhibits a handwritten ledger, with *B* and *S* signals noted. There is an *S* next to March 19, 1975, which is indeed one of the advertised sell dates. But there are also three *S*s and two *B*s over the next three months that have been crossed out and do not appear on the published record.

---

[4]If you bought silver for $1.40 in 1973, the police may be looking for you.

[5]"Incredible" is another favorite word in the investment business—as in "incredible track record." The people who say this are actually warning you, since the word "incredible" means, simply, "not to be believed."

Thinking the advisors' track record could be confirmed by what they had written in their newsletter, the *Forbes* writer read back issues.

[The firm] claims it took clients out of the market Dec. 12, 1972, for example, and kept them out for the next six months. The Dec. 22, 1972, newsletter, after some general discussion of economic trends, says: "Despite the lackadaisical performance expected from the Dow next year, we believe that over the near term, secondary-type issues may come to the fore and provide the best opportunities for capital appreciation."

If you had read that newsletter in 1972, you might have run out and bought secondary-type issues, lost money, and 12 years later discovered that the advisors meant for you to sell—not to buy.

The *Forbes* writer found the rest of the company's track record to be equally slippery. And he found similar problems with the published track records of the other firms he investigated.[6]

Vagueness

Many advisors create impressive track records by practicing the art of vagueness.

It *is* an art, since a recommendation won't impress the customers unless it *appears* to be clear-cut at the time it's made. A newsletter writer won't get many subscription renewals by saying, "I firmly believe the market may go up or down next month."

Instead, an advisor will give you such sage advice as "Buy on weakness" or "Buy more on dips." That seems clear enough when you read it or hear it.

But if the price falls, how do you know exactly when to buy? How do you know when the dip has dipped all it's going to? If you buy and then the price dips further, do you buy more? If you knew how to answer such questions, you wouldn't need the advisor.

Afterward, the advisor will say that *he* bought at the very bottom of the correction—no matter how deep or shallow it was—just as he told you to do.

Vagueness also serves the advisor when discussing longer-term possibilities. For example, a newsletter writer might reminisce about his

---

[6]"The Impossible Dream," by William Baldwin, *Forbes*, October 22, 1984, page 144. *Forbes* does not have copies of this issue for sale now, but you may be able to find it in a library. It is a very helpful article.

successful calls of the last few years—that oil prices would collapse, that bonds would be red hot in 1985, that blue chips would lead the stock market, and so on.

As you read his recollections, you may wonder why you didn't act on—or even notice—those juicy morsels when he first presented them. Why did you let these opportunities pass you by? But if you look through back issues of his newsletter, you may find that these weren't calls at all—just vague suspicions buried among other, long-forgotten conjectures.

If an advisor has to tell you what he said last year, he probably didn't say it then in a direct and forceful way—a way that would have prompted you to take notice and take action. If you had done what he now claims to have recommended, you'd have made a lot of money, and you wouldn't need anyone to remind you of it.

But, since most of his readers are new subscribers, he's free to add these "calls" to his track record.

Luck

Even if a track record is for real, there's no way to know how much longer it will continue.

If the fabulous coin-flipper in Chapter 2 had been an investment advisor or the manager of a mutual fund, he would have been besieged by people wanting him to invest their money. But he was only on a lucky streak that had a 50–50 chance of ending on the next toss.

Since no one controls the world or has perfect knowledge of it, every investment outcome reflects an element of chance. So every advisor's record has resulted partly from luck—which might have been good luck or bad luck. In either case, there's an even chance that his luck will be different tomorrow. It's no wonder that one year's star advisor or top mutual fund often turns out to be next year's also-ran.[7]

When you evaluate an advisor, find out how he deals with luck—especially how he allows for bad luck. The best advisors capitalize on good luck and limit the effects of bad luck, so that they do very well during good years and not too poorly during the bad ones.

If an advisor claims his method is too scientific to be affected by luck, look out—he isn't living in the real world.

---

[7]For the final quarter of 1985, Strategic Capital Gains was the #1 mutual fund tracked by Lipper Analytical Services. The very next quarter, Strategic Capital Gains finished 973rd—dead last. (*Barron's*, May 19, 1986, page 47.)

And if an advisor seems to have a "hot hand" right now, it may be because every advisor is entitled to a run of good luck. When an advisor registers with the Securities and Exchange Commission, he gets a form letter confirming his registration, together with a voucher for one hot streak.

Trading Contests

You sometimes read of a contest among investment advisors in which the winner produced a phenomenal result—perhaps doubling his initial capital within six months or so. Since the results were verified by the contest's sponsor, the outcome—and the winner's talent—seem to be on the level.

Realize, however, that any advisor competing in such a contest will handle his investments in a way that's far different from anything he could do with your investments over a period of time.

In the contest, he will take every risk imaginable in hope of being blessed by good luck and earning a spectacular return. If he fails, his poor result might show up once in the lower part of the contest results, and his participation soon will be forgotten. But if he strikes it rich, he can advertise the result for the rest of his career.

Obviously, you don't want him to approach *your* investments in this way. And, probably, he wouldn't. But whether or not he would, a spectacular contest result offers no hope to you.

Track Records

It isn't that most advisors lie, or that no one ever calls a market turn, or that all successful advisors are just lucky, or that predictions never come true, or that advisors never make money for their customers. Some track records may be exactly as presented to you.

But, unfortunately, there's no simple way for you to distinguish them from the fairy tales. So you have to take every claim with a grain of salt. No track record should convince you that you've found Mr. Right.

CREDENTIALS

When an advisor introduces himself as Mr. Right, he will present his credentials for your inspection. He doesn't expect you to be won over by the credentials themselves, but he knows that they can make you more receptive to the rest of his story.

Certification & Registration

One credential is membership in an organization that supposedly polices its members and insists upon high levels of competence and ethics.

I once heard an advisor on a TV talk show answer the question, "How do I find a reliable investment advisor?" by saying:

> Look in the Yellow Pages under "Financial Planners," run your finger down the column until you find one that says *"Certified* Financial Planner," and call him.

A few years later, I was amused to come across a man who had purchased from a trade association, by mail order, the titles "Certified Financial Planner" and "Certified Life Underwriter" for his dog.[8]

A financial planner might be valuable to you. But no organization will screen advisors according to your standards and tell you who's right for you. You have to judge for yourself.

Another apparent certification is registration with the Securities and Exchange Commission (SEC) or other regulatory agency. But about all a registration certifies is that the advisor knows how to fill out forms and submit them on time.

Unless you've been convicted of a felony or have run afoul of the law in other particular ways, *you* can become an SEC-registered investment advisor. Just fill out a form and pay $150. A knowledge of securities, exchanges, or commissions isn't required.

By the same token, when a regulatory agency accuses an advisor of wrongdoing, it doesn't mean he's actually done anything wrong—at least not by your standards. Regulators use words in strange ways. When they say an advisor is guilty of "fraud," for example, it may mean he holds opinions different from those of the regulators—or that he didn't submit his registration forms on time.

---

[8]The man was financial planner John J. Gargan of Tampa, Florida. He sent me a photocopy of his dog's certification. The dog's name was Boris "Bo" Regaard.

Awards

Another credential is the awards an advisor has received. Such honors tell you about the advisor's competence at collecting awards, but they don't tell you much else.

One famous investment advisor negotiates vigorously with the producers of investment seminars to get himself billed as the "keynote speaker"—and then tells his audience that he's touched to be so honored by his peers.

Another sometimes makes his appearance at an investment seminar contingent upon receiving a special award—such as "Advisor of the Year" or "World's Best Thinker"—and proudly advertises his trophies.

One newsletter's masthead says, "Declared 'Most profitable advisory letter,' *Hulbert Financial Digest*, March 1981"—even though the *Digest* has never declared the newsletter to be anything, and although the newsletter has never finished at the top of any list the *Digest* has compiled.

Even if an honor actually has been given, it provides no assurance that the advisor will do well in the future. In 1983 the City Treasurer of San Jose, California, was chosen "Treasurer of the Year" by the California Municipal Treasurers Association. The next year he lost $60 million of the city's reserves in bad investments.[9]

Advisory Committee

Some credentials are borrowed.

The publisher of a newsletter might recruit a group of famous economists and investment advisors to be his "Editorial Board" or to serve as "Contributing Editors." However, these celebrities don't review the newsletter's text or even see an issue before it's published, so they can't prevent the newsletter from giving bad—or even dangerous—advice.

Investment home-study courses often enlist famous people from the investment world to act as an advisory board. Here, too, the board is of no benefit to the investor. The members of the board usually are paid only for the use of their names—not for contributing anything to the course.

[9]San Francisco *Chronicle*, May 23, 1984, page 16.

Publishers can be rather loose about using names. My name has shown up in advertisements as an editorial advisor to two different newsletters—neither of which had even solicited my participation. If I *had* been approached, I would have declined, because I would have no advance knowledge of—nor be able to prevent—anything misleading, misinformed, false, risky, or dangerous that might be said in someone else's newsletter.

In a more bizarre example, a publisher launched a newsletter to investigate and report on the investment industry. In his advertising, he named a dozen former CIA agents as the publication's investigators. It turned out that he had made up all but one of the names.

GRAND IMPRESSIONS

Some advisors rise above the pettiness of mere track records and credentials, and present themselves as classy, expensive, authoritative institutions.

Such an advisor usually adopts a slightly stuffy-sounding name for his firm—perhaps including the word "Institute," "Econometric," or "Consultants." This is meant to imply that the firm receives six-figure retainers from multinational conglomerates, that its well-placed contacts around the world call in daily to report the secrets that are moving markets, that it uses a computer big enough to heat an apartment house, and that it issues its forecasts on parchment in editions that are limited and numbered.

The presentation can be overwhelming. This isn't some mutual fund salesman in the basement of a Sears store. It's a prestigious institution whose name, when mentioned, should be accompanied by a symphony orchestra.[10]

These people don't solicit new clients, they "accept" them. And if you learn that the price isn't as high as you'd assumed, you might rush to sign up before they change their minds.

One such firm drifted to earth in August 1985, when a newsletter interviewed the "Founder and Chairman" of a firm of "economic consultants." During the interview, Mr. F&C explained that "The models we use on a long-term basis have never been wrong."

Whew!

---

[10]"Prestigious" is another popular word in the investment world. Accept it as a warning, since its original meaning is "of, relating to, or marked by illusion, conjuring, or trickery"— *Webster's New Collegiate Dictionary*, 1973.

As he referred to the cyclical studies, historical patterns, and arcane techniques that enable the firm to predict the future, he made you feel you were in the presence of true genius—although you couldn't actually understand much of what he was saying.

Three fairly intelligible forecasts did emerge from Mr. F&C's August 1985 interview:

1. The Dow Jones Industrial Average was starting "a five to six month consolidation period from the July high." (Instead, the Dow began a 500-point advance the month after the interview.)

2. Gold would reach its low probably in the week of November 18. How low? ". . . we're showing a very sharp correction which could bring it back down to 276 or 280 very shortly." And "There's potential for gold to move down to $192." (The actual low came in December—at $315, only $5 below the price at the time of the interview.)

3. Silver's 1985 low "could" be $2.40 or $3.80. (The reason for having two possibilities wasn't explained. The actual 1985 low was $5.57.)

Of course, every forecast was couched in such imprecise, slippery terms that Mr. F&C will never be held accountable for the money a trusting investor would have lost betting on his advice.

Prestigious institutions can be wrong, too.[11]

MR. RIGHT

When you realize that most track records are at least partly fictitious, when you strip away the camouflage of credentials, and when you get past the impressive fronts, you're left with the simple truth that there is no Mr. Right—no one advisor who knows exactly what you should do.

Then you are ready to benefit from the many good things an investment advisor can do for you. In Chapter 34, I'll offer some guidelines for selecting an advisor and profiting from his help. If nothing else, a good advisor can provide a valuable service just by pointing out alternatives you weren't aware of.

---

[11]As I'll discuss on page 212, Mr. F&C may have been misquoted by an interviewer who reported what he would have liked Mr. F&C to say. In fact, Mr. F&C may be a reasonable fellow. But I'd still rather not bet on his "long-term models."

But he can't define your goals or make your decisions for you. If you let an advisor decide—by default—what your goals are, what techniques you should employ, and what financial risks and emotional burdens you should bear, then your investment plans are bound to go wrong.

5

Going Wrong
Trying to Be Scientific

It is often in the name of science that the most unscientific investment plans are laid.

An investment system, you're told, has been tested scientifically. Or a particular event is inevitable because economic science assures it. Or a forecast can be relied upon because it is the product of the scientific method.

But, somehow, when you bet your money on the investment systems and forecasts that proudly display the "Made with Science" label, they don't operate with the same reliability as the Universal Law of Gravitation.

It's understandable that investors believe science can be put to use in the markets, since it's employed effectively in so many other matters.

After all, science predicts the flow of tomorrow's tides and the very day that Halley's Comet will arrive in the 21st century. With the right economic theories, sufficient data, a large enough computer, and a scientific attitude, why can't we predict next year's inflation rate?

WHAT IS ECONOMICS?

Unfortunately, applying science to investing isn't quite so simple.

In the investment world, science means economics. And to understand and plan your investments properly, I think it's vital to understand what economics is and how it can help you. It's even more important to appreciate its limitations. A proper understanding of the scope and reach of economics can explain why so many of the best-laid plans go awry.

We need to begin with the two basic elements studied by economics: resources and desires.

Resources

An individual has certain resources simply by virtue of being human —such as personal energy, intelligence, knowledge, and time. However, those resources are limited. He has only so much energy, so much intelligence, and so much knowledge. And since he won't live forever, he has only so much time in which to use them.

In pursuit of his goals, he applies his human resources to the world around him. But the availability of natural resources (land, water, air, minerals, vegetation, and so forth) also is limited—because of the limits of nature, and because the human resources needed for the discovery and exploitation of natural resources are limited.

The application of human resources to natural resources yields the products and services that people want—either for immediate consumption or for use in producing other products or services for consumption.

The quantity of products and services produced also are limited— limited to what human resources can extract from the available natural resources. There may be enough timber growing in the world to supply every human being with a house, but there isn't enough manpower to harvest the timber, mill the lumber, manufacture the tools, and construct the houses—let alone cook lunch for everyone until the work is completed.

It can seem that some people possess unlimited resources. But in fact not even the richest man in the world can spend with abandon, and the most oppressive government quickly finds that there's a limit to the resources it can extract from its citizens.

Desires

The second element of economics is human desire.

Every individual has wants. His wants include short-term goals (such as what he wants to do in the next few minutes) and long-term goals (such as what he wants to do 20 years from now), as well as goals for periods in between.

His desires might be what we think of as self-centered—such as wanting to acquire a large house and a fancy car. Or they might be what people call altruistic—such as wanting to be a missionary or to feed the poor. Whatever they may be, they are *his* desires, and his efforts are aimed at satisfying them.

Unlike resources, which are limited, desires are boundless. Someone's desires might seem modest—a small list of things that would make him content. But we usually notice only the desires that clamor the loudest or that can be satisfied most easily. As soon as they're fulfilled, other wants become apparent—desires that were less urgent or were more difficult to satisfy, or that arose from satisfying the first desires.

An individual who's homeless and hungry might love the idea of spending a few weeks in Hawaii, but he won't concern himself with that while he's preoccupied with finding a meal and a place to sleep. Only when those more urgent desires have been satisfied will he give serious thought to sunny beaches and hula dancers.

Because each person's desires are unlimited, he has to place *values* on the things he desires—deciding which among them are the most important and should be satisfied even at the expense of the others.

But as one desire is satisfied, another moves up to take its place. The process never ends. An individual without desires is not what we think of as human.

Economics Defined

A human being's desires are unlimited, but his resources aren't. Thus only some of his desires can be satisfied, and satisfying them means neglecting others.

So an individual is forced to choose which desires he will try to satisfy, and to choose the means of satisfying them that will get the most from his limited resources. This is the concern of economics.

Economics is the study of the choices people make—how they allocate limited resources to the satisfaction of unlimited desires.

Economics tries to identify the effects that flow from each choice —particularly how each choice affects one's ability to satisfy other desires, and how the choices made by one person affect the opportunities available to other people.

Economic issues can be as seemingly trivial as the question of whether to use one's limited time to watch television or clean the house, or as far-reaching as trying to determine the cost to the nation (in other satisfactions that must be forgone) of a national program of compulsory medical care.

In short, economics tries to determine the *consequences* of decisions—including the wishes that would have to be abandoned or postponed in order to satisfy the desires being considered.

Behavioral Science

Economics studies how the choices people make today lead to the conditions of tomorrow. In this it is similar to other branches of science that foresee tomorrow's effects from today's causes.

But the physical sciences (such as physics or chemistry) are quite different from the behavioral sciences (such as economics, psychology, or sociology). In fact, it may be confusing things even to call economics a science.

There are four basic reasons that economics doesn't live up to the hopes of people who want to use it "scientifically" (meaning in the manner of the physical sciences) to predict the future or to construct reliable investment systems.

ECONOMIC THEORY

The first problem is the difference between economics and the physical sciences.

The physical sciences deal with *things*—particles, forces, masses, substances, structures—that are uniform and constant. Every electron is identical to every other electron—yesterday, today, and tomorrow —and each one is a perfect specimen.

Economics deals with *people*—human beings who think and learn and pursue individual goals, including goals that often aren't clearly defined. Each person is different, and each person changes from day to day.

In the physical sciences, experiments are designed to isolate each variable, so that scientists can identify and measure the separate influence and effect of each factor.

Because scientists are dealing with *things*, they can apply their discoveries to practical matters—confident that the relationships they've found are correct and will be exactly the same tomorrow. That's why most airplanes actually fly, and why so few microwave ovens produce ice cubes.

In economics, however, the "particles" are human beings, each different from all the others, and the "forces" are their many, changing desires—both spoken and unspoken.

Everything in economics deals with the actions and values of individual human beings. We may talk about economic issues that seem impersonal—such as the supply of wheat or the level of interest rates. But wheat doesn't plant itself, fertilize itself, harvest itself, or offer itself for sale. When we talk about wheat or interest rates, we're really talking about what thinking, purposeful *individuals* do—as producers, consumers, borrowers, and lenders.

Because economics deals with human choices that are constantly changing, there's very little in the methodology of the physical sciences that economics can use. You can't herd human beings into a laboratory for controlled tests to discover their reactions to every imaginable set of circumstances.

Human action is never suspended or brought to a standstill so that we can isolate, inspect, and analyze the elements of human activity. Thus the techniques of the physical sciences can't be used to verify an economic principle.

The Use of History

History gives us general clues to human behavior, but you can't use history to prove an economic theory.

No matter what one group of people did at one time, another group—with different values—may behave differently in a situation that seems similar. Even when the people are the same, the circumstances will be changed in some way. And even if the people and circumstances were both the same, the reactions will be different—because the people know how matters turned out the first time.

History can be used only to *refute* an economic principle. If you believe that event A must *always* lead to event B, you can see whether history provides any examples to the contrary. But no matter how many times A *was* followed by B, and even if you find no contrary examples, you can't be sure the relationship will hold tomorrow—when the circumstances and participants will be different.

Chemicals and metals don't think or make choices or learn from experience; that's why they're so predictable. Human beings do think and learn—both well and badly—which means that we can never be sure what they'll do tomorrow.

A common cliché says that "human nature never changes." Even if that's true, two aspects of human nature are (1) ever-changing desires, and (2) the ability to learn new ways to achieve whatever is desired.

Deduction

Because economic theories can't be tested and refined by the methods of the physical sciences, the principles of economics have to be developed through deductive reasoning. An economist attempts to apply to each question what he believes about the way human beings act.

The basic premise of economics is:

Each individual will do what he believes will best satisfy the desires that compete for his resources, whatever those desires may be.

Even though some people plan 20 years ahead while others think only of immediate gratification—even though each person's goals, priorities, talents, nature, and emotions are uniquely his own—this simple, universal principle is the premise upon which we build an understanding of human behavior.

Every individual uses his resources in the best way he can imagine. Whenever he buys, sells, or trades something, he does so to improve his situation.

From this premise, an economist works outward—trying to deduce further economic principles. Because only individual human beings act, the economist starts by pondering how one individual in isolation tries to satisfy his desires, and then how individuals interact and influence one another.

He eventually arrives at conclusions—such as principles of supply and demand, how the money supply affects inflation, how changes in corn prices affect the supply of hogs, what consequences ensue when governments prevent individuals from engaging in certain transactions.

But even the best economist isn't so wise or ingenious that he can be sure that each step forward in his theory is completely consistent with the nature of human action. He can't be sure that the economic "truth" he's discovered won't be proven false by events some time in the future.

So we begin with the limitation that we can never be sure the economic theories we use are perfect and eternal.

APPLICATION

The second limitation of economics is that the application of economic principles requires a particular kind of imagination and talent. It's quite different from relying on the laws of physics to drive a car or design one.

Despite my belief that no one can predict the future (expressed so adamantly in Chapter 3), it's true that economics' most important application is in looking into the future—looking for the effects of what has already happened, and trying to foresee how those effects will lead to further consequences.

Economics tries to recognize the not-so-obvious, long-run consequences of an act, as well as what happens immediately. It looks for the unseen effects, as well as the obvious. It attempts to see how choices made by one person today will affect the opportunities available to other people tomorrow.

As Frédéric Bastiat put it 140 years ago:

> There is only one difference between a bad economist and a good one: the bad economist confines himself to the *visible* effect; the good economist takes into account both the effect that can be seen and those effects that must be *foreseen*.[1]

And as Henry Hazlitt restated it 40 years ago:

---

[1]"What Is Seen and What Is Not Seen," by Frédéric Bastiat, from *Selected Essays on Political Economy* (Van Nostrand 1964 edition), page 1.

The art of economics consists in looking not merely at the immediate but at the longer effects of any act or policy; it consists in tracing the consequences of that policy not merely for one group but for all groups.[2]

Economics tries to foresee how an investment in a new machine will enhance a company's ability to do some things but take resources away from other valuable things—how it will affect its payroll, tax bill, product development, and maintenance costs.

Economics tries to identify what a nation will have to give up if the government decides that everyone is entitled to free milk and cookies, or decrees that no one may be hired whose labor isn't worth a minimum wage.

If the Federal Reserve System creates new reserves for commercial banks, will this increase the supply of lendable funds and cause interest rates to decline? By very much? Will the new money this creates cause lenders to fear a rise in inflation and to hold out for *higher* interest rates? If interest rates do go down, will deposits of banks decline—reducing the availability of credit to bank customers? What other consequences might ensue?

But to trace the effects of a cause through myriad tributaries is no simple task. For one thing, no economic principle operates in isolation; each event reflects many different principles.

As Henry Hazlitt said, economics is an *art*. To be a good economist requires far more than just a university degree and a knowledge of economic theory; an economist must have the imagination and creativity of a novelist.

It's no wonder that economists disagree about the future—and the present and the past. No one can be absolutely certain of the consequences of an act until long after the fact, if at all.

DATA

The third limitation in economics is that so little of the data needed to develop a precise forecast are actually available.

Some data *are* available. The supplies of some resources can be measured—up to a point. It's possible to make a fairly good estimate of how many bushels of wheat were grown in America last year, or how many barrels of oil are in storage right now.

[2]*Economics in One Lesson*, by Henry Hazlitt (Harper & Bros. 1946 edition), page 5.

But most of the important data in economics concern human beings—their motivations, preferences, and intentions—both as producers and as consumers. Human values aren't visible or countable. We can't look into the minds of people to examine their desires— much less know which desires they consider most urgent.

Surveys tell very little about the preferences of people. Individuals often won't—or can't—articulate their desires. Well-run companies have suffered great losses because the best market research yielded a false picture of what people wanted. The Edsel and "New Coke" are only two examples of extensive, sophisticated market research that failed to foresee actual choices.

And even if you're confident that many people desire something, there's no way to know how much they will give up to get it. Someone may claim to want something very much. But at the moment of truth—when required to give up some other satisfaction to get it—he may discover that he doesn't want the object as much as he had said.

For example, surveys over the past couple of decades have shown consistently that consumers want safer cars. This has encouraged governments to impose safety standards on automakers. But when manufacturers offer optional equipment that enhances a car's safety, consumers in general decline to pay the price. Greater safety is desired, but other desires are more urgent.[3]

The only way to measure an individual's desire for something is by what he's willing to give up to get it—which can be discovered only after the fact. Before the fact, expressions of wish and hope only hint at what people will do.

Consequently, what we know with certainty about individuals' economic preferences is knowledge only of the past, not of the future.

QUALITY VS. QUANTITY

The fourth reason that economics can't make precise, scientific forecasts is that economic theory deals only with *qualitative* relationships—while the physical sciences deal with *quantitative* matters.

Someone's preference of beef over pork is a qualitative comparison.

---

[3]Government programs to compel companies to provide certain services ignore the difference between wants in the abstract and wants worth paying for. The desires that prompt government action may be real, but too weak to prompt a consumer to give up other things when he knows he must pay for it himself.

A quantitative comparison would be a number that showed the *extent* to which he prefers beef to pork.

A qualitative economic principle is that, if it becomes more profitable to produce a commodity, the supply of it tends to increase. But economic theory can't determine the *quantity* by which a given price increase would cause the supply to increase. Any estimate will be a guess, educated though it may be.

Economics always comes back to the *values held by human beings*. Since value is subjective, in the eye of each individual, it can't be measured, quantified, or used for mathematical analysis.

How do you measure the demand for a commodity, the demand for money, or the intensity of desire for something? How do you know at what level of international tension how many individuals will dump how much of their stock portfolios and buy gold instead? And how do you measure tension?

Economics can deal with *comparisons*, but not intensities. We can't add an individual's wants to those of other people to arrive at a number that represents how intensely people in general want this or that.

If mortgage interest rates fall below 10%, we expect many homeowners to refinance their mortgages—but *how* many? We assume that the number will be larger than at higher rates, but there's no way to measure in advance how big the increase will be.

As the price of silver rises, more and more industrial consumers will look for substitutes—reducing the demand for silver. But no formula can tell us at what price the supply will outrun demand—or what price investors will think is high enough to warrant selling—or at what price other investors will buy because they think a bandwagon has started to roll.

Economic theory can only compare one situation with another; it can't measure the difference and give it a number.

Statistics

We can look at last year's sales figures for clues to what people want and how intensely they want it. But those numbers don't reveal today's values, they describe yesterday's actions. Today's desires can't be measured until after they've been revealed by what people do today.

Tomorrow won't repeat yesterday, because the circumstances now aren't the same as they were yesterday. That's one reason that sales figures for almost any product—cars, houses, entertainment, even foods—vary so widely from year to year.

Statistics tell us about the past, not about the present. And a great deal of the statistics that economists and investment analysts rely on —including such things as the Gross National Product, the Consumer Price Index, housing starts, and international trade figures—are only crude estimates.

SCIENCE

If you try to use economics to predict the future, you have four strikes against you.

First, our ideas of how the economic world works are imperfect because we can't confirm them through controlled tests.

Second, the application of economic theory isn't simple or unambiguous. It requires creativity and imagination, as well as an interest in the study of human nature.

Third, even if we could be sure that economic theory were being applied correctly, we couldn't obtain sufficient data about human values to predict the direction of the economy or investments.

And fourth, even if we had the data, we couldn't reduce an expected result to numbers—telling us precisely how high or how low an investment price, interest rate, inflation rate, or anything else will go.

Economic principles are observations about human action—such as that consumption of an item tends to increase as its cost is reduced— not formulas that can tell you by how much consumption will increase. Economics may explain reasonably that A generally leads to B, but it has no formula to tell how soon and in what quantity.

Investors and advisors who notice general principles and tendencies in the investment markets want very much to refine these generalities into fixed, reliable formulas.

For example, many investors have observed that an investment tends to draw the most publicity near the end of a bull market. Some of them have tried to take the "scientific" next step and develop procedures for measuring the extent of an investment's publicity—gathering numbers that should indicate when a bull market has ended. But there's no way in economics to translate a general observation into an explicit formula.

Observations about the way markets work are valuable. They can help you to be alert, keep you from rushing into an investment on the heels of a crowd, and keep you from getting carried away. But they can't tell you when a bull market will end—no more than a fortune cookie can.

Authority

I realize that you often read or hear the words of economists and investment advisors who *are* able to apply economics scientifically; who have developed formulas to measure the past, present, and future with precision; and who speak with the confidence that only success can bring.

But what you might not know is that some of these people have made some of the most unsuccessful forecasts imaginable.

If they speak authoritatively, it's not because they've been right in the past but only because humility isn't in their repertoires. No matter how many times they fail, their self-assurance never weakens. Their greatest (or only) talent is for speaking authoritatively.

One famous investment advisor, in the early 1980s, forecast again and again a resumption of inflation that again and again failed to arrive. But he still was able to begin a dissertation in 1984:

> The principal reason most commentators are confused about the economy, where it is and where it is likely to be in the next quarter, or next year, or the year after next, is . . .

No failure will make him doubt his profound understanding of economics and his superior insight into what's going on in the world.

ECONOMICS & INVESTMENTS

Economics may have its limitations, but it's still a valuable and fascinating study.

Economic theory can help you to understand the world, to be prepared for what might be surprises to others, to understand why the consequences of government programs are seldom those intended, to reject unrealistic investment plans, to disregard clichés, and to develop the strategy and portfolio with the best chance of protecting you in the unknowable future.

Economics can't tell you what *will* happen. But it can prepare you for what *might* happen.

Economic principles are especially useful in the investment world. It's a great help to understand how increases in the money supply increase the likelihood of inflation, or why large federal deficits cause interest rates to be higher than they would be otherwise, or how price controls usually lead to shortages and—eventually—to higher prices.

Economics is an even bigger help in rejecting nonsense. With an understanding of economics, you often can judge immediately that an idea you hear is inconsistent or logically flawed. You'll know that OPEC members can't raise oil prices just by wanting to, or that a population of 1 billion doesn't make China an economic power.

Just don't expect economics to unlock the secrets of the future for you. The value of economics is in its ability to reveal hidden consequences, to keep you open to *possibilities* that others ignore, and to help you prepare for potential futures that the arrogant refuse to consider.

6

Going Wrong
Acting on Superstitions

Suppose you could take a walk with the investment advisor you most respect—giving you the opportunity to see how a great mind works.

As you walk together down the street, he looks up at the sky and says, "The clouds are in a straight line across the horizon—a bullish sign for the stock market."

A little farther along, you come to a ladder propped against a wall. He steers you around it, explaining, "I don't want to walk under a ladder. The week ahead is going to be critical for our stocks."

You chuckle politely at his little joke. But when he glares at you, you realize he's serious. "The next week may be the crossroads," he says sternly, "determining whether stocks continue up or slip into a bear market. I don't want to take any chances."

You say to him, "You don't really believe that the pattern of the clouds or your path around a ladder has anything to do with the market's performance, do you?"

"Yes I do."

"How can you? What do clouds have to do with stocks? How does walking under a ladder influence the investment markets?"

"I don't know *how* these things work. But I can tell you this: I've been in the investment business for 14 years, and I know that they *do*."

There's no way to answer such an assertion. You can't investigate all the advisor's encounters with ladders and cloud formations over the last 14 years. But you don't feel a need to. You simply assume that any connections he's seen must be coincidence—since there's no conceivable tie between clouds and stocks, or between ladders and markets.

So, rather than argue with him, you resolve to spend the next week looking for a new advisor.

The Numbers Game

To find a replacement for the cloud-watcher, you take a friend's advice to see a trader who's known to have an excellent track record.

When you meet the trader, you're encouraged by his studious manner. Here's a man who uses his intellect.

During the conversation, you ask him about the outlook for gold. He says, "Gold looks good. The next uptrend should last 13 months and bring an increase of $144."

You're impressed by his precision; he must be one of those market geniuses you've heard about. Here's a chance to find out how he does it. So you ask him why he's so sure about gold's future.

He says, "In the last uptrend, gold gained $89, and 1.618 times $89 is $144. The number 1.618 is the Golden Ratio, you know. As to the timing, the last two uptrends lasted 5 and 8 months, respectively. Whenever 8 follows 5, 13 usually comes next—so the $144 rally should take about 13 months."

You wonder whether the cloud-watcher would be willing to handle your account again.

Numerology at Work

While this story is fanciful, its elements are more commonplace than you might think.

I haven't actually encountered much cloudophilia or ladderphobia, but the investment world is full of superstitions.

One of the more popular varieties is numerology—the belief that certain numbers or patterns of numbers have special significance. For example, an advisor who has been quoted frequently by newspaper wire services began a newsletter article in 1986 with:

> We forecast a new all-time high for gold in this cycle, much higher than the 1980 high of $850.

If you're interested in gold, that opening would certainly get your attention, and you'd want to know how he arrived at his opinion. Fortunately, he explains:

> In the early 1970s, gold rose from $35 to $180 (the orthodox Elliott Wave high). This was a factor of 5 (35 × 5 = 175), a Fibonacci number. From 1976 to 1980, gold advanced from $103 to $850, a Fibonacci factor of 8 (103 × 8 = 824). The price low of the 1980–1985 bear market in gold was $285. The next number in the Fibonacci sequence is 13. If the current bull market in gold continues its Fibonacci relationship, then it could peak to $3705 (285 × 13).

I'll explain Fibonacci numbers shortly, but for now please understand that the example isn't hypothetical or even exceptional. The superstitions I'll discuss in this chapter touch perhaps 75% or more of all investment advisors. There's a better-than-even chance that your favorite advisor is guided by some of them.

If you wonder why the best-laid investment plans seem to go wrong so often, part of the answer may be that many plans are founded on superstitions—including superstitions believed by advisors you may be depending on.

IDEAS

There are four types of ideas that you might act upon:

1. *The Verifiable:* You may not understand all the ins and outs of the law of gravity, but you can verify its central thesis at any time just by dropping something and watching it fall to the ground.

2. *The Reasonable:* You haven't actually tested the idea that you'll drown if you stay too long under water. But it is consistent with what you know about water, life, and breathing—and you can't imagine a way for the idea not to be true.

3. *The Authoritative:* You've never checked personally to be sure that Africa is located where the atlas says it is, but you trust Rand-McNally's version of the world—because you believe they've verified the matter using standards you would consider reasonable, and because you've never found them saying anything you know to be wrong.

4. *The Superstitious:* A superstition is a belief that hasn't been verified (and perhaps *can't* be verified)—for which no one has a reasonable explanation, for which you can't even imagine what a reasonable explanation might be, and for which no authoritative source has claimed that there *is* a reasonable explanation.

You don't accept the idea that breaking a mirror brings seven years' bad luck, because nothing you know about life suggests any connection between mirrors and misfortune. In addition, there's no body of authoritative opinion that accepts this idea, and it's doubtful that you'll spend seven years trying to verify it.

Superstition in Investing

Since you and I aren't superstitious, no one could convince us to worry over a broken mirror, or to act on the premise that "things happen in threes," or to pay attention to ladders or black cats.

But somehow we can be fooled into accepting more sophisticated superstitions by someone who leads us to believe that a particular investment rule *has* been verified, or explains it in a way that *seems* reasonable, or cloaks it in a mantel of authority.

As we saw in the preceding chapter, economics and investing depend very little on principles that are verifiable—ideas that can be proven once and for all.

Most of the economic principles you act on are accepted because they seem reasonable to you, or because you believe they've been checked out or thought through by someone you consider to be reasonable.

Because economics deals with the decisions and actions of human beings, an idea is reasonable only if it's consistent with what we know about the way human beings act. What electrons or planets do isn't relevant. Economic event A can be expected to lead to economic event B only if you can imagine how the actions of human beings create a continuous thread leading from A to B.

Selling Superstition

Because the principles of economics and investing can't be proven once and for all, there's a lot of room for pseudoscience and superstition. People who reject ideas about full moons and black cats readily accept superstitions pertaining to investments.

There are three principal ways that investors are induced to accept superstitions that have no reasonable explanations.

The first is with evidence that is incomplete. You're shown that event B followed event A four times in a row, but you aren't shown the seven times event A *wasn't* followed by event B. Or you aren't shown the nine times that event B occurred without event A preceding it. Or it isn't pointed out that events A and B are just two of a large group of events that seem to follow whenever event Q occurs.

The second is that the idea comes from a source you consider to be authoritative. You may respect the person who's promoting the idea because he is known to have an outstanding record, or because he once made a remarkable forecast that came to pass, or because his economic or political philosophy seems to be similar to yours. Or you may simply be bowled over by his credentials—as an economist, a scientist, or a famous person—or even by his confident manner.

The third possibility is that the idea comes wrapped in an authoritative package. It's claimed that the idea has been tested extensively and verified beyond question. Or perhaps the promoter of the idea dazzles you with mathematical and statistical techniques that are useful in the physical sciences but have no place in economics.

In other areas of life, one or more of these components might not be enough to overcome anyone's natural reserve and skepticism. But ideas that promise to make investing easy or simple generally are welcomed because most investors want so much to believe that they're true.

Investing isn't easy work. It draws more on judgment than on science. There is no skill, no technique that can be relied upon to work unfailingly—no rules that provide consistent knowledge of the way a market is going to move.

In order to find something they can count on, many investors are willing to set aside their skepticism, to give any idea the benefit of every doubt, to ignore the exceptions or logical flaws that would scream at them if the subject were something other than investing.

And so superstitions are accepted eagerly, are repeated endlessly, give birth to new superstitions, and become a large part of the "common knowledge" of the investing world.

Superstitions Widespread

The practice of "technical analysis" is overflowing with superstition. For one example, some technicians believe that an investment price plotted on a graph that forms a pattern similar to a drooping flag is a prelude to a rally—even though there's no reasonable explanation for this belief and no rigorous attempt (that I know of) has ever been made to test the idea.[1]

Superstition isn't confined to technicians, however. In fact, it pervades the investment world. Investors and advisors rely on trading systems, on supposedly fixed economic relationships, and on legends about how investment prices move—all without demanding an explanation of why they should be true, and usually without any serious attempt to determine whether history has refuted them.

The common explanation is, "I don't know *why* it works this way, but it always does."

But that's not much of an explanation. Even a witch doctor who forecasts the future by throwing chicken bones on the ground could argue, "I don't know why it works, but it always has." Every cult of magic, no matter how outlandish, has adherents who swear that it always works.

In most cases, the technique actually works only infrequently. However, when a person joins a cult, although he may not learn how to see the future, he does learn how to explain away the lapses between theory and practice.

Even if you see that an idea *has* worked on one or more occasions, the lack of a reasonable explanation makes the idea unreliable. Someone watching the coin-flipper from Chapter 2 (as he flipped heads time after time) might say, "I don't know why it works, but it *does* work."

Any cause-and-effect relationship must be explained in terms of what we know about how human beings act. You should remain unconvinced until someone explains how the actions of one person lead to the actions of another, to another and another, until you arrive at the effect that's supposed to flow from the original cause.

---

[1] I'll discuss further examples of superstition in technical analysis (as well as the more reasonable aspects of technical analysis) in Chapter 8.

Without such an explanation, the odds are very great that the evidence for the relationship is contrived or is the result of coincidence.

Realism vs. Superstition

Studying coincidences can be entertaining, but it isn't the highway to investment profits—any more than studying rabbits' feet is the key to avoiding accidents.

It's more productive to examine common rules of investing to see whether they're consistent with what you know about the way human beings act.

It's a common belief, for example, that gold is an inflation hedge. The idea that bull markets in gold tend to coincide roughly with periods of rising inflation *is* understandable because it's consistent with what we know about the way people act: (1) that many people around the world hold U.S. dollars as a store of wealth; (2) that people try to avoid losing wealth (to inflation or to anything else); (3) that gold— because it's liquid, portable, divisible, readily identifiable, private, and stable in supply—is a ready alternative to U.S. dollars as a store of value; and (4) that during periods when the U.S. dollar is losing value to inflation, gold's usefulness as a store of value increases by comparison.[2]

Even if someone should refute this analysis eventually, it wouldn't mean that it hadn't been reasonable to accept it.

On the other hand, it is mere superstition to believe, as many people do, that gold prices *foretell* the future of inflation; or that the scope of the next bull market in gold can be foreseen by measuring the last bull market; or that gold stocks are a leading indicator of gold bullion.

No one can explain why people in the gold market should behave in such a way as to make these things happen, no conceivable explanations seem possible, and all these ideas can be refuted by history. They are just superstitions that happen to be widely accepted.

Nor is there any reason to accept stock market superstitions such as "July is a bullish month" or "A chart gap must be filled eventually" or "The market always does well in years ending in 5"—until someone can explain, in terms of how the world works, why any of this should be so. I haven't seen anyone even try.

---

[2]The relationship between gold and inflation is discussed further in Chapter 25.

FIBONACCI NUMBERS

A few superstitions have the loyalty of occult-minded investors but are too bizarre for the average investor or advisor to swallow.

And yet once you stop demanding reasonable explanations for investment rules, you become fair game for just about anything anyone might dream up.

You could, for example, find yourself entranced by Fibonacci numbers—and you'd have plenty of company. Many investors and advisors believe that mathematics can unlock the secrets of the financial universe—and that Fibonacci numbers are the key.

Leonardo Fibonacci (approx. 1170–1230) was an Italian mathematician who devised a numerical sequence that begins with 1 and 1, which are the "seeds" of the sequence. These are added together to make 2, which is the third number. Then 1 and 2 are added to make 3; 2 and 3 to make 5; 3 and 5 to make 8; and so on. Thus the sequence runs: 1, 1, 2, 3, 5, 8, 13, 21, 34, 55, 89, 144, and on and on—with each number after the seeds equal to the sum of the two numbers immediately preceding it.

Modern witch doctors believe that Fibonacci numbers have a special status in nature and in the financial world, and they expect these numbers to show up at strategic places in an investment's future. In the example on page 87, the advisor saw (or thought he saw) 5 and 8, and concluded that 13 must be coming next—three Fibonacci numbers in sequence.

Fibonacci buffs offer no cause-and-effect explanation (that I've seen) for the significance of Fibonacci numbers. Instead, they "verify" its significance by collecting examples of Fibonacci numbers in the investment world, such as an uptrend lasting 8 months. Of course, it would be amazing if there *weren't* plenty of examples—since half the numbers between 1 and 10 are Fibonacci numbers.

Adherents also are awed by the fact that the result of dividing any Fibonacci number (after the first few) by its predecessor is approximately 1.618 ($55 \div 34 = 1.618$, $144 \div 89 = 1.618$, and so on). If there were nothing special about Fibonacci numbers, why is there a consistent relationship between every pair of numbers?

The number 1.618 is called the Golden Ratio or the Golden Mean. This number and its reciprocal .618 ($1 \div 1.618 = .618$) have special significance in the Fibonacci scheme of things. An uptrend might be expected to stop at 1.618 times its starting price, or a downtrend might be expected to halt at .618 times the price at which it began.

Some writers have composed rhapsodies about the frequency with which the Golden Mean shows up in life. A rectangle whose length is 1.618 times its width is said to be the proportion most pleasing to the eye, and so that shape is found in paintings, playing cards, windows, doors, books (but not *this* book), and many other things.[3]

Fibomania

Fibonacci fans say that mathematics can be used to project the past or present into the future—if only you know the right multiplier or have the correct sequence of numbers.

And it's true that there is something fascinating about the symmetry of the Fibonacci series and the tidy way in which each number is about 1.618 times the size of its predecessor. Once it's been called to your attention, it's easy to start seeing Fibonacci numbers under every bed. Somehow the world seems full of numbers like 3, 5, 8, 1.618, and .618.

Life itself seems to testify to the significance of Fibonacci numbers. And what could be more authoritative than mathematics?

But hold off before you enter limit orders to sell all your investments at 1.618 times their recent lows. What we've seen of Fibonacci numbers so far is true, but incomplete. The attributes of the Fibonacci series may be interesting, but they're far from unique. Mathematics is full of curious consistencies.

Bean Math

For example, let me tell you about the famous Italian mathematician Gabrielo Garbanzo (?–?).

His series runs: 0, 1, 2, 3, 6, 11, 20, 37, 68, 125, 230, 423, 778, 1431, and so on. It's similar to the Fibonacci series, but each number after 2 is the sum of the preceding *three* numbers in the series (6 = 1 + 2 + 3; 11 = 2 + 3 + 6; 20 = 3 + 6 + 11; and so forth).

After the series gets going, divide any number by its predecessor and—lo and behold—the answer is 1.839. We can call this constant the Golden Bean. I'm sure that, once we start looking, we'll find plenty

---

[3]However, if you walk around your home with a tape measure, you might not find a single example of the Golden Ratio. Of course, your house may have been poorly designed.

of Garbanzo numbers and Garbanzo's Beans in the investment markets—such as an investment trend that lasted 1, 2, 3, 6, or 11 months, and ended somewhere near 1.8 times the price at which it started.

Actually, *any* series in which each element is the sum of a given number of its predecessors will have a "golden ratio"—a constant ratio between each pair of adjoining numbers.

In fact, any series will produce *many* golden ratios. In the Garbanzo series, after 125, each number is 3.4 times the number that's two steps before it, 6.2 times the number that's three steps before it, and so on indefinitely.

The Proof of the Pasta

Another mathematical genius, Enrico Fettucini (?–?), created a series made up of the *squares* of numbers: 1 (1 × 1), 4 (2 × 2), 9 (3 × 3), 16 (you get the idea), 25, 36, 49, 64, 81, 100, and so on. This is the famous Fettucini Series.

Some years later, his son Alfredo used the differences between each pair of adjoining numbers in the series to create a second series: 3 (4 minus 1), 5 (9 − 4), 7 (16 − 9), 9 (got it?), 11, 13, 15, 17, 19, and so on.

What do you know? Each number is 2 greater than its predecessor. This is the famous Fettucini Alfredo Series.

Fun with Numbers

Mathematics is full of surprising consistencies, symmetries, and other curiosities. There are entertaining books full of oddities and games played with numbers. And there are numbers that seem to show up wherever you look.

The number 2 is the basis of almost all music phraseology in Western civilization. Musical phrases, fragments, songs, and sections fit into standard lengths of 2 bars, 4, 8, 16, 32, or 64 bars—all powers of 2. When a phrase is any other length—3 bars or 5 bars, for example— it sounds lopsided.

Literature is brimming with the number 3. You never read a story about someone posing 4 riddles or 7 riddles; it's always 3. The hero never has to face 2 tests or 5 tests; it's always 3. The trinity appears throughout literature—not just in Christian theology.

Because we use the decimal system, the number 10 appears espe-cially significant. We think of the numbers 10, 20, 800, 3000, for example, as being round—while 64 or 89, while not jagged, just aren't round. And numbers ending in 5 are usually considered round because they add up so easily in decimal arithmetic. But in octal arithmetic (a counting system that uses a base of 8 rather than a base of 10), 64 is as round as 100 is in decimal arithmetic.

Almost any number has its own claim to significance. There's 1 (unity), 2 (as in music), 3 (as in literature), 4 (seasons), 5 (round number), 6 (Satan's number), 8 (music again), 9 (3 squared), and 10 (there's nothing rounder). The only number between 1 and 10 without special significance seems to be 7—and you know what *it* means.

Fibonacci numbers have no special claim to being nature's dar-lings—and certainly are of no importance in the investment markets.

USE OF SUPERSTITION

If I've labored the matter of Fibonacci numbers too long, please forgive me—but there's an important point here. You can't identify the likely highs or lows of an investment trend by playing with numbers.

In addition, the Fibonacci enthusiasm points up how easily an au-dience with a limited knowledge of mathematics can be dazzled by numerical fireworks that seem to be proving something.

You might assume that bizarre subjects like Fibonacci numbers are of no particular importance, and that only the less-than-serious investor would give them the time of day. But that isn't the case. Many advisors set their watches by Fibonacci numbers.

Many of the investment forecasts you've read may have been con-structed using Fibonacci numbers—even though the forecasters didn't bother to tell you that. And Fibonacciphilia is only one superstition that guides investment advisors.

I know many advisors personally, and I know many more through reading their works. While I haven't made a methodical study of the popularity of superstitions, I estimate that:

—About 2% of investment advisors use astrology in their work;

—At least 15% of all advisors pay attention to Fibonacci numbers, with the figure closer to 50% among people in the futures and commodity markets;

—At least 35% believe that history repeats itself as if reading from a script, and so they study such things as 21-day cycles, 5-month cycles, 4-year cycles, the 54-year Kondratieff Wave cycle, or Elliott Waves;[4]

—Perhaps 75% adhere to one or more rules of technical analysis that have neither reasonable explanations nor verified records of predictive powers.[5]

These practitioners aren't found only on the fringes of the advisory business. Some of the best-known advisors take Fibonacci numbers seriously. And many well-known advisors act on rules of technical analysis that have no more foundation than the famous natural law, "Things always happen in threes."

Math

The fascination with Fibonacci numbers is part of something more popular and more dangerous—the widespread belief that economic questions can be answered by playing with numbers.

Most investment advisors believe that a great deal can be discovered by multiplying, adding, or dividing something with something else— even though there are no principles in economics that can be applied by mathematical calculation.

Attaching significance to certain numbers because they happen to be in the Fibonacci series may seem ridiculous to you. But the next time you draw a trendline on a chart, ask yourself why you're doing it. A trendline is nothing more than an attempt to use two significant numbers to create a series of other significant numbers.[6]

Mathematics doesn't have the mysterious powers hoped for by investors and advisors who read buy and sell signals in the moving averages of an investment price, or who measure the lengths and heights of previous bull markets to foresee the scope of the next bull market, or who try to discover next year's inflation rate by projecting the patterns of past inflationary periods.

Because mathematics is so important in the physical sciences, its significance for economics may seem self-evident. As a result, very few investment advisors even question whether mathematics is an appropriate tool in the many areas in which they use it.

The only legitimate meeting of economics and mathematical calculation is in the area of statistics. We use arithmetic to add up quan-

[4] All of which will be discussed in Chapter 9.
[5] A few of these rules will be discussed in Chapter 8.
[6] This will be discussed further in Chapter 8.

tities of wheat or total the money supply, to calculate gains and losses in investments, to compute yields from prices, to determine indices of market prices, to compute rates of growth. These uses are purely descriptive; the answers they give will be the same no matter what human beings may decide to do in the future.

But it's a misuse of mathematics to apply it to questions that will be answered in the future by the actions of human beings. No mathematical formula can tell you how much consumers or investors will value something in the future—or even in the present.

Rules that purport to use mathematics in this way have no credentials; they are pure superstition.

SUPERSTITION

Investment markets aren't moved by ratios, divisors, numerical series, cubes, or lines drawn on graphs—nor are they moved by chicken bones. They're moved by human beings buying and selling in accordance with their own private hopes, concerns, beliefs, and aspirations—values that change constantly and allow no measurement.

There is no way to verify absolutely the worth of any trading system, indicator, or investment rule. And, no matter how commonly accepted, no such system or rule should be considered to be authoritative.

So it's imperative that you apply the test of reason to any trading system, method of investment analysis, or rule you consider. There must be an explanation that shows how the rule evolves from the actions of human beings pursuing their own goals.

Statements like "It works," "History repeats itself," "The markets are moved by fear and greed," or "Human nature never changes" aren't explanations. They are merely slogans.

And as we saw in Chapter 2, a track record isn't a reliable guide to the validity of a system.

Even the ideas that do make sense aren't necessarily unyielding laws of nature. Plausible ideas, like the best-laid plans, often turn out to be incorrect or incomplete.

That's why the strategy I'll propose in Part II is designed to take care of you even when the best-laid plans go wrong.[7]

---

[7]Sorry, I can't provide a personalized strategy without knowing what your sign is.

7

Going Wrong with Fundamental Analysis

Fundamental analysis attempts to evaluate an investment without reference to what investors may think of the investment.

A fundamental analyst doesn't care about an investment's popularity or its apparent trend. His only concern is whether the investment's current price is "too high" or "too low" compared to what he believes is its *fundamental value*. That's the value that exists in an investment, apart from—and independently of—what investors may now think of it.

The value may be present because of the income the investment produces, because of the income it *will* or *might* produce, because of shortages that eventually should force the price of a product upward, or because of some other factor—any factor that doesn't depend on investor expectations.

The value is considered to be "fundamental" if it will bring profit to the investment's owner sooner or later—even if no one ever believes it will.

To identify that value, an analyst looks at production costs and volume, consumption levels, balance sheets, profit-and-loss statements, company managements, economic indicators, world events, and the like.

It isn't necessary to discuss here the ways analysts estimate the fundamental value of an investment. If you're curious, the methods are described in an appendix, "The Methodology of Fundamental Analysis," on page 534.

This chapter focuses on the problems that arise when fundamental analysis is used to select investments—whether you make the analysis yourself or rely on an advisor to do it. As with other tools for making investment decisions, it's easy to overrate the power of fundamental analysis—expecting it to provide answers it can't produce.

THE RELIABILITY OF DATA

The most important pitfall concerns the data that the analyst uses.

To make sensible estimates of future values, the analyst needs accurate information. In fact, fundamental analysts tend to pride themselves on dealing only with hard data from the real world. They have no time for mystical theories concerning "cycles," "killer waves," or "head and shoulders patterns"—just the facts.

But most of what we call "data" are really only estimates, and crude estimates at that.

The CPI, For Instance

The Consumer Price Index (CPI), which attempts to measure the general level of retail prices, is one example of information that's unwisely taken for granted and used extensively in drawing conclusions about the economy and investments. So I think it will be helpful to look closely at what the CPI really is.

Each month, the CPI is announced in a form that implies accuracy to 1/10 of 1%. And investment prices can make big moves, depending on whether the CPI has risen by one small amount rather than another—by, say, 0.3% instead of 0.5%.

But despite the uncritical acceptance of CPI figures by most analysts, the CPI actually gives only a very rough indication of the direction of retail prices. It just isn't possible to construct an index that will be precise or timely.

There are at least four big problems that muddy *any* general price index.

The first problem is that the individual prices used to compile the index are only samples of what's going on. The sampling isn't even large; there are just too many supermarkets to visit. So index compilers check a few prices here and there and then start adding.

The second difficulty is that improvements in products can't be taken into account accurately by the index. If a product that appears to be priced 10% higher today than it was two years ago includes improvements or extras, is it really 10% more expensive? Not for anyone who likes the improvements or extras. For some consumers, the product may be only 5% more expensive. Or, if they especially appreciate the changes, the product may even seem cheaper than two years ago.

In other words, many people may consider the 1988 Chevrolet the equivalent of a 1978 Cadillac—but the index will compare the price of the 1988 Chevy with the price of the 1978 Chevy.

A third problem is that any procedure for incorporating new products into a price index will be arbitrary. How do you compare today's prices for home videocassette recorders (introduced in the late 1970s, and falling in price ever since) with VCRs of 1960 or 1970?

The fourth problem is that the index can't treat all products alike. You wouldn't give the same importance to changes in the price of diamonds that you give to changes in the price of bread—since the price of bread is more important to most consumers than the price of diamonds.

The CPI tries, imperfectly, to give each product a weight commensurate with the amount consumed by the general population. But no one knows precisely what those amounts are. You have to estimate the physical quantities consumed, and convert them to dollar volumes based on recent prices—which also are estimates.

But consumption patterns change constantly—responding to many influences, including price. If the price of something rises, its volume of consumption probably will drop, and the item should then be accorded a smaller weight in the index. Obviously, no index can do a perfect job of keeping up with such changes.

Index compilers devise ways to deal with all these problems. But they necessarily have to make arbitrary decisions in doing so. Despite their best efforts, an index can provide only a very rough estimate of changes in the general level of prices.

Keep this in mind the next time you see a graph of inflation rates or a graph converting investment prices to ''real'' prices using the

CPI. A technical analyst might draw a trendline on such a chart to show precisely when a trend has been broken. This fictitious precision is comparable to using a sundial to time a 3-minute egg.

Other Indicators

The flaws inherent in the Consumer Price Index aren't unique or even special. All economic indicators—including the Gross National Product, industrial production, national income, corporate profits, commodity production and consumption figures, rates of saving—are imperfect estimates, drawn from limited samples.

Somewhat precise data exist for a few things (such as money-supply totals derived from banking reports), but these figures arrive months or years after the fact. The early data that investment analysts act on are only estimates—constructed from samples in the same rough way that the CPI is constructed.

Studies of Reliability

A number of statisticians and economists have investigated the reliability of national economic data—usually concluding that the data deserve skepticism.

Simon Kuznets, in a study for the National Bureau for Economic Research, estimated that the government's figures for national income could be off by 10% in either direction.

Noting that the error for one period could be in the opposite direction from the preceding period's error (an overestimate followed by an underestimate, for example), he concluded that the reported *changes* in national income (from one period to the next) could be very wide of the mark. A presumed gain could actually be a loss—or vice versa.[1]

Since we can't know the true figure for any period, we'll never know how far off the announced figures for any particular period are—or even what the maximum error might be.

The significance of the margin of error is considerable. How many times has the stock market moved dramatically upon hearing that the latest GNP growth rate is, say, 2.8% when a rate of 3.3% had been

[1]*National Income and Its Composition*, by Simon Kuznets, published in 1942 by the National Bureau for Economic Research, Princeton, N.J. The above points were cited in *National Income Statistics*, identified in the footnote on page 103.

generally expected? Ironically, the 2.8% figure might be revised later to a number *greater* than the original expectation.

Some figures are revised *years* after the fact. The Federal Reserve Board occasionally issues historical revisions of the money supply, providing new figures that go back several decades. And yet, how many times in, say, 1974 did the stock market react violently to a weekly announcement of the money supply total—a total still being revised even today?

Many times, the long-range revisions occur because of new ways of collecting or counting the data—suggesting that today's statistics will be thrown out eventually, when a better way of estimating them has been found.

Revisions

Oskar Morgenstern may have done more than anyone else to investigate the reliability of economic data. His book *On the Accuracy of Economic Observations*, published in 1950 and revised in 1963, offered scores of examples of meaningless data—data upon which millions of businessmen and investment analysts were basing their decisions.

He found that the "best" data series—such as aggregate employee compensation and national income—had average changes from one calendar quarter to the next of about 2.0%, but that later revisions usually changed the estimates by about 0.5% in either direction. Thus the "best" of the timely indicators of economic change will, on average, be revised later by one fourth—and the revision might be in either direction.

Meanwhile, for the least reliable data—such as that for business income or aggregate corporate profits—the average revision is as great as the average change that's first announced. An initial announcement of, say, 2.0% growth might be revised later to a 1.0% drop. Such data are virtually useless.

In other words, most of the economic data that investment analysts watch so closely are actually little more than wild guesses.

Consider the Source

Mr. Morgenstern also called attention to the fact that most statistics are issued by governments, often for partisan purposes. This point should be obvious but, strangely, it's rarely considered by people who like to rely on the numbers the government hands out.

In Japan after World War II, the Japanese government and the U.S. occupation force regularly decided on Japan's official national income figures *by negotiation*. They did this because U.S. economic subsidies were based on the figures. How many computer studies have run through that data and drawn conclusions about the dynamics of economic growth in Japan?[2]

Company Data

Even if it's obvious that national economic data are very crude, one can still imagine that a stock analyst works with firm numbers—company balance sheets, sales figures, profit-and-loss statements, price comparisons, and so on.

In general, the situation is better at the company level. But company data have problems, too—such as the variations in accounting methods from company to company.

And analysis of a company requires more than looking at just the company itself. Its fortunes will depend on what its competitors do. The company also will be affected by general economic conditions—which puts the analyst at the mercy of inaccurate national data.

Most important, an analyst has to make judgments about the company's management and its policies, since the quality of management will determine how much—or how little—is made of the firm's assets and opportunities. Of course, these judgments are the analyst's own; there are no formulas to do the judging for him.

The only truly reliable data an investment analyst works with are the prices at which investments have been traded. No other data in economics are truly "hard" and reliable; everything else is an estimate, and every estimate is based upon what someone has chosen to reveal.

MISSING PIECES

It may seem that, by doing the best he can, an analyst will at least get *close* to the truth. If he misses only one or two pieces of data, a stock

[2]A large part of this section was taken from *National Income Statistics*, by Oskar Morgenstern (an excerpt from *On the Accuracy of Economic Observations*), published by the Cato Institute, 224 Second Street SE, Washington, D.C. 20003; $3.00.

priced today at $40 might disappoint him by peaking at $95, instead of at his target of $100. Who would complain?

But a little missing data usually produces more than a little error. If perfect knowledge of a stock's future price requires 10 pieces of data, the analyst who finds 9 of them still may be miles from the truth.

The missing piece of data might be one that's crucial to the outcome. It could be something like: Will the citrus crop in Florida be destroyed by a freeze or won't it? Will the court award the $10 billion damage claim or won't it? Will Iraq destroy Iran's oil fields or won't it?

An analyst can only guess at answers to questions like these. And yet their answers may completely overshadow the hard data the analyst acts on.

And, rather than needing 10 pieces of data, one needs *millions* to be sure of an outcome in advance. The most important data in economics concern human beings—their motivations, preferences, and intentions—information that's locked inside the minds of people all around the world.

The best analyst will have information—imperfect information—on only a *handful* of the factors affecting an investment's value.

The fundamental analyst lives and works in the same uncertain world where *we* hang out. His desk may be tidier, but his judgments have as many loose ends as yours and mine. All he can do is assemble the clues that are available to him—and then try to gain a sense of whether the market has underpriced or overpriced an investment.

TIME IS MONEY

The search for an underpriced investment is itself a recognition that an investment doesn't have to sell for its fundamental value. But an analyst assumes that an underpriced investment will rise to its fundamental value sooner or later.

However, an investment that's underpriced today can be more underpriced tomorrow. And the further an investment falls after you buy it, the more it has to rise before you can start showing a profit.

If your only concern is the income the investment provides, you won't care how low the price goes—so long as the income continues. But if capital gains are the object, you might grow restless during the years it can take for the fundamentals to assert themselves.

If the investment does show a profit eventually, your grandchildren may thank you for your patience—even though the capital might have grown more if invested in Treasury bills.

DANGEROUS PLAUSIBILITIES

There are hundreds of ways of applying fundamental analysis. Most of them rely on cause-and-effect relationships that seem very plausible.

One system, which could be called the Warehouse Strategy, attempts to profit from underpriced commodities. It provides a good example because it's fairly simple and clear-cut. And it demonstrates how dangerous a plausible fundamental strategy can be.

There's no reliable way to know a commodity's fundamental value. So the Warehouse Strategy uses the "cost of production" as a stand-in for fundamental value.

To apply the strategy, an investor attempts to estimate how much it costs producers to bring a particular non-perishable commodity to market. If the commodity's price falls significantly below the cost of production, the investor buys the commodity. He might buy the physical commodity itself and have it stored, or he may buy futures contracts and roll them over as necessary.

The investor assumes that the low price will be answered by a drastic decline in production. When production has dried up sufficiently, the price will have to rise—possibly rising far above the production cost before full production resumes.

Like many fundamental systems, the Warehouse Strategy has a ring of truth about it. It seems to be based on sound economics, not on mysterious technical indicators.

But there are problems. Four of them have to do with the investor's expectations of declining production:

1. No single figure is the universal "production cost." Some producers can operate profitably at considerably lower prices than others.

The U.S. Bureau of Mines published a table in 1982 showing production costs of copper around the world. The cost for one major U.S. producer was over twice that for one major Canadian producer.[3]

2. Any producer's cost, if it's properly computed, allows for the amortization and repayment of his capital. But a much lower price might still allow him to operate with a positive cash flow—which could be a reason to continue producing. And in some industries, such

---

[3]The table was reprinted in *Common Sense Viewpoint* (October 1984), page 9.

as mining, it can be cheaper to keep operating at a loss than to shut down and reopen again later.

3. Some commodities are produced as by-products of others. For example, even if the price of silver is below the cost of mining it directly, silver might continue to come onto the market as a by-product of the mining of gold, copper, lead, and zinc.

4. Government subsidies in some countries might keep production flowing at below-cost prices.

In addition to the problems relating to production, the Warehouse Strategy suffers by neglecting the demand for the commodity. If demand is falling, the price may keep falling for years—no matter how high the cost of production.

Even if the price eventually recovers, even if you get your money back, even if you eventually make a profit, the return might not justify the length of time your capital has been tied up. Even if your expectation comes true, it may be that you could have earned more in Treasury bills than by betting on the commodity.

Roller Coaster Rides

Copper recently was a favorite commodity for applying this strategy. Its production cost was considered by some analysts to be around $.90. So when the price fell from $1.45 in 1980 to under $.80 in 1981, it seemed to be time to buy. But the price since then has been stuck in a range between $.54 and $.79, and no one's made a dime for six years of patience.

Another recent favorite was sugar. It had reached peaks of $.65 per pound in 1974 and $.45 in 1980. Production cost was estimated to be $.10. In 1982 sugar looked like a good buy at $.08. After falling to $.05½, it did rise to $.13 in 1983, but then the price collapsed—making it a good buy at $.08 again in 1984. But this time the price kept falling—to under $.02 in 1985. Finally, in 1986, the price rose back up to $.09½ before collapsing again to $.05.

The price movements of these two commodities demonstrate how distantly a price can roam from what people believe is the cost of production. If a commodity's price is tied to the cost of production, the leash is very long.

Production vs. Price

The Warehouse Strategy, like most fundamental strategies, comes with a plausible explanation of why a price that's low enough is guaranteed to rise eventually. But the investment graveyard is filled with plausible explanations that somehow didn't work out in practice.

Between 1974 and 1978, the price of silver fluctuated roughly between $4 and $5. In early 1978, a silver producer in Mexico explained to me that silver mines could produce vast quantities of silver at a cost of around $4.50. To him, this meant that whenever the price rose to $5, an abundance of new silver would be dumped on the market and the price would have to retreat. Thus the fundamentals of supply assured that the price of silver would never rise much above $5.

But, somehow, within two years the price had reached $48.

As with the Warehouse Strategy, the Mexican producer's plausible argument neglected the demand for the commodity. Investment expectations often seem plausible precisely because they overlook a critical element.

MARKET DISCOUNTING

Another type of problem comes from a kind of shorthand fundamental analysis. Instead of trying to determine an investment's fundamental value, an investor attempts to estimate how events should *change* the investment's fundamental value.

This can lead to trouble—especially if you buy an investment in response to the "latest" news—if you don't realize that the prices at which you're able to buy and sell reflect the judgments of other investors about fundamental value.

For example, if you hear that IBM is offering a new line of computers with certain features, you may judge that computer-buyers will respond favorably—which will cause IBM's earnings to increase.

Or you may believe that the political problems in South Africa will eventually reduce the supply of platinum to the world—driving up the price of platinum.

In either case, you might look only at the present price and assume that future events, by altering the supply-and-demand equation, will push the investment price upward.

Not Alone

But other investors have heard the news upon which you make your judgment. They're aware of the new line of computers or the problems in South Africa. If they arrive at conclusions similar to yours, and arrive at them sooner, their purchases will push the price upward before you buy.

Thus an investment's current price may *already* reflect what you expect to happen in the future.

Every large brokerage house employs analysts to monitor every industry—and to ponder facts, rumors, and theories about every commodity. These specialists may be better equipped than you are to understand all the ramifications of a piece of news. And they're ready to act on news much more quickly than you are.

If the specialists agree with your interpretation, you can be sure a great deal of money has been poured into the investment before you buy it. So you're buying at a price that already assumes the future you're expecting.

If expectations you share with large numbers of investors do materialize, the investment will rise a little further from the price you paid. But if the popular expectations fail to materialize, the price probably will drop substantially—to a level based on a more pessimistic future.

Thus investing on expectations you share with too many others puts you at a disadvantage. In effect, you win a little if you're right, and you lose big if you're wrong.

Your estimate of the future for a company or commodity can earn big profits only if it differs significantly from the prevailing market view. Only then does your judgment point to a higher fundamental value than the current price already represents.

SUBJECTIVITY

Fundamental analysts often speak of buying stocks or commodities that represent "good solid values." But value is in the eye of the beholder.

It's easy to believe that fundamental analysis is a straightforward study: be conscientious, obtain enough data, eat right, and you'll arrive at the one unavoidable correct answer. But that just isn't so.

We do know there is a single reality out there that can't be bent to our wishes, because we bump into it sometimes and stub our toes. But that doesn't mean we can map it accurately. Thus people see the same world differently, and make different guesses about what lies around the next bend.

Two intelligent analysts can disagree about matters of fact—such as the data on which investment analysis is based. Or they can disagree about matters of theory—such as the philosophy underlying an investment strategy, or even the way the strategy should be employed in a given situation. As a result, one analyst can be bullish and another bearish while they enlist the same data to support their opinions.

The pieces of most puzzles are scattered. An analyst seldom works with the same set of pieces as his colleagues. Each analyst is concentrating on whatever elements have fallen into his lap or seem, by his standards, to be the most important.

Faith in the Analyst

When you rely on an analyst's conclusions, you're assuming that he's judged the data as rigorously as you would, that he's checked his figures as meticulously as you would, that he's drawn the same inferences from the fragments of data that you would. Whether that's really so, you'll probably never know—especially since most investment writers don't even bother to tell you where they obtained their data.

I remember asking a popular investment writer where he had uncovered the central "fact" upon which he had based an entire article dealing with the future of gold. He answered matter-of-factly, "I don't know; I heard it somewhere." Yet his readers undoubtedly assumed that he was working with information he knew to be true.

In any area of life, each person examines the data and comes to conclusions that he's comfortable with. He decides what proof he will accept as sufficient, what exceptions he's willing to tolerate, and what lingering doubts he won't ignore. Inevitably, each person's standards are different.

But when you accept an analyst's research, you have accepted his standards by default—without even knowing what those standards are. You're assuming that he's as meticulous about facts as you are, that he can add and subtract competently, and that his computer is correctly programmed.

Telling Tales

Fundamental analysis can appear to be an objective study, but it often deteriorates into storytelling. The tale is fashioned to support whatever view an analyst already holds—or simply to satisfy the public's wish for plausible investment opportunities.

USING FUNDAMENTAL ANALYSIS

As you can see, I'm rather skeptical about the extent to which you can apply fundamental analysis in making investment decisions.

It's tempting to bet on an apparent disparity between an investment's current price and its fundamental value. The disparity seems to guarantee that the investment has to go up eventually.

But an apparent disparity doesn't deserve your attention unless it's very wide. Because of the inability to obtain all the data, because of the unreliability of the data that *are* available, and because the data are evaluated subjectively, the margin of error is tremendous.

Only a huge disparity can allow for the error that comes even with careful analysis.

In the early 1970s, silver offered a clear example of an extreme disparity between price and value. No one knew its fundamental value, but the U.S. government had been able to keep the price from rising only by selling huge quantities—indicating that the fundamental value was much higher than the government-imposed price. Even if the fundamental value were much less than analysts were estimating, a silver investment still could pay off handsomely.

As it turned out, the price rose far more than any analyst had estimated originally—reaching $48 in 1980 from $1.29 in 1971. (The economics for gold and several foreign currencies during that era were similar to those described for silver.)

Although opportunities like that are rare, they exemplify what one should be looking for. And their rarity is a reason to be skeptical when someone claims to have found another one.

Choosing Investments

As I mentioned earlier, events and possibilities that seem significant to you usually have already been digested by thousands of analysts.

If the analysts agree with your evaluation, it probably is already reflected in the price of an investment that interests you. So, unless you have a rare talent, you aren't likely to spot underpriced situations in particular stocks and commodities.

More useful to you will be your thoughts on the general direction of the economy—toward more inflation, less inflation, prosperity, recession, higher or lower interest rates, and so on.

The data on which you base your opinions are still imperfect, and they're available to everyone else. But the imperfections won't be important if you don't try to make precision judgments. And in general matters, there's room for an infinite variety of interpretations; so your interpretation may be unique, and it might earn a large profit if it turns out to be correct.

General opinions about the economy lead to opinions about broad investment categories—stocks in general, bonds, gold, currencies, and so on.

The errors associated with fundamental analysis can hurt you most when you try to pick individual stocks. You can't verify the data shown in a company's annual report or assess the company's potential with any precision. Stock specialists and mutual fund managers are in a better position to judge these things. That doesn't mean they'll be right, but they at least have a fighting chance.

So, when you think stocks are a good speculation, you're probably better off investing in a mutual fund, trading stock indices through futures contracts or options, or buying a bundle of different stocks.

Other investments are simpler. Any long-term Treasury bond is a vehicle to profit from a fall in interest rates. And if you think inflation and gold are going up, you simply buy gold.

PROTECTION

You may someday light upon a system of fundamental analysis (or other type of analysis) that seems to work especially well. If so, more power to you. But please don't get carried away.

No matter how well the system seems to work, realize that you might be sharing a lucky streak with it. Or the system might be succeeding for reasons you're not aware of—and that may not last.

So don't bet on your system with capital you can't afford to lose.

8

Going Wrong with Technical Analysis

Technical analysis studies activity within the investment markets. It looks at patterns of price, trading volume, and other traces of investor activity—in the hope of finding clues to an investment's future.

A fundamental analyst (whose efforts were discussed in the preceding chapter) studies activity in the whole economy and in the particular sectors of the economy related to a given investment. He wants to know about a company's markets or a commodity's history of production and consumption.

But a technician is interested only in what *investors* are doing, have done, or might do. At what price are they likely to buy more—or sell more—of an investment? At what price is buying power—or selling power—likely to be exhausted?

Of course, it isn't possible to poll investors about their intentions, even if they were able and willing to tell. Instead, the technician hopes to find indications of what investors are thinking from what has already happened to the investment—especially its price history and the fluctuations in trading volume.

Much of the information that interests a technician is put on charts (graphs) so that it can be studied more easily. Hence technical analysts are also called chartists.

This chapter provides an introduction to technical analysis. I'll describe the particular elements of technical analysis that I believe are helpful and then say a few unkind words about the rest.

If you have no interest in the subject, please feel free to skip over to Chapter 9, on page 135. Realize, however, that your favorite investment genius may be using some of the superstitions I'll be discussing in this chapter.

SUPPORT & RESISTANCE

The primary elements of technical analysis are the concepts of *support* and *resistance*.

A support area for an investment is a price range at which a falling investment should encounter an increased amount of buying—causing the price decline to slow or halt. A resistance area is a price range at which a rising investment should encounter an increased amount of selling—causing the price rise to slow or halt.

A support level exists for one reason only—because a large number of people want to buy at that price. A number of factors might cause potential buyers to congregate at or near a specific price:

1. Many investors may have sold at a particular price the last time it was reached. Seeing the investment move higher, they regret having sold—and they welcome the chance to buy back in at the price at which they sold.

2. There may be a particular price at which many investors decide (from an analysis of fundamental factors or because of some other reason) that the investment is a bargain.

3. There may be a particular price at which industrial users of a commodity believe it is profitable to buy the commodity and stockpile it.

4. If the investment is a foreign currency, the government that issues it might buy it in the open market to keep it from dropping below a particular price.

Resistance areas form for similar reasons:

1. Investors who bought at a particular price, only to see the investment fall, may welcome the chance to sell at the same price and break even.

2. Many investors may target a particular price as the place at which to take profits.

3. There may be a particular price at which producers of a commodity will be willing to sell their production in advance.

4. If the investment is a currency, the government that issues it might sell it in the open market to keep it from rising above a particular price.

Of course, the intention of any one investor to buy or sell at a given price is of no significance in technical analysis. What is important is a price level at which we should see a large concentration of buying (a support level) or a large concentration of selling (a resistance area).

Since we can't discover support and resistance levels by reading the minds of investors, we look at a price graph to see where trends have stalled in the past. If uptrends or downtrends were halted two or more times at a particular price, that price might be a support or resistance level.

The graph of the Swiss franc on the facing page provides an example. Thin lines have been added to mark prices that appear to be support or resistance levels encountered during the past decade.

Support & Resistance Interchangeable

A price area that provided some resistance when the price was rising probably will be a support area if the price falls. And a range that was a support area may be a resistance area later.

Support and resistance are interchangeable because both the buyer and the seller may retain an emotional tie to the price at which a transaction took place. For the buyer, the price is the dividing line between making a profit or taking a loss eventually. The seller, should the price go higher, may dwell on "what might have been" if he'd held on to the investment.

Wherever a great deal of buying has taken place, a great deal of selling has occurred as well. So any price that is of interest to many potential sellers must also be important to many potential buyers.

Thus a price range that was a support level usually is a resistance level, too, and vice versa.

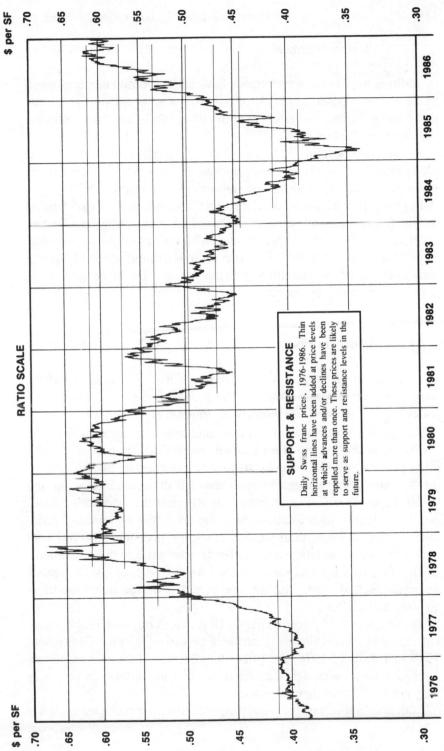

RATIO SCALE

$ per SF

SUPPORT & RESISTANCE

Daily Swiss franc prices, 1976-1986. Thin horizontal lines have been added at price levels at which advances and/or declines have been repelled more than once. These prices are likely to serve as support and resistance levels in the future.

Round Numbers

In addition to prices at which trends have stalled, round numbers (such as $2.00, as opposed to $2.13) often turn out to be support and resistance areas, because investors tend to choose them as target prices for purchases and sales.

An investor deciding in advance where he will take profits is less likely to choose $8.23, for example, than $8.00 or $8.50. Thus a rising price might run into a cluster of sell orders at a round number.

Support often occurs at round numbers, too, because bargain hunters are likely to pick round numbers when choosing buy points in advance.

Round numbers are of special interest when a price moves into new high or new low territory. In those regions, round numbers are the only clues to where support or resistance might lie, since there is no history of previous transactions.

Ideal Trends

The operation of support and resistance can give a price trend the appearance of moving in waves. The graph on the facing page illustrates this by showing a hypothetical uptrend.

The price moves upward until it runs into resistance at 60. The resistance pushes the price back down, but it finds support at 50. The price bounces off the support at 50 and resumes its upward movement—now strong enough to push through the resistance at 60 and go all the way to 70. The resistance at 70 sends the price into retreat, but the downturn halts at 60—where the price had encountered resistance before and now finds support, as some investors who had sold earlier at 60 now welcome a second chance to get into the investment.

This idealized uptrend makes it easy to see the principle of support and resistance at work. But the real world rarely produces anything so simple and clear.

The graph of gold prices on page 118 provides one remarkably clear-cut example of support and resistance in a real market. Throughout 1977 and most of 1978, the price of gold moved upward in clearly defined waves—although the waves weren't as uniform in height as they are in the hypothetical example.

Both graphs illustrate the interchangeability of support and resistance levels.

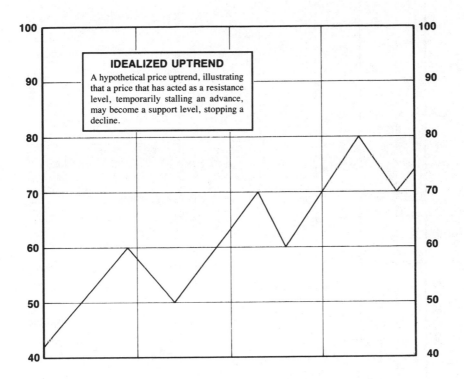

IDEALIZED UPTREND

A hypothetical price uptrend, illustrating that a price that has acted as a resistance level, temporarily stalling an advance, may become a support level, stopping a decline.

Permanently Renewable

Each transaction at a support-resistance level is an occasion for the buyer and seller to acquire or reinforce an emotional interest in that price level. So we can expect a support-resistance level to retain its potency if the price continues to return to that level.

Significance

Support and resistance levels are "alert" zones—areas where a price trend, up or down, should run into stronger opposition and have a greater chance of being reversed.

If the trend *isn't* reversed, the market may be providing a message. It may be telling you that the price trend is very strong—strong enough to move through the support or resistance.

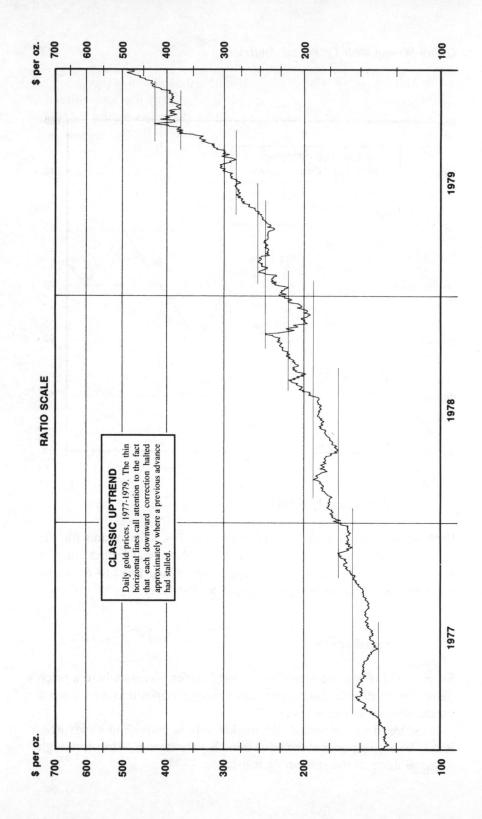

$ per oz.

700 600 500 400 300 200 100

RATIO SCALE

CLASSIC UPTREND

Daily gold prices, 1977-1979. The thin horizontal lines call attention to the fact that each downward correction halted approximately where a previous advance had stalled.

1977   1978   1979

$ per oz.

700 600 500 400 300 200 100

For further confirmation, you can examine the volume of transactions to determine how much support or resistance actually was encountered. If, in an uptrend, the volume increased as the price passed through the area, you know that indeed there was more selling pressure, but that the buying pressure was sufficient to overcome it. If the volume was only normal, no selling resistance was encountered.

On the other hand, if the price falls through what you believed to be a support level, an absence of high volume suggests that the imagined support wasn't there.

Use of Support & Resistance

Identifying support and resistance levels won't equip you to forecast the future. But it can increase the odds of making a correct trading decision.

For example, a price just above a support area is the least risky point at which to buy a speculative investment. The support may keep the price from dropping after you buy. And if it doesn't, the support level's failure is a signal that the investment is weaker than you had believed. You'd have good reason to abandon it immediately—and with only a small loss.

If you were to buy at a price far above the nearest support level, and the price were to fall, there would be no nearby price to tell you when to get out.[1]

Imprecision

A support-resistance level isn't a single number; it is a range or band of prices.

And its boundaries are neither precise nor permanent. As the price approaches an obvious support-resistance level, some technicians might expect the trend to halt, and buy or sell accordingly—causing the price to stall just ahead of what you believed was the support-resistance area.

In addition, an apparent support-resistance level may be an illusion. A previous uptrend or downtrend may have halted with weak volume, leaving very few investors interested in the price. Or many investors

---

[1] The use of support-resistance levels in a speculative strategy is described in more detail on pages 296–299.

who once had an interest in the price may have traded away that interest at some other price since then.

There's no way to be sure where support and resistance are waiting; we can only look for signs. In other words, support and resistance aren't a simple key to investment riches, waiting to be turned.

Technical analysis is a tool—one way to increase your chance of success when speculating. It's not a guarantee of success.

The Heart

As I see it, support and resistance are the heart of technical analysis. Of the many other chart-reading tools used by technicians, the few that make sense turn out to be applications of support and resistance.

For example, the chart of gold prices below illustrates what is called a "rectangle" formation. It is a trading range—bounded top and bottom by price levels that, for a while, aren't penetrated. Most technicians believe that when a price finally breaks out of a rectangle, upward or

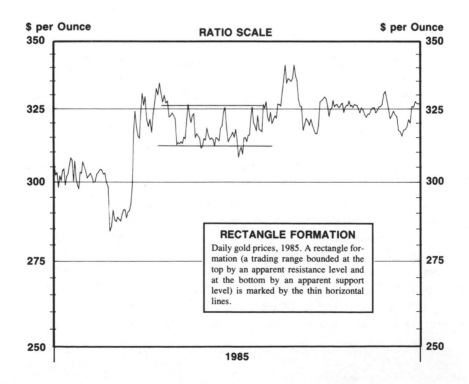

RECTANGLE FORMATION

Daily gold prices, 1985. A rectangle formation (a trading range bounded at the top by an apparent resistance level and at the bottom by an apparent support level) is marked by the thin horizontal lines.

downward, it's likely to continue for some distance in the same direction.

A rectangle is merely a combination of support and resistance—which is what the rectangle's lower and upper boundaries are. When the price finally breaks out of the rectangle, it's displaying new-found power to overcome support or resistance. This power offers hope that the move will continue a good deal further.

PROBLEMS WITH TECHNICAL ANALYSIS

Technical analysis attempts to anticipate how investors—who are people—may act. Consequently, every rule of technical analysis should evolve from what we know about the way human beings behave.

The concepts of support and resistance, for example, can be traced to the emotional interests that investors acquire in the prices at which they've bought and sold, to the way in which people select price targets, to the way in which businesses manage their inventories, and to the way in which the people who run government agencies often behave.

Superstitions

On the other hand, a "rule" that can't be explained in terms of the way people act shouldn't be allowed much of a claim on your thinking. It's a superstition—just like "break a mirror, get seven years' bad luck."

Suppose, for example, that someone were to tell you that, as an infallible market rule, "Whenever an investment rises five days in a row, it falls the next three days."

Your first reaction probably would be "Why?" What could occur in the minds of investors to cause them to sell heavily for exactly three days after a price has risen for five days?

If he responds, "I don't know why it works that way, but it always does," you aren't likely to accept his conviction as proof. You'll assume that he's simply wrong in believing that "it always does." Maybe he wants to believe it, or perhaps he's just generally gullible.

But suppose you find that the rule is very popular, and that it's cited in many investment books. Even so, without an explanation for the rule, you'll still view it with skepticism—suspecting it to be a superstition, rather than a description of reality.

After all, many people believe in lucky charms, old wives' tales, and witchcraft; or believe that a guru is the Messiah simply because the guru says so; or even claim that visitors from other planets have dropped in for tea. You know that popularity is a poor test of truth.

Even if someone shows you examples of the 5-days-up-3-days-down pattern, you'll probably dismiss them as an oddity akin to the performance of the Super Bowl Indicator.

You can't imagine any reason for the rule to be true; it isn't connected to what you know about the world, about people in general, or about investors in particular.

Many rules are cited over and over as tenets of technical analysis that are no more reasonable than the 5-up-3-down rule or the Super Bowl Indicator. They can't be explained by anything we know about the way human beings behave; they persist simply by habit or superstition.

Investors can get into trouble basing their investment decisions on rules of technical analysis that have no explanations, so we'll take a look at a number of those rules. We'll also see how easy it is to apply a reasonable rule where it doesn't belong.

Economic Indicators

Economic indicators sometimes are analyzed by technicians using rules that aren't appropriate.

Governments and private organizations prepare and publish thousands of indicators that summarize general economic conditions and activity in various industries. Included are such things as the Consumer Price Index, housing prices and sales, the Gross National Product, and so on.

Many technicians attempt to apply the concepts of support and resistance (and other technical tools) to these economic indicators. On a long-term chart of the rate of inflation, for example, they see peaks and valleys—levels at which inflation seems to have encountered support or resistance.

But no one buys and sells the Consumer Price Index or the inflation rate. A rising inflation rate isn't stalled at any point because of investors deciding to sell the Consumer Price Index, nor will a decline be halted by investors buying the CPI.

I know of no way that technical analysis can be applied to economic indicators.

Market Indices

In general, this is true also of market indices—such as the Dow Jones Industrial Average—since no one actually buys or sells an average.

Some investors may make decisions to buy or sell individual stocks because of the behavior of an index, especially a popular one such as the Dow. Such decisions might be based on round numbers (a Dow level of, say, 1800 or 1850) or historical high and low points for the average. If enough investors have the same idea, their trades of individual stocks could affect the index—causing movements in the index to slow down at areas that we could call support-resistance levels.

But the applications of support-resistance to market indices are very tenuous and very narrow—especially compared to an individual investment, about which investors make decisions that apply directly.

And support-resistance would be found, if at all, for only the most popular market indices (such as the Dow Industrials) that investors might use as guides to trading decisions. It won't be found in minor indices—such as those of industry groups.

In general, I wouldn't base investment decisions upon apparent support-resistance levels in a market index.

Mutual Funds

Mutual funds don't have support and resistance levels. A mutual fund's price is the net asset value of the fund's investments; it isn't determined by the purchases and sales of shares in the fund by investors.

Head & Shoulders Patterns

The operation of support and resistance can produce various patterns on a chart. The "rectangle" was discussed earlier. Another pattern is the "head & shoulders" formation.

A hypothetical example of this pattern is shown in the graph on page 124. In that chart, a rising investment runs into resistance at price B, then retreats to the support-resistance level it previously cleared at price A.

The investment then turns upward again and moves through the resistance at price B, rising all the way to point C. So far, the pattern is similar to the "idealized trend" in the graph on page 117.

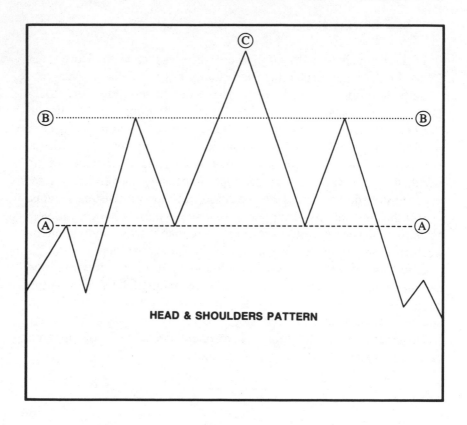

HEAD & SHOULDERS PATTERN

We would expect the investment to lose part of its latest gain—probably falling back down to support at price B. Instead, the investment falls through price B, dropping all the way back down to the support at price A. On the chart, these price movements trace out what vaguely resembles a shoulder and a head.

The investment rises again, but only up to price B, and then falls back down toward price A. The second shoulder is being added to the formation.

The dashed line drawn horizontally across the chart at price A is what technicians call the "neckline" of the head & shoulders formation. If the price falls below the neckline, technicians assume the uptrend is over and a bear market has begun.

There is some sense to this. But the significance of crossing the neckline wouldn't derive from any magic in the picture; it would lie in the fact that the support level at price A had failed to hold back the downturn.

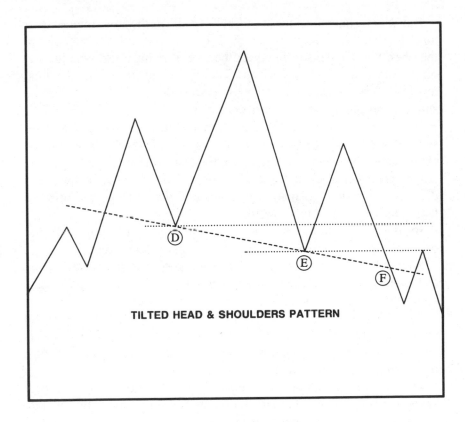

TILTED HEAD & SHOULDERS PATTERN

Tilted Head & Shoulders

Support and resistance can lead to a price pattern that looks like a head and shoulders. But if you attach significance to the *picture* of the head and shoulders—and forget about the investor actions that give rise to the picture—you will be ready to misinterpret a graph like the one on this page.

There we see what also looks like a head & shoulders formation. But whatever support was present at price D on the left shoulder fails to hold when the right side of the head is being formed. Instead, the second downmove halts at point E.

Even though the pattern indicates two *different* support levels, most technicians will draw a ''neckline'' anyway—the dashed line you see connecting points D and E. Then they watch to see whether the investment crosses the neckline around point F—with the future of the uptrend hinging on what happens.

But why? There's no reason to believe, from the investment's history, that human beings are inclined to buy (and provide support) at the price that happens to intersect the line at point F. So whether the price holds there isn't important. The significant events in the final downturn are the declines through prices D and E—places where support had previously been encountered.

For a line to show where the actions of investors might provide support and resistance, it must represent a price level where support or resistance has occurred already. Obviously, the line has to be horizontal, because a slanted line will create a different price for every date. Are investors so fickle that each day they change the price to which they have an emotional tie?

By drawing a slanted line, a technician may be creating a picture of a head & shoulders formation, but he hasn't found one.

Strangely, almost all the head & shoulders patterns identified by technicians are of the tilted variety shown in the graph on page 125. And in those cases, the head and shoulders are of no importance.

The only useful head & shoulders pattern has a horizontal neckline—the kind shown in the graph on page 124. But that kind is very rare. In fact, I searched through hundreds of charts and couldn't find a single real-life example to use as an illustration.

In all charts, it is the price levels at which there is reason to expect support and resistance that are significant—not the prices that fit into pictures someone has drawn on the chart.

Other Patterns

The lore of technical analysis includes a multitude of other chart patterns—pennants, wedges, scallops, saucers, gaps, fans, rounded or broadening tops and bottoms, multiple tops and bottoms, and more. Some of them, such as multiple tops and bottoms, are simply support and resistance in disguise.

But many are merely connect-the-dots pictures. Like magic charms, they come with legends about the results they lead to, but rarely can they be explained by what we know about the behavior of investors.

Measuring Devices

Technicians also believe that some chart formations tell them how far a price will move.

A completed head & shoulders formation, for example, is supposed to be followed by a price move equal to the distance from the top of the head to the neckline.

But I've never heard anyone try to explain what it is about investors' behavior that would cause one price move to lead to another price move of a specific size. Technicians simply assume that if a number is calculated from past prices, it must tell something about the future.

TRENDLINES

The most common charting device is the *trendline*.

An upward trendline is a straight line connecting low points (or bottoms) that seem to be part of a generally rising trend. A downward trendline connects high points (or tops) that appear to be part of a generally falling trend. The graph of gold prices below shows examples of upward and downward trendlines.

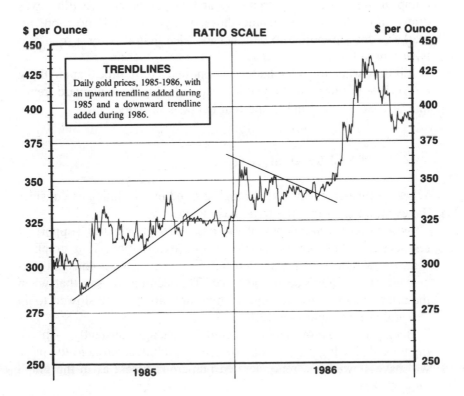

Most technicians believe that trendlines reveal support and resistance levels. When the price bumps into a trendline, from above or below, it is expected to stall. If the price passes through the trendline, the technician concludes that the trend has ended.

Trendlines as Support

Why should a trendline provide support?

A trendline is drawn at a slant and thus represents a different price every day. Why would potential buyers alter their plans day by day to keep their buy orders moving along the trendline? I can't imagine any reason that they would.

So why do technicians draw trendlines? It may be because trendlines *appear* to provide support and resistance—as in the chart on page 127. During 1985 the price moved down exactly to the trendline and away again—not just once, but twice.

But it's easy to overlook the obvious sometimes. The price didn't bump against an existing trendline at two points; the trendline was drawn *after the fact* to include those two points. It is no more remarkable for a trendline to be touched twice than it is for a square to have four sides.

It is only when the price nudges a trendline a third time that anything remarkable has happened (such as occurred with the downward trendline in 1986 in the graph), and that happens infrequently.

Trend Reversal

When an investment breaks through a trendline, technicians consider the event a signal that the trend has ended.

In addition to claiming that the breakthrough violates support or resistance, technicians provide a second explanation. If a graph is drawn to a ratio scale, a slanted trendline represents a constant percentage rate of increase in the price. The technicians say that when the price moves below an upward trendline, its rise has slowed to an extent that foreshadows a decline.

But a price's rate of increase is bound to change constantly—speeding up and slowing down. Long before a trendline is broken, the price will have slowed and reaccelerated numerous times, as in the graph on page 127.

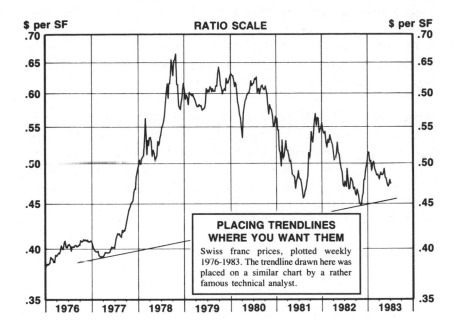

PLACING TRENDLINES
WHERE YOU WANT THEM

Swiss franc prices, plotted weekly
1976-1983. The trendline drawn here was
placed on a similar chart by a rather
famous technical analyst.

So a slowdown that breaks a trendline is just one of many slowdowns that occur during a trend. There is nothing particularly significant about that one slowdown.

Where You Like It

A trendline can't possibly have any meaning when the choice of where to draw it is so arbitrary. There are always many places where a trendline can be made to fit. If you are the one who draws the trendline, you get to decide where to put it.

The graph of the Swiss franc above is a re-creation of one that appeared in a well-known newsletter in 1983. The newsletter maintained that the long-term bull market in the Swiss franc was still alive because the price hadn't fallen below the trendline drawn on the chart by the newsletter's writer.

But look closely at the graph and you'll see how silly trendline talk can be. The second bottom on the trendline occurred only a few months before publication of the graph. How could the ending of a multi-year bull market be signaled by the breaking of a trendline that couldn't even have been drawn until recently? What was the signal a year earlier?

Furthermore, the trendline could have been drawn at many other places on the graph. If you take the bottom reached in early 1977 as the starting point, you could draw lines to low points reached in early 1980, early 1981, and mid-1981. The price had already fallen through those trendlines before the chart was published.

If trendlines mean anything, the "bull market" had already had three obituaries. Why was the technician waiting for a fourth?

Most likely, the trendline was drawn where it was simply because the artist wanted to believe that the Swiss franc was headed upward. Since there's no standard to tell him which trendlines should be heeded and which ignored, he was free to select the trendline he found most congenial.

Some technicians might contend that this was just an example of bad technical analysis—and they'd be right. But I've seen a great many technicians do similar things; I've picked an extreme example only to make it easier to see the fallacy.

No Trendlines

Nothing I know about the way investors act indicates that trendlines should mean anything.

But mine is only one man's opinion. Many a technician tends his charts by drawing trendlines wherever possible. And when a trendline fails to do what it's supposed to, he will draw another one—and then another and another—without ever wondering why he spends his time this way.

MOVING AVERAGES

Moving averages are another popular technical indicator. A moving average is the track of an investment's average price—the average being computed over a specified length of time. The length of time is whatever the technician chooses.

Some technicians plot an investment's price and the price's moving average on the same chart. They treat the moving average much like a trendline, expecting it to provide support and resistance. When the support-resistance fails—and the price and moving average cross—the trend is considered to be over.

The problems with this are the same as with trendlines. Why investors would buy (and create support) when a price touches its moving average, or how investors would decide which moving average to respond to, has never been explained. And I don't think you should consider yourself dull if you can't imagine what explanation there possibly could be.[2]

TECHNICAL INDICATORS

Technicians follow a number of other indicators, most of which wind up on charts of their own for easy monitoring.

Momentum

One is the "momentum indicator" (or "velocity"), which measures the rate of change in an investment's price.

A rate of change can be computed by dividing today's price by the price from a specified number of days before. For example, if today's price is $5.00 and the price 30 days ago was $4.00, the 30-day momentum would be 1.25 (5.00 ÷ 4.00).

When the investment is rising, the momentum will remain above 1.00. When the price falls for any length of time, the momentum will go below 1.00.

Of course, you can tell whether an investment's price is rising or falling just by looking at a chart of the price. But the technician wants advance notice of the direction of the price—which he hopes the momentum indicator will give him.

So he plots the momentum on a chart. When the momentum falls (such as from 1.35 to 1.30), he knows that the price is no longer rising as quickly as before—supposedly a warning that the price itself may soon start dropping.

Some technicians, after charting an investment's momentum, will compute the rate of change in momentum itself—meaning that they're charting the momentum of the momentum. This is called a "second

---

[2]Moving-average trading systems are discussed on pages 175–184.

derivative rate of change.'' When the momentum's momentum indicator starts to fall, the technician is warned that the momentum itself might fall, which would be a warning that the price might fall.

But then again, it might not.

A technician may even draw trendlines on the momentum chart or compute moving averages of the momentum. He expects support and resistance to develop for the momentum—and for the momentum's momentum. And if his momentum chart seems to show a head & shoulders pattern, he may need a tranquilizer to get to sleep that night.

The Trouble with Momentum

Momentum is charted for the same reason that trendlines are drawn —to call attention to the speed at which an investment is rising or falling. And so momentum studies suffer from the same conceptual problems.

In an uptrend, the rate of change in an investment price is constantly fluctuating. Some days the investment goes up, some days it goes down. Sometimes it leaps up quickly, other times it crawls.

Technicians find significance only in certain changes in the rate of change—such as a change that shows momentum breaking a trendline—even though the speed of an uptrend fluctuates throughout the trend's life.

A technician might work out rules to define which changes in momentum are significant. But, like almost all his rules, they are based only on what his experience happens to be—or what he remembers his experience to be.

Nothing we know about the way investors behave indicates that any specific change in acceleration will cause a trend to end. So a momentum chart is merely a look at history. Tomorrow will be different.

Relative Strength

Another favorite technical concept is *relative strength*.

A technician compares an investment with similar investments— such as other stocks in the same industry group. He wants to see whether the investment is rising faster or slower than its peers (or falling slower or faster than its peers). If it seems to be doing better than its fellows, the investment possesses relative strength and is considered a candidate for purchase.

Industry or commodity groups also are ranked against one another for relative strength.

A relative strength study is an excellent way to discover which investments you should have bought last month, but I've seen no evidence that it foretells which investments will do well next month.

"IT WORKS"

This chapter has attempted to explain some of the many patterns, indicators, and rules that make up technical analysis.

Some rules of technical analysis are grounded in the way human beings act. These rules can help you make decisions concerning when to buy and when to sell.

But many other technical rules simply float in the air. There are no foundations for them—nothing to distinguish them from superstitions.

Beyond support and resistance, most of what is called technical analysis is merely ritual that has no tie to the way investors act. Its only justification is "It works." But most of the time, it doesn't work.

Every technician has heard over and over that "It works." When it doesn't work for him, he assumes that *he*—not the system—must be at fault. And so he tries to improve his skills—knowing, because he's heard it so often, that the system itself works perfectly.

Because he's heard it so often, he too will echo the ritual "It works" whenever asked—even if he's never actually seen a chart pattern signal a market reversal. To him, technical analysis may be like a religion: as a matter of faith, it works—no matter what evidence to the contrary you or I might present.

The Evidence

For someone who wants to believe, there's always enough positive evidence.

After all, why do so many classic patterns show up on charts? Why are newsletters and investment books full of charts that prove how tightly the markets conform to the technical rules?

But those charts are a minuscule fraction of all the investment charts that could have been published. You've seen those few charts precisely because they contain the classic examples. The rest of the charts—showing the technical rules being violated—simply aren't printed.

Imperfect Tool

Technical analysis begins reasonably enough—attempting to discern the shape of supply and demand within the investment market itself.

But most technicians are carried away by a desire to believe that they're on to something. Having discovered that some lines provide perspective, they draw lines in all directions—plus arrows, circles, and much else—in their attempt to perceive the future.

Technicians unwittingly reveal the limitations of technical analysis when they point out that they monitor many different indicators because no one indicator is right all the time. Or when they maintain that different indicators work in different markets and at different times. Or when they assure you that they retest all their indicators periodically to see which ones are working best.

Without realizing it, they're saying that there's no link between the indicators and the way investors behave. If there were, the power of an indicator—even if not great—would at least be persistent.

The best technicians are those who use technical analysis in conjunction with other techniques, who use it cautiously, and who think of it as an art, not a science. There's very little science in technical analysis, because very little of it is based on what we know about the world—and because most of its rules must be applied arbitrarily, and hence can't be tested scientifically.

There are technicians who consistently do well in the markets over long periods. Some may have been blessed by chance up to now—and their luck may be about to run out.

But I believe there also are technicians who succeed because they focus on the realistic parts of technical analysis. They recognize that technical analysis is imprecise—and so they treat its signals as hints, not as revelations.

Above all, they don't base their investment decisions on superstitions.

9

Going Wrong with Cycles & Waves

Much of what science tells us about the physical world has to do with the regularity of cycles and waves.

The earth rotates on its axis and revolves around the sun in precise, regular cycles. The tides of the ocean ebb and flow with such regularity that almanacs announce their movements years in advance. Light propagates across the universe at a wavelength that's unaltered even by a journey lasting millions of years. The order, regularity, symmetry, and harmony of the universe are the wonders that science describes and that make science possible.

In many ways, human events seem to display a similar regularity. Enthusiasms come and go; nations rise and fall; war is replaced by peace, and peace by war.

Reaction and self-correction seem to be at the heart of economic matters. Boom is followed by bust, and then by a recovery leading to a new boom. Inflation gives way to disinflation or deflation, and then reasserts itself.

When a commodity's price moves too high, consumption of the commodity is reduced—leading to lower prices until the commodity is cheap enough to stimulate consumption again. Interest rates rise so far that most people want to save and few want to borrow—sending rates back downward again, discouraging saving and encouraging borrowing.

Investments seem to move in broad waves that take them to new highs, alternating with pullbacks that give up part of the gains.

Many things in the economic and investment worlds appear to swing back and forth—apparently sharing the cyclical patterns of the physical world. Just as Isaac Newton told us, what goes up must come down.

It seems obvious that the key to making money is to catch a rising wave, ride it upward, and then get out when the cycle turns.

Analysis

Cyclical analysis and wave analysis attempt to show you how. They try to foresee the course of a trend by identifying recurring patterns in the economic and investment worlds.

A pure cycle is a pattern that recurs on a fixed schedule, such as the earth's orbit around the sun or the rhythm of a healthy heart at rest. Cyclical analysis looks for investment patterns that recur on such regular timetables.

Wave analysis studies reversing *swings* in economic conditions or investment prices. Its principal difference from cyclical analysis is its disregard for the speed at which events occur. A wave analyst hopes to determine how far a particular price movement will go, without hoping to know how long it will take.

Cyclical analysis, by definition, presumes a regularity in timing. However, the word "cycle" is often applied, very loosely, to the pattern of anything that seems to move back and forth—including many patterns that, strictly speaking, are waves.

This chapter examines several varieties of wave and cycle theories.

WAVE THEORIES

Although the word "wave" is used less often than the word "cycle," wave theories are more numerous than cycle theories. We'll begin with brief descriptions of various wave theories, reserving my comments about them until later in the chapter.

Dow Theory

The famous Dow Theory was probably the first formal wave theory covering investments.

Newsletter writer Richard Russell has described the way Charles Dow came to develop his theory. Since many wave theories have borrowed heavily from Charles Dow, it might be helpful to quote Richard Russell at some length:

> [Charles Dow] noticed that stocks did not drift aimlessly, but seemed to rise and fall in definite patterns. To prove his thesis, he formulated the now famous Averages, and by plotting them back for a number of years, came upon the graphic proof for which he had been searching. . . .

Dow observed that a bull market in stocks has three phases:

> Phase one is the rebound from the depressed conditions of the previous bear market. Here stocks return to known values. In the second and longest phase, shares advance in recognition of improving business and a rising economy.
>
> During the third phase they spurt skyward on the hopes and expectations of a continuing rosy future. This is the traditional period of great prosperity and unbounded optimism. It is here that the public enters the market wholeheartedly for the first time. The low-priced "cats and dogs" historically make great moves in the third phase, and market volume becomes excessive. . . .

As with most financial wave theories, the Dow Theory is grounded in the idea expressed by Charles Dow that "The business community has a tendency to go from one extreme to the other."

> "The pragmatic basis for the theory," explained [William P.] Hamilton [a Dow theorist], "lies in human nature itself. Prosperity will drive men to excess, and repentance for the consequence of these excesses will produce a corresponding depression."
>
> In the depths of a depression the storekeeper will discover that he has become overly cautious; he has allowed his inventory to fall even below daily sales. He decides that prices are attractive and increases his stock above daily needs. The worker, now perhaps searching for a job instead of higher wages, becomes a saver, regardless of his reduced income. Thrift will be the order of the day, and the businessman, finding money cheap, will consider expanding.
>
> Dullness turns to activity, activity breeds optimism. Later, this gives way to speculation, then to inflation, spiraling wages, and higher money

rates. And again the entire structure, snapping under the strain of a myriad of economic ills, collapses, and the spectre of depression once more rides the air.[1]

In practice, the Dow Theory is concerned almost wholly with identifying the primary trend in the stock market. Simply put, the theory states that if, after a correction in the market, either the Dow Jones Industrial Average or the Dow Jones Transportation Average rises to a new high, without the other average also making a new high, a trend reversal has been signaled.

Elliott Wave Principle

The Elliott Wave Principle was developed in the 1930s by R. N. Elliott. Like the Dow Theory, it sees a bull market as containing three upward phases; but the Elliott analysis is considerably more complicated.

It breaks a bull market into five waves: up, down, up, down, up. And when a short-term downtrend interrupts a long-term uptrend, the correction will be comprised of three waves: down, up, and down. A wave might be of any length of time and cover any distance. A complete Elliott Wave pattern is shown in the graph on the facing page.

This pattern might occur on any scale—whether it be a price movement of a few percent or hundreds of percent—and over any period —whether it be a few minutes or many centuries. The important thing, according to Elliott theory, is that all movements follow this pattern or something derived from it.

The Elliott theory includes a number of techniques to forecast the price at which a wave is likely to end. Most of these techniques employ Fibonacci numbers or the Golden Ratio (described on pages 92–95).

Although it could be any length, a period comprising one bull market and one bear market (a 5-wave upward pattern and a 3-wave downward pattern) is called a "Cycle."

Within a Cycle, each of the three upward legs of the bull market contains a 5-wave upward pattern, and each downward leg contains a 3-wave pattern. And each of those waves is subdivided into its own 5-wave and 3-wave patterns, and so on to smaller and smaller magnitudes.

Above the level of the Cycle, there's the Supercycle—covering

[1]*The Dow Theory Today* by Richard Russell (Fraser Publishing Co., Box 494. Burlington, Vermont 05402; $9.00, cardcover); pages 4, 5, 20, 24, 25.

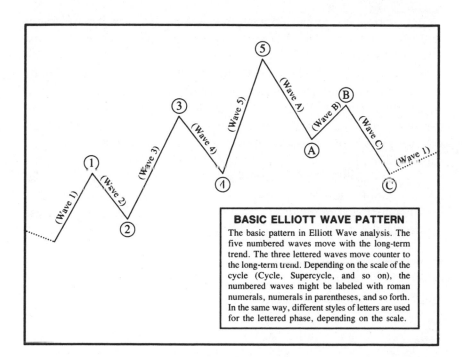

BASIC ELLIOTT WAVE PATTERN
The basic pattern in Elliott Wave analysis. The five numbered waves move with the long-term trend. The three lettered waves move counter to the long-term trend. Depending on the scale of the cycle (Cycle, Supercycle, and so on), the numbered waves might be labeled with roman numerals, numerals in parentheses, and so forth. In the same way, different styles of letters are used for the lettered phase, depending on the scale.

successive Cycles that are biased, respectively, up, down, up, down, and up—then down, up, and down. Then there's a Grand Supercycle, which is one magnitude greater and contains Supercycles—and follows a pattern that you probably can guess. Finally, 8 Grand Supercycles make up a Millennium Cycle (which, despite its name, isn't necessarily 1,000 years long).

According to Elliottologists, the late 1980s are particularly important. Sometime soon, the stock market (and the economy) will simultaneously hit the final peak of the Cycle that started in 1974, the Supercycle that began in 1932, the Grand Supercycle that started in 1789, and the Millennium Cycle that began sometime in the Middle Ages.

The U.S. and the world are condemned to head into the declining side on all four cycles simultaneously—sending us into an era so terrible that it can be compared only with the Dark Ages.[2]

[2] The Elliott theory is described in great detail in *Elliot Wave Principle* by Robert R. Prechter Jr., and A. J. Frost (New Classics Library, P.O. Box 1618, Gainesville, Georgia 30503; hardcover, 185 pages, $24.00).

Projecting the Future

A less formal, but more popular, wave technique is what we might call Projectionism. This is the simple practice of projecting the past into the future.

For example, if the Dow Jones Industrial Average rose 800 points in the last bull market, a projection might indicate that the next bull market will consist of a rise of 800 points. Or, if gold rose 500% in its first bull market in the early 1970s, and 700% in its second bull market in the late 1970s, someone might project a rise of 900% in the next bull market.

Projectionism looks for some kind of numerical sequence and projects it into the future.

This approach might seem simplistic, but investment advisors use it frequently.

"Business Cycle"

The most common variety of wave analysis deals with the "business cycle"—the economy's swings between prosperity and recession.

Because most analysts don't expect the business cycle to operate on a timetable, the "business cycle" would be better called the "business wave"—and some economists do in fact make a point of referring to "business fluctuations," rather than to "cycles."

Many investors and advisors believe that a repeating pattern is at work, each phase of which favors one or more specific investments. If you know where we are in the business cycle, you know which investments you should own right now—stocks when prosperity is beginning, switching to gold at the first sight of inflation, or into cash at the start of a recession.

CYCLE THEORIES

A cycle theory involves a definite period of time during which an investment makes a round trip from low to high and back to low again.

Time Cycles

The simplest cycle theories are what, for lack of a standardized name, I'll call "Time Cycle" theories. These have been popular mostly among commodity analysts, but lately they're being applied to the stock market as well.

A Time Cycle theory presumes that a commodity is tied to a recurring cycle that takes it from a low to a high and back again within a precise period of time. However, the commodity might not actually hit its lowest price at the low point of the cycle, nor actually hit its highest price at the high point of the cycle—since the price can be influenced by factors other than its cycle.

In other words, the commodity is moody—going through strong and weak periods on a regular timetable. The weak point of the cycle tends to depress the price while the upward phase acts as a stimulant. It's a kind of BioRhythm theory of commodities.

Time Cycle theories usually assume that several cycles of different lengths operate simultaneously on a commodity's price. For example, a price might be governed by cycles of 8 days superimposed on cycles of 6 weeks, superimposed on cycles of 8 months, and so on. In other words, the price is tied to a wheel inside a wheel inside a wheel.

Occasionally, all the cycles start moving upward at the same time, which is considered a particularly attractive time to buy.

The analyst's job is to identify where in each cycle the commodity is at any moment, so that he can forecast whether the price should go higher or lower, and how long the move will last [3]

Seasonalities

Seasonal patterns are similar to time cycles, except that they run on exactly a one-year schedule.

An analyst looks back to discover the month each year in which stocks (or some other investment) have done best, and which months were the worst. Usually no attempt is made to explain why a particular month is significant, other than to note that all of life is governed by the changing seasons.

---

[3] One book explaining Time Cycle theories in detail is *The Handbook of Commodity Cycles* by Jacob Bernstein (John Wiley and Sons, 1 Wiley Drive, Somerset, N.J. 08873; hardcover, 383 pages, $55.00).

Presidential Cycle

Probably the most popular cycle theory has been built around the 4-year Presidential Cycle. Unlike many others, this one does come with an explanation.

According to the theory, the year after a presidential election will be a down year for the stock market. The administration knows that sooner or later it will have to adopt policies of fiscal and monetary restraint to offset the excesses of the previous cycle. And it wants to be done with the bad news as far ahead of the next election as possible.

By the same logic, the fourth year of a presidential term (leap year) should be an up year. The administration will stimulate the economy in every possible way in order to get reelected.

Most presentations of this story are accompanied by graphs that highlight the gains of the Dow Jones Industrial Average in 1968, 1972, 1976, and 1980—and point out the declines in 1969, 1973, 1977, and 1981.

However, history was turned upside down when the Dow Industrials *fell* 3.7% in 1984 and *rose* 27.7% in 1985—the opposite of what it was supposed to do. As a result, the Presidential Cycle may be mentioned less often in the future.

Kondratieff Wave Theory

Just as the Business Cycle is a wave, the Kondratieff Wave is a cycle.

The Kondratieff theory was invented by the Soviet economist Nikolai Kondratieff in 1925. He said that capitalist economies went through up-and-down cycles lasting between 47 and 60 years.

Other writers, trying to refine Kondratieff's ideas, lit upon 54 years as the length of the "Long Wave." Accordingly, the stock market should peak and crash 54 years after the 1929 peak—in 1983, which will be upon us any day now.

Whether or not the "Killer Wave" arrives on anyone's schedule, most Kondratiovians are convinced that disaster is just around the corner somewhere.[4]

---

[4]Kondratieff's own text has been published (in translation) in *The Long Wave Cycle*. (New American Library, 120 Woodbine Street, Bergenfield, N.J. 07621; hardcover, 138 pages, $30.00).

THE TROUBLE WITH CYCLES & WAVES

A number of problems beset the cycle and wave theories.

Confusion of Sciences

The first is the supposition that what's true in the physical world should be true in the world of human behavior. If sound moves in waves, so should human behavior.

One proponent of the Elliott theory put it this way:

> Elliott ultimately concluded that mass human behavior is apparently such that a crowd acts the same way (and will always act the same way as long as people are people) in each situation where its members are betting against one another on the future course of prices.
>
> Its mood will swing from optimism to pessimism and back again in this sequence, which is natural to human beings and which occurs regardless of the surrounding extramarket news.
>
> That forms based on the same underlying principle have been observed throughout the natural sciences has merely added to the interest in Mr. Elliott's discovery.[5]

But, as discussed on pages 75–77, there's a vast difference between changing seasons and changes in human activity. The behavior of atoms, molecules, and electrons never changes; they continue to act exactly as they always have.

Human beings, on the other hand, are always learning, adapting, responding, and creating. It may be true that human nature never changes, but human beings do.

Cycle and wave theorists seem to believe that, no matter how many times investors repeat the process, they will always become overly optimistic and believe that a bull market will never end—carrying it to an excess that will have to collapse.

Even if that were true, the process needn't follow a timetable that would allow you to schedule your investment purchases and sales in advance. Nor will a wave conform to a recurring pattern that would allow you to measure the distance from here to its turning point with a mathematical formula.

[5]"From Now to '90," by Robert R. Pechter, Jr., *Reason* magazine (August–September 1986), page 37.

Human beings do learn from the past, from their mistakes, and from history. Otherwise, a graph of an investment price would show one simple pattern over and over again, instead of containing a random pattern that has to be "interpreted" by a cycle-wave translator.

It's fun to talk about crowd psychology, about investors acting like sheep—ruled by "fear and greed." But the fact is that crowds, even when they act as one, are as unpredictable as individuals.

Generalization

The second error is in overgeneralizing—taking an observation about the markets (for example, that bull markets end), and inflating it into a formula that tells exactly what is going to happen, or when it's going to happen, or how big it will be.

This is similar to observing that attendance at sports events is generally smaller on rainy days than on sunny days—an obvious truth—and constructing a formula to translate the amount of rainfall into the exact size of the turnout.

As I discussed on pages 80–81, human activity and human values aren't amenable to measurement. It's important to remember that trends *will* end, that swings *will* occur; but there are no scientific formulas to tell you *when* a trend will end.

Self-Correcting

A third general error applies to time cycles and seasonalities. They're based on the assumption that investors are blind to what happens in the markets.

Imagine that you actually discovered a seasonal pattern in some investment—finding, for example, that the price of something always rises during November. Every year in October, you'd cash in your savings account, increase the mortgage on your house, and buy as much of the investment as you could—using margin as thin as your broker would allow. And, at the end of November, you'd sell the investment, repay your debt, and enjoy your profits.

Sounds wonderful—every investor's fantasy.

But in the real world, millions of other investors share the same fantasy. And many of them are playing with their personal computers, looking for exactly that kind of easy opportunity.

And there are large organizations—mutual funds, pension plan managers, bank trust departments, brokerage houses, and more—who have really *big* computers that can look for seasonalities in every stock and commodity traded in the United States. Do you think they've overlooked what you found?

Well, maybe they found it and are making money on it, too. But while you scrape together $50,000 on October 31, they might pony up $50 million, $500 million, or more—on October 29. What happens then to the price? It starts rising in late October, instead of in November.

Then arbitrageurs will notice the rising price. They realize that they don't have to buy in October and get trampled in the stampede; they can buy as early as June and still profit handsomely from the November lift. Their buying causes the price to begin rising gradually during the summer—leaving less room for the price to rise in November.

Eventually, someone notices that he can come out ahead buying before June or selling after November. And pretty soon what was a large November bulge is only big enough to give an arbitrageur a return slightly greater than the cost of borrowing the money to finance the transaction.

The underlying reason for a November bulge may still be present, but the actions of investors and arbitrageurs have smoothed out the cycle. Whatever occurs in November that's bullish for the investment affects the price year-round, so that it no longer permits you to make an unusual profit.

In fact, that's what happens in the real world. That's why you can't make a killing buying frozen turkeys in June or frozen orange juice in September. If there really is a reason for the price to go up during a certain season, the actions of investors and arbitrageurs will flatten the cycle down to a nearly indetectable bump.

Cycle theories generally ignore this process. It doesn't matter whether you're talking about a seasonality, a fluctuating cycle, or a Presidential Cycle. If there's a clear reason for it (if it isn't just an illusion on someone's graph), the actions of traders and arbitrageurs will eliminate any easy opportunity for exceptional profits.

But a cycle buff wants to believe he's found a seasonal pattern that isn't common knowledge. Why did this pattern escape the world's attention? Because the cycles are so complex that only the cycle buff can interpret them.

That may be true. In fact, the cycles are so complex and so obscure that no one is making money from them—not even the cycologists.

FAILURES & FLAWS

Cycle and wave theories don't work, because the world just doesn't arrange its affairs in the tidy way the cycologists would have it.

Of course, any theory will seem to hold true occasionally, just by chance. And, tried long enough, any theory will give its practitioner a hot streak—a string of victories as impressive as flipping a coin that comes up "heads" 7 times in a row.

Then things go wrong—as with any attempt to outguess the future. But the analyst can never forget the hot streak, and he can never bring himself to believe it occurred by pure chance. He knows he's on to something—he just doesn't have the method quite perfect yet.

And so he may spend the rest of his life—and the rest of his clients' money—practicing and preaching an ill-conceived cycle or wave theory.

In this section of the chapter, I'll discuss what I know about the logical weaknesses in each of the popular cycle and wave theories, and the results some of the theories have produced.

Time Cycles

Commodities magazine (dealing with commodity and futures markets) used to carry articles on cycles frequently. These articles explained the way cycles work in individual investments or investment groups. Usually, an article would demonstrate the theory by forecasting when an investment's next bottom or top will arrive, or how strong the investment would be in the coming months.

I made a study of all the cycle articles appearing in the magazine in 1981 and 1982. I found a total of 50 specific forecasts. Only 16 (32%) could be considered to have come true even by the most generous system of grading.

Of course, as the practitioner of any system will modestly admit, no system can forecast the future 100% of the time. But of what meaning are projections that are right only 32% of the time?

The Business Cycle

When someone speaks of a "five-year" business cycle, he implies a regularity that doesn't exist. He really means that the cycles have lasted an *average* of five years.

LENGTHS OF U.S. "BUSINESS CYCLES"

	In Months		
Trough to Peak	Rising Period	Falling Period	Trough to Trough
May 1954 - August 1957	39	8	47
April 1958 - April 1960	24	10	34
February 1961 - December 1969	106	11	117
November 1970 - November 1973	36	16	52
March 1975 - January 1980	58	6	64
July 1980 - July 1981	12	16	28
November 1982 - *			

LENGTHS OF BULL & BEAR MARKETS

	In Months		
Bull Market Period	Rising Period	Falling Period	Trough to Trough
Stock Market (Dow Jones Industrial Average)			
April 1942 - May 1946	49	37	86
June 1949 - January 1966	199	52	251
May 1970 - January 1973	32	23	55
December 1974 - April 1976	16	48	64
April 1980 - April 1981	12	16	28
August 1982 - *			
Stock Market (N.Y. Stock Exchange Composite Index)			
April 1942 - June 1946	50	36	86
June 1949 - November 1968	233	18	251
May 1970 - January 1973	32	23	55
December 1974 - December 1976	24	14	38
February 1978 - November 1980	33	21	54
August 1982 - *			
Gold			
March 1968 - May 1969	14	15	29
August 1970 - December 1974	52	20	72
August 1976 - January 1980	41	61	102
February 1985 - *			

Business Cycles are periods of rising and falling economic activity. The trough is the very bottom of the cycle; the peak is the very top. The cycles listed are those recorded by the National Bureau of Economic Research (listed in the *Statistical Abstract of the United States, 1986*, page 531).

The dating of investment bull and bear markets is an arbitrary exercise.

* = Still in progress in August 1987.

The table on page 147 shows the lengths of business cycles since 1954. As you can see, the length is so variable that the data tell you only that there *are* fluctuations in business activity. There is no regularity in the severity or duration of the "cycles."

The table also shows the duration and extent of each bull market in stocks and gold. The only lesson I can draw from the table is that every bull market comes to an end. That in itself is important to remember; investors have been hurt by forgetting it. But it is hardly the key to the future.

For many years after World War II, there seemed to be a reason for a repeating pattern in business fluctuations—a reason grounded in the government's monetary policy, which alternated between stimulus and restraint. For a while, beginning in 1968, the repeating pattern seemed to be reflected in bull markets in gold and stocks.

But the monetary policy that caused the pattern wasn't a law of nature. Eventually, the monetary authorities learned from their mistakes (even if they learned no more than that they had been making mistakes). The monetary policy changed, and so did the shape of business fluctuations, which in turn upset the established patterns of bull and bear markets in stocks and gold.

There still are alternations of boom and bust, prosperity and recession. These "cycles" continue if for no other reason than by definition. If you mark the boundary between good times and bad as an unemployment rate of, say, 8%, the line will be crossed from time to time—signaling boom or bust.

However, recognizing that the economy alternates between these states isn't the same as knowing when the line will be crossed or how far the excursion will run.

The Dow Theory

The writings of Dow theorists are valuable reminders that all trends come to an end eventually. They help to keep one's feet on the ground while other investors may be losing their heads.

But Charles Dow apparently didn't intend for the "Dow Theory" to become a formula for market signals. Even if he had, the components of that formula would have to be changed to keep up with a changing world.

For example, the Dow Jones Industrial Average and the Dow Jones Transportation Average are equal partners in the Dow Theory. Charles

Dow apparently thought that the signal given by a new high in the Industrial Average wasn't sufficient unless confirmed by a new high in the Transportation Average.

The Transportation Average originally was the Railroad Average. Dow's preoccupation with the railroads was understandable, since the railroad boom of the late 1800s hadn't ended yet. In fact, Dow's first market average in 1884 was a single index that contained 9 railroads and only 2 industrials.[6]

That suggests that he wasn't thinking of transportation as an equal partner in the health of the economy. Rather, he probably considered the railroads to be more representative of the overall economy than the industrials were.

Today, the Transportation Average is dominated by airlines—with a little help from railroads and shipping companies. While airlines are an important industry, they are only one industry—nowhere near as important as railroads were in the late 19th century. It's not obvious why they should be more significant than, say, computers, chemicals, food, or entertainment.

Giving the airlines veto power in the Dow Theory isn't likely to provide the kind of double check that Charles Dow was looking for.

We also should realize that, in Dow's day, his Average was the only index in town. Having to add and divide the numbers manually, Dow picked just a handful of stocks that he hoped would represent the whole market. Today, alternatives such as the New York Stock Exchange Composite Index indicate the overall state of the market far better than the Dow Industrial and Transportation Averages combined.[7]

It's impossible to construct a track record for the Dow Theory, since the theory doesn't amount to a complete trading system; its application is a subjective matter. Determining whether a Dow signal has been given depends upon when you believe the current trend began, which phase of the bull market you believe we're in, and whether a recent decline was a significant correction. Each analyst has to decide these things for himself.

Dow theorists often disagree among themselves about the signals. So I don't think I, a non-Dow-theorist, can compile a performance record for Dow signals.

[6]The makeup of the indices is given in *The Dow Jones Averages 1885–1980*, edited by Phyllis Pierce, Dow Jones-Irwin Co., 1982. In 1970, the Railroad Average was transformed into the Transportation Average with a considerable change in its components.

[7]The Dow averages still serve to show at a glance the movement of the large capitalization stocks. My point here is only that they are poor spokesmen for the whole market.

However, two newsletters with "Dow Theory" in their names are tracked by *The Hulbert Financial Digest*—which measures the performance record of newsletters. Neither outperformed the major stock-market averages during the period between June 1980 and June 1987.

Although I haven't read the original writings of Charles Dow, I have the impression that he didn't intend for market analysts to become wrapped up in signals. Here is how Richard Russell (a Dow Theory practitioner) describes the evolution of the Dow Theory:

"Dow was almost too cautious to come out with a flat, dogmatic statement of his Theory . . ." observes [William P.] Hamilton. "It must be disinterred from those [*Wall Street Journal*] editorials, where it is illustrative and incidental and never the main topic of conversation." The way to the Dow Theory, it seems, was not easy even for Dow's protege. . . .

The phrase, Dow's Theory, was never used by Dow himself. It was coined by his friend and admirer, S. A. Nelson. Dow's complete editorials were assembled by Nelson in a little book entitled the "A.B.C. of Stock Speculation," which was published in 1902. A careful reading of this book will convince one that Dow did not envision his Theory as a device for predicting the trend of the market. He used his averages more as a guage of the current state of stocks and the economy.[8]

The ideas underlying the Dow Theory are realistic and valuable. They prepare investors for change. But they don't predict when the change will occur.

Elliott Wave Principle

The graph on page 139 shows the ideal Elliott Wave pattern. That graph makes the Elliott Wave Principle seem pretty straightforward. But the theory's practical application is something quite different.

For example, the graph on the facing page shows the Dow Jones Industrial Average since 1932, the beginning of the current Elliott Supercycle. On the graph, I've labeled the various waves exactly as a leading Elliott Wave proponent did in late 1986.

Note how arbitrary the labeling is. Note, too, that you would have had no way in the world of knowing which wave you were in at the time it was waving. And note that between 1966 and 1982 a market

[8]*The Dow Theory Today* by Richard Russell (described on page 138), page 16.

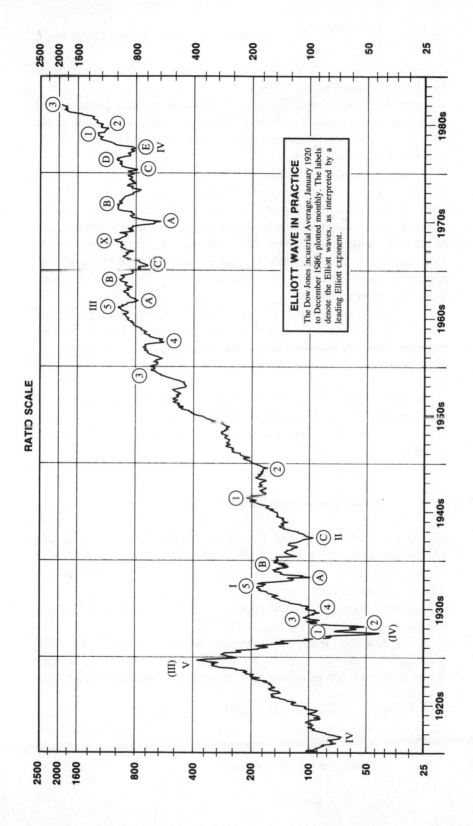

RATIO SCALE

ELLIOTT WAVE IN PRACTICE

The Dow Jones Industrial Average, January 1920 to December 1986, plotted monthly. The labels denote the Elliott waves, as interpreted by a leading Elliott exponent.

phenomenon (accompanied by new labels) occurred that isn't allowed for in the idealized graph on page 139.

An integral part of the Elliott Wave Principle is the significance of Fibonacci numbers and the Golden Mean of 1.618 (discussed on pages 92–95). If Fibonacci numbers are your cup of tea, Elliott invites you to a lifetime of tea parties.

In recent years, a practitioner of the Elliott Wave Principle has received a good deal of favorable publicity concerning his ability to call turns in the market. However, *The Hulbert Financial Digest*, rating only his market timing (since he doesn't recommend individual stocks or portfolio allocations), found his stock-market timing from 1980 to 1987 to be only slightly more profitable than a simple buy-and-hold approach, while his timing for bonds or gold was less profitable than a buy-and-hold approach.[9]

His 1978 book on the Elliott Wave Principle pointed toward 1982–1984 as the peak for all the cycle magnitudes I mentioned on page 139, but reality later forced him to revise this to the late 1980s. If the peak doesn't come in the late 1980s, I'm sure that more revisions will.

As most forecasters do, he points out that everything is subject to revision. But then why should we bother paying attention to his forecasts? How do we know which forecast is the final, and correct, revision?

Kondratieff Wave Theory

The Kondratieff Long Wave Theory is so vague and imprecise that it's difficult to discuss seriously. Of course, the imprecision will make it easy for someone to say in the future that it foretold something or other—no matter what happens.

However, there are a few specific criticisms to make about the theory.

To begin with, there's no theoretical reason to suppose that a 54-year cycle exists—in capitalist economies or anywhere else. Nothing in the nature of life or economics suggests that anything must recur every half-century.

The slogan "History repeats itself" isn't an economic principle. It has no practical meaning so far as investment markets are concerned.

---

[9]*The Hulbert Financial Digest* (July 1987), page 4.

Second, when Kondratieff made his original presentation, he had discovered one 60-year cycle and one 47-year cycle, and asserted that the capitalist economies were halfway through a third cycle. His fans have filled in the end of the third cycle and the first half of the fourth. That makes 3½ cycles.

There is nothing "scientific" in drawing conclusions from so few instances—none of which shows a length of 54 years. If you asked a statistician to evaluate the evidence for the Kondratieff theory, he'd tell you to ask again in 600 years—when there might be some evidence to evaluate. As the economist Murray N. Rothbard has pointed out:

> . . . Where real cycles exist, in physics, astronomy or biology, the scientist concludes that there are cycles after hundreds, if not thousands, of mutually confirming observations. But in the alleged "Krondratieff," there are, at very most, only 3½ cycles. What kind of analysis builds a cycle theory on only 3½ observations?[10]

Third, there's only flimsy evidence that the capitalist world has gone through even one cycle so far. Comrade Kondratieff chose isolated economic statistics on such things as savings bank liabilities and consumption of mineral fuel in France; lead, coal, and pig iron production in England; and so on. He even pointed out that he had discarded several other statistical tables that hadn't supported his hypothesis.

He presented graphs of only the "good" data. Even so, only the most devoted Kondratiovian could discern distinct cycles in those graphs.

But he shouted "Ergo!" (in Russian)—there's a half-century boom-bust cycle in capitalist economies.

But I do hand it to the man. Using questionable methods and insufficient data, and still drawing only a very vague conclusion, he conjured up one of the most popular investment superstitions of the 1980s.

SUPERSTITION

The study of history *is* important.

It helps to know what happened to governments that staked their survival on impregnable castles when—surprise—the cannon was invented. Or what happened to European civilization when the black plague arrived. Or what happened to inland canals (the original Amer-

---

[10]*Investment Insights* (September 1984), page 6.

ican growth industry) when the railroads blossomed. All these lessons teach you just how surprising surprises can be; they remind you that change is coming—unannounced.

History calls your attention to what is possible, including things you should allow for in your investment plans. And history arms you with concrete examples that refute the ideas that other people might accept.

But history isn't a roadmap of the future. Nothing in history (or economics) suggests that it is. In fact, history is riddled more with surprise and change than with repetition.

There is no reason for diverse, learning, changing human beings to repeat the past on either a fixed or a variable timetable. There's no truly authoritative body of work on the subject to impress us. And no evidence has been offered to show that cycles or waves provide reliable clues to the future. With no reason for being, no authority, and no verification, the belief in the market-timing power of cycles and waves is one more branch of superstition.

History Proves Anything

Some of a cycologist's time is spent trying to forecast the future. But a great deal more is spent trying to cram the square pegs of the present and past into the neat, round patterns of his theory. When he reconciles his theory with the facts, it's usually the facts that suffer the damage.

If a price explodes upward during the month when it was supposed to be heading toward its low, the practitioner merely says the price would have risen even more had it not been for the cycle's downward influence.

If a series of waves signals that a bull market is about to end, but the bull market continues, the wave theorist calls this an "extension"—or he may even call the upmove the first "downwave" of the ensuing bear period—although he never tells us in advance to expect an extension, inversion, or other irregularity.

Since he believes the theory to be true and never reconsiders the matter, an analyst always finds a way to explain market action in terms of the theory—no matter how farfetched the explanation might be to someone who examines it closely.

Even if the analysis were correct, it still would be after the fact—explaining only the past. It never warns you reliably of something to come.

As with any sect, cycologists have a bagful of logical tricks to explain what to us dullards appear to be contradictions. Here's one of the boldest strokes I've seen, straight from a well-known investment advisor who loves cycles:

> Our personal interpretation of the six year precious metal cycle would have called for a peak in the first quarter of 1986. . . .
>
> The six year precious metals cycle has both inverted and extended itself. When we say that this cycle has inverted, we mean that it recorded a cyclic low when a cyclic high would have been expected. . . . When we say that the gold cycle has extended itself, we are saying that the cycle has doubled. We predict that gold will be in a bull market from 1986 to 1992. The bear market in gold which began in 1980 doubled itself and gave birth to twins, a new six year precious metals cycle.

Have you got that?

10

Going Wrong
Misunderstanding
Success

By now you may be wondering whether I believe there's *anything* you can do as an investor.

I've said that consistent forecasting is impossible; that the track records of investment advisors should be taken with a grain of salt; that economic science has no formulas by which to calculate the future; that a great deal of investment advice is based upon superstition; and that the usefulness of all schools of investment analysis is severely limited.

That's *good* news—because it helps to explain why well-laid plans go wrong.

And there's even more good news. There *are* successful investors and speculators. And there are advisors who provide valuable services to their clients—services that help the clients make and keep profits.

I believe it's possible for you to succeed as an investor. And Part II will present a strategy that I think can help.

In fact, I have no bad news to give you—unless you have been hoping to make a fast killing in the market with a spectacular forecast, a foolproof system, or an advisor with the Midas touch.

Yet it's true that the first nine chapters raised questions that still need to be answered. Among them are:

1. Is there value in any school of investment analysis?

2. Why are some speculators successful?

3. How is it possible that some of them use analytical tools and rules that have never worked for you?

4. Can you learn to be a successful investor or successful speculator?

The best-laid plans often go wrong because an investor misunderstands the success he sees others achieving. So in this chapter we'll examine the elements that make a speculator successful—to show that simply imitating him won't work.

We'll begin by looking at the wide range of talents and personalities to be found among investment advisors—who represent here the wide range of investors and speculators.

THE GAMUT OF ADVISORS

There's no lack of variety in the kind of people who populate the investment advisory business.

Many advisors and writers are reasonable and helpful; a few are even wise. Others are chronically wrong in their information, in their logic, and in the recommendations they make.

There are noisy advisors who have little to offer but flamboyance and showmanship—although you'd never know that from hearing them describe themselves.

Some advisors are just plain dangerous. They are relay stations for rumor and misinformation. They stir your anxiety about real or imagined threats to the world. Their explanations are sloppy, and their suggestions often are deliberately ambiguous. Perhaps most important, their ideas, systems, and strategies could cost you dearly because they give no thought to the risks that go with their recommendations.

There also are advisors whose hearts are in the right place but whose judgments usually land elsewhere. They seem to have a knack for being in the wrong place at the wrong time. Fortunately, some of them have other virtues; they may be good educators, helpful in supplying information, or sources of ideas that you can transform to your own benefit.

Most advisors are neither saints nor great sinners. Some have particular strengths—as educators, informants, tacticians, entertainers, even tranquilizers. And each has his own weaknesses.

The Winners

Our concern here is with advisors who, from time to time, show flashes of genius. They sometimes have thoughts about the markets that are truly perceptive, original, and profitable.

They aren't always right. But sometimes they are spectacularly right—calling attention to possibilities that others have overlooked.

Generally, these advisors don't concern themselves with strategy or detail. Their primary concern is the question of where the markets are headed. And in that regard they seem to have more hot streaks than other advisors.

But in a number of puzzling cases, if you look closely at these people, it's hard to believe they could be successful at anything. Let me tell you about four of them.

Mr. Mystic

The first advisor seems to be two different personalities.

One side of him preaches and practices a kind of mysticism that explains the workings of the world by reference to one of the superstitious cycle-wave theories that make the rounds. In this persona, the advisor's comments and explanations are worthless.

But sometimes he sets aside his charts and magic spectacles, and speaks in English. When he does, he often provides remarkable insights into the markets—and even into the non-investment world. At such times, his ideas are worth hearing.

The record of his specific investment recommendations, while not outstanding, is above average—good enough that I'm willing to believe he has a feel for the way markets move.

Mr. Unappreciated

The second advisor might be described charitably as a manic-depressive paranoid schizophrenic. He is bitter, lonely, crying out for attention and recognition—the kind of person you'd like to have living next door.

And yet sometimes he comes up with spectacular forecasts that are both unusual and correct. He often sees things that others miss. And occasionally he has a hot streak in investment recommendations that runs for a year or more.

Of course, he's made the normal share of wrong guesses—which means quite a few. And some of those wrong guesses have been costly for his customers. You wouldn't be safe relying blindly on his recommendations. But if you can look beyond his self-pity, you often find good ideas lurking among the sniffles.

Mr. Occult

A third advisor loves to dabble in the occult. In his newsletter, he often plays with Fibonacci numbers and other mystical doodads.

But when it comes time to make a decision—to buy or sell—he forgoes the joy of witchcraft and relies on his sense of the market. That sense often has been remarkably right, and rarely very far wrong.

Mr. Other-World

The fourth advisor is so disconnected from the real world that he actually invited his newsletter subscribers to send him their personal experiences with changing retail prices—which he intended to use as data for a consumer price index he believed would be more accurate than the one compiled by the government.[1]

Despite this kind of thinking, for two years in a row he produced the best performance record of the advisors monitored by *The Hulbert Financial Digest.*

Strange Winners

For his faults, none of these advisors sounds very promising. But somehow each of them has earned a place in the upper ranks of the advisory business.

How could this be?

How could people with such silly ideas or troubled personalities do so well? Is there no justice in the world?

One possibility is luck, of course, But I've watched three of these advisors over a number of years. And each of them is pretty consistently right—or at least perceptive—in certain areas, while often wrong in others. Luck probably wouldn't be so discriminating.

[1]Maybe his circulation is larger than the government's.

And in the areas in which each one is generally right, his statements usually are at least reasonable. This leads me to believe that each of these advisors has a special aptitude in a certain area.

Sadly, the advisors aren't satisfied to accept their abilities for what they are and to concentrate on using them. They try to reduce their astute, general observations about the market to precise technical indicators. They often explain their success in ways that an intelligent person can't accept. And they roam into areas where their talents don't follow.

To understand the nature of their success, and to consider the possibility that you might be as successful, we need to examine the roles of talent and intuition—which are elements of success in any field.

TALENT

In every area of life, we recognize the importance of talent.

We know there are musicians, athletes, comics, writers, artists, architects, actors, and orators whose abilities go far beyond what they've learned from schooling or experience.

And this is true not only in glamorous occupations; we see the special brilliance that some people have as cooks, flower arrangers, woodworkers, mechanics, hairdressers. You undoubtedly know someone who has an unusually good memory, or who is "good with his hands," or who has an unusual ability to draw pictures or add large numbers in his head.

In each of these cases, the special ingredient that sets the person apart is a *talent* for a particular task—a talent the person "comes by naturally."

Mindful of the importance of talent, you wouldn't expect to become a celebrated pianist just by reading a book by Van Cliburn, Liberace, or Jerry Lee Lewis. In fact, you know that years of study with a great pianist might not turn you into a professional pianist, or even a very good amateur. The crucial question is whether you have a talent for music in general and for the piano in particular.

Talent is a factor in any job, craft, art, or hobby. You probably could learn to type 50 words a minute, but—no matter how smart you are or how long you practice—you might never catch up with the talented typist who turns out 100 words a minute.

Whatever degree of talent you have for something, training can make the talent more effective. But no amount of training will increase your talent or enable you to achieve things that your talent won't allow.

No one doubts this when the subject is music or athletics. Yet when the subject is investing, the point is overlooked.

Talent for Investing

But talent is just as critical a factor in the investment world. Some people were born to be speculators, and some speculators wish they'd never been born.

Writers and advisors often tempt you with the idea that you could become a great speculator, another Bernard Baruch, a millionaire many times over—just by following the rules practiced by the great (even though the person suggesting this hasn't accomplished it).

It's a wonderful idea, but it doesn't make sense.

Would you expect to make it to the stage of the Metropolitan Opera just by reading a book called *Luciano's Favorite Singing Tricks*? Would you expect to become an inventive genius like Thomas Edison just by watching an old Mickey Rooney movie?

Why should it be plausible, or even possible, that you (as well as millions of other investors) could become a stock-market whiz by learning the tricks of a recognized genius?

As I'll discuss on page 170, many elements of investing can be learned and put to use profitably without any special talent. But beyond these techniques lies an art that can't be taught or captured in a list of rules.

An art requires talent that no effort or education can produce. Some people study painting for years but never paint anything you'd want to look at. Others fill their schooldays with math courses but are never really at home with elementary algebra. And many people learn all they can about investing but always seem to buy the wrong things.

Apart from those who have simply been lucky, the people who achieve spectacular investment success do so because they have a talent for investing. Some of these winners are unrealistic, unattractive, even unintelligent people—but they have *a talent for sensing the movements of markets*.

Talent isn't everything. Because of other factors, some talented people are more successful than others. And the *lack* of a natural talent for speculating doesn't leave you helpless.

But any plans you may have to become a star speculator are empty if they disregard the importance of natural talent.

INTUITION

Not only is it impossible to copy the tricks of someone whose talents are different from yours, it's difficult even to identify what those tricks are.

Very few geniuses can explain their gifts, because so little of what they do operates solely on explicit, step-by-step reasoning.

This, of course, is true for most of what *anyone* does. For example, when you drive a car, you don't say to yourself, "Now I'll turn the wheel slightly to the left . . . now I'll turn it slightly to the right . . . now I should shift gears." Nor do you explain to yourself why you're doing these things.

You act automatically because your mind is taking in and processing information about the road, the traffic, and the speed and direction of your car—all without your having to make conscious decisions. In fact, if a passenger asked why you did a particular thing, you might find it difficult to explain. You might not even have noticed doing it.

When you make decisions without noticing the step-by-step process, you're using *intuition*—which is the unconscious processing of information and ideas.

There's nothing other-worldly about intuition. It isn't a strange gift for divining the future or reading minds. It's simply a faculty, that everyone has, to make a judgment—right or wrong—without paying attention to *how* you make the judgment. When intuition operates, you analyze information and ideas without noticing the process until the answer pops to the surface of your mind.

With intuition, you size up a stranger as honest or dishonest, or judge whether a house is one you'd be happy living in—without identifying all the factors that influenced your decision.

Most everyday activity runs on intuition—eating, walking, writing, talking, most physical labor and a great deal of mental labor. You don't focus on each step, you just move.[2]

---

[2]Habit also is involved in many activities. But habit and intuition aren't the same thing. Intuition is an activity of your intellect—a way by which you form judgments and opinions about what is true or what to do in a particular situation. Habit, on the other hand, is a condition that allows you to do repetitive things easily. Intuition is a natural function, but a habit is wholly learned (and can be unlearned).

Intuition in Speculating

A speculator acts intuitively, too.

He buys when he senses that he should—perhaps because his intuition notices a critical similarity between current market conditions and earlier situations (not explicitly remembered) that proved to be profitable. Or he may decide against an investment because he unconsciously detects a hazard that makes him uneasy—one that others haven't noticed.

If you ask him how he made his decision, he probably won't say, "It just felt right to me," even though that might be the most accurate answer. More likely, he will cite a half-dozen economic factors or technical indicators to explain his judgment.

But it's unlikely that those were the deciding factors. For one thing, there were similar indicators that pointed in the opposite direction. What he cites may be important; but his final decision was intuitive, and thus doesn't allow a complete explanation.

However, the fact that he can't explain his actions doesn't mean he didn't have good reason for what he did.

Experience

Investment talent operates intuitively, for the most part. And it draws on experience—which provides a fund of information to which intuition can refer.

Financial experience isn't the only kind that serves you. In making investment decisions, you draw upon what you know about human nature; on what life has taught you about making decisions; on what you've found to be logical or silly, careful or careless; on your ability to evaluate people's opinions and arguments; on your memories of how fads and fashions have changed; and on thousands of facts of life.

Experience of any kind contributes to your ability to make good intuitive decisions.

Intuition and "Gut Feelings"

Intuition has acquired a bad name—in part because many people try to dignify mere guesses, hopes, and wishes by citing the authority of their "instincts" or "gut feelings."

You can't convert a bad investment decision into a good one, or succeed with a sloppy strategy, by saying that your "gut feelings" are telling you to do something.

Intuition is valuable, and should always be respected. But it's no better than your talent, intelligence, and experience. And it doesn't have the power to overrule reality. In any conflict between feelings and logic, let logic prevail.

My purpose in discussing intuition isn't to encourage you to disregard logic. My purpose is only to explain why it is that some people succeed without being able to give satisfactory reasons for their success.

RULES

Some writers and advisors promise to turn you into a successful speculator by teaching you rules for beating the markets—rules formulated from the words of great achievers.

Doers & Teachers

But great achievers are rarely good teachers. They aren't necessarily even good thinkers. A financial genius would need a second great talent to be able to explain how his genius works.

This is true in any line of work. For example, ask a successful salesman how he does so well. He can't really explain his talent, but he won't want to seem stupid or unsociable.

For want of a better answer, he will probably repeat what he's read in the company manual or in books on selling. He'll tell you he makes extra calls every day, remembers everyone's name, never takes "no" for an answer, controls the interview—all the platitudes of selling.

But his answer doesn't explain anything, because most other salesmen do these things, too, as best they can. He doesn't know *what* to say, because he doesn't know *why* he's a superior salesman.

He can't explain how he senses which prospects are more likely to buy or which approach a given prospect will respond to, or how he knows when to ask for the order. Part of his talent is that such decisions are obvious to him. You might as well ask a bird how it flies as ask the salesman how to be sensitive to people's wants.

Few people would bother asking a great athlete how he runs so fast. We know that good training can improve his speed, but we also know that his speed is primarily a natural talent. So we don't expect him to concoct a recipe that will enable anyone to run a four-minute mile.

In the same way, but less obviously, some people are born mechanics, born designers, or born speculators. Such a person reacts intuitively to each situation as it develops; don't expect him to reduce his talent to a list of explicit rules.

Honest Answers

Some achievers believe they do know why they succeed, but their opinions aren't always correct.

Intuition can't be observed directly—even by the person using it. So it's very easy for someone to attribute his success to the wrong thing, to a rule that isn't really used, or even to an elaborate analytical system that's unworkable. I've seen an advisor or speculator attribute a successful investment, or even his entire career, to reasons that simply made no sense.

It would be a lot more helpful if the great achiever explained his latest coup by saying, "I did what I did because I *felt* it was the right thing to do." Hearing such an answer, no one would try to imitate his methods.

However, just like the salesman who answered with platitudes, few achievers are comfortable conceding that they don't fully understand their own success.

Exceptions to Rules

Rules are attempts to describe the methods of successful individuals. But even the most perceptive and articulate genius can't tell you what he would do in every conceivable situation.

Any rule he devises to help you will have many exceptions, since he can't imagine every circumstance that might arise. When he runs into an exceptional situation, he will adapt accordingly. But people who follow his rule have no way to know that a circumstance is exceptional until they trip over it.

In addition, a situation may appear to be governed by more than one rule. Accommodating contradictory principles and rules may be easy for the intuitive genius, but his followers aren't equipped to deal with such dilemmas.

This is one reason that technical analysis works for some investors but not for others who use the same written rules. Applying a rule requires judgments that everyone will make in his own way—using whatever talent he possesses.

Computer systems for technical analysis seldom work for any length of time because a computer's only talent is for calculation. And the computer calculates only according to the rules that have been programmed into it.

Not even the most successful trader can write a complete program of rules for the computer to follow, because he can't really pin down the rules by which he acts. Nor can he imagine in advance every circumstance that might arise. Consequently a computer program eventually runs into situations that its creator would handle differently.

Application

Formal rules are never complete answers. Even if a rule is correct, its application depends upon personal experience and present circumstances.

Because people rely so much on intuition, two investors can agree on a rule but disagree on its use. They both might say they "buy when blood is running in the streets" (buy an investment when all the news about it is bad), but one of them might think a pint of blood is a buy signal, while the other waits until he thinks the blood is knee-deep.

And even when one of them sees sufficient blood, some subtle factor may cause him to wait until he determines the blood type.

Rules do have value, however. "Buy when blood is running in the streets" can't tell you when to buy an investment. But if other considerations indicate that now is a good time to buy, the rule can remind you not to be deterred by widespread pessimism about the investment.

THE ROLE OF INVESTMENT ANALYSIS

By recognizing the roles of talent and intuition, it becomes easier to understand that a theory of investment analysis can work for one person but not for another.

It also means that no one can ever establish objectively how much value there is in such things as technical analysis.

For example, many academic studies have set out to test various rules of technical analysis. Most of them conclude that there's nothing about it that "works." And yet I'm convinced that some investors and advisors use technical analysis profitably; I believe I do so myself.

How can something fail a systematic test but still be useful in practice?

I think it's because a successful technician uses technical analysis in ways different from what he says—even in ways he doesn't realize. He succeeds by intuitively following rules he has never identified.

So the rules he recites to you probably will fail rigorous testing, because they aren't the rules by which he succeeds. The stated rules don't describe everything he takes into consideration—or might take into consideration tomorrow.

The technician's results tell you more about himself than about the rules he claims to follow.

Inspiration

But even that isn't the whole story. I doubt that any successful technician makes his decisions solely on the basis of what his charts show him.

I think he uses technical analysis not so much for the specific answers it gives, but as a routine for keeping in touch with the market—and as a tool of inspiration. The charts and indicators and other paraphernalia of technical analysis may be no more than exercise equipment for his mind.

The same is true for *any* type of investment analysis. The competent analyst studies the data to get his mind in motion, and to get a feel for what the market is doing.

He doesn't expect to find objective, scientific evidence that proves an investment or a market must go up, because no such proof is possible. If it were, thousands of other investors would see the evidence, too—and they would be bidding up the price.

The *un*talented analyst will analyze his research in accordance with rigid rules—and respond to what he believes should be clear, unequivocal buy and sell signals. The talented analyst knows that such signals don't exist; he studies the indicators to gain a sense of the market, but he doesn't consider his findings to be conclusive.

Viewing the same ambiguous indicators that the ordinary analyst follows, the talented analyst intuitively makes better judgments.

And, because opportunities come in *shades* of promise, part of the judgment he makes is whether to pass up buying opportunities that qualify by the "rules" but just don't seem right to him.

In many cases, an analyst may be using his research only to see whether it contradicts what his intuition is telling him—or simply to keep himself busy while his intuition does the real work.

When all the analysis is finished, a speculator enters a market because *it feels right to him*—no matter what his favorite tools and indicators tell him.

Mechanical Application

Those who make wrong judgments about the market fairly consistently do so, I think, because they're trying to apply an economic theory or system of analysis they believe in but lack the talent to handle.

Investing and speculating aren't mechanical activities, like Jazzercise. If they were, making money would be as simple as loading a video-cassette, turning on the TV, and jumping up and down. Speculating requires judgment, adaptation, and imagination.

In the late 1970s, two advisors I know, using elements of fundamental analysis, decided at about the same time that you could capitalize on the boom-bust business cycles by switching between common stocks and gold. The cycles had been produced with some regularity by the Federal Reserve's policy of stop-and-go expansion of the money supply.

But by the early 1980s, the Fed had changed its approach, other things had changed as well, and the character of the cycles was altered significantly. One of the advisors abandoned the strategy almost immediately, while the other continues unsuccessfully to try to make it work—even in 1987.

Those without the touch for speculating get no help from any school of investment analysis—no matter how much they study it—because the rules aren't sufficient, by themselves, to bring success.

MAKING USE OF A GENIUS

Some advisors seem to have the touch, and some don't. But no one is right all the time, nor is anyone always wrong.

Some people do have a special talent for imagining possibilities for the future that others overlook. But that doesn't mean they can predict the future reliably or in any profitable detail.

Even the best speculator will be wrong a good part of the time. For this reason, however great his talent may be, he won't succeed without a strategy that allows for losses.

Unfortunately, many advisors who have a good feel for the market are unconcerned about strategy. Following their suggestions consistently could lead eventually to bankruptcy.

So you can't succeed by simply doing whatever the genius is doing. Nor should you automatically bet against the chronic loser; now and then he will miscalculate and do something right.

However, it's worth knowing what these people are up to. When you're about to take a speculative position in the market, you'll want to reexamine your plans if you find that an advisor you respect is taking an opposite position—or if you find that you're marching arm-in-arm with the perennial loser.

LEARNING

You can't learn to be a market genius, but you can learn to be a better investor, and perhaps a better speculator, than you are now.

Investing & Speculating

First, we should recognize that investing and speculating aren't the same thing.

Investing is an attempt to earn a return by making your capital available to an investment market. An investor is willing to accept the same return (in yield and capital appreciation) that the market delivers to *anyone* who invests his capital there.

Speculation, on the other hand, is an attempt to increase one's profit by outguessing the market. The speculator hopes to earn a better return than he could achieve by simply making his capital available.

Buying a group of stocks and holding them through thick and thin is investing. Moving in or out of the market as the times look good or bad is speculating.

Buying a group of stocks or mutual funds that represent the overall market is investing. Choosing a few stocks or a mutual fund that you believe will outperform the market is speculating.

Holding some gold as a permanent hedge against bad times is investing. Buying gold because you believe inflation will come back this year is speculating.

Arranging and keeping a balanced portfolio to protect yourself against the unknown is investing. Trying to protect yourself by moving from one investment to another as you perceive the economy changing is speculating.

Learning to Invest

There is much about investing that can and should be learned: the mechanics and practices of various markets (in bonds, options, currencies, and so on), as well as principles for developing a good strategy, for hedging against things you fear, for creating balance and safety, and more.

Learning to Speculate

There also are many things you can learn about speculating: how to control risk, how to handle losses, how to let your profits run, and so on.

Learning these things won't increase your natural talent—but they can improve the results available with the talent you have, because a realistic strategy is as important as picking winners.

If you have a talent for speculating, you might learn from almost anything that has to do with speculation, including what other speculators have to say. Financial books and periodicals can stimulate your thinking—even if what you read is wrong, misguided, or unrealistic. You aren't reading to be told what to do; you're reading for inspiration—to prod your mind to clarify your own ideas about how markets move.

If you have no talent for speculation, none of that material will do you any good. And it might confuse or mislead you.

You can't learn how to spot a winner—not through education and not through experience. No one can teach you a feel for markets. But if you do have a talent, there's a great deal you can do to refine it and to make it more effective.

Your Opportunities

Although I've spoken of genius in this chapter, talent isn't an all-or-nothing matter. It comes in degrees—from a little to a lot. Most people have at least *some* talent for investing or speculating.

You don't have to be a genius to have enough talent to enjoy speculating or even to make money at it. So you may want to try your hand at speculating to see how you do.

If you're just beginning, go slowly. Start by speculating only on paper—making definite decisions to buy and sell, but without actually entering the orders. Keep track of the results. If you do actually make the investments, limit them to the minimum practical size, so that you can't lose very much.

If you find that you do well, then speculate in earnest. But never get carried away. *Always limit speculations to capital you can afford to lose.*

And no matter what kind of hot streak you find yourself on, realize that hot streaks end. Don't let yourself believe that you've found a system that can't lose—or that you're so smart you will never lose.

Be thankful for every profit you make, and treat each new speculation with the care and humility you gave your first one—because it has just as much chance to go wrong.

Motivation

On the other hand, you might have no desire to speculate.

Even if you're good at it, you might prefer to spend your time on other things. If so, accept the fact. Don't adopt a program that asks you to devote more time to your investments than you can give gladly.

If you like to spend hours studying the markets, do so. Enjoy yourself—but know that you're doing it by choice, not by necessity. If you like, subscribe to dozens of newsletters and stay in touch with all the telephone hotlines.

But if that sort of thing bores you or—worse yet—if it scares you, *don't do it.* You don't have to.

No matter what anyone says, you don't have to become a sophisticate, a daredevil, or a busy bee to protect yourself.

Don't Dare to Be Great

However, even if you have no talent or interest, you can't afford to neglect the subject of investing entirely.

You have to make some financial decisions just to hold on to what you have or to earn a conservative return on your capital. So, even if you have no aptitude for investing, you have to do *something*.

But you don't have to become a speculative genius. You can develop a relatively simple plan that's tailored to your own supply of talent and motivation.

In particular, you don't need to make clever investment decisions to set up a balanced portfolio that can protect you. You'll have to spend a few days working out the details; but from then on, you should be able to take good care of your portfolio with a minor touch-up only once a year.[3]

Whatever you do, recognize your own limits. When you resolve to do something you don't know how to do, don't have the talent for, or don't really want to do, you put yourself on the express train to financial ruin.

Your investment program will be successful only if it accepts you as you are.

Maybe You *Will* Be Great

But, as you evaluate your talents, don't judge yourself too harshly.

A few failures don't mean you're incompetent. They may mean only that you've been trying things that are over your head, or that might be unrealistic for *anyone* to attempt.

And with time, your knowledge and skills may grow—allowing you to be comfortable with things that now seem exotic, and allowing more of your natural talent to emerge. Some of that talent may have been overruled up to now by attempts to imitate the talents of others.

The strategy that's too sophisticated today may be a breeze tomorrow. So, if you want to be a better investor or speculator, take the time to read, consider, and test ideas and strategies.

But when you *act*, always recognize the limits of your ability at the time. Don't undertake investment plans today that go beyond the skills you have today.

---

[3]This will be discussed in Part II.

SUMMARY

I hope this chapter has helped to clear up some of the mysteries surrounding successful investors and speculators, and the theories and rules they profess.

Talent is the key to speculative success. Talent gives some speculators the ability to imagine possibilities that others miss, to foresee potential movements in markets, to sense whether the time is right for a move.

Talent can't be learned or profitably imitated. The decisions of a talented person can't even be explained satisfactorily, because talent operates largely through intuition.

Most explanations of speculative success are misleading—even those coming from a successful speculator. He can't identify all the reasons for his decisions, because so many of his decisions are made intuitively.

Although many successful investors and advisors attribute their success to some school of investment analysis or to a system, it's more likely that those methods are merely tools to exercise the mind—not roadmaps to riches. A successful speculator uses investment analysis to gain a general feel for the market and to get his mind in motion—not to arrive at clear-cut, yes-or-no answers.

So don't expect to succeed by copying the methods of the successful. Don't even expect to understand fully what those methods are. Don't expect to get an accurate and satisfying answer to the question, "How did you make this decision?"

Speculative talent can't be reduced to a set of rules. So don't expect to acquire such a talent through education.

However, education *can* show you how to be a better investor and a better speculator—to deal with risks more realistically, to satisfy investment needs more reliably, to protect what you have, and to speculate on the future without risking what's precious to you.

And, perhaps, to bring out of you the talent that *is* there.

11

Going Wrong with Trading Systems

The simplest to follow of the best-laid plans are trading systems—programs that tell you explicitly when to buy and when to sell as a result of automatic signals generated mathematically.

For many of these systems, a moving average of investment prices generates the buy and sell signals. Others use ratios or differences between investment prices, or some other statistical indicator, or even a numerical combination of several indicators.

A trading system is promoted as the easy way to invest—eliminating emotion and the agony of decisions. The system comes with an assurance that it's been tested scientifically—guaranteeing that you can beat the market, while reducing or eliminating risk at the same time.

Needless to say, any system to which you're introduced will have a fabulous track record. But please remember the first rule of trading systems:

The system that has worked perfectly up to now will go wrong when you stake your money on it.

The system's apparent success to date may be due entirely to coincidence or good luck. Unless you can point to a reason, based upon economic principles, that the system should work, you shouldn't expect its success to continue.

And just as some advisors selectively reconstruct their track records, so may the proponents of a trading system. The true record may not be as good as the one you're shown. And, of course, you won't hear today about the systems that were infallible yesterday—and then failed.

Indicators

Every system is based on at least one indicator—a statistic or formula that supposedly reveals whether an investment or market is currently in a bullish or bearish state.

Some indicators reflect certain kinds of activity within an investment market—such as the New York Stock Exchange "short interest ratio," which compares the volume of outstanding short sales with the average daily trading volume. Other indicators may be constructed from general economic statistics—such as the prime rate, the money supply, or the inflation rate.

Some indicators are fairly simple—tracking things like the difference, each day, between the number of stocks that rise in price and the number of stocks that fall. Others are quite complicated, involving perhaps dozens of pieces of data; they generally are monitored only by professional advisors and retired astrophysicists.

In this chapter, we'll take a close look at a few trading systems. Unfortunately, we probably won't touch on the exciting system you may run into tomorrow morning. But I hope you can generalize from the examples—enough to be a bit skeptical when someone claims he's found a map to Treasure Island.

MOVING AVERAGES

The most popular systems today use a moving average as the indicator. With no ifs, buts, or maybes, the moving average tells you when to buy and when to sell.

An investment's moving average is its average price over a specified period of time. The period might be of any length, from very short (such as a 5-day moving average) to very long (such as a 60-week moving average), whatever seems to be most reliable for the investment at hand.

For example, an investment's "50-week moving average" is its average price over the past 50 weeks. It is called a "moving" average because the average changes every week.

However, each week's change in price causes only a small change in the average, since the current price makes up only $\frac{1}{50}$ of the average. So the moving average is much less volatile than the actual price, and leaves a much smoother trail on a graph—as shown on the facing page. The longer the period spanned by the average, the slower and smoother its changes will be.[1]

Moving-Average Systems

Because the actual price is more volatile than the moving average, the price tends to "lead" the moving average. If the price is generally trending upward, the moving average (sooner or later) also will trend upward; but the moving average will trail behind the price, because it still includes lower prices from earlier days.

When a bull market begins (meaning when the price has reached bottom and is ready to start moving upward), the price is below the moving average—having led it downward. After the bull market has been under way for a while, the price rises up to and across the moving average. Eventually, the moving average will turn around and follow it. When the bull market ends (meaning when the price has peaked), the price begins dropping toward the moving average.

Since the price tends to lead the moving average, the price is expected to remain above the moving average for much of a prolonged bull market, and below it during much of a prolonged bear market. You can see this in the graph on the facing page.

In a moving-average system, a signal is given by the price crossing its moving average. The trading rule would be:

Buy the investment when the price rises above the moving average, and sell the investment as soon as the price falls below the moving average.[2]

The crossing of the price over its moving average is taken as confirmation that a definite trend is under way. By buying immediately

---

[1] An "exponential moving average" is weighted to give greater influence to more recent prices, and is thus more volatile than a simple moving average spanning the same period of time.

[2] With some systems, the buy or sell signal is triggered by one moving average crossing another moving average—such as a 10-week average crossing a 40-week average.

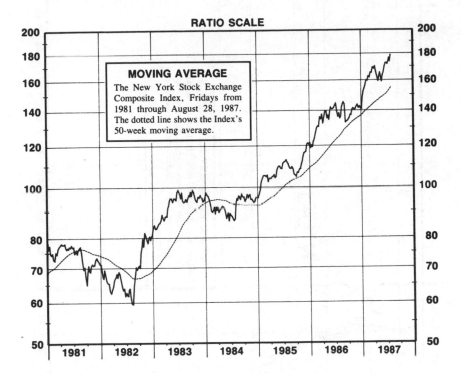

RATIO SCALE

MOVING AVERAGE

The New York Stock Exchange Composite Index, Fridays from 1981 through August 28, 1987. The dotted line shows the Index's 50-week moving average.

when the price rises above the moving average, you should be invested through most of a bull market—missing only its earliest stages. By selling immediately when the price drops below the moving average, you should avoid all but the beginning of the bear market.

The graph on page 178 illustrates this technique—showing the buy and sell signals generated for gold as the price moved above or below its 54-week moving average.

False Signals

Sometimes, however, the system produces a false signal.

This happens when the price rises above the moving average (calling for a purchase), only to fall back below the moving average (calling for a sale). Or the opposite can happen—with the system telling you to sell, and then telling you to buy again soon afterward. This occurred once during 1973 in the graph on page 178.

If there are too many false signals, you can run into a series of small

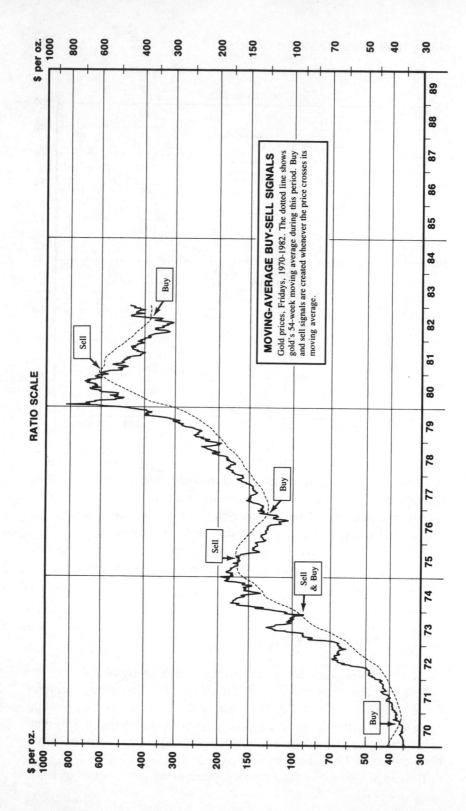

RATIO SCALE

$ per oz.

MOVING-AVERAGE BUY-SELL SIGNALS

Gold prices, Fridays, 1970-1982. The dotted line shows gold's 54-week moving average during this period. Buy and sell signals are created whenever the price crosses its moving average.

Buy

Sell

Buy

Sell

Sell & Buy

Buy

losses. It's possible, too, for a single false signal to inflict one large loss upon you.

The small losses occur when the price loops over and under the moving average—since a reversal of only ⅛ of a point could cause a stock to make a round trip across its moving average.[3]

The large loss can occur when the moving average continues to fall after the price has risen above it. The moving average could decline considerably further while the price—just above it—falls without giving a sell signal.

The graphs on page 180 illustrate these two problems.

Needless to say, false signals also can pull the investor out of a bull market too early.

Picking a Time Period

The person who develops a moving-average system chooses the length of time the average will span—40 days, 15 weeks, whatever.

Using a computer to examine the history of the investment's price, he tests every possible moving average—perhaps from 10 days to 80 weeks. He looks for the moving averages that have never produced false signals—or have rarely done so. Of those, he selects the one that has provided the earliest (and most profitable) signals to buy and sell.

When he's identified the "best" moving average, he may prepare a graph showing how reliably and profitably it would have guided an investor. The graph on page 178 is a typical presentation of a moving-average system that is infallible—meaning one that, at the time it was presented, had been performing magnificently.

No Economic Basis

When an analyst searches for the best moving average, he's hoping he will find one that produces excellent results. And the odds are great that he will. Mere chance suggests that, out of the 400 or so possibilities he might consider, at least one moving average will have a remarkable track record.

However, nothing in economics even remotely suggests that the

---

[3]Some investors try to avoid false signals by not buying or selling until the price has gone, say, 3% beyond the moving average. This reduces the number of false signals, but increases the cost of each one—since the investment has to drop further before the investor gets out.

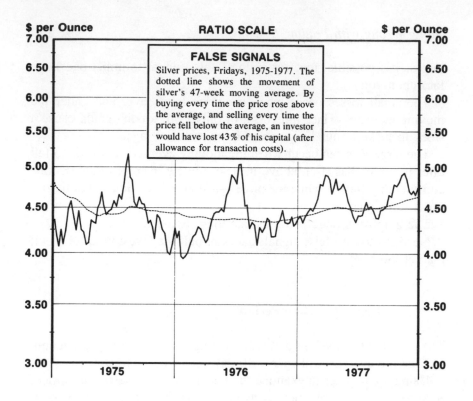

$ per Ounce
RATIO SCALE
$ per Ounce

FALSE SIGNALS

Silver prices, Fridays, 1975-1977. The dotted line shows the movement of silver's 47-week moving average. By buying every time the price rose above the average, and selling every time the price fell below the average, an investor would have lost 43% of his capital (after allowance for transaction costs).

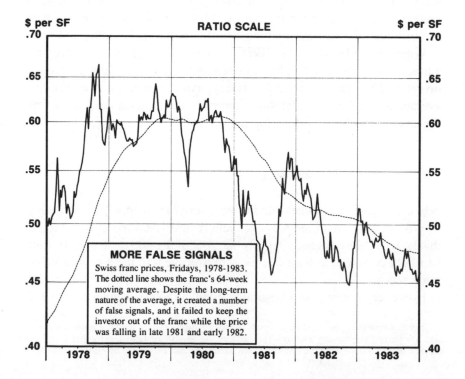

$ per SF
RATIO SCALE
$ per SF

MORE FALSE SIGNALS

Swiss franc prices, Fridays, 1978-1983. The dotted line shows the franc's 64-week moving average. Despite the long-term nature of the average, it created a number of false signals, and it failed to keep the investor out of the franc while the price was falling in late 1981 and early 1982.

crossing of an investment's price over *any* moving average confirms that a trend will continue. The event has no economic significance. It is an "event" only in the realm of statistics—a curiosity, like the year when your child's age becomes half of your own.

Any moving average brought to your attention will have a history of hypothetical success; otherwise, no one would bother telling you about it. But, no matter what it did before, the price is free to spend the coming year stumbling back and forth across its moving average. In fact, there's an even chance that the next signal given by the moving average will be false.

Moving Failures

The graph on page 178 shows a lovely moving-average system that for 13 years provided timely, profitable signals for entering and exiting the gold market.

Suppose that, having seen this graph, you decided in 1983 to let the moving average tell you when to buy and sell. The graph on page 182 shows what would have happened to you—as the moving average generated false and expensive signals from 1983 onward. Allowing for transaction costs, you would have lost 36% of your capital in just three years.

If you decide to let a moving average tell you when to buy and sell, you most likely will run into something similar to that graph—sooner or later.

At some point, the accumulated losses will discourage you from acting on the next signal—which might be the one that works again. Eventually, you'll throw in the towel and try something else.

However, the analyst who constructed the system is a professional who won't be so easily discouraged. He'll refine the system by adjusting the moving average—perhaps changing from a 54-week average to a 57-week average because the latter now seems to give better signals.

He'll tell his new customers that his system is based on actual experience. But the experience is a fantasy, having occurred only on the analysts's retrospective drawing board.

Looking at the graph on page 182, you might think that the losses incurred eventually would be a small penalty to pay for the profits that preceded them. But realize that no one acted on this moving average

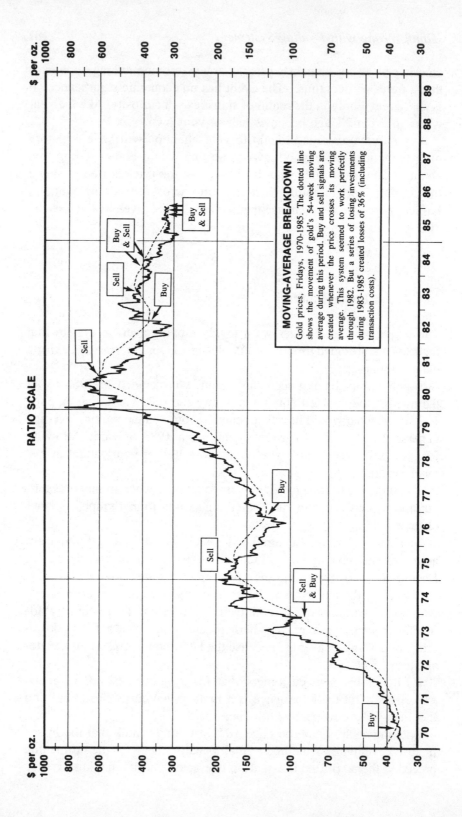

RATIO SCALE

$ per oz.

MOVING-AVERAGE BREAKDOWN

Gold prices, Fridays, 1970-1985. The dotted line shows the movement of gold's 54-week moving average during this period. Buy and sell signals are created whenever the price crosses its moving average. This system seemed to work perfectly through 1982. But a series of losing investments during 1983-1985 created losses of 36% (including transaction costs).

during its "successful" period. It is only *after* something appears to have worked well that anyone notices it and starts acting on it.

In fact, this is the case for *any* trading system.

Real-World Results

If you talk with other investors, you'll run across some who swear by moving-average systems. And they may cite profits they've made in the stock market over the last few years as the proof of the pudding.

But the past five years have been very good ones for the stock market, and a bull market guarantees good results for almost any trading system that includes the word "buy." Just about any system that kept you in stocks for most of the past five years would have shown a profit.

The question to ask about a system (of stock trading) is whether it outperformed a simple policy of buying stocks and holding on to them. And for moving-average systems, that doesn't appear to be the case. A number of investment newsletters do nothing but advise their readers on moving-average trading. But none of those tracked by *The Hulbert Financial Digest* from 1980 through 1986 beat the results for the New York Stock Exchange Composite Index.[4]

This doesn't mean that no moving-average system will do better than the NYSE Index next year. Very likely, more than one system will beat the NYSE Index. Some system may even beat the Index for several years in a row. But no one yet has devised a system for knowing in advance which moving-average system it will be.

Conservative?

Moving-average systems are sometimes promoted as a way to avoid risk. Whatever happens, the price can't drop terribly far before it crosses its moving average and tells you to sell; thus the system protects you against losing 30% or 40% of your investment in a bear market.

But a moving-average system merely replaces one risk with another. You can as easily run up losses of 30% or 40% if the moving average

---

[4]*The Hulbert Financial Digest* monitors the model portfolios recommended by several dozen newsletters and reports monthly on how well those portfolios do. Additional information for the *Digest* appears on page 449 of this book.

issues a string of false signals. The only difference is that you'll probably lose the money in several transactions, rather than in one.

Particularly costly are long periods when the investment's price moves sideways through a narrow range—as illustrated in the upper graph on page 180. The price and its moving average will be close together during most of the period, with many crossings and many false signals—any one of which might have been the start of a new bull market and, hence, had to be taken seriously by the system player.

In the upper graph on page 180, the 47-week moving average generated silver losses totaling 43% in 3 years—involving 21 transactions. In the lower graph on that page, the Swiss franc's 64-week moving average ate up half one's capital in just 6 years—with 30 transactions involved. In both cases, these results allow for the transaction costs incurred in the heavy trading.[5]

Moving-average systems provide decent profits actually only during dynamic bull markets—such as in the graph on page 178. They also work fairly well during severe bear markets (although they produce no profits then unless you sell short). But even the most volatile investment can fall into an extended trading range or a ragged trend— and that's when the system becomes very costly.

Moving-average systems don't improve the odds of success, nor do they eliminate risk. In the most fortunate circumstances, a moving-average system will give you a better return than a buy-and-hold approach. But in the worst circumstances, it delivers large losses on the installment plan.

I have dwelt at some length on moving-average systems because they are so popular today, and because they epitomize the simple, straightforward system that supposedly can't go wrong.

PLAYING THE SPREADS & RATIOS

Another common trading system uses spreads.

A spread involves two investments whose prices move more or less together. With a spread, you buy one of the investments and simultaneously sell the other short—anticipating that the price difference between the two investments will change to a large degree.

For example, you might buy a futures contract on the Standard &

---

[5]The calculations assume a 2% cost to buy and a 2% cost to sell—which allow both for commissions and a bid-ask spread surrounding the published price.

Poor's Composite Index and sell short a contract on the Value Line Composite Index. If blue chip stocks (represented by the S&P Index) do comparatively better than low-priced stocks (represented by the Value Line Index), your spread should produce a profit—as the S&P Index outperforms the Value Line Index.

Another example is the ''TED Spread''—using Treasury-bill contracts and Eurodollar contracts. When confidence in the health and stability of the international banking system weakens, Treasury-bill contracts become more valuable in comparison with Eurodollar contracts. You would profit from that loss of confidence if you had purchased Treasury-bill contracts and sold Eurodollar contracts short.

With any spread, the investment you've bought doesn't have to go up for you to make a profit; it need only do better than the investment you've sold—which it could do by falling a shorter distance.

An investor might enter a spread because he believes there are economic reasons for one of the investments to do better than the other. A spread is a valid medium for speculating on one's judgments.

Our concern here, however, is with spread *systems*. They involve no judgment about the market. Instead, the system automatically issues buy and sell signals—based on the price relationship between the two investments.

The Gold-Silver Ratio

A trading system using the gold-silver ratio has been quite popular. It provides a good illustration of how spread systems work.

The gold-silver ratio is the price of gold divided by the price of silver. For example, if gold is at $400 and silver is at $8, the ratio is 50.

The upper graph on page 186 shows the history of the gold-silver ratio from 1972 through 1978. It was around 1978 that many investors and advisors began to think of the ratio as the basis of a trading system.

They noticed that when the ratio rose above 40 or dropped below 30, it seemed to set in motion forces that would draw the ratio back toward its equilibrium in the mid-30s. So a simple trading system was born:

> Whenever the ratio rises above 40, buy gold and sell silver. When the ratio falls below 30, buy silver and sell gold.

Behind this system is the notion that, since both commodities are

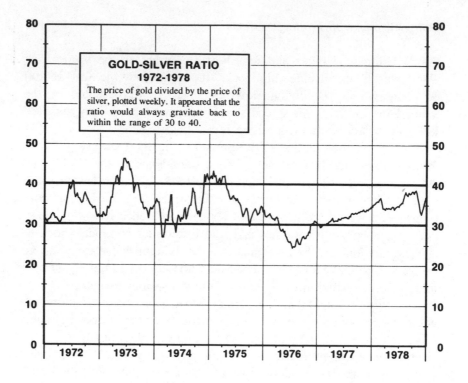

**GOLD-SILVER RATIO
1972-1978**

The price of gold divided by the price of silver, plotted weekly. It appeared that the ratio would always gravitate back to within the range of 30 to 40.

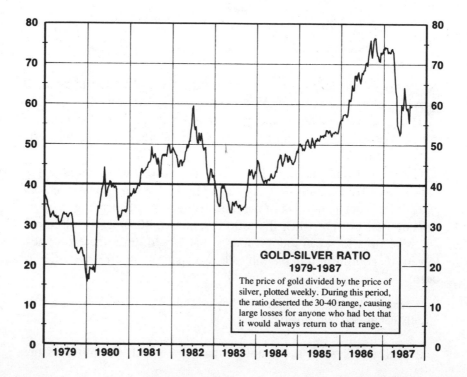

**GOLD-SILVER RATIO
1979-1987**

The price of gold divided by the price of silver, plotted weekly. During this period, the ratio deserted the 30-40 range, causing large losses for anyone who had bet that it would always return to that range.

precious metals, their prices should maintain a fairly constant relationship. An investor trades the spread when he believes the price ratio has deviated, temporarily, from the norm.

Anyone looking at the upper graph on page 186 could see that the system was a gold mine. Institute a position when the system says to do so, wait a year or two, and collect a profit equal to about 20% of the value of the gold and silver contracts—which might be a profit of more than 100% on the cash invested as a margin deposit.

Gold-Silver Problems

But the pattern began to break down almost as soon as it had become obvious. The lower graph on page 186 shows what happened through mid-1987.

The first spread would have been entered in 1979, when the ratio fell below 30. Unfortunately, the ratio just kept falling.

It finally hit bottom, at 17, in 1980 when both metals hit their all-time peaks—gold at $850 and silver at almost $50. Then the ratio started rising, and it crossed 40 in 1980—allowing a trader to realize a profit on his first spread, and telling him to enter a new spread in the opposite direction.

At a ratio of 40, the trader sold gold and bought silver. After a small rise, the ratio headed downward—as promised by the system. But the ratio never made it down to 30, so no profit was realized. Instead, the ratio headed back upward. It crossed 40 again, putting the system trader into a loss position, and reached 59 in 1982.

The ratio finally dropped for a while but, to this day, it still hasn't seen 30. Any ratio player who hasn't given up is still holding today the spread he entered in 1980.

Even as the system was failing, articles in financial publications were touting it as safe and sure. But given the fact that the trading signals at 30 and 40 weren't working anymore, the articles used levels of 35 and 45—and later 35 and 50. No mention was made of the old 30–40 trigger points or of the losses suffered by traders who had relied on them as the magic numbers.

In 1986, the ratio reached a new high of 77. People who had sold gold and bought silver when the ratio was at 40, 45, 50, or even 60 had to wonder what was going on.

Articles on the gold-silver spread still show up from time to time, but not nearly so often as they did when everyone knew it was a sure thing.

Risk in Spreads

Strangely, spreads are often presented as being "virtually riskless."

The principal rationale is that the two investments tend to move in the same direction; so if the one you buy drops, the one you sell short probably will drop, too, and so the loss and the profit will roughly offset each other.

But if such parallel movement keeps you from losing money, how are you supposed to *make* money? Why would the market reward you for outguessing the future if you can't lose when you guess wrong? It's as though a casino would let you keep your blackjack winnings but never collect your losses.

Another supposed comfort is that you enter a spread only when the ratio has reached an extreme. But the lower graph on page 186 is a reminder that *no* ratio is so extreme that it can't be followed by something even more extreme.

Nothing about spreads makes them less risky than other investments. The risk you take is determined by the capital you invest, and by the size of the loss you're willing to tolerate before you get out.

A spread (or any trading system) may be even more risky than other investments if, acting in the belief that it's inherently safe, you make no judgments about the investments involved and put your trading system on automatic pilot.

Gold-Silver Losses

The gold-silver ratio offers a dramatic example of how costly a spread system can turn out to be.

If you had bought $5,000 worth of gold and sold short $5,000 worth of silver when the ratio dropped to 30 in 1979, you'd have been $2,167 in the hole 6 months later. When the ratio finally rose to 40 in 1980, you'd have cashed in at a profit of $1,667 (less commissions).

You then would have bought silver and sold gold. If the spread again involved $5,000 of each, you'd have had a loss of $2,375 when the ratio hit 59 in 1982. When the ratio reached 77 in 1986, your loss would have climbed to $4,625.

A spread trader usually operates in the futures market. Using margin, he buys gold or silver worth several times the value of his cash investment. For him, the loss would have been well over 100% of his initial investment—unless he was fortunate enough to be sold out for failing to meet a margin call.

Economic Basis

A spread system is workable only if some economic force imposes minimum and maximum limits on the price ratio (or price difference) between two investments.

But I know of no economic reason that the ratio between gold and silver must remain within *any* limits. In fact, the contrary is true.

Gold is predominantly a monetary metal; people buy it as a form of security. The demand from industrial users exerts only a tiny influence on the price. As a monetary metal, gold profits from inflation—the worse the inflation, the better for gold. Best of all for gold is inflation that is strong enough to disrupt the economy.

Silver, on the other hand, is an industrial commodity. Investors wanting to hold silver as a financial asset exert only a temporary influence on its price. Severe inflation—which is good for gold—is bad for all industrial commodities, including silver.

Thus certain events, such as severe inflation, could send gold soaring while depressing silver. Since there's no limit to the severity of inflation or other economic disruptions, there's no limit to how *high* the gold-silver ratio could go.

General price stability and prosperity are usually very good for the economy and for industrial commodities, including silver. But the longer price stability continues, the less people fear inflation and the less enthusiasm they have for owning gold. So there's no limit to how *low* the gold-silver ratio might go.

Gold and silver have moved together much less than most investors imagine—as the graph of the ratio demonstrates.

Even when a case can be made that two investments (such as two related stocks) tend to move in tandem, it would be rare to find an economic reason to believe there are minimum and maximum limits to the ratio of their prices.

Change

Spread systems are based on the unstated assumption that the world doesn't change. But the world is in constant change—as values change, demand changes, supplies change. Otherwise there would be no price movements for investors to try to exploit.

A price ratio that goes to a new high isn't necessarily due for a fall. The weaker investment doesn't have to "catch up"—ever. The ratio's new high may reflect a fundamental change in technology or in the values of consumers. We might never again see the old high—let alone the old low.

In the 1950s some spread-system trader may have followed the ratio between the stocks of Xerox and the Careful Clean Carbon Paper Co. When he noticed that the ratio had moved in favor of Xerox, he probably took the CCCP side of a spread. Maybe today he's still waiting for the traditional relationship between carbon paper and photocopying to reassert itself.

For a real-world example, from 1955 to 1975 the German mark was consistently more expensive than the Swiss franc—the currency of an important trading partner. When the mark fell to a slight discount against the franc in the mid-1970s, many shrewd traders saw the op-

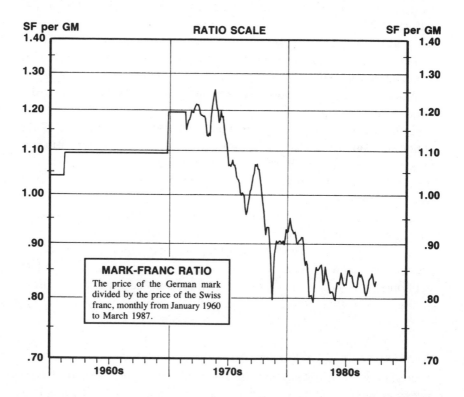

MARK-FRANC RATIO
The price of the German mark divided by the price of the Swiss franc, monthly from January 1960 to March 1987.

portunity for a sure profit. They bought the mark and sold the franc short—confident that the ''proper'' ratio would be restored.

Twelve years later, the old ratio has yet to return. As the graph on page 190 shows, the mark's discount over the franc has grown—reaching 20% on occasion. Obviously, times have changed.

Spreads

The spread system you'll be offered won't be one of those discussed here. It will be the platinum-palladium spread or bills-bonds or copper-lead or something else that's presented as a sure thing, backed up by the historical record.

Whatever the elements, try to remember that the gold-silver spread once was a sure thing, too.

There can be economic circumstances in which it might make sense to bet on a spread. But don't believe that your success is guaranteed, or that history imposes a limit on your potential loss.

A spread isn't a sure thing, nor is its risk inherently low. It is a speculation, like any other bet on the future.

SYSTEMS FOR SALE

Many trading systems are based on a group of indicators. The indicators are fed into a formula, and a single indicator comes out. When the indicator goes to a certain level, it's time to buy; when the indicator goes to another level, it's time to sell.

In many cases, the system's creator won't reveal the formula. Instead, he may sell the signals the system generates—perhaps through a newsletter or as a money management service.

Or he may sell the system itself—sometimes in the form of a computer program. A system might cost anywhere from $1, for one you buy through a classified ad in the *National Enquirer*, up to $300,000 or more. All are guaranteed to produce fortunes, and all have astounding track records.

These systems are part of the great tradition that has produced miracle hair-growth stimulators, bust creams, and pills you put in the gas tank to stretch your mileage.

As you might expect, trading systems come and go—while the people offering them are with us always. A system works for a while, then fails; its creator learns from the failure, and he fashions a new, improved system that will be everlastingly infallible—for a while.

Great Track Records

As I described on page 35, most indicators and systems are discovered by a computer's search through history for consistent relationships between potential indicators and investments or markets.

Even if the analyst finds an interesting relationship, he doesn't have an economic reason for believing that it will remain in force. He knows only that it prevailed during some period in the past.

But a system-builder takes history as proof that the system will be good forever. And to demonstrate his system's power, he will compile a track record showing how much money you would have made with it over the past umpteen years.

When you see the track record, you might assume that he's been using the system himself, and that all those dollars listed are his profits. But in fact he's saying only that if you (or he or Walter Mondale or anyone else) had happened to use the system, the user would have made so many millions.

But unfortunately for you, him, Walter Mondale, and everyone else, he didn't offer the system umpteen years ago. It hadn't even been thought of then.

Millions on Paper

One such hypothetical triumph was recounted in the *Forbes* article I referred to earlier.

The writer, William Baldwin, came across a system created by a famous money manager who advertised a track record showing a compound yearly gain of 27.3% over the ten years ending in December 1983.

Since the advisor's managed accounts were confidential, an outsider couldn't look at customer records to verify that the system worked. But the advisor also publishes a newsletter, so the *Forbes* writer looked at back issues to see how well the advisor had employed his own system.

He found that, for some of the periods listed as buying times in the track record, the advisor's newsletter was telling people to stay *out* of the market. The reporter asked the advisor about the discrepancy, and was told that a different trading system had been employed in the earlier period.

Where, then, does the new system's track record come from? According to Mr. Baldwin:

> The performance figures that [the advisor] uses in his sales literature are clearly marked hypothetical. But a prospect could easily infer that this caution merely relates to [the advisor's] having managed money for less than the whole period. He might think that if someone had hypothetically used [the advisor's] signals to get in and out of the market, the profits would have been as indicated.
>
> The unreality of the hypothesis runs much deeper than that. The [system], in the jargon of technicians, was "backfitted" [created by discovering what *would* have worked during the period of time under study].
>
> Think about that a minute. The formulas are not public, and they were created by looking backward. They could be, for all we know, a string of 56 rules like "Buy when T-bills are between 15.2% and 15.7% during March in a leap year." There is no way to verify whether [the system's] "hypothetical investment performance" represents anything more than what [the advisor] wishes he had signaled. If hindsight brought profits, we could all be rich.[6]

So when you run across a system that sports a wonderful track record, keep in mind the possibility that you will be the first person to use it.

SYSTEMS & INDICATORS

In your investment career, you'll come across dozens—or hundreds —of infallible indicators, proven systems, and virtually riskless investments. Tomorrow someone might offer you an amazing discovery that represents a breakthrough to profit and safety. Or maybe someone will offer you a perpetual-motion machine.

Moving-average systems and spread systems, like cycle theories and wave analysis, assume an essentially static world—in which all movement is merely a deviation from, or a return to, norms that remain the same year after year, even century after century. But in fact we live in a world in which the underlying causes of prices—technology, human wants, and existing resources—change constantly.

---

[6]"The Impossible Dream," by William Baldwin, *Forbes*, October 22, 1984, page 144.

Thus no track record, covering the past, can tell you what works today; no indicator can foretell market movements; no system can take the uncertainty out of investing; and no investment can truly promise a profit without threatening a loss.

You may find a system of trading that doesn't seem to have the flaws I've discussed in this chapter. When you do, I won't be there to rain on your parade. So please try to remember that no system is riskless, and that no indicator can give you an inside track to the future.

The first rule of trading systems is:

The system that has worked perfectly up to now will go wrong when you stake your money on it.

As I'll discuss in Chapter 21, no system of any kind should be used without a clearly defined bail-out point for each investment you make (a maximum loss, a definite circumstance or limit) at which you'll abandon your position, rather than allowing a loss to grow.

12

Going Wrong
Trying to Be
Sophisticated

The best-laid plans are doomed from the start if they require expertise you don't have, or if they demand more effort than you're willing to give.

When you read investment newsletters and books, you'll encounter techniques and strategies that seem clever, or that are presented as being essential to your financial safety, but which you don't really understand. It can seem as though every advisor and writer wants to turn you into a sophisticated speculator—even if it isn't your destiny to be a financial wizard.

Many an advisor or writer is oblivious to the problems he creates for his customers by urging them to use schemes they're not prepared to handle—either because he's unwise or just inconsiderate.

Or he may do it simply to show off—presenting himself as "shrewd," "savvy," and "street smart." He'll talk about what the "big money" and the insiders are doing—to encourage you to feel that you and he are part of an elite group of sophisticates.

Whatever his reasons, it's important that you not be lured into investment plans you can't carry off.

You can get into trouble trying to employ strategies or investments that require more investing aptitude or speculative talent than you have.

As we saw in Chapter 10, both investing and speculating involve an element of talent—just as any other endeavor does. Recognize the limits of your talent, knowledge, skills, and interest. Don't let anyone persuade you that speculating is a simple, mechanical process that involves nothing more than following a set of instructions.

INVESTMENT RULE #1

At times it may seem that you *must* do something you don't understand, or that you must evaluate an investment alternative that calls for more sophistication than you possess. What do you do then?

What should you do when someone says you must make a decision *now*—and you feel you could lose your life savings if you jump the wrong way?

No matter what else you may know, I hope you will hold on to one suggestion. I call it Investment Rule #1:

> *When in doubt about an investment decision, it is always better to err on the side of caution.*

If it turns out you're wrong, be wrong on the safe side. If you wind up losing something, let it be only an opportunity that was lost—not precious capital.

Few people go broke playing it safe. But many go broke taking great risks or making investments they know too little about.

I don't mean that you should never take risks. Such a policy isn't even possible. Every investment, every action—even inaction— involves risk of some kind. Which risks to accept, how much to risk, and how to lessen risk are some of the subjects we'll cover in Part II of this book.

But whenever you aren't sure what to do, the answer is: *Play it safe*. If you're hesitating, it's because you don't yet know enough about the investment or the problem to make a confident decision.

Wolves vs. Sheep

Some people will tell you that you can't afford to play it safe—or even that there's no such thing as safety.

They may say that risky, unfamiliar investments and strategies are your only hope for survival. For example, we heard often in the 1970s that the poor sheep who left their life savings in banks would lose everything to inflation. As it turned out, those poor sheep managed to survive.

Over the decade of the 1970s, inflation averaged 7.4% per year. The poor soul who left his money in a bank passbook savings account earned an average of only 4.8% per year.

So, for the worst financial decade since the 1930s, it cost him 2.6% of the purchasing power of his capital each year to remain free of alien investment strategies and continue to do what was familiar.

That wasn't a very good bargain. But, for someone who wanted to stay with what he knew, it wasn't such a bad bargain either—not as bad as the losses that can come from playing with investments you don't understand.

And the cost of safety would have been considerably less with almost any other simple strategy—such as leaving one's money in Treasury bills (which would have cost only 0.2% per year in purchasing power), or keeping just a tiny, fixed share of one's capital in gold coins.[1]

And with any of these simple approaches, the investor did manage to hold on to most of his capital.

Meanwhile, many people who thought they were being sophisticated lost heavily by buying precious metals or real estate at the wrong time with borrowed money (expecting to repay it later with "cheaper dollars")—or trying to master the art of short-selling in the stock market or day-trading in the commodity markets—or buying exotic investments such as strategic metals, diamonds, or colored gemstones—or trusting international money managers who turned out to be better promoters than managers.

I'm not suggesting that you leave all your money in the bank, or even in T-bills; those investments have their own risks and drawbacks. Nor am I saying that it was wrong to invest in precious metals or real estate.

I *am* saying that history provides no evidence that only the bold and adventurous survive financially. I *am* suggesting that you stay clear of stampedes into investments you don't understand. I *am* saying that you

[1]The inflation rate cited is the compound annual change in the Consumer Price Index from December 1969 to December 1979. The T-bill return was converted to a true yield from the average yearly bank-discount rates, quoted in the *Annual Statistical Digest, 1970–1979*, page 162 (Federal Reserve System). The average passbook savings rate was taken from the various legal maximums in force during the decade—listed in the *Federal Reserve Bulletin*, September 1973 and March 1980, table A10.

should ignore anyone who claims that your only route to financial survival is with an investment or strategy that scares you.

It's true that some people made fortunes in precious metals in the 1970s. And many people coped with inflation in ways that allowed them to hang on to all of what they had. But it's unlikely that anyone in either group played with investment strategies he didn't understand or couldn't easily execute.

You aren't a failure if you miss the boat. If you're not sure about the situation, just let the opportunity pass you by. The world won't end tomorrow; there will be more opportunities.

Taking Chances

There's nothing wrong with taking chances.

Once you have a safety net in place, don't be afraid to take a flyer when the odds seem to be in your favor—provided you're using money you can afford to lose, provided you understand what you're doing, and provided you enjoy the excitement.

But don't feel that *any* situation ever requires bold action. Don't feel that you must fling everything into the pot and hope that some advisor's judgment will prove to be correct.

You don't have to be courageous; you don't have to emulate the masters of finance. If you come up against something you don't want to do with your investments, *don't do it*. When your stomach says no, obey it.

Pay no attention to advice that says, to survive today, you must be a speculator—or short seller, option trader, international expert, ballet dancer, whatever. There's nothing that everyone must be. There are eager, ambitious people—with a feel for speculation—who have tried to carry out sophisticated plans and have lost heavily. Someone who's reluctant or untrained or has no talent for speculating has almost no chance at all.

As for those crucial moments that seem to require big decisions, there usually are more alternatives than any single person presents to you. One choice that's seldom mentioned is to invest less than the amount suggested by the urgency of the presentation.

Whenever someone pressures you to strike while the iron is hot, remember Investment Rule #1:

> *When in doubt about an investment decision, it is always better to err on the side of caution.*

13

Going Wrong
by Being Contrary

During your odyssey through the investment world, trying to lay the best plans, you're bound to run into one of the most seductive methods for outguessing the market—the Theory of Contrary Opinion.

The gist of the Theory is this.

> Whenever we see that most people are bullish on an investment, we can conclude that almost everyone who might buy has already done so, which means there's very little buying power left to move the price higher. Conversely, when we see that most people are bearish on an investment, we can conclude that nearly everyone who might want to sell has already done so, leaving little possibility of further selling to depress the price.

The Theory makes sense. In general, investors and advisors are the most bullish about the investments they already own. Only investors who have just become bullish are likely to be buyers. So when the public seems to be overwhelmingly bullish, all the buying may be over, and the rising trend may be about to run out of gas.

Like many investment principles, the Theory can alert you to opportunity, and it can caution you against being carried away. But, as with most observations about investing, it can't be applied to the markets with any precision. We have no reliable way to measure at any time *how* bullish or bearish the public is—because there's no way to read the minds of investors.

INDICATORS OF CONTRARY OPINION

This doesn't stop investment advisors from trying, however. To apply the Theory of Contrary Opinion, they've devised numerical indicators that tell them exactly when an investment is over-popular or over-shunned.

Advisory Sentiment

The most widely used indicator of investor sentiment is based on the published recommendations of investment advisors. Someone reads many of the reports turned out by advisors and brokerage houses, rates each report as bullish or bearish, totals up the score, and publishes a Sentiment Index. He might find that, say, 60% of the advisors expect stocks to go up.

To provide perspective, each week's score is plotted on a graph. By studying the chart, the contrarian can decide how high (80%, for example) the sentiment can go before the market tops—and what low score (say, 30%) represents the extreme limit of pessimism. Then he will be ready to dump his holdings whenever the sentiment indicator goes up to 80%, and he will be ready to buy whenever the sentiment indicator drops to 30%.

It seems clever, but an index of advisory sentiment may be little more than a straw in the wind. Advisors may be recommending one thing while investors in general are doing something else.

A great many investors don't read newsletters or listen to brokers. Those who do receive investment recommendations don't necessarily act on all of them. And a large share of stock investing is done by mutual funds and other institutions that retain their own investment advisors, and thus don't act on newsletter recommendations.

Cash Position

Another contrary indicator for the stock market is the size of the cash positions held by mutual funds.

If mutual funds specializing in stocks have less than, say, 5% of their assests in cash (the rest being invested in stocks already), they have little buying power left with which to push up stock prices. If they have more than 15%, perhaps they've already sold all the stocks they're going to sell, and their cash is restless buying power waiting to propel a rally.

This indicator is closer to being useful, because it measures actual money—not just talk. But it has plenty of problems, too.

Mutual funds aren't the whole market. Even if they were, bearish fund managers can become more bearish—and increase their cash holdings from high to higher. And a mutual fund with 0% in cash might receive millions of dollars in new buying power from customers tomorrow morning.

GIMMICKS

These indicators are a little too popular to suit a true contrarian. He doesn't want to act on an indicator that many other investors use.

So investment advisors try to devise new methods for discerning market sentiment.

The Old Best-Seller Trick

Some of them are almost intentionally cute.

One, for example, advises doing the opposite of what is recommended in any investment book that appears on a national list of best-selling books (such as *The New York Times* best-seller list). The book's popularity is evidence that nearly everyone who is inclined to act on its advice has already done so.

While this seems plausible, the truth is that best-selling investment books usually have been published a little early—rather than too late.

The Money Game, a 1968 classic by Adam Smith, was skeptical of the stock market, which was in its "go-go" phase then. Seeing the popularity of such a negative book, a contrarian would have had to be bullish on stocks—just as they were heading into a severe, two-year bear market.

And best-selling books encouraging investors to buy gold appeared in 1970, 1974, and 1978—all poor years in which to sell gold short.[1]

Cover Stories

Another old adage says to sell an investment when it's touted on the cover of a major magazine or is otherwise highlighted by the press.

One newsletter writer, an avid contrarian, tried to apply the cover-story rule in February 1985. He cited a headline from the financial section of an unnamed Chicago daily newspaper: "Not Too Late to Jump into the Market," and another headline from *USA Today:* "Dow at 1500 by Year-End?"

The contrarian argued that such enthusiasm from the establishment press should be interpreted as an obituary for the stock market, and shrewd investors should sell out before the funeral actually took place.

This kind of argument can be compelling. The newsletter's insight seemed pretty foxy—being contrary to the expectations of the dumb sheep.

But in this case, as in so many others, the insight was really an illusion. The Dow Jones Industrial Average (around 1300 at the time of the newsletter article) *did* reach 1500 by year-end, just as the innocents at *USA Today* had suspected it would. And twelve months after the newsletter article had appeared, the market was up 500 points, at 1800.

Somehow, the dumb sheep had outsmarted the fox again.

Experts & Amateurs

In March 1980, after the price of silver had fallen to $30 from $50, I heard a silver expert tell an audience of investors that silver was going higher again. As evidence, he cited the fact that the public was lined up on sidewalks outside stores, trying to *sell* its silver heirlooms. Since the public must be wrong, this obviously was a time to buy.

As it turned out, the hayseeds apparently knew what they were doing.

---

[1]I'm hoping *this* book will make the best-seller list, if only for one week. That will force thousands and thousands of contrarians to buy it in order to know what to be contrary to.

Silver kept falling until it landed at $10. Those who were sophisticated enough to buy silver at $30 took quite a beating.

Pro & Con

Of course, there are opposing examples—cases of the public or the mass media being clearly wrong about the future. Famous examples include the cover headlines on news magazines—such as "Super Dollar" in October 1984, just 5 months before the end of the dollar's 6-year bull market—or "The Death of Mining" in December 1984, almost at the very end of the bear market in mining stocks—and many others.

But there have been plenty of times when the so-called boobs have turned out to be right, and the insiders or specialists or sophisticates have turned out to be wrong.

The Theory of Contrary Opinion isn't a reliable guide to the future.

PRECONCEIVED NOTIONS

As frequently as Contrary Opinion is cited, I rarely see anyone actually base a decision on it. I've never read anything like this from an advisor:

> As you know, I was bullish on the market last month. But now 80% of the advisory services are bullish. The market must be headed downward, and so I'm selling out.

The Theory generally is important to an advisor only when it confirms what he wants to believe anyway. He's contrary only to what he already disagrees with, while stoically tolerating any majority view that agrees with his. In fact, I *have* read statements similar to this:

> The only negative in the bullish picture is that the latest reading of advisory services shows that 80% are bullish. This is reason for caution. But since the rest of our indicators point upward, we're going to plunge in and buy. We'll keep an eye on the bullish consensus, but as of now it appears to be an aberration.

A reader might have put a different perspective on the bearish contrariness of the newsletter mentioned on page 202 if he'd known that the newsletter had predicted a severe bear market just a month earlier.

Whatever you want to believe, it's no trick to find evidence that the majority is contrary to it. As a result, you often see two advisors, with opposite points of view, each justifying his position by claiming that it's contrary to the majority view.

Standing Alone

Pledging his troth to Contrary Opinion is a wonderful gambit for an advisor. It allows him to strike a favored pose—that of the independent, cool-headed, can't-be-bought, we've-always-been-ahead-of-the-pack maverick.

An advisor loves nothing more than to tell you that he's "going against the crowd." No matter what his opinion, even if all he's decided to do is to chew gum, he's somehow always in that lonely, independent minority that's the home of all great thinkers.

The most crowded corner in the world is the one where all the investment advisors "stand alone" with their predictions, analyses, and maverick forecasts.

BETTING WITH THE MAJORITY

At the root of the Theory of Contrary Opinion is a grain of truth. It is the realization that you can't make money acting on what everyone believes.

A prevailing belief that stocks are going higher doesn't mean that stocks must go lower; it means only that prices already are so high that you aren't likely to find any bargains. You'll bet a lot to make a little—the opposite of what you should be doing.

A good example of this principle was the belief, so popular around 1980, that the way to beat inflation is to buy gold or other hard assets with borrowed money and repay the loan later with cheaper dollars. Actually, that's a very poor strategy during a time of high inflation.

The time to speculate on gold or other hard assets with borrowed money is *before* inflation has arrived in full force. The prices of the investments will be low, and so will be the cost of borrowing money. If your expectation of high inflation turns out to be correct, other people will want the things you own and will pay a high price for them; you can pay off the margin loans and pocket the profits.

In the early 1970s, you could buy gold for $35 or $40 per ounce, paying 8% interest on the money you borrowed for the purchase. By 1980, you had to pay $600 or more for the gold and 18% on the money you borrowed. You had to pay more because, by 1980, a lot of other people were trying to do the same thing.

The popularity of the strategy didn't mean that gold couldn't go higher, nor did the 18% interest rate mean that inflation couldn't get worse. But they did signify that the gold-on-margin tactic was no longer an efficient one. Gold would have to go a good deal higher just to pay the 18% interest on the money you borrowed. You might still make a profit, but you had little chance to make a big profit.

Whenever you're about to enter a speculation, ask yourself what you know or believe that's different from what other investors think. If you're simply acting on what you've read in the press, you should assume that the price of the investment already reflects your expectations. If so, even if everything you anticipate does come true, the best result will be a modest gain.

Whatever it is that seems to make an investment a hot prospect, if you know about it and I know about it, there probably isn't much money to be made from it.

Majority Not Necessarily Wrong

Not wanting to bet with the majority is quite different from assuming that the majority is always wrong.

The statement that the public is always wrong is a smug slogan that offers no insight into the task of investing. The idea is defended only with platitudes about the loneliness of success or "the man who stands alone." But no one (to the best of my knowledge) has explained *why* the majority must always be wrong.

In truth, the majority isn't always wrong. For one obvious example, during World War II most Americans based their business and investment plans on the assumption that the U.S. would win the war—and they were right. A true contrarian would have bet on the Nazis.

HAVING FUN

One danger in the Theory of Contrary Opinion is that it appeals to vanity.

Many investors and advisors love to believe that they're members of a small elite of wise, savvy, street-smart insiders—and that the majority of investors are lemmings who know no better than to follow one another off the investment cliff.

This is part of the fun of investing—to feel so much smarter than the other players in the market. Even if it costs money, your ego gets a boost.

We look down our noses at the odd-lot short-sellers, the news magazines, the institutional money managers, the establishment forecasters, the public, everyone. Whatever these people are doing must be wrong. We are wise; they are stupid.

They are slaves to their emotions. Their investing decisions are dominated by "fear and greed." But, of course, *our* decisions are determined by a rational desire to avoid losses and to maximize profits—motivations somehow different from fear and greed.

Greed afflicts other people, not me. I'm not greedy if I hope my stock will double in a year. But any investor who holds on to an investment too long, trying to let his profits run, is too "greedy" for his own good.

"Fear & Greed" may be the longest-running act on the investment stage. Their presentation is entertaining, but it doesn't help us to find safety or profit.

Advisors know many ways to pander to the desire to feel superior. But no matter how delightful the feeling, vanity earns no dividends that you can spend. As an investor, I have to do more than feel superior; I have to make superior decisions.

FANTASIES

If only it were true that everyone else is so stupid and I'm so smart. I could make money just by acting opposite to the boobs. If only investors, ruled by their passions, spent all their time stubbing their toes and providing bargain prices for me to take advantage of.

But in the real world, speculating isn't simple. There are no sheep waiting to be sheared. Successful speculation involves risk, hard work, hours of study, and the humility to admit one's mistakes.

Not surprisingly, these are the requirements for achieving *anything* important in life. The investment markets aren't a Fantasyland in which you can get something for nothing.

It may be fun to coin epigrams about the ignorance and emotions of other investors. But a successful investor doesn't waste time chuckling about other people's "Fear & Greed." He's too busy watching *his own* emotions—trying to overcome his own pride, wishfulness, and readiness to join a stampede.

If I'm such a smart fellow, I should know more next year than I do now—which means I don't know everything today. I have to remember this whenever I make a decision—as an investor or an advisor. I have to be prepared for the possibility that I'll see tomorrow how wrong I was today.

ORIGINAL THEORY

So far as I know, the Theory of Contrary Opinion originated with a writer named Humphrey B. Neill.

His book *The Art of Contrary Thinking*, first published in 1954, was an attempt to open minds to wider perspectives. Speaking of the Theory, he said:

> [It] certainly is not a system to beat the horse races, or the stock market. Nor is it a crystal ball. It is plainly nothing more than developing the habit of doing what every textbook on learning advises, namely, to look at both sides of all questions.
>
> . . . The chief "catch" in the Contrary Opinion Theory seems to be that readers persist in looking upon it as a forecasting tool or system, whereas, in actuality, it is an antidote to careless and fruitless predictions.[2]

The original Theory encouraged you to see the other side of an issue—not just the side opposed to the majority view, but the side opposed to *your* view.

It suggested that you imagine ways by which events could unfold in a pattern opposite to your expectations—and that you be skeptical about anything that "everyone knows" is true. You couldn't find better advice than that.

Eventually, however, the Theory evolved to a second stage. This was the idea, stated at the beginning of the chapter, that too much bullish sentiment implied that there's too little buying power left to push prices higher.

That, in turn, degenerated into the third stage in the life of the Theory—the simple-minded idea that the majority is always wrong.

[2]*The Art of Contrary Thinking*, by Humphrey B. Neill (The Caxton Printers, Box 700, Caldwell, Idaho 83606; $4.95, cardcover), pages 67 and 173.

What has happened to the Theory of Contrary Opinion is an illustration of one of my favorite maxims:

There is no idea so good that someone won't carry it to an absurd conclusion.

However, since the Theory has gone through three stages, it must be about ready to pass away. As every scientist knows, things come in threes. I don't why they do, they just do.[3]

INDEPENDENCE

It's wise to remain skeptical of popular ideas—even ideas that appear to be skeptical.

The investment arena, like the rest of the world, is crowded with clichés and superstitions whose only authority is repetition. That doesn't mean that everything you hear is wrong, only that you shouldn't allow an idea's popularity to disarm your skepticism.

You have to make your own decisions. You can't choose an investment because the majority favors it—or because you believe the majority opposes it.

The Theory of Contrary Opinion, as it's practiced today, isn't a method for thinking for oneself. It's a method for pretending to do so.

People use it in the hope of simplifying a complicated world—and as a trick to take the work and risk out of speculating—and as a ploy to demonstrate their superiority to the mythical "crowd."

According to the current incarnation of the Theory of Contrary Opinion, any idea that has achieved widespread acceptance is about to fade away.

Since the Theory itself has achieved such widespread popularity, maybe *it* is on the way out.

Well, we can hope.

[3]Only kidding. See page 88.

14

Going Wrong with Instant Advice, Instant Wisdom, & Instant Evidence

In the spring of 1986, a television financial program featured an interview with a renowned investment advisor.

The host treated his guest with great respect—pointing out that the guest had a phenomenal track record of calling the direction of the stock market. During the interview, the advisor pointed out that he had been bullish on stocks throughout a recent big rally—for which he was duly congratulated by the host.

But when it came time for viewers to phone in their questions, one caller said:

> I saw you the last time you were on this program—three months ago. At *that* time, you said the market was about to collapse. I sold all my stocks because of what you said. Now you tell us you've been bullish throughout the rally. I don't understand.

The advisor replied:

> Yes, when I was on this show I was bearish on the market. But a week later, all my indicators turned bullish, and so I sent out a special alert to my newsletter subscribers—telling them to buy heavily. We got in right at the bottom.

Whether or not the advisor actually did get his readers in at the bottom of the rally is something we'll never know and don't need to know. More important is that neither the host, the advisor, nor the viewer called attention to the obvious: *If the advisor might reverse his position next week, why should you act on any opinion he holds today?*

Capsule Advice

The incident I've described is an example of what might be called *instant advice* or *capsule advice*. It's as common as sin, and it comes in as many varieties, some of which are:

—A financial expert delivers an authoritative-sounding forecast for the market, without telling you what underlies his judgment, or what would cause him to change his mind.

—A press or television feature includes an advisor's one-line prognosis for some investment.

—A newsletter or magazine offers the distilled wisdom of the experts, packed into one-paragraph "digests" of what various financial experts currently think.

—Some digests make things even easier by giving the reader a table that cross-references advisors with investments, displaying an arrow or numerical value to show how bullish or bearish each advisor is about each market.

Reporters aren't the only people who are fond of capsule advice. Invariably, at an investment seminar, someone will ask me, "Is this a good time to buy gold?"—as if any intelligent person would stake his financial future on my one-word answer.

In all these cases, what the investor receives is worthless. It's a prime-rib dinner with just the rib—and none of the extras, such as the meat, that might make the meal worthwhile.

An investment one-liner lacks all the details, qualifications, and nuances of its source. It can't begin to tell you what an advisor believes about the subject on which he's been quoted.

For example, suppose an advisor tells his newsletter subscribers that he thinks a particular bond would be a bargain if it could be bought at a particular limit price. Even though the advisor might caution his reader to realize how risky the trade is, and to bail out quickly if the bond falls to a specified level, a report elsewhere may simply announce that the advisor has "turned bullish on bonds."

If you happen to respect the advisor's judgment, the capsule report might inspire you to buy bonds—on the assumption that bonds have entered a big bull market. Long after the advisor and his readers have bailed out of the bond with a small loss, you might be holding on—running up larger and larger losses—relying on what you were led to believe was the advisor's "bullish" attitude.

Capsule advice is useless—except when it inspires you to investigate an idea further. A summary opinion doesn't tell you how strongly the advisor feels about his expectations, the circumstances in which he might change his mind, or whether his reasons are sound.

What You Read

It's particularly important to be on guard when someone presumes to relay the views of someone else.

Reporters (financial or otherwise) are no more omniscient than anyone else. With the limited information available to them, they try to turn out stories people will want to read. They don't have the time or the desire to verify all the assumptions that underlie their stories. Nor do they waste much effort on details or thoughts that are counter to the points they want to make.

And as a rule, the stories are worth printing only if they're exciting enough. Thus anything that would dampen the excitement, no matter how relevant, tends to be omitted.

I've had firsthand dealings with the press, both the general press and the financial newsletter industry, for many years. My experience has convinced me that if all I know about something is what I read in the papers, then I don't know anything about it. Very seldom is the reported version accurate and complete.

Many times I've read a description in the press that was totally different from—sometimes exactly opposite to—what I'd witnessed firsthand. Bear with me as I give you a few examples of events I know best—my own experience.

In 1981, a *Wall Street Journal* reporter covered a big investment conference that's held every fall in New Orleans. His report appeared on the front page of the *Journal* on December 10, 1981, and discussed the spirit of gloom and doom generated by many of the several dozen speakers at the conference.

To make the point, the article cited my speech: "Buy Swiss francs, he advised, and store food and gasoline because the 'great climax' may be at hand.'' A number of subscribers to my newsletter called to find out why I hadn't given these hot tips in the newsletter.

I don't know which speaker at the conference actually said those things—or if *anyone* actually did. But it wasn't I. My only reference to Swiss francs was a comment that I didn't see any profit in the franc in the near term; my only interest in food was "When do we eat?''; and I'm much too refined to discuss gas in public.

At that same conference, a *Money* magazine reporter interviewed several speakers for its annual forecast issue. I agreed to be interviewed on condition that I be given the chance to verify any quotes attributed to me before they went to press.

When the reporter's story was submitted for me to examine, I found that the advisors and their opinions had been mismatched—so that each forecast was attributed to the wrong advisor. The confusion was resolved before the story was printed, but only because I had insisted on seeing the story before publication—something that most journalists wouldn't allow. In fact, the reporter had been rather put off when I'd demanded that safeguard as a condition of the interview.

Supporting Evidence

Often the mixup in a press story has nothing to do with incompetence, tight deadlines, or limited information. Instead, the writer wants support for his own viewpoint—and so he cites a confirming opinion from someone he hopes will carry some weight with his audience.

A bizarre example of that happened to me in 1984. I had been cool toward gold for several years. In my newsletter, I had made fun of forecasts of $1,000 gold—since inflation was falling and there was no reason to expect a 1970s-style bull market in gold. You can imagine my shock when I read the following in an investment newsletter digest:

> Harry Browne's Special Reports, 12/26/84, reports: On December 18th, "it was suddenly obvious that federal deficits would have to lead to immediate inflation and, in turn, to higher gold prices. It was very clear that the wanton, unrestrained, profligate monetary stimulation of the past few years must inevitably lead to higher gold prices—and soon. It was obvious to me that there is every reason for gold to go to $2,000, $3,000, or higher. Gold has to go up,'' he says.

An article in my newsletter had indeed contained those words. But the digest didn't mention that it had reprinted less than half of my words—nor that the whole passage was a joke that would be obvious to any subscriber. Unfortunately, the joke turned out to be on me. The digest editor had managed to find just the right words to support his own position.

These anecdotes might seem trivial. But they're examples of what you may be reading all the time without realizing it. They are much closer to the rule for journalism than to the exception.

Summaries of what someone is reported to have said, or snippets of what he's shown to say, mean nothing and can easily mislead you. Just as TV journalists edit their interviews so that the "consumer crusader" will look like St. George and the businessman will look like a dragon, so does a financial reporter use quotations to further the point he wants to make.

Don't buy any investment on the basis of an opinion you hear on radio or television, or because of a secondhand quote you read. If what you see or hear seems important, get the source and read it for yourself. You may find that the quotation's meaning is quite different in context. You may also find that you don't agree with the reasons for the opinion.

INSTANT WISDOM

When you do have in hand all the reasons for an opinion, you may find that the "food for thought" is really junk food.

The nuggets of wisdom that float around the investment world often are just slogans that have been polished up to resemble reasoned arguments. Similar to capsule advice, an investment slogan is a form of capsule wisdom—a complex matter, full of qualifications and complexities, that is reduced to a phrase that's supposed to be self-evident and irrefutable.

The investment world is full of such clichés and slogans. Here are just a few that may sound familiar to you:

"Federal deficits cause inflation, and the deficits are out of control."

"Real estate is the one investment they're not making any more of."

"The Federal Reserve will never allow a big U.S. bank to go under."

"No one ever went broke taking a profit."

"The public is always wrong."

These statements might be ideal for bumper stickers or greeting cards, but they aren't arguments. Each of the issues they evoke is considerably more complicated than the one-line wisdom allows for.

Such statements usually are presented as the *coup de grâce*—and are meant to be so convincing that they require no elaboration. They are marvels of self-sufficiency—the beginning, middle, and end of the argument.

If investing really were so simple that one could learn what to do by consulting a one-line platitude, we'd all be billionaires—several times over.

Unfortunately, there's much more to any issue. Often overlooked about a slogan is that it was delivered just as persuasively last year or the year before—after which the inevitable result it implied didn't come to pass.

I hope you'll catch yourself the next time you start to nod in agreement to one of these epigrams.

INSTANT EVIDENCE

Slogans and other one-liners make statements of a somewhat general nature. Sometimes, they're accompanied by what appears to be supporting evidence.

Unfortunately, financial writers rarely explain how they came by the "facts" they cite to support their case. There's very little documenting or footnoting in financial journalism—or, in fact, in any journalism.

Because of this, a capsule "fact" sometimes appears out of nowhere and makes a tour of the investment world—stopping briefly at the word processor of any writer who needs a little help.

For example, in early 1985 the dollar finally began falling against major foreign currencies, after more than six years of strength. One writer, who wanted very much to make a case that inflation was on the way back, was inspired to say, "Historically, every 10% drop in the dollar results in a 1% rise in the Consumer Price Index."

No evidence was cited to support this claim, but it was catchy and sounded like the fruit of serious research. And so it was picked up by other writers who wanted to show that inflation was imminent—to support a bullish position on gold, or a bearish position on stocks or bonds, or some other position the advisor had taken. Eventually, the statement was preceded with the phrase, "It's a well-known fact that"—as by then it certainly was, even if no one could prove it.

But in early 1987, after the dollar had fallen more than 30% in two years against other major currencies, the inflation rate was even lower than it had been before the dollar's fall.

Another "fact" appeared in 1986, when the price of platinum had run up to $680 from a price of $450 just six months earlier. Someone reported that the world was consuming 100,000 ounces more of platinum each year than it was producing.

The "100,000 ounce shortage" idea started making the rounds of investment newsletters—where it was used as evidence that the rise to $680 was just the beginning of a long bull market, since there was no hope for the shortage to be alleviated.

As a matter of fact, there was no shortage—or at least no evidence of any shortage. The primary industry data on platinum are published by Johnson Matthey of London, and their reports showed a consistent *surplus* of platinum from 1982 forward.[1]

As it turned out, the price of platinum began to plunge shortly after the "100,000 ounce shortage" stories appeared. Within two months, the price had fallen to $460—a drop of over 30% from its top.

GRAPHIC DECEPTIONS

If a picture is worth a thousand words, a good graph must be worth at least 50 slogans.

A graph is a spray can of instant knowledge that can be used to make almost any point—true or false.

Consider the graph on page 216, showing the obvious, documented, indisputable relationship between government deficits and consumer price inflation. Anyone who looks at that graph and still thinks that federal deficits don't cause inflation should have his head examined.

But then look at the graph on page 217. This one shows irrefutably that inflation is caused by people going to the movies.

In fact, we have no way of knowing with either graph whether one line is the cause of the second, or the second line is the cause of the first, or whether both lines are caused by some other factor that isn't

[1]Johnson Matthey PLC, New Garden House, 78 Hatton Garden, London EC1N 8JP, publishes an annual review of the platinum market.

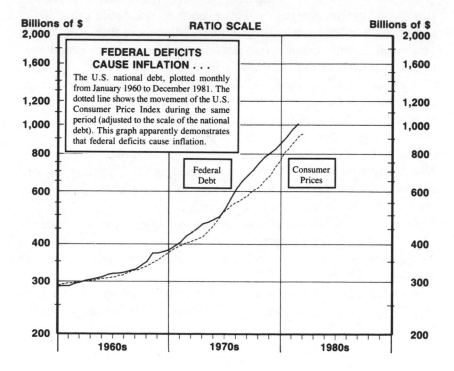

Billions of $ RATIO SCALE   Billions of $

**FEDERAL DEFICITS
CAUSE INFLATION . . .**

The U.S. national debt, plotted monthly
from January 1960 to December 1981. The
dotted line shows the movement of the U.S.
Consumer Price Index during the same
period (adjusted to the scale of the national
debt). This graph apparently demonstrates
that federal deficits cause inflation.

Federal
Debt

Consumer
Prices

shown on the graph, or whether the whole thing is simply a coincidence.

Graphs are wonderful tools. A graph can make it easier to understand
something that might otherwise require pages to explain. But in the
hands of someone who's careless with the truth, it can be used to
mislead, overemphasize, misinform, or just plain deceive.

Be particularly wary of graphs that attempt to prove a cause-and-
effect relationship between two things—such as an economic condition
leading to an investment result.

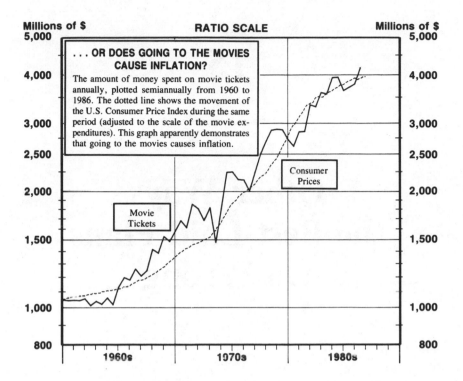

... OR DOES GOING TO THE MOVIES CAUSE INFLATION?

The amount of money spent on movie tickets annually, plotted semiannually from 1960 to 1986. The dotted line shows the movement of the U.S. Consumer Price Index during the same period (adjusted to the scale of the movie expenditures). This graph apparently demonstrates that going to the movies causes inflation.

INSTANT DISASTER

The investment world is full of instant advice, instant arguments, and instant facts. None of this instant knowledge is worth very much. You have to take with a grain of salt the research that's handed to you in a pretty package.

Fortunately, you don't have to rely on the validity of what you read. In Part II, I'll suggest a strategy that should free you from dependence upon anyone's accuracy, honesty, or goodwill.

15

Other Ways
the Best-Laid Plans
Go Wrong

The list of ways by which the best-laid investment plans go wrong is endless. I couldn't count all the ways, let alone discuss them. In the preceding chapters, I've tried to deal with the investment traps that most often catch investors and their money—especially the traps that I haven't seen discussed elsewhere.

There are a few more I don't want to neglect, even though there's room only for brief comments.

GOING WRONG WITH POSITIVE THINKING

The following appeared in an investment newsletter:

> The first step to investment success, or success in almost any endeavor, is the right mental attitude. If you want to accomplish a great task, you must really believe that you can. Skeptical people seldom achieve the same results that believers do. They do not try as hard. They are less committed. They reduce their effort when they face minor road blocks.

It's probably true that if you see no possibility of success in something, you'll proceed half-heartedly—since any real effort would seem futile. But you rarely find yourself trying to do something that seems hopeless.

More often, you're involved in an endeavor in which the outcome is in doubt. And in those situations, a positive mental attitude has little to recommend itself. It can't make investment prices go up or down, since prices are moved by the actions of other investors. It can't even make you think more clearly.

And a positive mental attitude can cause several bad things. The sense that you're sure to succeed can encourage you to hang on to a losing investment too long, to ignore defects in your strategy, and to be careless when checking investment systems and proposals. Focusing on your mental attitude can cause you to pay too little attention to the world outside you—where investment results are determined.

Negative Thinking

I've had a good deal of success in my life—as an investor, an advisor, and a writer. And I would call myself a negative thinker. My main concerns always are the things that can go wrong and the unexpected problems that might be encountered.

If the circumstances seem promising, I may be optimistic. But I've never approached any matter with a positive attitude   smiling at the facts in order to make them smile back at me.

That hasn't stopped me from investing, speculating, or doing other things. In fact, sometimes I've pushed ahead with projects I felt had very little chance of success, because the potential rewards were compelling. And some of those projects succeeded, despite my attitude.

My negative attitude has made me skeptical, and skepticism has saved me from biting at a lot of hooks that caught friends and colleagues.

But the benefits of a negative attitude aren't just negative. My attitude helps me spot the problems associated with a plan, so that I can allow for them. Having done that, I'm free to proceed enthusiastically—knowing that the inevitable surprises can't destroy me.

Of the successful people I've known in my life, I can't offhand remember one who would be called a positive thinker. But I can recall many who were preoccupied with the possibilities for failure.

I'm not suggesting that you be a defeatist; I *am* suggesting that you be ready for *some* defeats. As the old saw goes, "Prepared for the worst, you can hope for the best."

And as Shakespeare said, "To fear the worst oft cures the worse."[1]

GOING WRONG BY SETTING GOALS

The newsletter I just quoted went on:

The second step to investment success is to have a goal. . . . The selection of a goal (like a particular average growth rate) will help you to maintain your effort and allow you to measure the degree of success you have achieved to date. . . .

This is a locker-room platitude—repeated often, certainly plausible, correct for some undertakings, but totally unrealistic for investing and speculating.

An investor setting a goal is a different matter from a runner aiming to cut 10 seconds off his time every week, or a piano student committing himself to master one new piece a month. Their results depend mostly on the effort they make. Your results as an investor depend on the effort you make, but also on what the market will permit you to achieve each year.

Suppose that you choose a growth rate of 20% per year as your goal for stock speculation. How do you reach the goal during a year when stocks are in a bear market? Do you buck the trend? Learn to be a short-seller? Turn to other, unfamiliar markets?

Sometimes droughts beset the entire financial world. From late 1980 through the middle of 1984, for example, there were practically no bull markets *in anything*—only about 11 months for stocks, 8 months for gold, and 5 months for bonds—with all the uptrends concentrated between June 1982 and June 1983. The rest of the time everything was dropping.

Obviously, the best speculative strategy for most of that period was to sit on one's hands, collect interest on Treasury bills, and wait for better days. A yearly goal could have goaded you into making losing investments.

[1]And you know what a great track record *he* has. (*Troilus and Cressida*, Act III, Scene 2.)

A goal keeps you from recognizing how dependent you are on circumstance—and from developing a strategy that allows for circumstances you can't control.

Even if you're a good speculator, you may have a spectacular year only occasionally, middling years often, and disappointing years sometimes. The spectacular year happens because you do the right things consistently and, eventually, circumstances permit a big payoff.

If you take a yearly goal seriously, you'll be tempted to take extra risks when circumstances are unfavorable and you're falling behind the goal. Or you may pass up opportunities during good times if your yearly goal has already been achieved.

GOING WRONG
BETTING WHAT YOU CAN'T AFFORD

Believing that trying to outwit the future is the only way to invest, investors fail to separate the funds that are available for speculation from the precious funds they can't afford to risk.

Bets on the future should be made only with money you can afford to lose. You need not and should not bet any more than that.

We'll discuss this further in Chapter 17.

GOING WRONG IN A CATTLE STAMPEDE

An easy way to go wrong is to let someone convince you that today is your last chance to make the investment of the century.

I have from time to time regretted that I failed to buy something that I'd considered. But I've never been hurt by not buying.

Meanwhile, I've seen plenty of money lost by investors who were convinced that an opportunity demanded immediate action. But there never really is a "last chance." Even if you miss out on a good investment, there always will be other opportunities.

It's harder to resist the stampede when others seem to be raking in profits. But you don't really know how well other people are doing. Even if you're convinced that someone is doing very well, he may be taking risks that aren't right for you.

Investment Rule #1 says:

When in doubt about an investment decision, it is always better to err on the side of caution.

People don't go broke being too cautious, but they can be hurt badly by jumping into something they don't understand, haven't thought out, or can't afford.

GOING WRONG WITHOUT A STRATEGY

Most investors operate without a strategy. Their portfolios are the accumulated result of years of isolated decisions, as one idea and then another has seemed good enough to prompt a purchase of this or that.

It's important to have a strategy—an overall plan—by which to evaluate potential investments. Only then can you know whether a particular investment suits you, how much of it to buy, and the circumstances in which you should sell.

The lack of a well-defined strategy usually leads to one or more of these symptoms:

1. You have no standard against which to evaluate an investment. This makes you susceptible to every hotshot scheme, trading system, idea, and proposal that comes along. A clearly defined strategy would enable you to sort through all those schemes and investments to find the ones that make sense and fit your needs.

2. When you find an investment you want to buy, you don't know what should be sold to make room for it, because your present investments aren't serving clearly defined purposes.

3. You have no basis on which to decide how much of your portfolio to allocate to any given investment.

4. You have no idea how much you could lose on a speculation you're about to make—because, without a strategy, you have no basis for choosing in advance the point at which you would bail out and take a loss.

5. You find yourself holding on to every losing speculation seemingly forever—waiting and waiting for it to turn around.

6. You're dependent upon someone's ability (yours or an advisor's) to forecast the future infallibly because, without a good strategy for controlling risk, a single mistake could be fatal.

7. You're frequently tempted to act on claims that this is your "last chance" for an investment.

8. Investing interferes with the rest of your life, because your investment plan can't take care of itself and let you focus on other things. Every investment decision must be reevaluated daily, to be reconsidered in the light of every forecast and opinion you hear about the economy, the markets, and individual investments.

9. You find that, too often, you've acted in accordance with the values, ambitions, and capabilities of other people—rather than your own.

10. You wonder frequently whether you're doing the right thing, because you have no basis on which to evaluate what you're doing.

Investing without a good strategy is like placing bets at random and whim on a roulette table. Sometimes you win, but in the long run you're bound to lose.

No strategy can eliminate investment losses or guarantee profits. But a good one can assure that you never incur intolerable losses. And it gives you the opportunity to make gains that far exceed the losses.

A well-defined investment strategy is like a well-defined philosophy of life. It provides a standard by which to evaluate decisions, so that they aren't made in isolation or without regard for all the possible consequences. It keeps you from taking risks you can't afford, and from acting in ways that aren't in keeping with your nature and your objectives.

Part II of this book is devoted to the strategy I've developed for myself. I hope you'll find it reasonable, and adapt it to your own requirements. If you already have a workable strategy, the ideas in Part II may help you refine it.

GOING WRONG WITH INSIDE INFORMATION

It's easy to believe there are people in the world who possess such power, position, or influence that they know of market-moving events before they occur. How nice it would be if one of those people tipped you off to a big price move just before it happened.

Because you can easily imagine the profits that would be yours, you might be an eager recipient if someone appears to be passing out information from the inside. But inside information is more likely to be a source of loss than of profit.

It's true that some people have greater and quicker access to information than you do, and some people have more talent for interpreting the information than you do. But seldom does anyone have reliable, advance knowledge of anything other than what he controls directly —which is always very little.

The president of a company knows the plans of his own firm, but he isn't likely to know the plans of his competitors or what the general economy will do next year—all of which will influence the fortunes of his firm. And even his company's plans can go awry or need to be changed. Not even the president of IBM knows what the price of IBM stock will be tomorrow.

In 1986 a handful of stock traders were found to have been buying information that was, in effect, stolen—in that they bought the information from people who didn't have the right to sell it. How wonderful it would have been to have shared in their information without sharing in their misdeeds.

But not quite so wonderful as you might imagine. In the investigation into the affairs of these traders, it was learned that they were far from infallible. Even with the privileged information they possessed, they often bet incorrectly—sometimes losing tens of millions of dollars at a stroke.

Tips

Many times in my investment career, someone has told me about information that came from a special source. And I've read dozens of tips in newsletters that were touted as coming from reliable sources inside government or among the movers and shakers. But I've never seen an inside tip turn out to be worth anything.

My favorite example came from the chief gold trader at a "Big Three" Swiss bank. In 1970 he guaranteed to a friend of mine that gold would never go above $40 per ounce. Asked how he could be so sure, the banker replied, "Because *we* control the market."

Risking your money on information that supposedly comes from authoritative, "savvy," or inside sources means that you're gullible, not smart. Using a hot tip is like buying a map of treasure buried in Ethiopia, or buying diamonds at an unbelievable discount from a man wearing a black shirt and white tie.

There are better things for us to be concerned about. For example, there's this device you install on the carburetor of your car and you get 150 miles to the gallon, but the big oil companies have been suppressing it. . . .

GOING WRONG AVOIDING LOSSES

One of the qualities of a successful speculator is his readiness to accept losses.

If you make a speculation because you believe the time has come for an investment to go up, you should be ready at all times to concede that it isn't working out and run for the door.

To say "I can't sell because I don't want to lose money" is to hide from the problem. You already have a loss if the investment's value has declined from the price at which you bought. Selling only acknowledges the loss, it doesn't create it.

It's true that selling now destroys all hope that the investment could someday be a winner. But keeping the investment makes you a prisoner to it, while selling the investment frees you to buy anything you want.[2]

GOING WRONG WITH THE GAMBLER'S ITCH

You can't always find an investment that satisfies the standards of a good speculation. At such times it's better to sit on your capital than to throw it at rainbows.

You don't have to be in the market all the time; other forms of entertainment are available. Speculating just to be speculating is a sure way to lose money.

For a speculator, patience is a survival skill. So wait for opportunities that tilt the odds in your favor.

GOING WRONG DEPENDING ON STOCKS

Too many investors think the world of investing includes only stocks and cash.

As a result, most strategies for dealing with good times and bad times turn out to be a simple plan for moving money between the stock market and a money market fund.

This is understandable—especially since stocks have been the best performing investment over the past few years. But no bull market lasts forever.

Even during the awful 1970s, most investors held on to their stocks while they waited out the bad times. At best, they reduced their hold-

---

[2]As we'll see in Part II, there are investments you should buy as insurance, in which case a loss is offset almost automatically by a larger gain elsewhere in your portfolio. Losses are not reasons to sell such investments.

ings. The idea of holding gold instead was rejected as too risky. And so they continued losing money while the price of gold went up.

Gold seems risky because it fluctuates so much—as demonstrated by its 134% rise in 1979 and its 31% fall in 1981. But that would be frightening only if you were considering putting everything you own into gold—something you should never do with any investment. A more sensible approach is to use gold as a way to reduce the risk associated with stocks.

Balance

Suppose, at the end of 1969, you had put 80% of your net worth into a portfolio of low-risk, blue-chip common stocks such as those in the Dow Jones Industrial Average. A decade later, at the end of 1979, your stocks would have appreciated 4.8%. Dividends would have brought the total return on the stocks to 53.8%, or a compound yearly average gain of just 4.4% during a decade when the inflation rate averaged 7.4%.

And suppose that you had put the other 20% of your capital into gold at the end of 1969. The 10-year result for your *combined* holdings of stocks and gold would have been a gain of 313.9%, or a compound annual average of 15.3%. Quite a difference—just from hedging with a little gold.

Maybe it seems implausible that you could have been persuaded in 1969 to put 20% of your net worth into gold. But if you had put only 10% into gold and kept the rest in stocks (perhaps because you had a policy of always keeping 10% in gold), your entire portfolio would have appreciated 183.8% for the decade. With only 5% in gold, your net profit would have been 118.8%.

Of course, the 1970s were the decade for gold. And who could have foreseen that? Afterwards—between the end of 1979 and the end of 1986—gold lost 23.4% of its value. But the economic events that depressed gold also elevated the stock market. Consequently, an 80/20 division of capital would have gained 98.4% during that 7-year period.

As you can see, spreading your capital among different markets doesn't immobilize it. Handled properly, a balanced portfolio can come out ahead in almost any economic environment.

In Part II, I'll suggest a strategy that's more elaborate and more effective than just splitting your money between stocks and gold. But the point we've seen here is an important one.

The investment world is bigger than the stock market. By diversifying into other areas, you can increase the safety of your portfolio substantially. And, as the examples show, you don't have to give up the hope of profit.

MANY WAYS TO GO WRONG

This list of ways to go wrong isn't complete. But I hope it will help clear away some of the logical debris that clutters so much of what you read about investing.

16

Beyond the
Best-Laid Plans

The best-laid investment plans usually go wrong because they're based on an empty hope—the hope that some system, advisor, technique, indicator, or mysterious art will take the uncertainty out of investing.

By and large, the investors and speculators who make money consistently are those who have ignored the fantasies and accepted the world as it is. Many of them have no extraordinary aptitude or special ability to sense market movements.

They succeed because they've developed realistic investment strategies that leave room for uncertainty. Or they use speculative strategies that allow profits to pile up when things go well, and cut losses when things go poorly.

If you want to join them, you'll have to set aside the dream of easy money. You'll have to realize that forecasts, trading systems, numerical projections, advisors with "hot hands," and other miracles aren't going to make you rich. Then you'll be free to turn your attention to the important job—which is to devise a strategy for safety and profit that works in the real world.

Respecting Uncertainty

The feature that distinguishes an investment strategy from a fantasy is its attitude toward uncertainty. Fantasies purport to eliminate uncertainty; strategies deal with it.

The worth of a strategy can be judged by how well it *allows for* uncertainty—rather than how it claims to *overcome* it.

And it's only when you accept uncertainty that you can do anything constructive about your investments.

So long as you pine for an authoritative forecaster with a proven track record—or wonder whether the latest newsletter promotion is on the level about its spectacular results—or hope that someone out there can make it all work perfectly for you—or pray for science to find a cure for uncertainty—your efforts to design a realistic strategy will be half-hearted. You'll still be wondering whether the latest investment miracle you've heard about might actually help you to hit the jackpot.

That's why I've pounded so hard and thumped so long in these pages. I want you to be convinced beyond all question that no one can show you what's coming next. What I've said could have been presented in a few sentences:

1. No one accurately predicts human behavior in other matters, so there's no reason to expect anyone to predict future investment prices.

2. Coincidence and luck play a big part in any investor's results, and they can make a nonsensical technique appear to have been confirmed by history. So be skeptical of "past performance."

3. The truth often is stretched in the investment business, just as it is elsewhere—so take all claims for an advisor, a trading system, or a method of analysis with a grain of salt.

4. Any assertion that a particular method of investment analysis is "scientific" should be ignored. Controlled tests aren't possible for economic theories.

5. Don't believe an investment rule simply because it seems to be widely respected.

6. If there were a single trading system or school of investment analysis that could beat the market, investment advisors and system creators wouldn't be continually devising *new* systems they hope will beat the market.

7. If anyone had found the magic key to investment riches, he wouldn't be telling you of the profits his system *would* have produced (hypothetically), he'd be telling you of the profits it *did* produce.

8. Testimonials for investment systems and advisors are of no more value than they are for gurus, astrologers, or used-car dealers.

9. Some people are especially talented as investors or speculators —just as some people are talented athletes or musicians. Don't expect to imitate them successfully unless you have similar talents.

10. Since we don't expect an athlete to be able to explain how he runs so fast, we shouldn't expect a successful speculator to show us how to acquire the Midas touch.

If I had stated these points so concisely, I might have saved your time and still won your agreement—but I might not have won your conviction. I've approached these matters from many different angles because I'm hoping you'll do more than say "Of course." I'm hoping you'll see through the promise of wealth that may come in tomorrow's mail—a promise posing as an exception to these points.

I've tried to give you enough examples and to reveal enough of the tricks that are used to make fantasies believable so that, once and for all, you'll shake free of the Impossible Dream—so that you'll smile knowingly the next time you hear someone talk about his fabulous track record—so that you'll ask the next forecaster you encounter for a copy of *last year's* predictions—or so that you'll simply walk away when someone offers to sell you the secrets of the future.

Only then can you get on with the business of finding safety and profit in an uncertain world.

THE ONE IMPOSSIBLE DREAM

It may have seemed that we've roamed halfway around the world in Part I.

But a common thread runs through predictions, trading systems, numerical projections, cycle theories, most rules of technical analysis, rules for success, and all the other panaceas we examined. They are all aspects of the same delusion, and many traits are common to most of these fantasies.

1. Grain of Truth

A fantasy usually is founded on a principle that makes sense as a generality—an observation about life or the investment markets that seems self-evident when called to your attention.

The principle might be that investments generate the greatest publicity when they're about as high as they can go. Or that science predicts the future in many areas of our lives. Or that regular cycles abound in the physical world. Or that there are universal qualities in human nature. Or that people tend to repeat the mistakes of the past.

2. Over the Edge

The second common trait is that the general principle is stretched beyond the limits of its usefulness.

Instead of using the principle as a reminder—a way of keeping oneself from getting carried away or as a clue to potential opportunity—it is pumped up into an entire school of analysis or a complete trading system.

Thus advisors start "measuring" investor sentiment or counting waves or projecting price peaks. The generality is transformed into a prediction of what will come, and a formula is created to tell you when and where.

3. Scientific Posture

The name of "science" is invoked to justify what is really superstition. Pages of mathematics may be presented to demonstrate the scholarly approach of the fantasy's creator.

4. Coronation

Eventually, the fantasy is enthroned.

The market pattern that now and then holds true is proclaimed to be a tenet of natural law. It is elevated to a universal truth that "happens too often to be coincidence" and is too well established to be disputed.

The advisor who once made a perceptive observation about the future, and was proven right, becomes an authoritative forecaster with a fabulous track record. He now spends half his time trying to outguess the future—and the other half trying to persuade us that he can.

Whatever the fantasy may be, it no longer is merely a curiosity or a technique that may be useful occasionally. It is something around which a career, a system, or even an "institute" is built.

5. Sweet Superiority

Those who follow the system, the school, the forecaster, or the advisor become part of the elite—the illuminati—the small band of people who are in on the secret.

They look down at the boobs and yahoos who still believe the conventional interpretations and share the common expectations. No matter how many times the well-laid plans of the elite go wrong, they have the satisfaction of knowing that everyone else *must* be worse off.

6. Dogma

In fact, however, the elite never need to acknowledge—to themselves or to anyone else—that their plans have gone wrong. They know, beyond a shadow of a doubt, that what they're doing *works*.

If you naively believe that their principle, system, forecast, or plan has been contradicted by events, then you simply don't understand. There is always an explanation at hand. Such as:

A. "It really did work, but it was offset by other factors that were stronger in this case." (Then why did you have me bet my precious capital on it?)

B. "The system is perfect, but human beings practice it imperfectly." (Then wouldn't I be better off with a system that doesn't expect me to be perfect?)

C. "This was the exception that proves the rule." (How many more times must the rule be "proved" before it starts working?)[1]

D. "It happened exactly as expected; you must have misunderstood the expectation." (Since I never seem to understand what to expect, shouldn't I look for a method I can understand?)

E. "It was a clear-cut, textbook example of the principle working on an inverted/extended/reversed basis." (If it's so simple, why didn't you warn me that this time it would invert/extend/reverse?)

F. "The result has been delayed, pressure is building up, and the result will be twice as dramatic when it finally comes." (And if we wind up waiting 100 years, it will *really* be powerful.)

---

[1]Contrary to the old saying, an exception can't prove a rule. An exception can *call attention* to a rule. When you see a Japanese tourist without a camera, you're aware intuitively that something is unusual. After thinking about it, you realize that—as a general rule—Japanese tourists have cameras hanging from their necks. The rule had passed unnoticed until an exception caused you to recognize it.

And on and on. The catalog of justifications is a long one—with new supplements being issued regularly.

7. Irrefutability

Since there's an explanation for every apparent failure, the fantasy becomes irrefutable. No matter what happens, it can't be proven wrong.

If the facts seem to contradict the theory, you must not be reading the facts correctly. If a technique doesn't work, you must be using it incorrectly. If part of it makes no sense to you, then maybe you're not bright enough.

The devotee sees every outcome—up or down, back or forth—as a confirmation of his belief. He's like the Marxist who sees the riches of ordinary workers as evidence that capitalism exploits them, or the doctrinaire feminist who interprets a thoughtful gesture from a man as a condescending act.

No evidence can contradict the believer's faith. Events, logic, and reason no longer have the same meaning to him that they do to us. And so there's no longer any useful communication.

ORDER AND LAW

Fantasies aren't found only in the investment world. There are people everywhere who hope to find a secret way to put themselves ahead of everyone else.

They look to ESP, astrology, reincarnation, utilitarian religions, biblical prophecy, or any of dozens of other doctrines to get the edge. These ideas can be interesting and entertaining—even fascinating— but they don't help us deal with reality or make decisions.

One motivation behind the search for mystical answers, I believe, is that the answers seem to bring order to a chaotic world. They make things tidy, simple, easier to deal with.

But successful people don't put everything into convenient compartments and pretend that nothing is sticking out over the edges. They do something harder, which is to deal with the particulars and the peculiarities of things as they find them—not as they expect them to be. They're able to live with variety, disorder, randomness, luck, uncertainty, even chaos.

They accept diverse possibilities, they're prepared for the unexpected, and they treat an unknowable future as a challenge—instead of taking comfort in false predictability. They succeed largely because they accept uncertainty and disorder—and find ways to deal with them.

THE REAL WORLD

The study of the paranormal and the para-economic can be fun. But at some point we have to beam down to the real world—the one in which we live.

In the real world, there are principles of logic and truth that can't be overruled by a catchy phrase or a get-rich gimmick. Applying those principles to investing, you have to ask of every idea, "Can this be explained by what I know of the way human beings act?"

Can you imagine any process by which human beings would be moved suddenly to acquire an investment when its price touches a trendline—or to dump their stocks when a price falls below a particular moving average—or to keep buying until a price rises to exactly 1.618 times an earlier level and then start selling? Have you found evidence of a hormone that causes the bullishness of profit-seeking investors to rise and fall in cycles and waves like those on a biorhythm chart?

A valid relationship exists between two events (such as between an "indicator" and an investment's movement) only if it can be shown, step by step, how the first event induces human beings to act in such a way as to bring about the second event.

If there's no explanation in terms of the actions of human beings— the two-footed, happiness-seeking, lunch-eating *Homo sapiens* you're familiar with—the idea being proposed is merely superstition.

ONE WORLD

But, of course, this skepticism isn't new for you. You invoke similar standards of logic and proof constantly in other areas of your life. I'm simply suggesting that you approach investing in the same way.

The investment world isn't separate from the world you know—the world in which you've already succeeded and earned the capital you wish to nourish. Investing doesn't have a logic of its own.

In the world you know, there are no pundits who can see into the future. There aren't any here either.

Where you live, there's no successful way to bypass hard work, logic, or uncertainty. And that's true here as well.

In your world, people offer you arcane philosophies, secrets of life, mysterious ways of anticipating the future—but none of those things ever works out. It's the same here; you won't save your fortune or build a new one with a trendline or a Fibonacci number.

Just as in the world you know, there are no Messiahs with perfect knowledge in the investment world, no secret decoders that unravel the mysteries of market movements.

In your world, you've achieved what you have because of a philosophy of life that has helped you to deal with problems and complications, to allow for what you don't know, and to handle conflicts between competing ambitions and desires. *That* is what will help you here.

You'll succeed here by using your philosophy of life and your sense of realism to construct an investment strategy—one that will help you make decisions, help you deal with uncertainty, help you resolve conflicting claims and competing opportunities.

You *can* succeed with your investments—if you avoid the fantasies that underlie all the well-laid plans. Depending only on reality, you can develop a strategy to achieve what you had in mind when you bought this book.

PART II

A Strategy
for
Safety & Profit

17

Investing in an Uncertain World

Over and over, I've been saying that you must respect uncertainty and allow for it; you can't eliminate it. Your plans must be based on the fact that the future is unknowable.

But how can you protect yourself from whatever is coming if you don't know what it is? And how can you increase your wealth without staking it on a judgment of what the future will bring?

The strategy presented in this part of the book won't turn you into a stock-picking genius. Nor will it guarantee to double your money every year—nor in *any* fixed number of years.

But it does allow you to protect yourself, and to earn a profit, from whatever might come. And, if you so desire, it lets you reach for more dramatic profits without endangering the money you can't afford to lose.

INVESTING & SPECULATING

The strategy recognizes the difference between investing and speculating.

When you *invest*, you provide capital to the financial markets. You say, in effect, "Here's my money; use it as you think best, and pay me the return—in dividends, interest, and capital appreciation—that you're paying to everyone who invests."

The return on your investment will be determined primarily by the economic condition of the nation and of the world.

As an *investor*, you make no attempt to time your investments— to buy low and sell high. Nor do you try to identify the particular stocks, bonds, or other issues that will do best. You simply buy the items that, taken together, seem to be representative of each market—a collection of stocks that will move as the overall market moves, or a group of bonds that will do well whenever interest rates fall, and so on.

An investor does make a number of decisions in planning his portfolio. But he doesn't try to decide which investment will do best. Nor does he try to time his purchases and sales.

A *speculator* attempts to earn more than what the market is paying an investor. He tries to be in a market when it's going up, and out of it when it's going down. And he attempts to choose stocks or other investments that will outperform a market, rather than just reflect it.

Investing, Speculating, & Safety

A great deal of what's called investing is really speculation.

An idea may be promoted as "low-risk" investing or even packaged as "protection." But whenever you try to outguess the future—to switch into and out of investments in a timely fashion—you're speculating, not investing.

It's easy to be drawn into speculation, even if you're looking for safety. Many advisors contend that you'll be safe only if you understand that the future is sure to be dominated by inflation or deflation or something else—and bet everything on the one certain outcome.

Or you're told that safety comes from agility—from being in the right investment for each financial season, and moving quickly to the next investment as the season changes. This leads to a series of speculations on which you stake everything—over and over again—on someone's ability to read the future correctly. One or two wrong guesses could cause you to lose a great deal. This strategy also comes with the "safety" label.

But no matter what label is on the package, trying to beat the markets by outguessing the future is speculation.

The Universe of Investing

Despite its risks, agile speculation can seem safer than the more traditional methods of investing.

During the 1970s, traditional investors seemed to be eaten alive. For the decade, the Dow Jones Industrial Average lost over 25% of its purchasing power—even after allowing for dividends. And bonds did no better.

From this experience, many investors concluded that holding stocks and bonds through thick and thin is dangerous. Outguessing the future seemed to be the only alternative, and so they began dancing in and out of stocks, and in and out of gold, and in and out of real estate or bonds or foreign currencies—hoping to catch the right investment each time conditions seemed to be changing.

But the result for many of these jitterbugging investors has been worse than if they had simply stood still with the worst single investment.

SAFETY & PROFIT

Fortunately, there is a better way.

Your investment strategy can be both safe and profitable if you respect three principles:

1. Investing and speculating must be separate endeavors that are never combined or confused.

2. You should speculate only with money you can afford to lose— never betting with money that's precious to you.

3. The money you're not willing to lose should be invested so that it's protected, and able to grow, in any conceivable economic climate—without your having to foresee what the climate will be.

TWO PORTFOLIOS

The first step in the search for safety is to separate your investment capital into two different portfolios. I call them the Permanent Portfolio (for investing) and the Variable Portfolio (for speculating).[1]

The Permanent Portfolio is a permanent, balanced collection of long-

[1]A portfolio is a collection of investments—such as a number of different stocks, a quantity of gold, parcels of real estate, cash, and so on.

term investments. Its main purpose is to assure that you're financially safe no matter what the future brings. Once established, it remains virtually unchanged for many years—even as the economy bounces from recession to prosperity to inflation. If properly arranged, it should produce a profit; but its primary goal is safety.

The Variable Portfolio is a separate, changeable portfolio, funded with money you can afford to lose. Its contents vary as conditions change. With the Variable Portfolio, you attempt to beat the market and earn a sizable profit by acting on your judgments about investment trends. You vary the portfolio's investments as you see the opportunities for profit changing.

It is vital that the two portfolios be treated separately when you make investment decisions. The choices you make for one have nothing to do with the decisions you make for the other. Each portfolio has its own purpose and its own rules. They are as unrelated as the portfolios of two different investors.

THE PERMANENT PORTFOLIO

The primary purpose of the Permanent Portfolio is to preserve your capital no matter what economic circumstances descend upon us—more inflation, runaway inflation, deflation, stability, giddy prosperity, whatever.

This safety is created through careful diversification—pointing the portfolio in several different directions—so that any economic climate will cause at least one of the portfolio's investments to be a big winner.

The components must be chosen thoughtfully, so that they actually produce the safety that's expected from them. A scatter-gun approach won't work. And the particular investments must be selected so that the winners will win more than the others lose.

If you assemble the Permanent Portfolio properly, its structure can remain virtually unchanged for many years—requiring only minor attention once a year. You should be able to walk away from the portfolio without being afraid that changing times will make it vulnerable or obsolete.

THE VARIABLE PORTFOLIO

The Variable Portfolio begins with a supply of cash. It remains in cash until you're willing to risk some or all of it on an attractive speculation.

The speculation might be almost anything. It could be a specific stock or commodity that you believe shows exceptional promise. Or a mutual fund or stock index option when you feel stocks are in a bull market. It could be gold, a foreign currency, bonds, or put options—whatever looks attractive at a particular time.

The investment might be very short-term—such as a trade in the futures market that you expect to complete in a few days. Or it might be a bet that a bull market will last for a few months or years.

Depending on your current judgment, the portfolio might be completely invested in one item, or divided among two or more. Or it could be partly in cash and partly in one or more investments. Or it might be entirely in cash—waiting for an opportunity that meets your standards.

On occasion, the Variable Portfolio might contain something that's also represented in the Permanent Portfolio. But the investment would be serving a different purpose in each portfolio. An investment is held permanently in the Permanent Portfolio to provide long-term protection. If you hold the same investment temporarily in the Variable Portfolio, it is because you expect it to appreciate soon and you're willing to risk some money on your judgment.

DIVISION BETWEEN THE PORTFOLIOS

You don't have to speculate at all. You should do so only if you want to and can afford the risk.

You may prefer to forget about the Variable Portfolio and have only a Permanent Portfolio—if you have no interest in speculating, or you don't have the competence or the time to do it intelligently, or you have no capital you can afford to risk.

If you do choose to have a Variable Portfolio, it should be funded only with money you are prepared to lose. With a suitable Variable Portfolio strategy, you probably won't lose all the money—even if every speculation turns out badly. But it would be foolish to risk money that's precious to you.

If you don't now have capital you can afford to lose, you shouldn't set up a Variable Portfolio until your wealth has grown to where you have a surplus you can risk.

If you do have funds you can risk and you want to speculate, but you aren't sure how well you'll do, you might put a small amount into the Variable Portfolio as a trial. If you're eager to speculate and can afford to do so, you might put more into the Variable Portfolio.

Providing a Cushion

Although the Permanent Portfolio is designed for safety, there are bound to be periods when the portfolio will depreciate in value temporarily. Between 1980 and 1982, for example, virtually all investment prices declined. During such times, *any* portfolio (except one that's all in cash) must decline in value as well.

So if, say, 60% of your net worth is precious to you, you might allocate 75% to the Permanent Portfolio and put only 25% in the Variable Portfolio. The extra cushion will make it easier for you to tolerate a temporary decline in the Permanent Portfolio's value.

Try to Be Objective

When you decide on the division between the two portfolios, try to do so without considering any particular speculation. You'll be more objective about questions of risk and possible profit if you aren't thinking about the riches that will flow from the speculation that seems attractive right now.

In fact, a big advantage of dividing your wealth into two portfolios once and for all is that, thereafter, the capital that's precious to you can't be seduced by a hot opportunity. An investor (even one who recognizes the risks involved in speculating) is inclined to reopen the question of how much to speculate every time he finds an opportunity—trying at that moment to decide how much he can afford to risk. And if the speculation looks attractive, it's easy for him to overstate the amount he's willing to lose.

That's an important reason for making the division between the two portfolios now, and keeping the portfolios separate. That way, you'll never be tempted to bet more than you should on any speculation.

SAFETY & SPECULATION

A Permanent Portfolio provides much greater protection from the world's uncertainties than does anyone's ability to guess the future.

It isn't foolish to speculate. But speculate intelligently, betting only with Variable Portfolio money—money you can afford to lose—and only when the odds seem to be stacked in your favor.

Far from constraining you, the two-portfolio approach liberates you.

If you've placed a firm limit on the amount you can lose, you probably will speculate more calmly, more intelligently, and more profitably than if you have to fear the terrible consequences of making the wrong bet with too much of what you own.

MORE TO COME

This chapter probably has raised a number of questions—even objections—about the strategy. I hope that all of them will be answered in the chapters to come.

In the next three chapters, we'll see how a truly diversified Permanent Portfolio can protect you from virtually anything. Then I'll describe a strategy for making the most of a Variable Portfolio.

Part III will look at the individual investments that go into the portfolios, and make suggestions for handling them.

Part IV will take care of some details—tax considerations, where to keep investments, and where to get help.

And finally, in Chapter 36, we'll bring everything together and take a last look at the entire strategy.

18

Safety
Through the
Permanent Portfolio

To be safe, a portfolio must be permanent. The protection you *might* need someday must be in the portfolio now, and must be there to stay. Once the Permanent Portfolio has been arranged, you should be able to set it aside and forget about it—confident that you're safe from all threats. If you can't do that, it isn't safe.

You may think that you don't need to be prepared ahead of time— that you're agile enough to deal with any national or worldwide economic crisis as it occurs. But that approach should be filed among the best-laid plans as one more recipe for ruin.

Many worries about the economy never materialize; they only threaten. But when a threat appears, you don't know whether it will grow into real trouble or just blow over. You can't tell whether it's Judgment Day or just April Fool's Day.

If your portfolio isn't already insulated from whatever is threatening, you'll have to hurry to protect yourself. But that will be the most expensive time to acquire the protection, because other people will be bidding up its price.

It doesn't matter whether what threatens is a banking crisis brought on by hints that foreign governments will repudiate their debts, or the imposition of exchange controls, or a deflationary collapse and stock-market crash, or wage and price controls and suppressed inflation, or something else. Once the threat is visible, you can acquire protection only by buying certain assets at premium prices and dumping other assets at a discount.

And when the threat has passed, the assets you bought for protection will tumble in price, and the assets you dumped will once again be expensive.

Even if expense weren't important, you might not take steps quickly enough. The crisis might occur overnight, over a weekend, while you're on vacation, or when you're occupied with other matters. Or it might emerge so slowly that you fail to take it seriously until it's too late. Or the government might suddenly impose regulations that prohibit you from obtaining protection.

You can relax only if you prepare now, and keep your preparations in force permanently.

Permanent protection will be expensive and cumbersome if it's not arranged properly. But handled carefully, it can be part of a program for long-term profit, rather than an expense.

DIVERSIFICATION

The first step in creating a Permanent Portfolio is to allow for all possibilities. This means *real* diversification.

To stock-market investors, diversification means buying 20 different stocks—or buying a few "defensive" stocks along with growth issues—or maybe having some bonds along with one's stocks—or, more sophisticated yet, keeping some convertible bonds.

But this is little more than a parody of diversification. It protects you only from the isolated problems of individual companies. Most of the investments are pointed in one direction—providing no protection from inflation or recession. And to whatever extent the diversification *is* effective, it tends to cancel out the gains of the principal investments and neutralize the portfolio.

Diversification has to reach beyond traditional investments to deal with all the possibilities for the future. And the portfolio must be arranged so that it can achieve a net gain overall—no matter what the future brings.

Protection

Thorough diversification requires substantial holdings in four investment categories—each of which responds reliably to particular economic conditions. The four categories are:

1. Common stocks—for profit during periods of general prosperity and/or declining inflation;

2. Gold—for profit during periods of rising inflation—and, during those periods, to profit from other kinds of problems as well;

3. Bonds—for profit during periods of falling interest rates, such as when inflation is declining and especially in the later stages of a deflation; and

4. Cash—to provide stability when no investments are doing well, and to provide gains in purchasing power during periods of deflation.

Each of these investments is a cornerstone of a Permanent Portfolio because each has a clear and reliable link to a specific economic environment.

Volatility Needed

Diversification isn't a matter of buying a little of this and a little of that. You could easily buy too much of the losers and too little of the winners.

Somehow you have to assure that the winners win more than the losers lose, without knowing in advance which will be which. The key is to select, for each investment category, particular investments that are highly volatile. These are investments that will move a great distance, up or down, as conditions change.

Over a period of several years, the winners are likely to appreciate by several hundred percent—but the worst loser can't cost you more than 100% of its starting value. With a package of volatile investments, each purchased for cash, the gain from a single winner can outweigh what is lost on a number of losers—giving you a net profit overall.

During the 1970s, for example, the gold in a Permanent Portfolio doubled over and over again—far outweighing losses of 30% to 50% for the portfolio's stocks and bonds.

On page 226, we saw the example of an investor who kept only 20% of his portfolio in gold throughout the 1970s. His portfolio managed to outrun inflation during an inflationary decade, even while his large stock-market investments were losing a quarter of their purchasing power. And then, though he continued to keep 20% of his portfolio in gold, he was able to profit from the bull market in stocks in the 1980s.

Stocks and gold didn't nullify each other; they complemented each other. It was possible for an investor with a Permanent Portfolio to profit in two very different economic environments—*without changing the portfolio's structure, and without foreseeing when or how the environment would change.*

Perspective

Volatility works for you most effectively over long periods.

During a short period, an investment might go up a little or down a little—or even up a lot or down a lot. But the potential gain is no more than the potential loss, since no investment is likely to appreciate more than 100% in a matter of only a few months.

Over longer periods, however, a volatile investment has the power to go up a great deal—even though the potential loss, if the investment is purchased for cash, is limited to 100%. For example, in a long bull market, stocks might double or triple in value—but they're unlikely to lose more than half their value in a bear market.

The same is true for gold. It rose roughly 450% between 1972 and 1974, then fell 50% during the next two years, rose 700% between 1976 and 1980, and then fell 65% over the next five years. The gains were enormous, but the potential loss for an investor entering the market at any particular time could never be more than 100%.

Two investments held over a period of time, if they're sufficiently volatile and of contrasting natures, can generate a net gain. One investment may lose, but the gain from the other probably will offset that loss and add a profit to boot.

CHOICE OF INVESTMENTS

Stocks, gold, and bonds *as a package* can provide profit, and thus protection, in most economic circumstances. But it's important to use each in the way that provides the greatest volatility.

Gold

Gold is the preferred choice for inflation protection because, by itself, it provides all the volatility you need.

During the inflationary 1970s, gold rose 20 times over. In the next inflationary period, its gain might be considerably less—but a small commitment to gold still would provide powerful protection.

You would have to pay dearly to achieve similar protection against inflation in any other way. For example, using a group of commodities as an inflation hedge would demand a much larger portion of your portfolio, since no group of commodities is as volatile—or as reliably sensitive to inflation—as gold.

Gold's potential for spectacular gains will allow it to overwhelm the losses likely to be incurred by the portfolio's other investments when inflation reigns.

The connections between gold, inflation, and trouble in general are discussed in Chapter 25. ·

Bonds

The price of any bond tends to rise as interest rates in general fall. But the amount by which a particular bond rises depends on several characteristics of the bond—the most important of which is the time left before the bond matures.

The longer the time to maturity, the greater the effect a change in general interest rates has on a bond's price. High-grade bonds with 25 or 30 years to maturity are far more sensitive to changes in interest rates than bonds with only 5 or 10 years to maturity. Because of this volatility, a long-term bond is far more appropriate for a Permanent Portfolio.

An important function for bonds is to protect the portfolio in the event of a deflation—when both stocks and gold should be suffering. In order to provide that protection, the bonds must be absolutely immune to default—which means that only U.S. Treasury bonds should be considered.

The choice of bonds is discussed further in Chapter 28.

Stocks

The selection of stock-market investments is a bit more complicated.

Buying a group of stocks that represents the Dow Jones Industrial Average would be like buying a group of commodities as a hedge against inflation. Your stocks would move only to the degree that the general market moves. As with gold, you need stock-market investments that will provide a lot of movement from a small part of the portfolio.

The most appropriate stock-market investments for a Permanent Portfolio are:

1. Stocks that normally are highly volatile—that usually move further, up or down, than the market as a whole moves.

2. Mutual funds that invest in volatile stocks.

3. Warrants—which are, in effect, long-term options, and thus are very volatile.

These are discussed further in Chapter 26.

Cash

Together, stocks, bonds, and gold provide protection and profit potential for most economic climates—but not all climates.

Sometimes no investments are rising, as was the case from late 1980 through the summer of 1982, and again from mid-1983 through mid-1984.

At such times no portfolio can appreciate, because none of its components is appreciating. And if any of the components is falling, the portfolio itself must lose value.

Cash helps cushion such shocks to a Permanent Portfolio—enhancing the portfolio's stability. And if the cash is drawing interest, the interest can offset some of the damage to the other investments.

Cash also provides additional protection against a deflation, because dollars become more valuable as the general level of prices falls.

Treasury bills are the best medium for holding cash. They draw interest, and they're virtually free of credit risk. To earn a higher yield than that paid on Treasury bills, you would have to evaluate other investments for credit risk, and you'd have to monitor those investments to be sure the risk hadn't grown. That would be contrary to the idea of a portfolio that's permanently safe—one you can set up and then walk away from.

A money market fund investing only in Treasury securities is an acceptable substitute for Treasury bills.

We'll discuss this portion of the portfolio further in Chapter 27.

BALANCE AND SAFETY

Volatile stock-market investments, long-term Treasury bonds, gold, and Treasury bills combine to provide balance and safety.

Apart from Treasury bills, each has the ability to rise by more than 100% over a period of time, while the decline of any investment is limited to 100%. So a Permanent Portfolio comprised of these investments has a natural tendency to gain in value. And this upward bias is augmented by the interest earned by the Treasury bills and bonds.

Because of the upward bias, we would expect to find that, at any given time, one rising investment should be sufficient to pull the entire portfolio upward—even if the other investments are stagnant or falling.

The past can't tell us what will happen in the future. But it can show us whether history has already disproved what we believe to be a general rule.

The graph on page 253 shows the result during 1970–1987 for a simple, hypothetical Permanent Portfolio that invested 25% of its capital in each of the four essential investments—stocks, long-term Treasury bonds, gold bullion, and Treasury bills.

It also shows the individual performances of stocks (represented by the New York Stock Exchange Composite Index), bonds (represented by 20-year Treasury bonds), and gold. During any period in which at least one of these three investments was rising noticeably, the overall portfolio gained.

And because the investments are pointed in different directions, there rarely was a time when none of them was doing well. The only exceptions were short periods during parts of 1974 and 1980, and longer declines from late 1980 through mid-1982 and from 1983 through mid-1984.

The most striking aspect revealed by the graph is the stability of the portfolio's growth—rarely dramatic, but plowing inexorably upward. Obviously, diversification didn't neutralize the portfolio; even when one or more of the investments was falling, the portfolio continued to profit.

RATIO SCALE

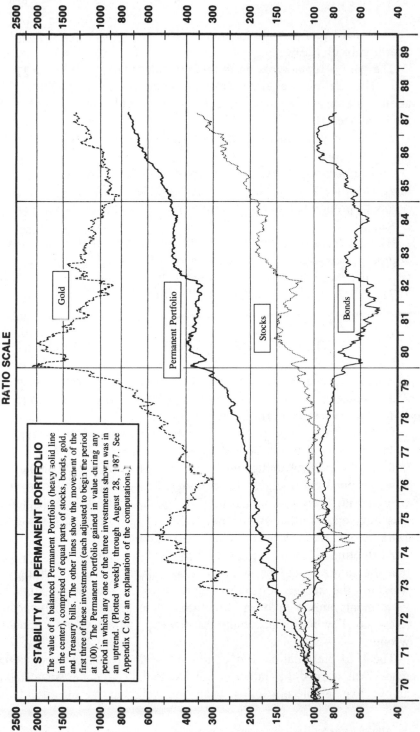

STABILITY IN A PERMANENT PORTFOLIO

The value of a balanced Permanent Portfolio (heavy solid line in the center), comprised of equal parts of stocks, bonds, gold, and Treasury bills. The other lines show the movement of the first three of these investments (each adjusted to begin the period at 100). The Permanent Portfolio gained in value during any period in which any one of the three investments shown was in an uptrend. (Plotted weekly through August 28, 1987. See Appendix C for an explanation of the computations.)

Gold

Permanent Portfolio

Stocks

Bonds

For the 17-year period, the gain was 639%—which is a compound yearly gain of 12.0%.[1]

The gain is remarkable when you consider that:

1. The portfolio required virtually no attention by its owner. No attempt was made to outguess the future; no speculative decisions were made or needed.

2. The 17 years included periods that were particularly turbulent for the economy.

3. The portfolio suffered no sharp losses during the 17 years. The largest decline from a high to a low was 15%. The longest period without a profit (the longest time from one high to the next) was exactly 2 years.

By contrast, stocks suffered one decline of 51% and went 7 years without a new high. Bonds had a drop of 57%, and gold had one of 61%. In 1987, bonds had yet to regain the high they had reached in 1971, and gold was still below its 1980 high.

EVOLUTION OF THE PERMANENT PORTFOLIO

In addition to the hypothetical portfolio shown in the graph on page 253, actual experience from the past 10 years provides further evidence of how a Permanent Portfolio performs.

I introduced the concept of the Permanent Portfolio in my newsletter in late 1977, and in my book *New Profits from the Monetary Crisis* in the fall of 1978. Although the basic concept has remained unaltered, it was refined considerably for *Inflation-Proofing Your Investments*, written with Terry Coxon and published in March 1981. And then it was developed further in my newsletter in an article in September 1981. More refinements are being introduced here.

At the time of the first presentations, in 1977 and 1978, I believed that the future would be dominated by inflation, and accordingly I weighted the sample portfolios heavily toward precious metals. The investments aimed in other directions were given only supporting roles—to allow for the possibility that my expectations would be proven wrong.

The 1981 presentations moved toward much greater balance, as the reader was warned that inflation wasn't eternal. A choice was offered among five sample portfolios, each one weighted toward one of the

---

[1] After allowing for inflation, the average yearly gain in purchasing power was 5.2%.

five possible futures for inflation: (1) level inflation, (2) continued rising inflation, (3) runaway inflation, (4) deflation, or (5) a soft landing (gradually declining inflation without a crash).

Each portfolio was fully hedged against the possibility that the expectation on which it was based was wrong. A sixth sample portfolio was labeled "uncertain"—for use by anyone who had no strong opinions about the direction of inflation.

Over the 10 years since I first introduced the Permanent Portfolio, my thinking has moved steadily toward greater balance. And although all the sample portfolios previously suggested have worked out well, I now see no reason to aim a Permanent Portfolio in any particular direction.

Results

All results so far confirm that a balanced portfolio will do well in any economic environment.

The upper graph on page 256 show the results for a Permanent Portfolio that followed the suggestions I've given—first those in my 1977 newsletter article, then the average of the sample portfolios in my 1978 book, and then the average of the sample portfolios in the 1981 book. (The results for the portfolios suggested in the 1981 newsletter article were almost identical to those for the 1981 book.)

The contents of all the portfolios, their results, and details on the computation of the results are given in Appendix C on page 513.

In addition, the Permanent Portfolio Fund (a mutual fund described on page 446), has made its own application of the Permanent Portfolio concept. The fund uses the four essential investments, plus silver, Swiss francs, and stocks of natural resource and real estate companies. In both a portfolio simulation running from 1970 to 1982, and in its actual operation since late 1982, the fund's results are consistent with my own.

The lower graph on page 256 shows the progress of the Permanent Portfolio Fund since its inception in December 1982.

Each Permanent Portfolio I've suggested (especially from among the balanced portfolios suggested in 1981), as well as the Permanent Portfolio Fund, has performed as you would expect a Permanent Portfolio to perform. Any major investment in a bull market will pull the entire portfolio upward, but the portfolio is bound to depreciate during periods in which all its investments are falling.

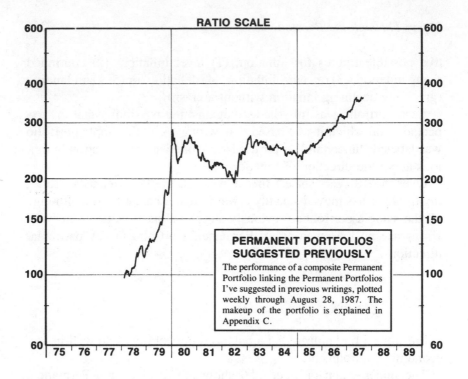

RATIO SCALE

**PERMANENT PORTFOLIOS
SUGGESTED PREVIOUSLY**

The performance of a composite Permanent
Portfolio linking the Permanent Portfolios
I've suggested in previous writings, plotted
weekly through August 28, 1987. The
makeup of the portfolio is explained in
Appendix C.

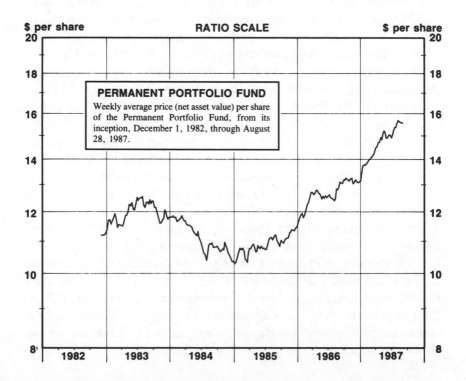

$ per share   **RATIO SCALE** $ per share

PERMANENT PORTFOLIO FUND

Weekly average price (net asset value) per share
of the Permanent Portfolio Fund, from its
inception, December 1, 1982, through August
28, 1987.

Simplicity

Along with an increasing respect for balance, my thinking has evolved toward greater simplicity. In 1981 I felt that it was important to diversify as much as practical. So I suggested silver, Swiss francs, and real estate to accompany gold as inflation hedges.

But none of those investments is the pure inflation hedge that gold is—and none has the reliable volatility of gold. Nor does any have the additional virtue of responding positively to non-economic crises during inflationary periods. However, you still might want to consider them for the Permanent Portfolio—a matter we'll take up again in Chapters 25, 29, and 30.

I think now that it's most important to have the portfolio dominated by the four essential investments—gold, stocks, long-term Treasury bonds, and Treasury bills.

So I would start the process of designing a Permanent Portfolio by assuming, at least provisionally, that the portfolio will be divided as follows:

Stock-market investments:	25%
Long-term Treasury bonds:	25%
Gold:	25%
Treasury bills:	25%

I think it's also valuable to have some cash and silver coins as further protection against such things as runaway inflation, bank closings, and other extreme events. Some amount less than 5% of the total portfolio would probably be sufficient.[2]

Additions

You might also own real estate or a business that would need to be accounted for. And you might decide to add foreign currencies, foreign stocks, silver, or some other long-term investment.

These other investments aren't essential to a Permanent Portfolio, but they might be included to provide additional diversification, or

---

[2]The holding of cash and silver coins is discussed further on page 350.

because they play important roles in your life. We'll discuss them further in Part III.

GEOGRAPHIC DIVERSIFICATION

In addition to investment diversification, I believe it's important to diversify geographically.

Keeping some investments outside the U.S. provides safe and easy protection against extreme events that might happen anywhere—confiscation of gold holdings by the government, exchange controls, civil disorder, even war.

My first choice is Switzerland—using a Swiss bank to hold a portion of your assets. The most appropriate asset to hold in a Swiss bank account is gold, but it wouldn't hurt to have some of the other assets there also, at least in small quantities.[3]

PEACE OF MIND

The test of a Permanent Portfolio is whether it provides peace of mind.

A Permanent Portfolio should let you watch the evening news or read investment publications with serenity. No actual or threatened event should trouble you, because you'll know that your portfolio is protected against it.

When you read of the "alarming parallels" between the 1980s and the 1920s, you shouldn't wonder whether you need to sell all your stocks. You'll know that your Permanent Portfolio will take care of you—even if 1989 turns out to be 1929.

When you read that the inflation rate is headed toward 20%, you shouldn't wonder whether to dump all your bonds. You'll know that the gain in your Permanent Portfolio's gold would far outweigh any losses incurred by the portfolio's bonds.

When you read that a politician is pushing to fight the terrible trade deficit by building a wall around the U.S. with foreign exchange controls, you shouldn't get a bad feeling in the pit of your stomach. You'll know that you already own gold sitting outside the United States.

---

[3]Swiss banks are discussed further in Chapter 32, and additional comments about where to keep things are given in Chapter 33.

When someone says the Latin American debt crisis could destroy the U.S. banking system, while someone else says the Federal Reserve would never let the banks fail, you shouldn't have to worry over who is right. You'll know that very little of your wealth would be affected by a banking crisis.

When someone announces that a new bull market is starting in stocks, bonds, or gold, you shouldn't feel pressured to decide whether he's right. You'll know that the Permanent Portfolio will respond favorably to any major bull market. And you can take your time deciding whether to try to exploit the situation further with your Variable Portfolio.

Whatever the potential crisis or opportunity, your Permanent Portfolio should already be taking care of you.

The portfolio can't guarantee a profit every year (no portfolio can). And it won't outperform the hotshot advisor in his best year. But it can give you the confidence that no crisis will destroy you, and the knowledge that you're no longer vulnerable to the mistakes in judgment that you or the best advisor could so easily make.

19

Managing the Permanent Portfolio

Setting up a permanent portfolio seems simple enough so far. But there are further points that we need to consider.

ANNUAL ADJUSTMENTS

Protection, stability, and steady growth are a Permanent Portfolio's great virtues.

The stability comes from allocating a substantial (but not overwhelming) share of the portfolio to each of the four essential investments. A portfolio that's mostly in stocks, or 50% in gold, or overloaded with bonds would behave erratically; it would be far less dependable.

The more or less steady growth of a Permanent Portfolio comes from the contrary movements of the investments it includes. The investments take turns contributing to the portfolio's value.

But, ironically, as each investment has its day, it tends to distort the portfolio—making it less and less balanced, less able to grow, and more vulnerable.

For a simple example, suppose that you begin by dividing capital of $1,000 equally among the four essential investments—$250 in each of gold, stocks, bonds, and T-bills. And suppose that, over the ensuing year, stock prices double, while bond and gold prices remain unchanged.

Your portfolio's value will grow to $1,250, which is 25% more than you started with. The stocks, now worth $500, represent 40% of the portfolio's increased total value—with the other three investments each representing only 20% of $1,250.

You decided at the outset that the portfolio would be properly balanced if it had 25% in each of the four investments. By that standard, you're now over-invested in stocks. It is just as imprudent to have 40% of your capital in stocks now as it would have been at the outset.

Your large stock holdings leave the portfolio vulnerable to tight credit, a deflation, a return of inflation, and other hazards that are bad for stocks. And the holdings of the other investments are too small to adequately protect the new, larger value of your portfolio against these things.

To rectify the imbalance that success has brought, you need only respect the percentages you decided upon at the outset—just as if you were starting anew today, but with a larger portfolio. So simply alter your holdings of each investment to conform to its designated percentage.

In this example, you would sell enough stocks to *reduce* your stock-market holdings to 25% of the portfolio's new value. With the proceeds of that sale, you would buy additional quantities of the three other investments—to *increase* your holdings of them, each to 25% of the portfolio's new value. Your holdings of every investment in the portfolio, including the Treasury-bill portion, should be adjusted—upward or downward—to its designated percentage.

The table on page 262 shows another example. In maintaining a Permanent Portfolio, you can use such a table to figure quickly the adjustments the portfolio will need.

You might decide at the outset not to split the portfolio evenly among the four investments, and you may want to include additional investments. Whatever percentages you choose for each investment, that is the percentage to which it should be restored when you make an adjustment.

If an investment's actual share of the portfolio is larger than its designated percentage, sell the excess. Use the proceeds to buy enough of the other investments to bring your holdings of them up to their designated percentages.

ANNUAL PERMANENT PORTFOLIO ADJUSTMENT

(#1) Investment	(#2) Value Now	(#3) % Now	(#4) Designated %	(#5) Designated Value	(#6) Buy or (Sell)
Stock-market items	$ 30,300	27.7%	25%	$ 27,375	$ (2,925)
Treasury bonds	29,100	26.6%	25%	27,375	(1,725)
Gold	23,800	21.7%	25%	27,375	3,575
T-bills, money fund	26,300	24.0%	25%	27,375	1,075
Totals	$109,500	100.0%	100%	$109,500	$ 0

Column #1: Name of the investment.

Column #2: Current dollar value of the investment.

Column #3: Percentage of the total value of the portfolio represented by this investment.

Column #4: Designated percentage for this investment.

Column #5: Dollar value corresponding to the designated percentage.

Column #6: Dollar amount of the investment that must be bought or (sold).

When to Make an Adjustment

You need to make an adjustment only once each year. If you make the calculations for the adjustment in December, you can decide then whether to make the sales immediately or delay them until January for tax purposes.[1]

In earlier presentations of the Permanent Portfolio concept, I suggested making an extra adjustment whenever one investment had risen or fallen by 30% from its price as of the last adjustment. But experience has indicated that this extra attention doesn't materially improve the outcome.

However, if you're aware that either gold, bonds, or a major stock-market index has doubled—or fallen by 50%—since the last time you made an adjustment, your portfolio probably would benefit from an immediate adjustment.

Objections to Adjusting

Some investors have objected to the idea of adjusting the portfolio. The most common protest is that adjustments squander opportunity by causing you to sell an investment at the best time to be owning it—when its price is rising.

But an adjustment causes you to sell only a *portion* of what has been a winning investment. Any profit you take is profit on what has already happened. And having made the adjustment, you'll be no less able to profit from price increases than when you started the portfolio—because the investment will command the same percentage of the portfolio it had at the outset.

If you don't make the adjustment, you could become more and more over-invested in one investment. If its price continues to rise, you'll enjoy it for a while—but only temporarily, only so long as the investment continues upward. As soon as it begins to fall, your portfolio will suffer badly—while an adjusted portfolio will be able to continue its stable growth.

The graph on page 253 showed how stable the growth of a Permanent Portfolio can be. That portfolio was adjusted at the end of each year.

The graph on page 265 shows that portfolio again. A separate, dotted

---

[1]For a corporation or other entity that's not on a calendar tax year, make the calculations during the last month of the entity's tax year.

dotted line on the graph depicts the performance of a second portfolio that initially was identical to the first—but was never adjusted.

The remarkable stability of the adjusted portfolio isn't present in the unadjusted portfolio. By becoming over-invested in gold during 1974 and 1975, the unadjusted portfolio reaped a greater profit in the 1977–1979 gold bull market. But that simply set it up for the big fall of 1980–1982, during which it lost 43% of its value.[2]

And after the 1982 rally in gold, the unadjusted portfolio (still over-invested in gold and under-invested in stocks and bonds) failed to profit from the bull markets in stocks and bonds. Meanwhile, the adjusted portfolio was continuing to grow, and overtook the unadjusted portfolio. Not until gold rose again, in 1985, did the unadjusted portfolio return to life.

You might feel that you would have reduced your gold holdings in 1980, once the top in gold had been reached. But how would you have known that the peak had arrived?

If you really could know such things, you could have made a fortune selling gold short—with your Variable Portfolio. You wouldn't have needed to compromise the Permanent Portfolio.[3]

Being Under-Invested

For similar reasons, even if you believe an investment is in a bear market, don't drag your feet bringing it up to its designated percentage. You don't know when the investment's price will turn upward. If you think you do know, apply your opinion to the Variable Portfolio.

It seemed foolish to many investors to own stocks, bonds, or Treasury bills as 1980 began. Anyone could see that those investments would hold a portfolio back, since inflation was in double digits and gold was soaring upward. But during 1980 gold fell by 40%, stocks roared upward, the inflation rate began falling, and interest rates stabilized. It was a good time to have a balanced Permanent Portfolio.

---

[2]During the 17 years, the largest single decline for an adjusted portfolio was only 15%.

[3]Even if you're positive you can time investments profitably, at least refrain from trying to time Permanent Portfolio investments until after you've proven that you really can do it successfully by making big, actual profits with the Variable Portfolio.

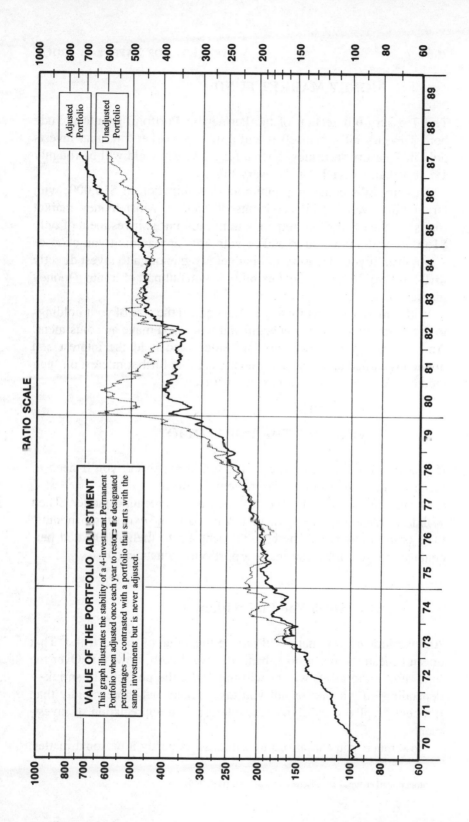

RATIO SCALE

VALUE OF THE PORTFOLIO ADJUSTMENT

This graph illustrates the stability of a 4-investment Permanent Portfolio when adjusted once each year to restore the designated percentages — contrasted with a portfolio that starts with the same investments but is never adjusted.

Adjusted Portfolio

Unadjusted Portfolio

MONEY MARKET FUND

The Treasury-bill section of the Permanent Portfolio should include both Treasury bills themselves and a money market fund that invests only in Treasury securities. Such a fund's yearly yield will be roughly 1% less than the yield on Treasury bills.

Treasury bills come in a minimum denomination of $10,000, with larger bills available in increments of $5,000. Most money market funds, on the other hand, require a minimum initial investment of only $1,000—and allow you to add or withdraw any amount you choose.

So, even if your Treasury-bill budget is big enough to invest directly in T-bills, you'll have more flexibility if you put part of it into a money market fund.

With a money market fund, you can control the size of your holdings to the penny, both when you begin and when you make an adjustment. And the money fund account can collect and hold the interest and dividends earned on other investments, earning further interest on such income until you make the next adjustment.[4]

LIVING OFF THE PORTFOLIO

If you rely on your investments for living expenses, you'll need to make withdrawals from the Permanent Portfolio.

Decide on an amount to be withdrawn per calendar quarter. Then withdraw that amount from the money market fund every three months. (The cash holdings will be brought back up to their designated percentage the next time you make a portfolio adjustment.)

How Much You Can Withdraw

Any withdrawal you make will reduce the value of the portfolio. That doesn't mean the portfolio is headed toward zero, however. Over the long run, withdrawals will or will not cause the portfolio to shrink— depending on whether or not you take money out more rapidly than it's being replaced by dividends, interest, and appreciation of investments.

How much you can afford to withdraw is partly a personal matter,

[4]Money market funds are discussed further on page 349.

depending on factors such as how long you expect to live and how much capital you want to leave for your heirs. Some people are willing to let their capital run down somewhat, so long as they are sure it won't run out. Others are determined to conserve their capital even as they live off it.

Were there no personal factors to consider, the question of how much you can afford to withdraw still would be difficult to answer. You can't forecast the portfolio's earnings (the total of interest, dividends, and appreciation of investments), nor do you know how deeply inflation will dig into the purchasing power of the earnings.

As a starting point, I believe it's reasonable to expect a Permanent Portfolio to earn, over a period of years, an average yearly return of at least 5% above the inflation rate. That is, if inflation averages 6% over the next decade, the portfolio should earn an average return of at least 11% per year.

Although the actual return could easily be greater, I prefer to play it safe by counting on no more than 5% per year above the rate of inflation. There will be years in which the portfolio's after-inflation growth falls short of 5%, and even some years in which the portfolio's value falls. But those periods should be offset by years in which the real growth is much better than 5%.[5]

Of course, in inflationary times, there will be years of very high growth in the portfolio's *nominal* value (the number of dollars). But the real return, after allowing for inflation, may be no better than 5%.

Given this minimum rate of return, you should be able to withdraw 5% of whatever the portfolio is worth each year, and your capital will retain the same purchasing power that it started with.

If, as I consider likely, the portfolio's overall return exceeds the inflation rate by more than 5%, the portfolio's purchasing-power value will grow—even while you make withdrawals.

If you withdraw money from the portfolio for living expenses, you have to keep your eye on the long-term growth of the entire portfolio, but that's all you have to worry about.

It doesn't matter whether the money you withdraw was earned as interest, dividends, or appreciation. It doesn't even matter whether the portfolio has appreciated before you withdraw the money you need. The only consideration is that you don't, over a period of years, withdraw so much that you're spending capital you'll wish you had held on to.

[5]For the 1970–1987 period, the average growth rate in the hypothetical portfolio was 12.0%, or 5.2% above the inflation rate.

How the Income Is Produced

There's no special connection between the interest and dividends the portfolio earns and the money you withdraw. Interest and dividends are just two ways by which the portfolio produces value; a third way is through increases in the prices of investments.

If you think the money you spend must be limited to earnings from interest and dividends (in accordance with the age-old advice to "live off the income, not the capital"), you'll most likely choose investments on the basis of their interest or dividend yield.

Doing so can lead you unintentionally to *consume* capital, rather than conserve it—because you'll wind up with a portfolio that falls far short of providing the safety, balance, and profit potential a Permanent Portfolio must have.

Suppose that in 1970 you had put your capital into long-term Treasury bonds yielding 6%, with the thought that you would live on the income and preserve the capital. Consumer prices doubled during the 1970s—cutting the purchasing power of the bond interest in half, and cutting your standard of living in half as well.

Replacing the bonds in 1980 with issues that offered a higher yield wouldn't have restored your standard of living. Higher-yielding bonds were available, but higher interest rates had cut 20% from the market value of the bonds you already owned.

You thought you were "living off the income, not the capital," but your capital had shrunk 20% in dollar value—and 60% in actual purchasing power. And the income was buying only half the living standard expected of it.

Meanwhile, the value of a safe, balanced Permanent Portfolio—containing stocks, gold, Treasury bills, and Treasury bonds—grew during the 1970s by 13.2% per year. You could have withdrawn 6% of its starting value every year even as your capital was doubling, and thus stayed even with inflation.

If the Income Isn't Enough

If you believe you need more income than a balanced and diversified portfolio would deliver, the problem doesn't lie with the concept of the Permanent Portfolio. The shortfall means that your capital isn't large enough to provide both safety and the level of income you want.

In that case, you have to choose among (1) living on less, (2) earning income in addition to what your investments provide, (3) drawing down the capital over the years, or (4) taking chances by relying on an unsafe portfolio. There are no other choices.

Tax Benefits

The Permanent Portfolio has a further advantage over the "high-income" portfolio. By living off capital appreciation, rather than only current yield, you pay less in tax—even if you spend all the appreciation.

When you sell part of an investment that has appreciated, you pay tax only on the excess of the selling price over the buying price. Thus only part of the proceeds is taxable; the rest is a tax-free return of capital.

As a result, you need less gross income from the portfolio, since less of the income will go to the tax collector.

AGE, GENDER, & WEALTH

Whether you're young, old, single, married, divorced, widowed, male, female, rich, poor, or none of the above, the makeup of your Permanent Portfolio shouldn't be affected much by who you are.

The principal difference between you and the rest of the population is in how much you can afford to devote to a Variable Portfolio—or whether you even want to have a Variable Portfolio. In addition, if you're retired, you may want to draw living expenses from the Permanent Portfolio, as I've just discussed.

Otherwise, the Permanent Portfolio concept serves the same purpose for everyone—to provide safety and a modest profit. Taking risks to make bigger profits is the business of the Variable Portfolio.

COMPLETE PORTFOLIO

Investment planning disregards personal-use items such as autos, furniture, clothing, and other things that you wouldn't sell except to avoid imminent starvation.

But aside from personal items, every part of your wealth normally is considered when planning your investments. This includes any real estate you own (including the house you live in), a business, artwork and other collectibles held as investments, and non-marketable interests in limited partnerships.

All these things are part of your net worth. Changes in their values affect the size of your wealth and influence what needs to be done with the rest of the portfolio.

Inflation-Proofing Your Investments (which I wrote with Terry Coxon) deals solely with the task of establishing and maintaining a Permanent Portfolio. Among other things, it shows how to account for nearly every type of asset you might own. Only part of that will be covered here; to go into all of it again would double the size of this book.

Part III of this book explains how to integrate a number of different investments into the Permanent Portfolio. The guidance it provides should be sufficient for almost everyone. But if you need more help, please consult *Inflation-Proofing*.[6]

CHANGING THE PERCENTAGES

Most likely, you'll spend a few days pondering the structure of your Permanent Portfolio before you start assembling it.

After you've decided what to do, respect your decision. A Permanent Portfolio, by definition, is meant to be permanent. It needn't and shouldn't be altered when your opinions change. If you have strong opinions about coming trends, act on those opinions through the Variable Portfolio.

If you've weighted the percentages a little toward a particular outcome for the economy (such as toward more inflation), I won't argue with a later decision to make the percentages more neutral. Nor would I argue with a decision to reduce the share of the portfolio allotted to any investment beyond the four essential investments.

But I do advise against changing the designated percentages to make the Permanent Portfolio *less* neutral, or to reduce the importance of the four essential investments, or to favor an investment you think will rise in the near or distant future.

Having established a neutral Permanent Portfolio—divided somewhat evenly among the four essential investments—don't fool with it. Let it do its job, and save the tinkering and betting for the Variable Portfolio.

[6]Details of *Inflation-Proofing Your Investments* are given on page 447.

STRATEGY VS. SYSTEM

The two-portfolio strategy differs considerably from an investment "system" of the kind I criticized in Part I.

First, the Permanent Portfolio wasn't designed to re-create what would have worked best in the past. It was created to accomplish certain ends (balance and profit) by means that economic theory indicated were likely to work—and that the past didn't contradict. History was consulted only to discover whether it had already disproved the assumptions I was making.

Second, changes in the strategy weren't made in response to bad results. In fact, the strategy has worked well from its first use in 1977. And no changes were instituted to increase profitability. All changes have been in the direction of greater balance and safety—even at the expense of profitability, and even though the original safety factors hadn't yet been put to an extreme test.

In addition, changes have been made for the sake of convenience and simplicity—because the more complicated the strategy is, the less likely you are to use it consistently.

20

Starting the
Permanent Portfolio

In Part III, we'll look more closely at each investment that might go into a Permanent Portfolio. But it may be easier to understand the concept of a Permanent Portfolio if we take a preliminary walk through the process of establishing and maintaining one.

So imagine that you've finished reading this book and are setting up your own Permanent Portfolio.

WHAT YOU HAVE NOW

The first step is to evaluate what you have now.

You need to estimate the size of your net worth. It isn't necessary to prepare a detailed balance sheet, but it is important to know about how much capital you have, after allowing for debts. Add up the current value of all your investments and other assets—excluding only personal-use property you wouldn't consider selling. Subtract any investment debts (such as margin loans) and major consumer debts. The result is roughly your net worth.

272

DIVISION BETWEEN TWO PORTFOLIOS

The next step is to decide how you'll divide your net worth between the Variable Portfolio and the Permanent Portfolio.

The Variable Portfolio should be funded only with money you can afford to risk losing. Nothing that is precious to you should be permitted to wander outside the Permanent Portfolio.

Some people will decide that everything—100% of their net worth —should go into the Permanent Portfolio, because:

1. No money is available to risk, since everything they have is precious to them; or

2. They have no desire to speculate; or

3. They don't feel competent to speculate and have no desire to learn.

No one *must* have a Variable Portfolio. You don't need to speculate to survive financially; a balanced Permanent Portfolio should take care of you nicely. You should speculate only if you hope thereby to achieve a substantial increase in your wealth—or if you enjoy the adventure.

CREATING THE IDEAL PORTFOLIO

The next step is to choose the fixed, designated percentages for the Permanent Portfolio.

For our purpose in this chapter, we'll assume that you own no illiquid assets—such as a home or a business—that would complicate your decisions. Thus the entire amount allocated to the Permanent Portfolio is available to be used exactly as you think best. (We'll make room for the illiquid investments later.)

No two investors' needs are the same. Consequently, no advisor can prescribe a portfolio for you without first spending time to understand your financial and emotional circumstances. I've had numerous consultations with investors that required several hours to work out a portfolio tailored to the investor's situation.

But I've also come to the conclusion over the years that most investors would be well served by a simple Permanent Portfolio containing nothing but equal measures of the four essential investments.

Of course, this isn't true of everyone. You may have such strong feelings about the direction the economy will take over the next decade that you wouldn't be comfortable unless you weighted your portfolio accordingly. Or you may want to diversify with additional investments.

Or an illiquid investment (or more than one) may dominate your portfolio—making you extremely vulnerable to certain risks, and calling for special planning. The most common example is the ownership of a business or home that makes up 50%, 70%, or more of one's net worth. Or you may have unusual problems, or opportunities, involving tax planning or estate planning that bear on your investment decisions.

Each of these situations calls for different portfolio percentages. We'll discuss some of the possibilities in Parts III and IV.

If you want or need to include other investments in the Permanent Portfolio, I believe their total value should be limited, if practical, to no more than 15% of the total.

Even if you believe that a particular path for the economy is especially likely, I hope you'll consider establishing a neutral portfolio. It will reward you whether you're right or wrong. But if you're determined to weight the portfolio in one direction, please don't give any investment more than 35%. And don't reduce any of the four essential investments to less than 20%.

If you have strong feelings about the future, refer them to the Variable Portfolio. If you can't afford to put enough into the Variable Portfolio to satisfy the desire to act on your opinion, then you can't afford to risk having too much of the Permanent Portfolio in one investment.

SETTING UP THE PORTFOLIO

The next step is to draw up a table that includes the portfolio you have now, the portfolio you want to have, and the changes that will take you from the one to the other. An example of such a table appears on page 275—using, for simplicity, $270 as your entire net worth.

For purposes of this example, we'll continue to assume that your new portfolio is to be divided equally among the four essential investments.

Column 1 names every investment you own now, plus every investment you plan to acquire. Column 2 shows the designated percentages you've worked out for the Permanent Portfolio. Column 3 translates the designated percentages into dollar amounts—the desired holdings of each investment.

Column 4 lists the dollar value of each investment you now hold. And Column 5 shows how much must be bought or sold to arrive at the desired holdings.

ESTABLISHING THE NEW PORTFOLIOS

(#1) Investment	(#2) Desired %	(#3) Desired $	(#4) Current Holdings	(#5) Buy or (Sell)
Gold	25%	$ 50.00	$ 24.26	$ 25.74
Stock-market items	25%	50.00	148.24	(98.24)
Treasury bonds	25%	50.00	8.00	42.00
T-bills, money fund	25%	50.00	29.20	20.80
Silver	—	—	6.20	(6.20)
Corporate bonds	—	—	22.26	(22.26)
Utility stocks	—	—	12.80	(12.80)
Swiss francs	—	—	4.36	(4.36)
Futures contracts	—	—	14.68	(14.68)
Permanent Portfolio	**100%**	**$200.00**	**$270.00**	**(70.00)**
Variable Portfolio	—	70.00	—	70.00
Grand Total	**—**	**$270.00**	**$270.00**	**$ 0**

Column #1: Name of the investment.

Column #2: Designated percentage for the Permanent Portfolio.

Column #3: Dollar amount represented by the designated percentage.

Column #4: Value of current holdings.

Column #5: Dollar amount to be bought or (sold) so that the investment will be at its designated percentage of the Permanent
Portfolio (column #3 less column #4).

If you're going to have a Variable Portfolio, the tabulation will show more to be sold overall than to be bought for the Permanent Portfolio. The difference is the amount that will be going into the Variable Portfolio; it is noted in the final section of the table.

Spring Cleaning

You may decide that some of the investments earmarked for sale could find a place in the Variable Portfolio for now.

In fact, if you're overloaded in one of the essential Permanent Portfolio investments, it may be because you're bullish about its prospects. Rather than sell the excess, you might decide to transfer it into the Variable Portfolio.

But please don't rush to that decision.

This may be the best time for a general housecleaning and financial garage sale. Your current portfolio may include a lot of odds and ends you've picked up over the years, one at a time, making investments without an overall plan. Now may be the easiest time to sweep all that out and get a fresh, organized start.

Try to begin the Variable Portfolio from scratch, with a sum of cash. Once you've actually dumped all the baggage you've acquired over the years—the Edsel stock, the strategic metals, the Imperial Russian bonds, and the Vegematic—you'll probably find that you're delighted to be rid of it all. With the cash in hand, you can buy for the Variable Portfolio whatever seems best *now*—rather than living with what you did two or three or ten years ago.

TAKING ACTION

The next step is to sell everything that won't be kept for either portfolio. If you're like many people, you might find this step to be the hardest.

For one thing, you may be reluctant to sell an investment at a loss—preferring to wait until the price rises, so that you can get your money back. But the fastest way to earn back your loss usually is to sell the loser now and invest the proceeds in something better.

The second reason for reluctance is the opposite of the first. If an investment shows a profit, you might not want to pay income tax on a sale. Although tax considerations are always important, refusing to sell is self-defeating. You obviously don't want to hold on until the price of a winning investment drops—eliminating the profit along with the tax liability.

Whether an investment shows a gain or a loss, the time to sell is when you've decided the investment no longer belongs in the portfolio.

However, after you've identified what needs to be sold, evaluate the tax consequences. Some of the taxable profits may be offset by losses. If there's a sizable net profit overall, you may need to reduce the size of the Variable Portfolio or Permanent Portfolio to provide for the tax you'll have to pay. If so, you might set aside some of the proceeds of the sales in a separate money market fund account until the tax is due.

Buying What You Need

With the sale proceeds in hand, the next step is to buy what you need to bring your holdings in each investment category of the Permanent Portfolio up to its designated percentage.

IN MOTION

Having done all this, you'll have a Permanent Portfolio and—if you want one—a Variable Portfolio.

After the Permanent Portfolio has been established, you don't need to concern yourself with it, except for the once-yearly adjustments.

WHEN TO BUY THE INVESTMENTS

I've often been asked questions like this one:

> I'm setting up my Permanent Portfolio. Should I buy the bonds [or gold or stocks] now, or should I wait until prices are lower? It seems like a bad bargain to buy bonds [or gold or stocks] at these high prices.

I understand the feelings that prompt such a question. But don't look at the bonds (or any other item) as though they were the only investment you're going to make. You are buying a *package* of investments, not betting on any one of them.

If you buy the bonds now and they do indeed decline, the loss probably will be more than offset by a profit on gold. That isn't guaranteed, and it doesn't work day by day, but the process is far more reliable than anyone's forecast of bond prices.

You might have opinions about investment trends at *any* time—not just on the day you start your Permanent Portfolio. But if you fiddle with the portfolio whenever you think you know what's coming, you won't have a Permanent Portfolio; you'll have a Variable Portfolio in disguise. You won't have the stable growth a Permanent Portfolio provides; instead, you'll have erratic swings in value.

I realize that the future can seem pretty obvious at times. But when you get that feeling of omniscience, you might reread Part I of this book—because no matter how obvious the future may seem, it rarely turns out as we expect it to.

In 1978, gold seemed to be very expensive when it rose to over $200 from $103 two years earlier. Why buy gold for the Permanent Portfolio when the metal obviously was close to its peak? But then gold rose above $300. If it was overpriced at $200, it was grossly overpriced at $300. But it continued to rise—to $450, to $600, and on and on until it reached $850, a level beyond the dreams of the most optimistic goldbug.

In the meantime, stocks and bonds were going nowhere, and a portfolio without gold was rapidly losing ground to inflation. Many investors passed up the protection gold provides because they knew gold was no bargain at $200.

The same principle applies to stocks or bonds. In late 1982, the Dow Jones Industrial Average bumped for the sixth time against its historical ceiling of 1000. Who would be foolish enough to buy stocks at an obvious peak? But four years later the Dow was at 2000—double its "ceiling."

In the same way, it often seems that interest rates have gone as low (or as high) as they possibly can—but then they go to a further extreme.

If you decide to wait for a better price before buying something, you could easily wind up waiting a year or two years or several years—losing the profit that a rising price would have brought to your portfolio.

A Permanent Portfolio makes sense only as a whole, with all the parts taken together. It is a complete meal; you won't benefit by treating it as a smorgasbord from which to pick and choose.

MORE TO COME

Part III will discuss the choices to be made for each category in the Permanent Portfolio. And Part IV will discuss some special problems.

Then in Chapter 36 we'll apply the additional information of Parts III and IV to the task of setting up and maintaining the Permanent Portfolio. Having looked at the individual investments that go into the portfolio, we'll be able to be more specific about the process of starting it.

21

Profit Through the Variable Portfolio

It is with the Variable Portfolio that you speculate on investment trends. The portfolio begins with a quantity of cash, from which you draw to act on attractive speculations as they present themselves.

You can learn some things about picking and timing speculations from the lore of fundamental analysis, technical analysis, or other investment schools, but your final decisions about what to buy will be intuitive. So no hard-and-fast rules can be given for choosing speculations.

But a great deal can be learned about the *strategy* of speculation— about limiting losses, letting profits run, and waiting for the best opportunities. We'll cover these topics here and in the two chapters that follow.

This chapter discusses principles I believe any speculative strategy should observe. The next chapter explains some of the methods I use in my own Variable Portfolio strategy. And Chapter 23 will cover some matters that arise in operating the Variable Portfolio.

Everything discussed in these three chapters refers to the Variable

Portfolio (and not to the Permanent Portfolio), except where I've explicitly indicated otherwise.[1]

LIMITING LOSSES

When you make an investment, it's natural to focus on the profit you hope to make. But it's more important to be concerned with the potential loss.

Any speculation can turn out to be a loser. No matter how careful your analysis, no matter how shrewd your system, no matter how favorable conditions seem to be, no matter how sure you are, the truth remains that *anything can happen*. There are no sure things in investing or speculating.

The key factor in a speculative strategy is the way in which losses are allowed for, accepted, and limited—in other words, the way in which you control risk. You must have a way to keep any loss within acceptable limits, and thereby assure that no series of losses will wipe out the entire Variable Portfolio—nor even prevent the portfolio from showing a profit overall.

This means that you must have a way to measure in advance how much you might lose on each speculation you consider.

Historical Method

Some investors think it's enough to study the history of an investment or a trading system. They might discover that the average loss for a given investment or system was quite modest—or even that the largest loss was tolerable.

But this approach only prepares you for what is normal; it doesn't allow for everything that's possible. History may be saving its worst case for you to sample personally.

"Lowest Possible Price" Method

The most common method for measuring potential loss is to try to estimate how low an investment might go. Here's a hypothetical example:

---

[1]As I've said before, you don't have to have a Variable Portfolio. If you have no desire to speculate, please feel free to skip over to Chapter 24 on page 311.

The price of Xcorp stock is now $40. Because of [whatever reason], the lowest possible level to which it could drop is $36. Thus, for an investment made now at $40, the maximum possible loss is only $4, or 10%.

But this isn't a method for limiting risk. It's simply an assertion about the future.

The lowest possible price for any investment is zero. Every investment has the potential to be a total loss—because some unforeseen event or circumstance makes the investment eminently unpopular, or because the product related to the investment becomes worthless, or the dealer holding the investment fails, or the government intervenes in some way to prevent you from trading the investment for money.

The full value of any investment is at risk at all times. The Permanent Portfolio handles this risk by diversifying in a number of different ways. But the Variable Portfolio focuses on individual opportunities —and so is more exposed and more vulnerable.

I realize that investment prices rarely drop to zero. But above zero there's no firm floor that provides an absolute minimum price. The financial graveyard is filled with investors who relied on "price floors" that collapsed—prices at which central banks certainly would support the price of gold, levels below which the Federal Reserve wouldn't possibly let bond prices fall, prices below which commodity production inevitably would dry up.

A belief in a floor price below which an investment can't go isn't the same thing as a limit to the loss that might be suffered.

Bail-Out Point

And a limit on the loss is essential to a profitable strategy.

Many strategies fail because an investor or advisor, while claiming that he accepts losses when necessary, actually enters an investment with only the vague idea that he will sell if the investment "doesn't work out."

What's missing is a clearly defined *bail-out point*—a specific price or event, defined in advance, that tells the investor when the time has come to abandon the investment, sell out, and take his loss. This is the only reliable method for limiting one's loss.

For the bail-out point actually to limit risk, it must be determined before you buy the investment. Once you've paid your money, you have an emotional tie to the investment, and your objectivity is compromised. From then on, there always will be a good reason to delay accepting a loss for another day or another week or another month— which can drag on into years of watching a loss grow larger and larger.

Defining Your Reason

The choice of a bail-out point follows from the reason for making the speculation. So you first must define that reason.

The vague thought that the price of some investment ought to go higher eventually isn't sufficient. You must define your reason precisely, so that you can establish a standard by which subsequent events can tell you whether you were correct.

Here are some examples of different reasons an investor might have had for speculating in gold in early 1985, when the price had fallen to around $300. By being clearly defined, each reason points to a specific bail-out point:

1. "A 29-month price decline halted around $300 in 1982. It appears that $300 is a support level at which many people want to buy. This buying power could hold gold at around $300 until inflation picks up and triggers a new bull market—and I believe inflation *will* pick up. I'm willing to take a chance and buy around $300. But a decline much below $300 would mean that the support wasn't strong enough for my plan to work. So I'll commit myself to getting out if the price drops to $275."

2. "The decline has lasted a long time and is now slowing down. So we may be overdue for gold to turn upward. I'm willing to risk a loss of about 10% on that possibility. Thus, if the price drops to $270 (from a $300 purchase price), I'll get out."

3. "Gold may still be in a bear market, but it should be ready for at least a bear-market rally. The fall has already slowed somewhat, which may be the prelude to a rally of $50 or more. I'd be willing to risk $10 per ounce on such a possibility; the potential reward doesn't warrant a larger risk. So, if the price drops to $290, I'll give up and sell out."

4. "We must be getting close to the turnaround for gold, but I don't believe I can foresee when the bear market will end. So I'll allocate a certain amount to speculate that we're close to a turnaround. I'll invest half of that amount now—at $300. If the price drops to $250 *or* rises to $350, I'll invest the other half. But I'll get out in any of the following cases: (a) if the price drops to $225; (b) if the second

half of the gold budget hasn't been invested by June 1986; or (c) if the price is still under $275 at the end of 1985.''

In each of these examples, the rationale for the investment is defined precisely (not just ''Gold is a good buy at these prices''), and it clearly points to a specific bail-out point (not just ''I'll sell if things don't work out'').

I'm not saying *I* would act on all four rationales—only that each example clearly defines the investor's reasoning and the allowable loss.

Always a Bail-Out Point

Any number of considerations might tell you that an investment is attractive and timely—such as that its price is below your estimate of its fundamental value, or that technical analysis reveals an upward breakout. It may even be just that the market ''feels right'' to you.

But, whatever your reason for making the investment, you must define it in a way that sets a standard for deciding when your opinion has been disproved. And that should lead to the pegging of a precise bail-out point.

No speculative position can be open-ended, to be kept however long it takes to succeed. Such a speculation could immobilize your capital for a long period—rendering it unavailable for attractive alternatives.

There has to be a bail-out point, chosen in advance, at which you'll give up, sell the investment, accept a loss, and free the remaining capital for other opportunities.

Faint Heart

When a losing investment falls to the sell point you had chosen, you may feel that only your timing has been wrong—that the price is falling just a little further than you had imagined it might, and taking just a little longer before doing what you'd expected of it.

But that might be true of anything at any time. If you invoke that possibility as an excuse for not selling, you can assume that your Variable Portfolio will run out of money eventually.

To be successful, a speculator has to be able to say, ''My expectation was wrong; the investment isn't doing what I'd hoped for it, so I must get out.''

This is the case whether the expectation was for an investment to rally "this week"—or for interest rates to fall "soon"—or for a deflation to occur "this year"—or a runaway inflation to start "within the next few years."

No matter what you expect or how long you expect it to take, you must establish a precise standard for each speculation—some event whose occurrence would tell you that your expectation hasn't worked out and that you should abandon the investment.

Once you've defined the event that would prove your expectation wrong, you can translate that into a specific price at which you'll bail out. And that tells you, in advance, how many dollars you would lose if the investment should turn out badly.

Now your loss is limited.

When an investor tries to limit his loss with a promise to sell if the investment "doesn't work out," the eventual loss usually turns out to be much greater than he believed likely.

And even if a losing investment does eventually come back and produce a profit, the gain still could be too small to compensate for (1) the length of time the investor had to keep the investment, (2) the size of the loss he endured while waiting, and (3) the discomfort in carrying the loss for so long.

POTENTIAL GAIN

The potential loss for an investment can be identified fairly closely—since it's simply the difference between the buying price and the bail-out point.

The potential gain, on the other hand, is harder to pin down.

I could target a price at which I believe I'll sell and take a profit. But I don't know that the price will be reached. Nor do I know whether I'd still want to sell if it *were* reached. And something might cause me to get out with a profit at a price lower than the target.

The potential gain is always vague. You may feel strongly that the price is going up, but there's no way to know how far or how fast.

Fundamental analysis can't help, because an investment price rarely rises to its fundamental value and then stops. And measuring devices of technical analysis or wave analysis are simply attempts to endow mathematics with a role it can't play.

We can't know in advance where an uptrend will end. But we can get an idea of the magnitude of the potential gain. And we can use that to decide whether the investment seems to be a good gamble.

Estimating Potential Gain

An estimate of the potential gain is always made with one eye on the past.

For example, if a given stock has barely doubled in previous bull markets, you wouldn't estimate its potential gain now to be 400%—unless you believed that something had happened to alter its character.

Usually, if you think an investment is entering a bull market, or is already in one, the gain achieved in its last bull market is the starting point for your analysis. You then consider factors that suggest the investment might do better or worse than it did last time.

From this, you make a soft, fuzzy, imprecise estimate of what the top of this uptrend could be—which is the best that anyone can do.

Your estimate of the potential top isn't a prediction, nor a promise to sell if the price reaches that level. The estimate is only an attempt to establish the *magnitude* of the potential gain.

REWARD-RISK RATIO

Neither the potential loss you've defined nor the potential gain you've estimated means anything by itself. It's the comparison of the two, the reward-risk ratio, that tells whether the investment makes sense.

For example, if the potential gain seems to be around 120% (of the amount of the purchase) and the possible loss can be limited to 15%, the reward-risk ratio is 8-to-1 (120 ÷ 15 = 8).

It's important to identify the reward-risk ratio for any investment. It's even more important to establish a minimum standard against which to judge the reward-risk ratio of every proposed investment. Otherwise, you can be lured into speculations in which the odds aren't really in your favor.

For example, here's a comment typical of many that I've read:

> The potential gain on this transaction is $3 per share, while the potential loss is only $2 per share. Thus the risk-reward ratio is favorable.

The statement takes for granted that any speculation is worth considering if the potential gain is greater than the potential loss.

Here's a fancier example that amounts to the same thing:

> Buy gold at $390 with a stop-loss at $380. If the price reaches $400, reverse and go short with a target of $385 and a stop-loss at $410.

In either of these examples, by the time you allow for commissions, bid-ask spreads, and ragged executions, the potential gain may be smaller than the potential loss. More than half of such speculations must succeed for you just to break even.

This stacks the deck against you. In an uncertain world, you have no reason to expect more than an even split between wins and losses—and you could easily lose a majority of your bets. So if your victories are no bigger than your defeats, you'll lose overall.

Most successful traders have more defeats than victories. Success is achieved by making more money from the winners than is given up to the losers—by letting the winners run up big profits while selling the losers quickly.

You have to look for profits that are big enough to overshadow the losses you'll incur.

5-to-1 & 10-to-1

A high reward-risk ratio is an essential part of a speculative strategy. My minimum is 5-to-1 (a potential gain 5 times as large as the potential loss), but I prefer 10-to-1.

There are several reasons for choosing such a high standard:

1. *The frequency of losses:* The losses could easily outnumber the gains; so the gains must be bigger than the losses.

2. *The possibility of a larger loss:* A loss might turn out to be larger than you've allowed for; the market could fall sharply, causing the investment to be sold below the bail-out point.

3. *The possibility of a smaller profit:* Your estimate of the potential gain is only a guess. The investment might succeed but produce a smaller profit. No matter how high it goes, you're not likely to sell at the very top.

Not only should the gains outweigh the losses, you should be shooting for large gains in the portfolio overall. Your return on the Permanent Portfolio probably will average 10% or more per year while requiring almost no attention. If you're going to trouble yourself with a Variable Portfolio, you should hope that the capital you divert to it will produce a better return than it would earn in the Permanent Portfolio.

And the return should be *much* better to warrant the effort involved. Consider the money and time you spend on newsletters and investment books; remember the guilt you feel when you see them piled up in the corner, unread. Weigh the time you spend thinking about your investments, struggling to stay awake during speeches at investment seminars, arguing with your spouse over where the money should be invested, putting a good face on your results at cocktail parties.

No one *has* to have a Variable Portfolio. If you undertake the risk, the effort, and the expense to have one, your objective should be large profits. A yearly gain for the Variable Portfolio of 10% to 15% or so isn't worth the trouble—given that the money would have earned almost as much in a Permanent Portfolio with little effort and risk.

Despite your best efforts, the Variable Portfolio may wind up the year with a small gain (or even a loss), but the goal should be much higher.

And a large overall gain isn't likely to come from a series of small gains. You can be nickel-and-dimed to death earning small profits that don't outweigh your losses—with transaction costs nibbling at both the winners and the losers.

I think the Variable Portfolio should sit in Treasury bills or a money market fund until an exciting opportunity comes along—one with a reward-risk ratio of at least 10-to-1, one that might produce a big change in the value of the portfolio.

I haven't always honored the 10-to-1 ratio, nor will I always in the future. But it provides a standard—one that assures that I won't risk 5% to make 6%.

And under no circumstances will I act on a ratio smaller than 5-to-1.

Potential Gain & Reward-Risk Ratio

It's easiest to begin your evaluation of an investment by establishing the potential loss. Then you can estimate the potential gain and, finally, determine whether the reward-risk ratio is large enough.

You also can reverse the last two steps. Having established the potential loss, you could multiply that amount by 10 (the ideal reward-risk ratio) to see what minimum potential gain would be acceptable. Add that to the current price, and decide whether it's reasonable to expect the investment to reach such a target.

Very often, doing this will make you realize that an investment that seems attractive at first glance doesn't really have the potential to justify the risk.

FINDING BIG ODDS

One way or another, you first limit the potential loss of an investment to an acceptable size. Then the size of the reward-risk ratio will depend upon how great the potential gain seems to be.

And the potential gain will be larger when your thinking differs from the prevailing opinion. When your expectations agree with those of the majority, the potential gain usually won't be large enough to satisfy your reward-risk standard.

For example, in 1984 many investors feared that large federal deficits would push interest rates upward. But everyone knew about the deficits—and so interest rates *already* were high enough to reflect the widespread concern.

Consequently, rates were likely to rise a good deal further only if the deficits were considerably larger than expected—or if some other surprise altered the picture. So there wasn't a great deal to be gained from betting on higher interest rates.

But someone betting that rates would *drop* could hope for a large gain because, if it turned out he was right, the market would be caught by surprise and interest rates could move a great distance.

Being in the minority doesn't make you right, but it usually means that you have more to gain if you *are* right.

In general, the market offers big odds only when your interpretation of the situation differs from that of most other investors. When you share the prevailing opinion, the price of the investment probably already reflects what you expect—leaving little room for profit even if things turn out exactly as you expected.

As I said earlier, it's usually best to take the attitude, "If you're aware of it and I'm aware of it, there probably isn't much profit to be made from it."

STOP-LOSSES

I've said that you can limit the potential loss of a speculation only by committing yourself to bail out if the price drops to a certain level.

The most reliable method for enforcing your commitment to sell is to use a stop-loss order—which is an instruction to a broker or dealer to sell your investment automatically if the price drops to a specified level.

A stop-loss is more reliable than a mere intention to sell, for at least two reasons.

First, the stop-loss will be executed automatically, rather than giving you a chance to change your mind. You decided on the bail-out point at a time when you were objective—when you didn't own the investment and it didn't matter personally whether it went up or down.

Now that you own the investment, you don't want to lose—and selling now will make the loss final and irreversible. So when the bail-out point is reached, it's easy to hope, wish, and pray that the price will go up tomorrow, and to hold on for just one more day—and another and another. A stop-loss circumvents those emotions and triggers the sale automatically.

Second, your attention could be elsewhere when the price drops to the bail-out point, and the price could continue downward. By the time you know what's happened and issue a sell order, the price could be 2%, 5%, or more below the bail-out point. But a stop-loss is executed for you as soon as the price touches the specified level.

Don't Lower the Stop-Loss

Once you set the stop-loss, don't lower it—unless you realize that you made a mistake in setting it where you did.

The fact that the price is nearing the stop-loss isn't a reason to lower the stop-loss. It's a reason to suspect that any argument for lowering the stop-loss is just an excuse for hanging on.

Price Gaps

A stop-loss isn't a perfect instrument. It doesn't always limit your loss to the penny, and it doesn't solve every strategic problem.

For example, a stop-loss can't overrule a price gap—a single, sudden leap downward in the price, with no trades in between. A gap usually occurs between one day's closing and the next day's opening, although a gap can occur between one instant and the next.

If your stop-loss falls between the two prices, it will be executed at the lower price—since no one offered to buy your investment at the stop-loss price. Thus your actual loss may be greater than the potential loss you defined before making the investment.

Price Reversal

After your stop-loss has been triggered and the investment sold, the price may turn around and head upward—leaving you behind.

To point out this possibility isn't to criticize the use of stop-losses. It's just a recognition that market actions aren't always consistent with your actions. The market can contradict your actions the day after you buy—or the day after you sell through a stop-loss—or the day after you sell without a stop-loss.

The fact remains that you do have to bail out of a losing investment at some point. A stop-loss is the safest way to assure that you bail out at a price that doesn't break you.

SELLING AT A PROFIT

Since you can't know when an uptrend will end, you can't hope to sell at the very top. But if the speculation prospers, you'll have to sell at some point and take your profit. Deciding when to do so is another critical part of speculating.

If you set a target at which you'll sell and take a profit, your target might not be reached. And while you wait for it, the price might drop far from its actual peak. Or you might sell at your target only to see the price continue upward.

Fortunately, you don't have to pick a selling price. Stop-losses are just as useful with winning investments as they are with those that don't work out.

When the price moves upward, you can cancel the stop-loss order and replace it with a new one that specifies a higher price.

For example, suppose you buy a stock at $31 and place a stop-loss order at $27.50. When the stock has risen above, say, $42, you can raise the stop-loss to, say, $37.50. If the stock should retreat to $37.50, your investment would be sold automatically—leaving you with a profit of about 20%.

If, on the other hand, the stock continues upward (rather than dropping to $37.50), you can raise the stop-loss again and again until, eventually, the stop-loss is triggered by a price decline—which would close out your investment at a substantial profit.

This method is usually called a "trailing stop-loss," because the stop-loss trails behind a rising price.

My best experience with trailing stop-losses occurred when gold was rising in the late 1970s. From an initial level of $155, in 1978, my newsletter raised its suggested stop-loss many times. Finally, the gold was sold in the spring of 1980—when stop-losses were triggered at $565 and $600 per ounce (each stop-loss covering half the Variable Portfolio gold holdings).

I would never sell an investment solely because it seemed to have reached its peak, since that would involve joining the fortune-tellers. It's more realistic, and more profitable, to let your profits grow until the market says "Sell now" by triggering your stop-loss.

The price could go still higher after you sell. But it's less likely to do so after a notable drop has occurred than after you've announced that the peak has been reached.[2]

ENTRY POINTS

Controlling losses is the most important element in a speculative strategy.

As I've discussed, the success of that effort relies on selling before the price drops too far. It also depends a great deal on buying at the right price.

You can't control risk if you buy without regard to price—if you buy just because you're convinced an investment probably will rise eventually. The price at which you buy affects the potential loss and the potential gain—and thus affects both sides of the reward-risk ratio.

A purchase should be made only at what I call an *efficient entry point*—a buying price just above a level at which there's good reason to place a stop-loss.

In the next chapter, I'll discuss my approach to identifying an efficient entry point, and I'll give my thoughts on where stop-losses should be placed. Here I'll point out only that it isn't enough to feel that an investment is cheap at current prices. You have to buy at a price that contributes to an attractive reward-risk ratio.

[2]Some market conditions might make it necessary to sell without using a stop-loss. These are described on page 299.

Limit Orders

Once you've chosen an efficient entry point, the best way to buy is with a limit order.

A limit order is an instruction to a broker or dealer to buy only if the price is at or below a specified point. A limit order states the maximum price you're willing to pay.

As with a stop-loss, a limit order relieves you of the need to watch the investment continually until it drops to the price you're willing to pay. You're assured that the broker will buy for you whenever the price is at or below the level you've specified.

A limit order also assures that you won't pay more than you're willing to pay. If you issue a limit order to buy a stock at $31 or less, you can rest assured that the stock won't be bought if the price shoots upward to $32 or $34 before the purchase can be made.

An investment could have an acceptable potential loss (and reward-risk ratio) if purchased at one price, but be too risky if bought at a price only 5% higher. So a limit order is an important tool.

There's no Variable Portfolio investment that *must* be made. It's far better to be left behind because the investment can't be bought at your limit price than to buy on terms that entail too much risk or offer too little gain.

If you become impatient or afraid you'll miss out if you don't get in now, you expose yourself to a larger potential loss, and you reduce the potential profit—each of which cuts into the investment's reward-risk ratio.

Availability of Limits & Stops

Limit orders and stop-loss orders can be given to a broker or dealer for any investment traded on a stock or commodity exchange. In addition, they're available at most Swiss banks and at some U.S. and Canadian dealers for transactions in gold, silver, and foreign currencies.

You can give a broker an instruction that includes both a limit and a stop-loss, such as:

> For my account 00000, purchase 000 shares [or $00,000 worth] of XYZ stock at a price of $31.00 or less. If this order is filled, place a stop-loss at $27.50 on the shares covered by this purchase.

SUMMARY

Your Variable Portfolio strategy has to include a method for controlling losses—of making sure that no potential loss is open-ended. Even the best stock-picker or market-timer can suffer a series of losses; so he must assure that no individual loss will be fatal.

In addition, any speculation should offer a potential gain that's far greater than the limit you've placed on the loss. I don't consider a speculation attractive unless the potential gain is at least 5 times greater than the potential loss—and a 10-to-1 reward-risk ratio is more likely to make me enthusiastic.

To make sure the reward-risk ratio is large enough, you must pay careful attention to the price at which you enter an investment. Limit orders assure that you never pay more than you've decided you can afford to pay.

Although there's no way to prove it, I believe that more speculative profits are made by limiting the price paid and limiting the loss to be tolerated than by astute selection of investments.

22

Tactics for the Variable Portfolio

This chapter discusses some of the trading methods I use—methods that implement the principles explained in the preceding chapter.

You might decide to use these techniques, those of someone else, or new methods you develop yourself. In any case, I hope you'll evaluate all trading techniques by the principles set out in Chapter 21.

FINDING A STOP-LOSS LEVEL

A stop-loss should be located at a price that, if touched, would tell you that your expectation was wrong and that you should get out of the investment.

This rule assumes that some price levels represent critical junctures for an investment. A fall below such a level would be a signal to sell out.

Support & Resistance

On pages 113–121, I discussed support and resistance, which I believe are the most useful concepts in technical analysis.

A support level is a price area at which you would expect buying volume to increase by enough to stall or stop a price decline. A resistance level is a price area at which you would expect selling volume to increase by enough to stall or stop a price rise. Support and resistance levels are interchangeable; a given level most likely would stall a trend coming from either direction.

How an investment actually behaves when it reaches such a level tells you something about the strength of the current trend. Expect a support-resistance level to halt a price movement and send the price back a ways before the trend resumes. If the price goes right through the level, it's an indication that the trend in that direction is very strong.

Stop-Loss & Entry Point

When considering a speculation, the first thing I look for is an escape route—a logical place for a stop-loss that will get me out of an investment inexpensively when it's going in the wrong direction.

The most efficient place for a stop-loss normally is just below a support level. If the price falls through that support level, I assume that the downtrend is strong and that I'm probably better off getting out of the investment.

So I look for a support level near the current price. I usually would place a stop-loss around 5% below the support level, but it depends on the volatility of the investment.

If I make the investment, the potential loss will be the difference between the stop-loss and the entry point. To keep the difference small, I choose an entry point just above the support level—usually around 5% above it.

Then I consider whether there's good reason to think the investment might rise from the entry point to a price at which the gain would be 10 times the potential loss. If it seems so, I probably will place a limit order to buy the investment at the entry point. The buy order would be accompanied by a stop-loss order.

The Entry-Point Rule

This approach to finding entry points can be used whether an investment is dropping toward a support level or rising toward one.

In either case, the rule for picking an entry point is the same: *Always buy at a price just above a support-resistance level, not below it.*

For example, suppose you see support-resistance for an investment only at prices of $20 and $30. An efficient stop-loss point would be around $19. This makes the area between $21.50 and $30 a no-man's-land. A purchase made at $25, for instance, would entail a potential loss of 24%—which I would consider intolerably large.

Rather than buy between $21.50 and $30, I'd wait for the price either to fall to $21.50 (and buy there with a stop-loss at $19) or to rise to $31 or so (and buy there with a stop-loss at $28 or $29).

Thus there are times when it's better to wait for the price to *rise* before buying. It's safer to buy just above a resistance level than just below one—because the distance to an efficient stop-loss is smaller when you're just above a support-resistance level.

So don't be hurried into buying something by the fact that the price has started moving upward. Missing one buying opportunity doesn't mean you won't have another, and you can limit your loss more effectively after the price has cleared the next resistance level.

Finding Support & Resistance

Although I've spoken of looking for support-resistance levels, they aren't always easy to find.

In many cases, all you see are many little jagged reversals in the trend, with no areas that have clearly stalled major price movements. Or the price may be a long distance from the nearest clear-cut support-resistance you can spot.

My policy is to stay out of a market unless I see a well-defined support-resistance level that allows me to use the entry method I've described. Because of this policy, I'm sometimes left out of rallies I had been expecting.

But I see no alternative. The easiest way to run up a series of losses is to buy without regard to entry prices and bail-out points.

RAISING THE STOP-LOSS

On pages 291–292, I suggested using a trailing stop-loss (raising the stop-loss as the price rises) in order to let your profits run until a price decline stops you out. This involves a number of judgments.

The first question is when to raise the stop-loss. I believe the time to do so is when the price has successfully cleared a resistance level. If there's resistance at $20 and $25, for example, the stop-loss would remain just under $20 until the price has cleared $25.

Another judgment is whether to raise the stop-loss every time a resistance level is cleared. You might not want to do so if there seem to be several resistance levels close together.

A further judgment concerns how high the price must go to establish that a resistance level has been surpassed. If the resistance level appears to be around $40, for example, you shouldn't raise the stop-loss as soon as the price reaches $40.05—because a resistance level isn't a pinpoint.

If you're unable to make such a judgment, I suggest that you consider the price to have cleared the resistance level when it rises 5% above the resistance level's center. That is, if the resistance level is in the area of $40, you would raise the stop-loss only after the price had reached $42.00. Of course, this is only a rule of thumb.

Where to Place the Stop-Loss

Another decision to be made in protecting a successful investment is where to place the new stop-loss.

Normally, as with the original stop-loss, I'd place it 5% or so below the support-resistance level that has just been cleared.

However, there may be times when I believe I can tolerate the risk of setting the stop-loss below the *second* support level beneath the current price—rather than just below the nearest support level.

Whether to allow room for so great a fall will depend upon how volatile the investment is, upon how confident you are about the first support level, and upon how strongly you feel that prices are going higher eventually. Ordinarily, I think it's best to keep the stop-loss under the nearest support level.

The distance to allow between the market price and the stop-loss also depends on how big you expect the hoped-for price rise to be. If you're trying to scalp just a few cents, each stop-loss should be very close to the current price. But if you're looking for a big price rise (as I usually am), you'll want to give the price plenty of room to fluctuate.

In other words, the potential gain limits the potential loss you can tolerate. In addition, no matter how great the potential gain, I'm not likely to give a new speculation the chance to lose more than 10%. Only after an investment has proven that it's in an uptrend am I likely to give it much room to wander.

STOP-LOSS EXCEPTIONS

In a few circumstances, I would sell a successful investment outright—despite my general rule to wait for a stop-loss to be triggered.

One such circumstance is a market that's extremely volatile. If the price has been rising 10% or more per day, it could drop a long way between one day's closing and the next day's opening—with the opening price far below your current stop-loss. The dent in your profit would be larger than you had allowed for.

To avoid this, you might make a sale at the current price, rather than wait for the stop-loss to be triggered. However, I probably would sell only half the investment outright, and take my chances with a stop-loss on the other half—leaving open the possibility of further profit.

Another special situation is a price that's far above the nearest support level. If the price of your investment has gone straight upward for some distance and is in new, high territory, you can't know where support and resistance might show up, or where you should place a stop-loss.

Still, you should place a stop-loss somewhere, perhaps 10% or so below the current price, in order to limit the amount of profit you'll risk giving up.

A third exception is an investment that doesn't seem to be going anywhere. If the price has dallied too long in one area, you might conclude that your expectations of a rally were misguided and sell the investment outright—without waiting for a stop-loss to be triggered. You might simply want to be rid of it, or you might want to switch to a speculation that promises a bigger or quicker profit.

Although I might sell an investment without a stop-loss, I wouldn't hold on to one without a stop-loss—or at least a clearly defined bailout point.

23

Operating the Variable Portfolio

This chapter covers questions you might encounter in operating a Variable Portfolio.

SHARE OF PORTFOLIO TO INVEST

The portion of the Variable Portfolio to risk on any one speculation will depend upon three factors:

1. *Alternatives:* If two or more attractive speculations are competing for your attention, you may want to divide the portfolio among them. The Variable Portfolio can be involved with more than one investment at a time.

2. *Loss potential:* The magnitude of an investment's potential loss should affect the amount of money you give it. An investment might offer a potential gain of 200% and a potential loss that can't be limited (for some reason) to less than 20%. The 10-to-1 reward-risk ratio would be attractive, but you still wouldn't want to risk losing 20% of the entire portfolio on a single speculation. So you might allot 50% or

less of the portfolio to the investment—even if it's the only speculation that interests you now.

3. *The chance of success:* The stronger your belief that the investment will succeed, the more you want to bet on it. But your enthusiasm always should bow to the magnitude of the potential loss.

No formula can measure the confidence you have in a speculation or compare your confidence with the risk. Your decision of how much to invest will be subjective and informal.

Whatever your standards in determining the size of Variable Portfolio investments, the first step should be to decide how much of the portfolio you're willing to risk losing on one investment.

In general, I think that a potential loss of 10% of the *entire* Variable Portfolio is the most I would risk on any single investment. For one thing, I know that a price gap or some other surprise might make the actual loss greater than the potential loss I've estimated. And I prefer to keep the potential loss closer to 5% of the portfolio.

OPTION CONTRACTS

I've discussed the use of limit orders and stop-losses to control risk. Another way to limit risk is with a call option—an instrument that gives you the right to buy an investment at a specified price for a limited period of time. The potential loss is limited absolutely to what you pay for the option.

Options can seem attractive, but their prices often make for poor reward-risk ratios. And their principal attraction—the limitation of risk—can be achieved less expensively by a disciplined use of stop-losses. Consequently, I've seldom employed options or suggested them to readers of my newsletter.

But they remain an alternative to be used on the rare occasion when the price is right. With an option, your hopes remain alive until the option expires—whereas a stop-loss, once executed, is final.

However, even with an option, I prefer to buy only when the underlying investment is priced just above a support level. This reduces the likelihood of buying just before the underlying investment takes a large drop, which would put the option in a loss position at the start of its short life.

Evaluating Options

Because an option can lose so much of its value so fast, the option's entire cost should be considered at risk. You can sell a losing option before its expiration and recoup some part of your cost, but there's no minimum amount you can be sure of recovering.

If you have a reason to expect the investment's price to go up almost immediately, you can reduce the risk by using an option that is fairly short-lived (an option that will expire fairly soon). A short-lived option costs less than a similar option with a longer time to maturity.

But an expectation of quick results is exceptional. Normally, unless a particular option seems especially cheap, you would pass up the short-lived options and choose from among those with the longest life remaining—giving the investment as much time as possible to succeed.

There will be several striking prices among the longest-life options, and you will need to choose among them on the basis of their reward-risk ratios.[1]

To make this choice, first establish a potential price for the underlying investment. Then compute the profit that this would create for each available long-life option. Finally, compare each option's potential net profit with its cost to determine the reward-risk ratio.

Don't be surprised if no option offers an acceptable reward-risk ratio. If that's the case, don't buy any. Otherwise, buy the one with the highest ratio.

Successful Options

When a direct investment is successful, you raise the stop-loss behind the rising price. This locks in a large part of the profit, while leaving the door open to more. Options require a slightly different approach.

When the price of the underlying investment goes up, so does the value of the option. When a successful option approaches its expiration, you can sell it for more than you paid for it—and for more than a new option with a higher striking price would cost.

As each successful option nears expiration, sell it and buy a similar long-lived one with a higher striking price. Bank the difference between the price at which you sell the old option and the price at which you buy the new option.

---

[1] An option's *striking price* is the price at which you're entitled to buy the underlying investment.

Don't use the profit to buy a greater number of options. If you do, you'll simply bet your profits over and over until you lose them.

Eventually, an option will expire worthless. This ends the speculation, just as when the stop-loss for a direct investment is triggered. The profits you've banked along the way will still be yours.

Quantity of Options

Usually, when an option investment doesn't work out, the entire cost of the option is lost. So if you decide to devote, say, 50% of the Variable Portfolio to a speculation, and you choose to invest through options, don't invest 50% of the Variable Portfolio. That would risk losing half the portfolio on one speculation.

Instead, approach the question as though you were investing directly. Determine the quantity of the underlying investment you could buy with the share of the portfolio allocated to it—how many shares of stock, ounces of gold, or whatever. Then buy the number of options that will cover that quantity of the underlying investment.

This way, if the speculation fails, your loss will be approximately what it would have been had you invested in the underlying investment rather than through options.

If the speculation succeeds, your final profit probably will be a bit less than if you had bought the underlying investment. The difference is the cost (or time premium) for the privilege of using options.

SELLING SHORT & PUT OPTIONS

Every example I've given in these chapters has pertained to purchases of investments. The same principles can be applied to selling short, or to buying put options rather than call options.

MARGIN BUYING

Sometimes an investment with a small potential gain and a small potential loss doesn't seem worth the trouble. In such a case, buying on margin (increasing the size of the purchase by using borrowed money) may be the answer.

For example, suppose an investment seems to offer a potential gain of 25% and a potential loss of only 3%—for a reward-risk ratio of 8-to-1. You might want to buy on, say, 33% margin—increasing the potential gain to around 75% and the potential loss to about 9%.

The decision to use margin should be based only on the size of the potential loss, not on the extent of your confidence in the investment.

In considering a margin investment, be sure to allow for the amount of interest you can expect to pay during the probable duration of the investment—subtracting the interest expense from the potential gain, and adding it to the potential loss.

Interest expense can seem negligible until you take the trouble to include it in your calculations. You may be surprised how it alters the economics of an investment.

Don't use margin unless you're sure you understand how it works.

FUTURES MARKETS

Many investments that ordinarily are purchased outright also can be traded in a futures market—where you buy only a claim on the investment. Futures markets are attractive because they're usually highly liquid and the transaction costs are comparatively small.

But I've found that investors sometimes have trouble keeping a proper perspective when they deal in the futures market.

In the futures market, you don't ordinarily pay out the full price of an investment. Instead, you're required to make only a small deposit (5% to 10% of the amount of the purchase), with more payable only if the price of the investment declines.

Investors sometimes think of the deposit (the "margin") as the entire investment—even though they're liable for much more. Thus an investor who intends to put, say, 50% of his Variable Portfolio into a given speculation can wind up with a futures position amounting to 5 to 10 times the size of his Variable Portfolio.

The small decline that triggers a stop-loss could cost him most of his Variable Portfolio, rather than the insignificant percentage he would have lost on a cash investment.

Approach every Variable Portfolio investment as a cash investment—as though you were going to buy the item outright and pay the full price in cash. If it happens to be expedient to buy a particular investment in the futures market, *purchase contracts covering the quantity of the investment you would have purchased in the cash market*.

Don't use the futures market unless you're sure you understand how it works. Otherwise, you could lose your entire Variable Portfolio, or more, in a day.

Futures markets, if you do understand them, can be a convenient medium for Variable Portfolio investments. But they also have their drawbacks.

One is that futures contracts cover only round-number quantities, whereas most investments can be purchased in the cash markets in odd lots. The quantity covered by a single futures contract might be much greater than what you want, or the round numbers may fall considerably above or below the quantity you want.

TYPES OF INVESTMENTS

Because speculations require monitoring and wide-open escape routes, a Variable Portfolio investment must be liquid. This rules out real estate, collectibles, businesses, and partnerships. If you buy them at all, they belong in the Permanent Portfolio.

LOCATION OF PORTFOLIO

The Variable Portfolio doesn't have to be restricted to a single investment account or location, but such a restriction can make the portfolio much simpler to deal with.

Some brokers or dealers handle a wide enough range of investments for almost anyone's Variable Portfolio. These institutions include many stock and commodity brokers, Swiss banks, and some mutual fund families.

Such institutions allow you to switch into or out of a Variable Portfolio investment with a phone call. This saves you the trouble and delay of transferring money from one place to another.

The ideal is to deal with an institution that handles all the investments you're likely to consider for the Variable Portfolio—and preferably one that allows you to use stop-losses and limit orders.

TRANSACTION COSTS

In evaluating any investment, allow for transaction costs—the commissions and, if buying through a dealer, the spread between buying and selling prices. These costs add to the potential loss and diminish the potential profit.

In some cases the costs are insignificant. In others, transaction costs amount to 5% or more of the price of the investment, and reduce the reward-risk ratio substantially.

LEARNING

If you're new to speculating, start slowly. Use only a small portion of the Variable Portfolio on each speculation as you learn. As you go along, you'll discover many things about speculating that neither I nor anyone else bothered to tell you.

Whenever you're in doubt about what you're doing, simply step back and let the opportunity pass. Don't fool with investments, tricks, or markets you don't understand.

LOSSES & MISTAKES

In these chapters on the Variable Portfolio, I haven't referred to a losing investment as a "mistake" or a "failure."

If you've carefully considered your expectations, established a clear-cut bail-out point, and honestly calculated a worthwhile reward-risk ratio, your investment decision is correct.

If a particular investment made with such care results in a loss, the loss isn't an indictment of your reasoning. There's no way by which anyone can know whether a price will rise.

An investment decision *is* a mistake if you buy it only because you're afraid of missing the bandwagon. Or if you make it without establishing a bail-out point. Or if you disregard your reward-risk standard. Or if the reasoning leading to the investment is logically flawed.

In that case, not even an eventual profit can justify the decision.[2]

RECAP

Let's review the main points concerning speculation that have been covered in Part II.

[2]But you don't have to give the profit back.

1. *Speculate only with money you can afford to lose.* Separate your capital into two portfolios. The Permanent Portfolio is a balanced portfolio designed to protect you against whatever may come—earning a modest profit while it does so. The Variable Portfolio uses money you can afford to lose, and is available for speculating on short-term and mid-term trends.

Once you have the safety net of the Permanent Portfolio beneath you, you can afford to be adventurous with the capital in your Variable Portfolio—knowing that you aren't risking what you can't afford to risk.

I believe that the separation of capital between two portfolios is by far the most important requirement for speculating safely.

2. *Have a strategy.* Don't respond one at a time to things that sound good. If you do, you'll discover one day that you have no capital left to respond with.

Establish standards for evaluating speculations, for deciding how much of the Variable Portfolio to invest at one time, for deciding the price at which you will buy and sell.

Develop a strategy by reading the ideas of others; adopt the tactics that fit you, and reject those that don't.

3. *The key factor in any speculative strategy is the way in which losses are limited.* You must decide in advance when you will bail out of a losing investment.

4. *The choice of a bail-out point usually follows from the reasons for making the investment.* But if you buy an investment merely because someone tells you it eventually will go up, there is no deadline, and no event can prove the opinion wrong.

5. *The most effective method of enforcing your plan to bail out, should the market go against you, is to place a stop-loss order.* A stop-loss is an instruction to a broker or dealer to sell the investment automatically if the price drops to a specified level. A stop-loss eliminates the need to watch the market continually, and it eliminates the possibility that you'll delay selling when the bail-out point is touched.

6. *Assume that your losses will outnumber your gains.* Even the best speculators are wrong more often than they're right.

7. *Speculate only when the potential gain appears to be many times the potential loss.* Small gains will be soaked up by the inevitable losses. To make money overall, you need to win big now and then. I never speculate unless the potential gain appears to be at least 5 times the potential loss; and I prefer a 10-to-1 ratio.

8. *Normally, big gains are possible only if your opinion differs from*

the prevailing view. Don't expect to make money just by being contrary. But when you share the majority's view concerning events that affect an investment, the current price probably already reflects most of what you expect. If you're right, the price might not rise very far; and if you're wrong, the price might drop quite a distance.

9. *Use a limit order when you buy.* A limit order is an instruction to a broker to buy only if the investment is at or below a specified price. A limit order assures that you won't increase your potential loss and reduce your potential profit by buying at too high a price.

10. *Support-resistance levels are areas where uptrends or downtrends have been halted in the past by large volumes of trading.* These are price levels that are likely to challenge any future trend, from either direction. When a price goes through such an area, it's an indication that the trend is very strong.

11. *It is best to buy just above a support-resistance level.* An investment dropping through a support level is a signal that the downtrend is strong and that you should get out. By buying just above a support level, and placing the stop-loss just below it, you can limit your potential loss to a tolerable amount, while reducing the risk of being stopped out prematurely.

12. *If the investment rises, raise the stop-loss behind it so that you don't have to guess when to sell.* Don't try to decide when an uptrend is over. Let the market tell you when to get out.

SYSTEMS & OTHER STRATEGIES

The speculative strategy I've presented isn't the only one that makes sense, of course. I've offered it to help you get your thoughts in motion. Books and newsletters offer many other plans for speculating, as will your own imagination.

Whatever strategy you follow, I believe three rules should be respected always:

1. Establish a balanced, diversified, safe Permanent Portfolio before taking any Variable Portfolio risks. Make sure the funds used for the speculative strategy or system are separate from those in the Permanent Portfolio.

2. Have a clearly defined bail-out point to assure that the loss on every speculation is limited.

3. When in doubt about what you should do, wait for the next opportunity. It will be along soon enough.

PART III

Investment
Vehicles

24

Using Investments Efficiently

This part of the book discusses the four investments that are essential to a Permanent Portfolio. It also covers other investments that investors often decide to include in a Permanent Portfolio, as well as fixed investments (such as a home or a business) that an investor might have to accommodate in his planning.

I won't burden you with my expectations for investments. That would just be "capsule advice," since my opinions might change even before this book comes off the press.

Our purpose in this part is to understand why gold, stocks, cash, and long-term bonds are both necessary and sufficient for a Permanent Portfolio, to evaluate the particular forms in which each investment can be purchased and held, and to decide which forms are suited for the Permanent Portfolio and which are suited for the Variable Portfolio.

And we'll look at silver, other precious metals, real estate, foreign currencies, foreign stocks, collectibles, annuities, life insurance, and a closely held business—in case you're considering one or more of these for your Permanent Portfolio, or in case you already own one that you want to keep or don't know how to get rid of.

CRITERIA

As we look at each investment, we need to keep in mind the requirements of the two portfolios. This will make it easier to decide the form in which an investment should be purchased for either portfolio.

Permanent Portfolio Requirements

For the Permanent Portfolio, the five most important requirements are:

1. *Safety:* A Permanent Portfolio is meant to protect you no matter what happens. So, in weighing alternatives, the decision must always go to the safest.

This means, for example, that you should choose the bond that is least likely to default—not the one with the highest yield.

2. *Economic tie:* The object of the Permanent Portfolio is to have investments that, *as a package*, will protect you no matter what the economy does. This is achieved by having investments that are each tied to a specific economic climate—a climate in which you can count on the investment profiting. You have to be confident that an investment you're relying on will come through when you need it.

That means, for example, that you need gold itself in the portfolio—not gold stocks. When inflation is raging and gold bullion is rising in price, individual mining companies might be hurt—by political edicts, by management errors, by civil disorder, or by other events that prevent gold-mining companies from profiting from inflation.

3. *Fixed character:* Once it is established, you should be able to walk away from a Permanent Portfolio—confident that no event, political or economic, can render it out-of-date. You can't do this unless you're sure that each investment in the portfolio will retain its economic character for the indefinite future.

Thus you shouldn't, for example, include the bonds of an issuer whose credit standing might deteriorate, or the shares of a mutual fund whose investment policy is variable.

4. *Liquidity & Divisibility:* Your Permanent Portfolio will be simpler to manage if most of the investments it holds in each category are easily salable and easily divisible. Although the investments are meant to be held permanently, you will be making small adjustments each year to restore the investments to their designated percentages.

Adjustments will be easier if you own some small-denomination gold coins, along with bullion or one-ounce coins. And it's helpful to have some mutual funds among your stock-market investments, because you can buy or sell an odd number of mutual fund shares without commission or inconvenience.

5. *Volatility:* Except for cash, each investment in a Permanent Portfolio should be capable of wide fluctuations in price. Only then can the small share of the portfolio devoted to the investment have the power to pull the entire portfolio upward.

Thus you need stock-market investments that are more volatile than the standard market averages, as well as Treasury bonds of the longest maturity possible. And nothing less volatile than gold should be trusted to respond adequately to inflation.

Variable Portfolio Qualifications

To be suitable for the Variable Portfolio, an investment should have these attributes:

1. *Public trading:* The investment must trade in a public market—so that you can monitor its price and cut your losses as soon as the price tells you it's time to get out.

2. *Loss limitation:* You must be able to limit the potential loss on every speculation. Thus it makes sense to use investments for which you can place limit orders and stop-losses, or to use an investment such as an option or a warrant—whose purchase price is small compared to the potential gain.

3. *Low transaction costs:* Transaction costs must be small, since you may have to move in and out of the investment several times in order to profit just once.

4. *Divisibility:* The investment should be available in small pieces, so that you can buy roughly the amount you want. You shouldn't have to bend your Variable Portfolio budget to fit a particular contract size or round lot.

STANDARDS

Not all the qualifications for either portfolio will be met in all situations. But they provide standards by which we can judge any investment. They tell us what to look for.

25

Gold

Gold is essential to a Permanent Portfolio. No other investment responds so powerfully and reliably to broad changes in U.S. inflation.

This chapter explains why gold is tied so closely to inflation, how gold responds to non-inflationary crises, and why the price of gold is so volatile. We'll also look at the safest ways to hold gold for the Permanent Portfolio, and the most convenient and economical ways to buy gold for the Variable Portfolio.

GOLD & MONEY

In nearly every country of the world, the type of money most widely used for commerce, and the money most extensively held as a store of value, is the currency issued by the country's government. Whether it be marks in Germany, dollars in the United States, pula in Botswana, or even cruzados in inflationary Brazil, the local currency is used throughout the economy.

To supplement holdings of their own country's currency, a substantial number of people want to hold some portion of their wealth in a foreign currency—either because the home currency is losing value to inflation, or to protect against that possibility.

This demand for foreign money is what concerns us here.

The U.S. Dollar Is #1

Worldwide, the most popular form of foreign money is the U.S. dollar.

Bank accounts denominated in U.S. dollars are commonplace in every country where they're not prohibited by exchange controls or other regulations. Where such accounts aren't legal, U.S. banknotes —$20 bills and the like—are widely circulated.

The U.S. dollar is liquid, acceptable almost everywhere, and— normally—relatively stable in value. So long as the dollar's stability seems likely to continue, the dollar is the first choice of individuals everywhere who want an international form of money.

But the dollar becomes less attractive when it appears that price inflation will diminish its value. And concerns over the dollar's purchasing power affect foreign holders as much as Americans, because persistent U.S. inflation usually causes the dollar to fall in value against other currencies. If that happens, foreigners can expect to get less of their own currency back when the day comes to sell their dollars.

When inflation muddies the future of the dollar, alternatives to the dollar seem brighter—to people both inside and outside the U.S. And the brightest alternative always is gold.

Gold Is #2

Gold is the second most popular international money.

Currencies such as the Swiss franc, the German mark, and the Japanese yen are attractive to investors in many countries. But none offers the liquidity, the instant recognition, the non-dependence on institutions, the history of long-term stability, or the assurances of continued stability that gold provides.

Thus people with dollars tend to move a larger part of their holdings into gold—the second most popular form of money—during periods of U.S. price inflation.

Since the fixed parity between gold and the dollar ended in 1968, the dollar has had plenty of problems with inflation. A dollar buys less today than it did in 1968, while an ounce of gold buys more. Still, the purchasing power of the dollar is much more stable over short periods than that of gold. Month-to-month or year-to-year changes for the dollar have been slight compared to the changes for gold.

The price of gold has been chronically volatile. It can drop more in a bad week than the purchasing power of the dollar drops in a bad year.

But when U.S. inflation heats up, the melting away of purchasing power raises the long-term cost of enjoying the dollar's short-term stability. That higher cost makes gold more attractive than it is when inflation isn't a concern.

This is why gold responds to U.S. inflation—because, during inflationary periods, gold takes (or shares) the place of the U.S. dollar as an international currency for many people. This also explains why gold generally responds primarily to inflation in the U.S.—not to inflation elsewhere.

Crises

Gold's response to non-inflationary crises (such as international tension, military confrontations, political instability or scandal, and the like) depends mostly on the condition of the U.S. dollar. Gold responds bullishly to these crises only when U.S. inflation already has made gold attractive.

A crisis—military, political, or financial—is bullish for *money*. Anyone who feels threatened by the crisis will seek the liquidity, stability, and safety that money provides.

Since the dollar is the world's most popular form of money, a crisis normally is bullish for the dollar—and it appreciates against other currencies. The price of gold responds very little or not at all.

But when U.S. inflation makes the dollar seem less reliable, a good part of the increased demand for money generated by a crisis is directed toward gold. Thus the price of gold jumps upward on bad news—even non-financial bad news—during periods of rising U.S. inflation.

When inflation was weakening the dollar during 1972–1974 and 1977–1979, gold became a more attractive form of money. Those were the days when gold jumped $25 or more in response to a single piece of bad news about banks in trouble or hostages in the Middle East.

But with inflation at 1% to 3% in the mid-1980s, neither an invasion of Grenada, the bombing of Libya, nor the hounding of a U.S. president by the press and Congress could make gold jump.

A crisis is bullish for money. But whether that increased demand for money will be directed toward gold or toward the dollar depends on the confidence people generally have in the dollar's future purchasing power.

So when inflation isn't threatening the U.S. dollar, the price of gold doesn't respond to bad news—no matter how bad the news may be.

Fundamentals & Speculation

The demand for money is the *fundamental* factor that pushes gold upward during a bull market. People around the world buy gold when they believe it is likely to be more stable in the near future than the U.S. dollar. They are looking for protection, not necessarily for profit.

The rise in gold can be intensified by *speculative* activity—speculators buying because they believe an upward trend is in progress. The speculators are looking for profit, not protection.

Gold sometimes rises on bad news during non-inflationary periods because speculators *believe* the bad news will be bullish for gold. But if there's no fundamental underpinning for the rise—no inflation to cause those who are threatened to prefer gold to the dollar—the rally in gold is short-lived.

In Summary

When U.S. price inflation is low, and prospects are good that it will stay low, the U.S. dollar—and not gold—is the beneficiary of the world's troubles.

When inflation is high or threatens to rise, gold is an attractive alternative to the U.S. dollar. During such times, gold is the principal beneficiary of anything that increases the demand for money.

The U.S. dollar is the leading money of the world, and gold is its principal challenger. It hasn't always been that way, and it may not always be. Sufficient inflation in the U.S. could dethrone the dollar —making way for gold or another currency to be king. But, in the late 1980s, we're quite a distance from such an event.[1]

---

[1] What I've said here contradicts some things I've said in previous books, but that's just part of growing up. I'm grateful to Terry Coxon for first calling my attention to gold's role as a competing substitute for the dollar. Needless to say, neither of us presumes to have said the last word on gold.

OTHER PRECIOUS METALS

As we've seen, a direct monetary link runs between gold and U.S. price inflation. But no such link ties inflation to silver, platinum, palladium, or any other precious metal.

Few investors buy silver or platinum for monetary stability. They buy these metals primarily as a speculation—looking for profit. And most of the time, investors are only a minor influence in the markets for these metals.

The fundamental demand for silver, platinum, and palladium is for industrial use, which overwhelms any monetary interest in them. The amount of silver or platinum going into coins—even if you think of those coins as money, rather than as collectible curiosities—is much less than what is consumed in industry. The industrial demand for gold, on the other hand, is a drop in the ocean compared to the monetary demand.[2]

All precious metals rose during the inflationary 1970s. But all other commodities rose, too. Gold and silver did especially well, because they had special reasons: the U.S. government had controlled the price of each for decades, ending the controls in the late 1960s, and this led to explosive, post-control price increases.

There have been lengthy periods when gold and silver have moved in different directions. For example, from mid-1974 to mid-1978, silver spent most of its time between $4 and $5; during that same period, gold rose from $145 to $200, fell back to $104, and then rose to $175, on its way to much higher prices. And gold was in an uptrend during 1985 and 1986—rising from $300 to $400—while silver drifted downward from $6 to $5.

Investing in Other Precious Metals

Any precious metal might seem attractive at any time, and so might be a candidate for the Variable Portfolio. When that seems to be the case, consider the situation, compute a reward-risk ratio, and decide whether the speculation makes sense.

[2]According to Handy & Harman, New York, the 1986 industrial consumption of silver was 380,700,000 ounces, while the world's coinage used only 22,800,000 ounces. And according to Johnson Matthey, London, industrial uses of platinum consumed 2,400,000 ounces in 1986, while investment bars and coins used only 450,000 ounces.

But I see no need to keep any metal other than gold in the Permanent Portfolio. Only gold responds so powerfully and reliably to inflation.

During the 1970s, I suggested both gold and silver for the Permanent Portfolio. But now that silver has compensated for the decades of price control, it no longer has a built-in reason for appreciation. Future long-term price appreciation for silver will depend on the fundamentals for the future—next year's industrial consumption and new production—which aren't matters of concern to the Permanent Portfolio.

DEFLATION

Given the monetary relationship between the dollar and gold, there's not much reason to expect gold to profit from a deflation (a fall in consumer prices), nor even from a financial panic that might accompany a deflationary crash.

A deflation probably would entail a number of problems beyond the purely economic—including fear of civil unrest and political upheaval. But the increased demand for money would be aimed at the dollar, because of its rising purchasing power—not at gold.

On the other hand, a general deflation would raise the threat of widespread U.S. bank failures. And since most dollars are kept in U.S. banks, the fear of bank failures could spark some demand away from the dollar and toward gold—an asset that's independent of the banking system.

But I believe it's safest to assume that the price of gold will fall during a deflation, no matter how much bad news the deflation generates.

PRICE VOLATILITY

There is more price volatility in gold than in perhaps any other investment. The volatility arises from the unusual nature of the supply and demand fundamentals for gold.

The existing stockpile of gold—the quantity held in bank vaults, treasuries, and private hands by investors, dealers, and governments—is roughly 2 billion ounces. The annual production of new gold is 40 to 50 million ounces—only 2% to 2½% of the existing stockpile.

And that newly mined gold does little more than offset the gold consumed by industrial users.[3]

Thus changes in production and consumption—the usual elements of fundamental analysis—are insignificant compared with the huge existing stockpile of gold. Because the supply is virtually fixed, any substantial increase in the demand for gold as money or as a speculation can be satisfied only by sales from *existing holders* of gold.

Most commodities are traded between people whose motives, interests, and considerations are quite different. Normally, the seller of the commodity is in the business of producing it, while the buyer intends to consume it—either directly or by incorporating it into another product. Each party has his own interests, and those interests complement each other—making a mutually profitable exchange possible.

But the demanders and suppliers of gold are largely the same group of people. Their decisions about gold are based on the same central issue—whether the dollar is going to lose purchasing power.

This is why gold is so volatile. Most of the market's participants are weighing the same evidence and acting with the same motivations. They do not pursue opposing, complementary interests that can offset each other.

The considerations that motivate investors to buy gold may also motivate the potential sellers to hold on to what they have. This can force the price upward sharply, since there are many anxious buyers and no willing sellers. The reverse, a steep fall, occurs when the considerations motivate holders to sell but there are very few interested buyers.

The volatility of gold is demonstrated by the fact that, from its low of $35 in 1970, gold rose to a high of $850 in 1980—which was 24 times its price of 10 years earlier. A comparable rise in the Dow Jones Industrial Average from its 1974 low of 577 would take it to 14,027.

This also means that the more traditional fundamental factors—new mining discoveries, government sales of gold, new uses of gold for industry and coinage, and so on—are insignificant matters in the gold market.

For gold, Demand is the senior partner in the firm of Supply &

---

[3]Production and consumption figures are from annual industry reviews by Consolidated Gold Fields, London. The International Monetary Fund estimates the total gold held by governments of the "free world" to be 939 million ounces at the end of 1986 (*International Financial Statistics,* March 1987, page 32). Most estimates of holdings of private parties and Communist governments range around 1 billion ounces—bringing the total existing supply to somewhere around 2 billion ounces.

Demand. Supply is virtually fixed, and so the price rises and falls as demand rises and falls. And the primary demand is the demand for gold as money—egged on by speculative interest.

THE SECURITY OF GOLD

If the future brings extreme problems—runaway inflation, political upheaval, war—gold is the investment your Permanent Portfolio will need the most. It is the one investment that isn't someone else's paper promise.

Most financial assets are obligations due to you. A bond, bank account, or Treasury bill is someone's promise to pay you a number of dollars. A stock is a piece of paper that entitles you to a share of a company's assets and profits—if any.

And unless you maintain a private army, even real estate is a paper promise—since its value depends on the government's restraint in respecting your deed, and on the performance of its promise to protect your property.

Gold is the only investment that stands on its own. It is real money—portable, independent, divisible, durable, and recognizable—and so it survives when everything else fails. Welcome in far more places and circumstances than your American Express card, it is the most reliable source of financial security.

That doesn't mean gold will always have today's value. But it will always have *some* value—no matter what happens to governments or currencies.

It is your portfolio's asset of last resort.

PERMANENT PORTFOLIO GOLD HOLDINGS

Since gold is the last line of defense for your portfolio, you have to be sure to handle it properly.

Don't throw away the benefits of gold by treating it too casually. Don't put too many pieces of paper, too many people, or too many institutions between you and your gold. Buy gold that you can hold in your hand.

Gold stocks, for example, are only partly an investment in gold. Although a gold stock's value is affected by ups and downs in the price of gold, it also is affected by the management of the company, accidents of geology and engineering, relationships with workers, and government policies.

Political problems can cause gold stocks to fall at the very time gold bullion is rising. This was the case in 1985 and 1986, when South African gold stocks were falling while gold was rising.

Gold coins and gold bullion are the only two gold investments appropriate to the Permanent Portfolio. Each gives you possession of the metal itself, rather than someone's promise to deliver it later.

Safekeeping

However, you have to be concerned about the protection of your holdings, and you'll need to find a safe place to store coins and bullion. I believe the following storage arrangements are the only ones to consider:

1. Gold coins in your own possession;
2. Gold bullion or coins stored in a Swiss bank;
3. Gold coins stored in a safe deposit box;
4. Gold bullion or coins stored with a U.S. bank acting as a custodian or trustee.

On page 323, there's a list of U.S. banks that store gold, that deal with the public, and that are monitored closely for safety by the leading gold wholesalers or the futures exchanges.

No matter where you buy the gold, you can arrange to have it shipped to the storage location you choose.

Under no circumstances would I store Permanent Portfolio gold with a U.S. gold dealer. There are many honest and conscientious gold dealers, but there have been too many scandals in which many people have lost gold they thought was completely secure. Guarantees backed up by reputations, and even guarantees supposedly backed by insurance policies, have proven to be meaningless. However, some dealers will arrange storage for you elsewhere, where the gold will be kept by a bank in an account in your name and you're not vulnerable to the gold dealer's policies.

A Swiss bank allows you to store some of the gold outside the country in which you live—where it cannot be fondled by your government. Even if your government were to prohibit you (and every other resident of your country) from holding gold, you probably could

BANKS THAT STORE GOLD

These banks store gold for individual customers, as well as for gold dealers.

Bank of Delaware
519 North Market St.
Wilmington, Delaware 19801
(302) 429-2144
Contact: Stephanie Fortunato

Chase Manhattan Bank N.A.
Precious Metals Vault Service
1 Chase Manhattan Plaza — 2B
New York, New York 10081
(212) 552-1327
Contact: John Monroe

Citibank N.A.
399 Park Avenue — Level C
New York, New York 10043
(212) 599-3630

Iron Mountain Depository Corp.
26 Broadway
New York, New York 10004
(212) 912-8531
Contact: Joe Gilhooley

Republic National Bank of N.Y.
1 West 39th Street
New York, New York 10018
(212) 930-6439
Contact: Dick Ray, Dick Loeffler

Rhode Island Hospital
  Trust National Bank
Precious Metals Department
15 Westminster Street — Suite 915
Providence, Rhode Island 02903
(401) 278-8000, (800) 343-8419

Swiss Bank Corporation
P.O. Box 395
Church Street Station
New York, New York 10008
Attn: Private Clients
(212) 574-3696

Wilmington Trust Company
Rodney Square North
Wilmington, Delaware 19890
Attn: Precious Metals
(302) 651-1000

take your time about complying with the edict—if the gold were beyond the easy reach of your government.[4]

GOLD COINS

Gold coins make it easier to manage the gold budget of the Permanent Portfolio.

The smallest standard bar of gold bullion is 1 kilogram (32.15 ounces) which, at a price of $500 per ounce, would cost $16,000. Most gold coins come in units of 1 ounce or less. This allows you to buy almost exactly the amount of gold you want. Coins also accommodate the small purchases and sales often needed for annual portfolio adjustments.

It isn't necessary to hold all your gold in coins, but they should comprise at least one fourth of your gold budget. Beyond that, you may prefer to use bullion.[5]

Coin Premiums

The table on page 325 provides data for the most common gold coins.

The final column in the table shows the recent *premium* for each coin. This is the percentage by which a coin's price exceeds the market value of the gold content (the gold within the coin).

For example, when the price of gold bullion is $500 per ounce, a coin that contains 1 ounce of gold might sell for $515. The extra $15 is the premium—the price you pay for the convenience of holding gold in small, standardized, recognizable packages. Since $15 is 3% of $500, the premium is stated as 3%.

A coin's premium is not a sales charge or commission. It's more like a deposit on a bottle. Normally, you get the premium back when you resell a coin.

However, premiums fluctuate—just as the price of gold does. So it's wise to buy a coin with a small premium—thereby leaving little room for the premium to become smaller. At a minimum, the coin

---

[4]Swiss bank storage is discussed on pages 401 and 417. A few U.S. dealers are listed on pages 443–444.

[5]Some Swiss banks sell fractional units of gold bullion—making bullion as divisible and convenient as coins.

BULLION COINS
(Gold coins priced close to the value of the gold they contain)

Coin	Gold Ounces	Ask Price	Bid Price	Spread	Premium
American Eagle — 1 oz.	1.0000	$487.25	$476.25	2.3%	4.9%
American Eagle — 1/2 oz.	.5000	248.50	242.50	2.4%	6.9%
American Eagle — 1/4 oz.	.2500	128.25	125.50	2.1%	10.3%
American Eagle — 1/10 oz.	.1000	53.75	52.75	1.9%	15.6%
Canadian Maple Leaf	1.0000	485.75	472.75	2.7%	4.5%
S.A. Krugerrand — 1 oz.	1.0000	473.75	460.75	2.7%	1.9%
S.A. Krugerrand — 1/2 oz.	.5000	240.75	233.75	3.0%	3.5%
S.A. Krugerrand — 1/4 oz.	.2500	121.25	117.25	3.3%	4.3%
Mexican 50-peso	1.2057	584.00	568.00	2.7%	4.2%
Austrian 100 Crown	.9802	462.00	449.75	2.7%	1.4%

Gold bullion: $465.00 per ounce

Gold ounces: The weight of pure gold in the coin, not including any other metals the coin contains.

Ask price: The price at which you can buy from a dealer.

Bid price: The price at which a dealer will buy from you.

Spread: The difference between the bid and ask prices, stated as a percentage of the ask price.

Premium: The amount by which the ask price exceeds the value of the gold contained in the coin. Premiums fluctuate from day to day, but the premiums for these coins are likely to remain somewhat close to the levels shown. To calculate the premium, [a] divide the ask price of the coin by the ounces of gold in the coin; [b] divide the result by the price of gold bullion; [c] subtract 1; and [d] multiply by 100. For the American Eagle 1/2-ounce coin, for example, the calculation is: [a] 248.50 ÷ .5000 = 497.00; [b] 497.00 ÷ 465.00 = 1.069; [c] 1.069 − 1 = .069; [d] .069 × 100 = 6.9%.

Commissions may be charged in addition to the spread.

Source of prices: Monex International, Newport Beach, California, May 29, 1987.

will always be worth the value of its gold content—less the small cost of melting the coin and refining the bullion.[6]

Small Coins

As the table on page 325 shows, the premium is larger for the very small coins. However, you probably should have a few of them.

In the worst kind of circumstance, such as runaway inflation, gold coins might become spending money. In addition, if your Permanent Portfolio is small, the small coins might make it easier to buy the amount called for by gold's designated percentage.

Premiums on 1-ounce coins generally are less than 5%. For the smaller coins, you may have to pay 10% or so. Again, realize that—in most cases—you will recapture the premium when you sell the coin.

IRAs

As of 1987, the American Eagle coins are unique in being permissible holdings for Individual Retirement Accounts (IRAs).

It's important that you don't hold all your gold in a pension plan. Some gold should be in your own possession, or at least beyond the reach of the government.

But you may have occasion to put part of your gold budget into an IRA, in which case American Eagles are the only choice.

Numismatic Coins

Numismatic (rare) coins are inappropriate for the Permanent Portfolio, because they have large premiums that could evaporate.

For example, the U.S. Double Eagle had a premium in early 1987 of around 25%—all of which conceivably could disappear. In fact, the premium used to be over 100%, and was 65% as recently as 1985. If the current premium shrinks, the price of the coin could fall—even as the price of gold remains steady or rises.

Many coin dealers regularly promote new issues of gold coins, such as the commemorative issues of governments. Although the premium

---

[6]In 1987, the refining cost was about 70 cents per ounce.

is never discussed in the advertising, you should assume it's very large. You can use the formula given in the table on page 325 to calculate the premium for any gold coin.

VARIABLE PORTFOLIO HOLDINGS

If you decide at any time to buy gold for the Variable Portfolio, you don't need to be so concerned with the somewhat remote hazards of less-than-perfect storage. You will be betting that the price will increase soon—not buying gold as a hedge against the worst possible conditions.

You'll want small transaction costs, convenience in issuing buy and sell orders, and the availability of limit orders and stop-losses. So you might find it convenient to buy in the futures markets; through a dealer, using his storage facilities; or through a Swiss bank.

The futures market, with low commissions and microscopic buy-sell spreads, is an economical place to trade gold. But if you consider the futures market, please read—and take to heart—the cautionary remarks on pages 304–305.

26

Stock-Market
Investments

Stock-market investments are essential to the balance, stability, and long-term growth of the Permanent Portfolio.

The stock market can provide large profits during periods of general prosperity or gradually declining inflation. Without a healthy stake in the stock market, a Permanent Portfolio wouldn't be sufficiently diversified. Prepared only for the worst, the portfolio could fall victim to good times.

This chapter examines various types of stock-market investments—evaluating each of them by the standards of the Permanent Portfolio and the standards of the Variable Portfolio.

REQUIREMENTS

In Chapter 24, I said that to be suitable for the Variable Portfolio, an investment should be divisible so that you can invest just the amount you choose, and it should trade with low commissions and buy-sell

328

spreads in a liquid market that allows you to limit the potential loss conveniently and cheaply.

For the Permanent Portfolio, a stock-market investment should have these attributes:

1. *Market relationship:* The investment should have a strong tendency to move in the same direction as the general stock market, so that you can count on the investment profiting from general prosperity. The Permanent Portfolio's stock-market investments, as a group, should reflect a broad spectrum of American enterprise; they shouldn't be tied to a single industry or narrow group of industries.

2. *Volatility:* The investment should move further and faster than the general stock market. With this volatility, a small budget can earn a large profit—more than offsetting the losses prosperity would inflict upon other parts of the portfolio.

3. *Convenience:* The investment should be easy to buy, easy to sell, easy to keep track of.

4. *Divisibility:* The investment should be divisible into lots small enough that you can buy roughly the amount called for by your plan for the portfolio, without incurring special transaction costs or other expenses.

5. *Permanence:* Since a Permanent Portfolio shouldn't require regular supervision, the investment should be expected to retain its character for many years. It's not enough that the first four requirements are satisfied today; you should be confident that the investment will continue to satisfy them for the indefinite future.

EVALUATING THE CHOICES

We can apply these criteria to any stock-market investment available —to see whether it should be considered for either the Permanent Portfolio or the Variable Portfolio.

1. Blue-Chip Stocks

The straightforward way to invest in the stock market is to buy a selection of blue-chip stocks—shares of large, well-established companies.

But a Permanent Portfolio requires stocks with high price volatility, so that a small portion of the portfolio can pull the entire portfolio upward during a bull market. Blue-chip stocks don't have the volatility of smaller or more adventurous companies.

You might try to achieve a superior result by picking the "right" blue chips—the stocks that will be the next bull market's star performers. But stock-picking isn't the business of the Permanent Portfolio. You need stocks that will do the job 5 or 10 years from now, as well as next year.

2. Volatile Stocks

Some stocks are especially volatile by nature. They go way up in bull markets and way down in bear markets. Such stocks enable you to get more power from a small stock-market budget.

For example, stocks of stock-brokerage companies normally do exceptionally well during a bull market. Trading volume rises spectacularly during a bull market—producing much greater commission income. In addition, the companies have large holdings of stocks that serve as inventory, and those holdings increase in value during a bull market. It isn't unusual for a brokerage stock to more than double when the Dow Jones Industrial Average rises by only 50%.

A list of highly volatile stocks appears on page 336.

3. Listed Options on Stocks

A call option on a stock entitles you to buy the stock—if you eventually decide to—at a specified price during a specified period of time.

It is now easy to use these options, since they are available for hundreds of stocks, and the options themselves are listed on stock exchanges. But listed options have short lives (nine months at the most), and thus are ill-suited for a Permanent Portfolio.

When the price is right, a listed option may find a place in the Variable Portfolio. But, usually, the reward-risk ratio isn't attractive —for reasons discussed on pages 301–303.

4. Index Futures

Another alternative is to buy futures contracts on stock-market indices.[1]

Futures contracts are available covering the Standard & Poor's 500-Stock Index, the New York Stock Exchange Composite Index, the Value Line Index, and many industry indices. The value of such a futures contract rises and falls with the index on which it's based.

Using a stock-market index eliminates the need to select stocks. But it provides no special price volatility, since the investment corresponds to the market itself. As such, it isn't appropriate for the Permanent Portfolio.[2]

If, based on your expectations for the stock market, a stock index seems to offer an attractive reward-risk ratio, an index futures contract could be useful for the Variable Portfolio.

5. Options on Index Futures

It's also possible to buy a call option on a futures contract covering a stock-market index.

Since the futures price for an index closely follows the index itself, a call option on the futures contract is effectively a call option on the index.

Index options are similar to options on individual stocks. The risk is limited, with an unlimited potential gain. Buying an option on an entire index is more attractive than buying options on individual stocks, because it eliminates the need for picking stocks.

All listed options are too short-lived for the Permanent Portfolio. For the Variable Portfolio, although the reward-risk ratio normally is unattractive, occasionally it may not be so. Thus it's a good idea to evaluate index options whenever you're considering a speculation on the course of the stock market.

---

[1] A futures contract is a contract to buy an asset (or receive its equivalent dollar value) in the future at a price determined in the present. I won't try to explain the workings of the futures markets in this book, because that would take us too far afield.

If you consider using the futures markets for any purpose, learn before you leap. It's possible that more money has been lost in the futures markets through simple misunderstanding of terms and practices than through faulty forecasting.

[2] You can obtain greater volatility by using margin (as though you were buying with borrowed money), but doing so increases the potential loss beyond 100% of the stock-market budget.

6. Warrants

Warrants are a type of option. Like a listed call option, a warrant gives you the right to buy a share of stock in a company at a predetermined, fixed price. But a warrant differs from a listed option in two principal ways.

First, a warrant is issued by the company whose stock the warrant covers—while an option is issued ("written") by another investor or a dealer.

Second, a listed option is short-lived, lasting no longer than 9 months. A warrant normally runs for many years, and a few have no expiration date at all. A warrant's longevity makes it better suited than an option for the Permanent Portfolio.

Warrants were the preferred method for stock-market investments in my newsletter from 1975 to 1984 and in my last three books. The warrants did quite well—providing large gains whenever a substantial stock-market rise occurred, as in 1975 and 1982.

However, warrants are somewhat messy.

For one thing, they're hard to find. A lot of research is needed to ferret out the details of particular issues.[3]

Second, the companies that issue warrants don't happen to represent a broad spectrum of the U.S. economy. By and large, they represent the fringes. Although they generally should profit from any economic boom, there could be a significant disparity between the fates of the major market indices and a group of warrants.

Third, the volume of trading for most warrants is rather small, so careful attention is required in order to avoid buying or selling at unexpected prices.

Fourth, it isn't easy to find the current prices of some warrants.

Although warrants have served me well, I prefer to use something more convenient.

7. Dual-Purpose Funds

In previous books, I also suggested dual-purpose investment funds— which are closed-end investment companies that issue special classes

---

[3]*Value Line Convertibles*, a weekly publication, provides a great deal of information on warrants, but you need to study the information carefully to judge whether a warrant suits your own purposes. Subscription information is on page 441.

of shares. They are designed to be very volatile, but these funds operate on charters of limited life, and there are only a few in existence now.

8. Mutual Funds

Conventional mutual funds have some obvious advantages.[4]

With a single fund, you get a wide diversification of stocks. By using several funds, you also have diversification of management.

Some mutual funds are highly volatile. They move far more in either direction than the general market. But, of course, the risk is always limited to the amount invested.

The minimum investment in most mutual funds is small, and many funds impose no minimum at all on sales and additional purchases— making the yearly Permanent Portfolio adjustments simple. And since some mutual funds charge no commissions, you don't have to worry about large costs on small transactions.

Dealing with three mutual funds is, on the one hand, easier than dealing with a large collection of stocks, warrants, or options. But, on the other hand, the latter can all be handled through one broker, while you have to deal separately with each of the three funds; money has to be transferred to or from each fund whenever there's a transaction.

For the Variable Portfolio, a further drawback is that you can't place a limit order or a stop-loss order for mutual fund shares. You have to issue buy and sell instructions when the time comes.

For most people, I think that mutual funds provide a convenient medium for at least the Permanent Portfolio.

CHOICES

No one stock-market medium is perfect. But I believe you can get along nicely with what's available.

For the Permanent Portfolio, the best alternatives are volatile stocks, volatile mutual funds, and warrants. For the Variable Portfolio, I prefer volatile stocks, mutual funds, and index options.

Most investors should find mutual funds to be the most convenient and efficient medium for the Permanent Portfolio. But for the Variable

---

[4]The use of a mutual fund is explained on page 334.

Portfolio, mutual funds aren't as handy. There's no way to place a limit or stop-loss order. And you need to transfer money into and out of the mutual funds as it comes time to buy or sell.

However, if you use the same mutual funds for both portfolios, the funds become a little more convenient for the Variable Portfolio. The accounts already will be open when you want to make a Variable Portfolio investment, and you may be able to buy the Variable Portfolio shares with a telephone call—even before you send the money to pay for them.

Volatile stocks are advantageous for the Variable Portfolio. They are convenient, since they can be purchased through any stockbroker. They also make sense for a Permanent Portfolio, but you need to buy at least twenty to have sufficient diversification.

Warrants, though cumbersome, are a highly volatile, long-term investment. They are appropriate for the Permanent Portfolio of someone sufficiently ambitious, energetic, and conscientious to handle them. Large transaction costs rule out warrants for the Variable Portfolio, however. Warrants are purchased through a stockbroker.

On pages 335 and 336, you'll find tables listing warrants with long lives and volatile stocks.

Index options are useful for the Variable Portfolio when the reward-risk ratio is satisfactory. They are inappropriate for the Permanent Portfolio because their lives are too short.

The rest of this chapter explains the mechanics of investing in mutual funds and offers suggestions for choosing among them.

MUTUAL FUNDS

An investment company is a firm whose only business is to place its shareholders' capital in other investments—usually securities. If the investments are successful, the shareholders should profit.

A mutual fund is a particular type of investment company. Unlike a corporation, which has a fixed number of shares outstanding that are bought and sold among investors, a mutual fund sells its shares directly to investors. It issues new shares, as needed, to anyone who wants to buy them, and it redeems (buys back) the shares of anyone who wants to sell.

A mutual fund's policies and investment strategies are set forth in its "prospectus"—a legal document that is sent to anyone who inquires about the fund.

LONG-LIFE WARRANTS
(with expiration dates)

Angeles Corp. (1-15-91)
ASARCO, Inc. (8-15-91)
Atlas Corp. (Perpetual)

Bristol-Myers Co. (12-31-94)

Cetus Corp. (6-30-93)
Chieftan Development (10-19-96)
Clabir Corp. (7-29-91)

Federal National Mortgage Assn. (2-25-91)

Genesco Inc. (2-15-93)
Genesco Inc. (10-15-93)
Geothermal Resources International (11-15-91)

Intel Corp. (3-15-92)
Intel Corp. (5-15-95)

Keystone Camera Products (5-7-91)

Eli Lily & Co. (3-31-91)

Michaels Stores (11-15-91)

Navistar International (12-4-92)
Navistar International (12-15-93)

Pan Am Corp. (5-1-93)
Public Service of New Hampshire (10-16-91)

Rymer Co. (10-15-92)

Student Loan Marketing Assn. (8-1-91)

Tri-Star Pictures Inc. (6-1-92)
Tri-Star Pictures Inc. (12-31-93)
Turner Broadcasting Systems (12-15-91)

Varity Corp. (5-31-91)

Wickes Cos. (1-26-92)
World Airways Corp. (5-15-92)

Xidex Corp. (4-16-93)

Source: *Value Line Options & Convertibles*, May 18, 1987.

VOLATILE STOCKS
(with Betas)

Brokerage Services

Advest Group (1.40)
Edwards, A.G. (1.65)
First Boston (1.45)
Hutton, E.F. (1.70)

Merrill Lynch & Co. (1.75)
PaineWebber Group (1.70)
Quick & Reilly Group (1.80)
Salomon Inc. (1.80)

Computers & Computer Software

Apple Computer, Inc.[2] (1.55)
Ashton-Tate[2] (1.50)
COMPAQ Computer Corp. (1.85)
Cray Research (1.40)
Cullinet Software (1.55)
Gerber Scientific (1.70)

Lotus Development Corp.[2] (1.70)
NCR Corp. (1.30)
Prime Computer Inc. (1.35)
Storage Technology (1.50)
Telex Corp. (1.50)
Wang Labs Inc. "B"[1] (1.45)

Drugs

ALZA Corp. "A"[1] (1.50)

Forest Laboratories[1] (1.40)

Electrical, Electronics, & Communications

Advanced Micro Devices (1.60)
Avnet Inc. (1.35)

Aydin Corp. (1.45)
MCI Communications[2] (1.45)

Financial Services & Insurance

American Express (1.50)
Comdisco, Inc. (1.30)
Dreyfus Corp. (1.40)

First Executive Corp. (1.50)
Grubb & Ellis (1.30)
Integrated Resources (1.30)

Leisure Time

Canon Group (1.45)

Reeves Communications (1.40)

Manufactured Housing & Recreational Vehicles

Coachmen Industries (1.65)
Fleetwood Enterprises (1.45)

Redman Industries (1.50)
Winnebago Industries (1.60)

Medical Services & Supplies

American Medical Int. (1.40)
Beverly Enterprises (1.50)
Community Psychiatric (1.35)

Flow General Inc. (1.40)
Humana, Inc. (1.30)
National Medical Enterprises
(1.35)

Real Estate Development & Building

Deltona Corp. (1.50)
Kaufman & Broad (1.80)

National Enterprises (1.50)
Pulte Home (1.50)

Retail

Action Industries[1] (1.35)
Circuit City Stores (1.50)
Home Depot (1.30)

Jamesway Corp. (1.40)
Limited, Inc. (1.45)
Wal-Mart Stores (1.30)

Savings & Loan

Ahmanson, H.F. (1.60)
Gibraltar Financial (1.75)

Golden West Financial (1.55)
Great Western Financial (1.45)

Steel

Bethlehem Steel Corp. (1.45)

Florida Steel Corp. (1.30)

For an explanation of the beta ratings, see *Beta* in the Glossary.

[1]Listed on the American Stock Exchange
[2]Over-the-counter
All other stocks are listed on the New York Stock Exchange.

Source: *The Value Line Investment Survey*, May 15, 1987.

Purchases and redemptions of mutual fund shares are made at prices tied to the fund's "net asset value per share"—a figure that is computed every business day. The net asset value equals the value of all the mutual fund's assets, minus any liabilities, divided by the number of shares outstanding.

When you buy the shares in a fund, you pay the net asset value for that day—plus, with many funds, a sales charge. When you redeem (sell) any shares, the fund buys them back from you at that day's net asset value—minus, with a few funds, a redemption charge.

Subject to the fund's minimum, you can invest whatever sum of money you choose. The amount you invest is divided by the current price to determine the number of shares you receive.

Loads & Redemption Fees

About half of all funds impose a sales charge—commonly referred to as a "front-end load"—on every purchase of shares.

The sales charge pays commissions to salesmen and brokers, and is used also to cover advertising costs. Since the load is spent for sales promotion, it doesn't contribute to (or detract from) a fund's performance—although it obviously reduces the return on your investment.

The typical sales load is 8½%, with reduced rates applying to large purchases. A few "low-load" funds impose a flat 1% or 2% sales charge.

Some funds impose a charge when you redeem your shares. In some cases, it is as high as 5%, but 1% is more common. The redemption charge usually applies only to sales made within a certain time after the purchase—which might be 60 days, several months, or even several years—depending on the fund.

Standards

The standards for choosing a mutual fund are roughly the same for both the Permanent Portfolio and the Variable Portfolio. Here are the attributes I believe you should look for:

1. *Volatility:* The fund should move in the same direction as the general stock market—but farther and faster. For reasons discussed in Chapter 2, past performance isn't a sure guide to future volatility. But if a fund has a stated policy of pursuing high growth and has achieved

high growth during past bull markets for stocks, it probably will be volatile in the future.

2. *Fully invested:* The fund should, as a matter of policy, be fully invested in stocks at all times. You don't want the fund to decide *when* to invest in stocks. Instead, you should be able to rely on it to *stay* in stocks—so that you won't miss a bull market because the fund manager doesn't happen to believe one is under way. The fund's prospectus will tell you whether the fund remains fully invested at all times.

3. *Consistency:* If the fund measures up to your standards, you want to know that it won't change its policies. There's no way to know this for certain, of course. But if the fund hasn't changed its management in many years, the chances are good that its policies aren't in the process of change.

Also, the fund's prospectus will state its "fundamental investment policy," which can't be altered without shareholder approval, and which will mention whether it intends to remain fully invested at all times.

4. *Loads:* Generally, the fund should not have a sales load. There are enough no-load funds from which to choose, so that you don't need to pay an 8½% sales commission. A low-load fund should be considered only if it offers a rare feature that you especially want. Any load above 2% is out of the question for a Variable Portfolio investment, which might move into and out of a fund several times.

5. *Availability:* Each state government has its own individualized security laws, which require a mutual fund to register and gain legal acceptance before offering shares to investors within the state. A fund has to weigh the difficulty and expense of registering in a state against the potential market there. Only a minority of mutual funds are registered for sale in every state.

Some funds won't sell shares to investors in certain foreign countries, because of the securities laws prevailing in those countries. But most funds will sell to a Swiss bank, and most Swiss banks will handle mutual fund accounts for you.

6. *Size:* Up to a point, the size of a fund has no particular effect on either its performance or its volatility. But a fund with $1 billion or more in assets loses its flexibility in choosing stocks in which to invest. It can't specialize in the more volatile, low-priced stocks, because it can't buy enough shares without pushing up the price before it has finished buying.

7. *Diversification:* I think you should split the stock-market budget among at least three funds. Diversification protects against a multitude

of unforeseen possibilities. But the diversification must be authentic. Two stock-market funds that are in the same "family" of funds, or that use the same investment advisor, are only partly independent of each other. Buying both wouldn't give you any more management diversification than buying one.

8. *Switching:* Primarily for the Variable Portfolio, it is helpful if a fund is part of a family of funds that includes a money market fund, a bond fund, possibly a gold-stock fund, and so on. This allows you to keep all or part of your Variable Portfolio in one spot. You can then make changes for the Variable Portfolio with a single phone call to the fund.

9. *Qualified for both portfolios:* It is convenient to use the same mutual funds for both portfolios. That way, the account will already be open when you decide to buy shares for the Variable Portfolio; you'll need only to make a phone call to purchase those shares. So, if you have two portfolios, anything that rules out a fund for one portfolio argues against using it for the other portfolio.

Fund Suggestions

For several years, I have monitored growth mutual funds in my newsletter. Page 340 lists seven no-load stock funds that I've found to be useful for at least the past 3 years—and that are likely to remain useful for the indefinite future.

All eight funds appear to be competently managed. But please bear in mind that I don't mention them because I believe the management has some special skill, talent, or ability. I mention them because their character seems to fit the needs of the Permanent Portfolio or Variable Portfolio.[5]

Picking the Funds

For the Permanent Portfolio, I suggest that you use three to five mutual funds. Select them at random from the eight suggested.

Split the stock-market budget equally among the funds you select. Don't try to pick next year's winners.

[5]Mutual fund prices are listed in a table appearing in most daily newspapers. Manhattan Fund is listed under Neuberger Berman, W. L. Morgan under Vanguard, and Tudor is listed under Weiss Peck Greer.

MUTUAL FUNDS APPROPRIATE
FOR BOTH PORTFOLIOS

Each of these seven funds is very volatile, remains fully invested in stocks as a general rule, has no sales or redemption fees, and is available in virtually every state. Minimum initial investments range between $500 and $2,000. All offer IRAs and Keogh plans. None (except Twentieth Century) has over $1 billion in assets. All (except Manhattan and Tudor) offer quick-redemption procedures.

Columbia Growth Fund
1301 S.W. Fifth, P.O. Box 1350
Portland, Oregon 97207
(503) 222-3600, (800) 547-1037

Scudder Capital Growth Fund, Inc.
345 Park Avenue — 26th Floor
New York, New York 10154
(617) 439-4640, (800) 225-2470

The Evergreen Fund, Inc.
550 Mamaroneck Avenue
Harrison, New York 10528
(212) 828-7700, (800) 235-0064

Tudor Fund
One New York Plaza
New York, New York 10004
(212) 908-9582, (800) 223-3332

Manhattan Fund, Inc.
Neuberger & Berman Mgmt., Inc.
342 Madison Avenue
New York, New York 10173
(212) 850-8300, (800) 367-0770

Twentieth Century Growth Investors
P.O. Box 200
Kansas City, Missouri 64141
(816) 531-5575, (800) 345-2021

W. L. Morgan Growth Fund
Vanguard Financial Center
Valley Forge, Penn. 19482
(215) 648-6000, (800) 662-7447

This information was correct as of May 26, 1987, but is subject to change.

For the Variable Portfolio, use at least three funds at a time. Split the money equally among the funds and don't switch from one to another—moving into the one that did best last week. During a bull market, leadership among the funds will change many times.

Getting Started

To use a mutual fund for the Permanent Portfolio, just call or write to each of the funds you want to use and ask for a prospectus.

From each one, you'll receive a prospectus, sales literature, and an application form. Read the prospectus and the sales brochure carefully and completely. You may discover a reason that a fund I've suggested isn't right for you.

If you plan to use a fund only for the Variable Portfolio, get the prospectus and other information ahead of time—so that you can move quickly when the time comes to buy. If the fund requires only a small minimum investment and accepts telephone additions, you may want to open a small account in advance—so that you can purchase additional shares by phone when you're ready to speculate.

Redeeming Shares

When you're ready to sell mutual funds from the Variable Portfolio, you will want to act quickly, before the market falls further. So you need to arrange ahead of time to get out in a hurry.

The normal procedure for redeeming (selling) shares in a mutual fund is to submit a request in writing, with your signature guaranteed by an officer of a commercial bank or a brokerage firm that's a member of a national stock exchange. You *can't* use a notary public, a savings & loan association, or a credit union.

While it's an inconvenience to get your signature guaranteed, the procedure is a safeguard to protect your account from unauthorized redemptions. The fund wants to be certain that a request to exchange shares for cash is coming from you—not from someone falsely claiming to be you.

Some funds offer a simpler procedure as an alternative. You may give redemption instructions by telephone or telegram, or by mail without a signature guarantee—and have the proceeds of the sale wired to your bank, rather than mailed to you in a check. But a fund will do this only if you agree to two conditions: (1) that you accept the responsibility for any mistakes; and (2) that the proceeds be sent only to a bank account that you've identified in writing in advance. If a fund offers simplified redemptions, mark the shareholder application form to authorize them.

Mail Redemptions

If the Variable Portfolio invests in a fund that redeems shares only by mail, write the redemption letter ahead of time so that it will be ready to send as soon as you want to sell.

The letter can be very simple. If you have only Variable Portfolio shares at the fund, you can say:

Sell all the shares in my account #00000.

If the account at the fund contains shares for both your Permanent Portfolio and Variable Portfolio, say:

Sell 000 shares from my account #00000.

Write and sign each letter in the exact name (or names) in which the account is registered. Leave off the date until later. Address the envelope, but don't seal or mail it.

Get your signature guaranteed ahead of time. If the guarantor balks at guaranteeing the signature on an undated letter, write in that day's date. It shouldn't matter to the fund that the date isn't current.

When the time comes to sell, send the letter by a courier service such as Federal Express (being sure to use the fund's street address) or by the Postal Service's overnight Express Mail. This is not only faster, it's more reliable and it's traceable.

Before you prepare a redemption letter, reread the section of the prospectus concerning redemptions. Mutual funds are sticklers; they often will reject a redemption request because some formality hasn't been observed. If you have any questions, call the fund for guidance.

Then test your redemption letter by redeeming a few shares ahead of time.

VOLATILE STOCK-MARKET INVESTMENTS

It may strike some investors as a little strange to suggest volatile stock-market investments for a Permanent Portfolio, whose first purpose is safety. But the portfolio would be *less* safe without them.

You need gold to protect against inflation. But when inflation is minor or falling, gold can take a beating. That's when stocks take over; but the stock-market investments need to be powerful enough to overcome the losses to gold and pull the entire portfolio upward.

27

Cash
& Cash Equivalents

"Cash" is the supply of dollars you hold as paper currency and checking-account deposits. A "cash equivalent" is an interest-earning investment that is readily spendable, and has the stable value of cash. Examples of cash equivalents include Treasury bills and money market fund accounts. For simplicity, I'll refer to both cash and cash equivalents as *cash*.

Cash enhances the stability of a Permanent Portfolio during those occasional periods when the other essential investments all do badly. A dollar is always a dollar; its price doesn't fluctuate. So the presence of cash will moderate any decline the portfolio suffers. In addition, the interest the cash can earn helps to offset losses suffered by other investments during such a period.

A second benefit of cash is its instant liquidity. It allows you to withdraw money from the portfolio on short notice, if necessary, without cost or inconvenience.

And cash adds protection against a deflation. If consumer prices are falling, the purchasing power of dollars will rise. The purchasing power of cash in the investment markets also rises—which means that the annual portfolio adjustments would add to your Permanent Portfolio's holdings of stocks and gold at bargain prices.

There are many cash equivalents, including commercial paper and negotiable certificates of deposit (CDs). But because a Permanent Portfolio must be protected from credit risks, its cash should be kept in U.S. Treasury securities.

These normally would be Treasury bills, but they also can be Treasury notes or Treasury bonds that will mature within a year. The short maturity is necessary to keep the value stable. You can purchase Treasury securities directly, or invest in them indirectly by buying shares in a money market fund that invests only in Treasury bills.

This chapter explains the workings of Treasury securities and money market funds, discusses the frail underpinnings of the U.S. banking system, and suggests the forms of cash equivalents most appropriate for each of the two portfolios.

TREASURY SECURITIES

"Government securities" are debt instruments (IOUs) issued by a U.S. government agency or department.

Treasury securities are one kind of government security—those issued by the United States Treasury. They include Treasury bills, Treasury notes, and Treasury bonds.

Treasury bills (T-bills) are short-term debts. They are issued with maturities (payoff dates) that are 13 weeks, 26 weeks, or 52 weeks away. The minimum face value (size) of a T-bill is $10,000; larger sizes are available in increments of $5,000 ($15,000, $20,000, and so on).

A T-bill is issued at a discount from its face value, and pays the face value at maturity. The difference between the issue price and the face value is the interest the investor will earn.

Treasury notes are issued with maturities ranging from 2 to 10 years. Most come in denominations of $1,000 and multiples thereof. They are issued at face value (or very close to it), with interest paid twice yearly until maturity.

Treasury bonds are identical to Treasury notes—except that bonds are issued with maturities ranging from 11 to 30 years.

Bonds and notes become short-term instruments (like T-bills) when they are within a year of maturing.

Yields

Unlike some other government securities, Treasury securities are "full faith and credit" obligations of the U.S. government—meaning that the government guarantees to pay them under all circumstances.

If necessary, the U.S. Treasury, in effect, could print the money to pay its debts. And so, next to actual currency, a Treasury security has the smallest credit risk of any dollar instrument. Because of this, Treasury bills pay less interest than commercial paper, certificates of deposit (CDs), and other cash equivalents issued by private companies.

Normally, Treasury bills pay about 1% or so less than large ($100,000 or greater) bank CDs. It makes no sense to jeopardize the long-term safety of a Permanent Portfolio by reaching for the slightly higher return offered by a CD or other instrument.

And because of the unusual way a Treasury bill's interest rate is quoted, its yield is higher than it may appear. The rate quoted in newspapers and by brokers for T-bills isn't the true yield—and it can't be compared directly with rates quoted for CDs, commercial paper, or other debt instruments.

Continuing an archaic practice, T-bill rates are usually quoted as a "bank discount rate." This rate is the difference between the buying price and the face value (stated as a percentage of the face value), multiplied by 360, and divided by the number of days to maturity.

The true yield is always higher than the quoted rate. For example, a 52-week bill selling for 94% of face value would be quoted at a discount of 5.9%, but its actual annual yield would be 6.4% of the amount invested. The size of the difference between the quoted rate and the actual yield depends mostly on where the rate is—the higher the rate, the bigger the difference between the quoted rate and the actual yield.

The "coupon equivalent yield" that is sometimes quoted also understates the actual yield you earn on a Treasury bill. In fact, the true yield is rarely quoted in the financial press. The formula for converting a bank discount rate to a true yield is given in the Glossary on page 493 under "Bank discount basis."

Maturities

When interest rates rise, the prices of existing notes and bonds fall—so that they can remain competitive with new issues offering the higher current interest rates.

The longer its time to maturity, the more a debt instrument's price is affected by changes in current interest rates. A 1% decline in interest rates can cause the market price of a 20-year bond to rise by 10% or more.

A debt instrument is considered to be a cash equivalent only if it matures within a year, because a maturity that close assures that the market value of the instrument won't change much—even when interest rates are changing rapidly.

For the Permanent Portfolio, use 52-week Treasury bills—or use Treasury notes or bonds (which can be bought in denominations of only $1,000) that mature in about a year.

As each item matures, replace it with a new instrument that will mature in about a year. Normally, a broker will do this automatically for you if you ask him. If you use a money market fund, it will do the reinvesting for you—so you don't have to worry about maturities.

Where to Buy Treasury Securities

Treasury securities can be purchased through any stockbroker, U.S. bank, or Swiss bank. Or they can be purchased directly from the Treasury through the Federal Reserve System.[1]

U.S. BANKS

Deposits in U.S. banks or savings and loan associations, including CDs, aren't safe enough for the Permanent Portfolio—even deposits insured by the Federal Deposit Insurance Corporation (FDIC) or other government insurance agencies.

From time to time, bank problems make the headlines—when the Brazilian government stops making debt payments to U.S. banks, or when a large bank announces a big quarterly loss from bad loans. Then the news blows over and we turn to other things.

But the problems of the U.S. banking system are inherent in the way the banks do business. Those problems won't disappear because of good news, good times, or even government bailouts.[2]

---

[1]For information concerning purchases from the Treasury, call any Federal Reserve Bank branch or write to the Board of Governors, Federal Reserve System, Washington, D.C. 20551. Ask for a "Tender for Treasury Bills."

[2]In this section, references to banks apply as well to savings & loan associations and other thrift institutions.

Mismatching Maturities

The principal source of trouble is the banks' mismatching of maturities—better known as borrowing short and lending long.

If you put money into a time deposit due on April 1, and the bank lends the money to someone for repayment by April 1, the bank is matching maturities. You can't demand your money before the bank has a chance to obtain the money by collecting its loan.

But a bank commonly takes from depositors money that's repayable *on demand* and then lends it out on 1-year notes or, worse yet, on 30-year mortgages. The bank thereby makes itself vulnerable to anything that might inspire depositors to withdraw money sooner than expected.

U.S. banks have also created problems for themselves by underestimating the credit risks of borrowers—most notably of Third World governments. But the mismatching of maturities is a more critical problem—one that won't go away, no matter what is done about problem loans and debt suspensions.

It's possible that 90% of the banks in the U.S. are vulnerable to anything that could cause depositors to want to withdraw unusual amounts of money—while the banks are powerless to recover the necessary funds earlier from their borrowers.

Federal Insurance

The assurance that your bank account is safe up to $100,000, given by the Federal Deposit Insurance Corporation, isn't on a par with the safety of Treasury bills. Since the FDIC's insurance fund equals only 1.1% of the deposits it presumes to cover, a widespread run on the banks could quickly exhaust the FDIC's financial resources.[3]

Even if the FDIC somehow finds the money to pay everyone eventually, there might be substantial delays before you could get your hands on your own money.

I realize that everyone knows the government won't let any large bank fail. But if enough banks get into trouble, the cost of keeping them all afloat will be too great—and one more truth that "everyone knows" will bite the dust.

Treasury bills are more secure because even a one-day tardiness in

[3]As of December 31, 1986, according to the *1986 Annual Report* of the Federal Deposit Insurance Corporation.

paying off maturing T-bills would bring the government's own financial machinery to a dead stop. Consequently, Treasury securities should be the last dollar asset to default.

Dealing with Banks

The shaky condition of U.S. banks is one of the factors that might cause a deflationary crash and panic. So you can't depend on banks to protect you against a deflation.

I prefer to minimize my dependence on U.S. banks by keeping no more in the bank than one month's normal expenditures. It isn't inconvenient to keep a low balance. You can replenish your bank account easily just by writing a check on a money market fund.

MONEY MARKET FUNDS

A money market fund is a special type of mutual fund. It invests only in cash equivalents—short-term debt instruments maturing in one year or less—such as Treasury bills, commercial paper, CDs, and the like.

A money market fund earns interest on the investments it makes, and distributes this to its shareholders by declaring daily dividends. For the shareholder, it is much the same thing as having a bank account on which interest compounds daily.

A money market fund account is highly liquid. Once opened, you can add to it or withdraw from it on demand in any amounts. A withdrawal may be mailed as a check to you, or wired to your bank account. But the easiest way to withdraw money is by writing a check drawn on the fund—just as you would write a check drawn on your own bank account.

For many investors, a money market fund is a substitute for a bank—a place to earn interest on ready cash. But the two types of institutions differ considerably.

Unlike a bank, a money market fund can't mismatch its maturities. A money fund assures that it can deliver your money whenever you want it by investing only in money market instruments that it can sell almost instantly. The fund doesn't invest in personal loans and mortgages that are repayable over periods of years.

If every shareholder in a money market fund suddenly wanted to withdraw his money, the fund would be able to liquidate its assets and pay off everyone within a day or so. A "run" would reduce the size of a money market fund, but it wouldn't drive it into bankruptcy—as it would most banks.

However, some money market funds are heavily invested in certificates of deposit. In a banking crisis, some of those CDs may prove to be uncollectable—which would translate into a reduced share price and losses for investors in the fund. That's why I prefer to use only money market funds that restrict their investments to Treasury securities.

Some funds that appear to invest only in Treasury securities actually do so through repurchase agreements ("repos," defined on page 508). It's possible for a fund's entire assets to be in a single repo—a practice I don't consider to be safe. Since you can't easily monitor a money market fund to see how it's handling repos, I think it's best to avoid altogether funds that use repos.

If it's convenient to use more than one fund, I suggest you do so—for a further hedge against the unthinkable.

Three money market funds that invest only in Treasury securities, and that do not use repos, are listed on pages 445–446.

CURRENCY & COINS

To further your independence from the banking system, I believe it makes sense to keep some physical banknotes ($5-bills, $20-bills, and so on) in your own possession, in case there's a bank holiday.

If all banks were closed temporarily by government edict, there would be no medium through which you could withdraw money from your money market fund, nor could you sell your Treasury securities, for so long as the banks were closed. Even though your assets would be safe, they would be inaccessible until the banks reopened.

You wouldn't be the only person without cash, of course. But rather than enjoying misery's company, it would be better to avoid the problem entirely by always having enough cash on hand to cover the expenses you normally incur in a month. The money could be kept in a safe deposit box in a company that isn't a bank or in your home—whatever seems practical.

I also think it's wise to hold some "junk silver coins"—U.S. dimes or quarters that were minted prior to 1965. These coins are 90% silver (unlike the copper-nickel coins in circulation today), and they sell at a price based on the current price of silver bullion.

Having $100 or $200 face value of coins (400 or 800 quarters, for example) provides a hedge against the remote, but not fantastic, possibility of a runaway inflation. During such a period, retail prices would be rising daily, and cash (actual currency) would be virtually worthless. It's possible that silver coins would be the only practical spending money.

Some dealers that sell silver coins are listed on pages 443–444.

CASH IN THE VARIABLE PORTFOLIO

Since the Variable Portfolio should be funded with money you can afford to lose, and since the money may be in cash only part of the time, the safety requirement for cash holdings isn't so strict.

It's convenient to have the uninvested money in a place and a form that permits it to be moved into an investment quickly. So you might use a money market fund operated by the broker with whom you do business or a money fund that's part of a family of mutual funds, or you might keep the money in a dollar account at a Swiss bank.

If it's convenient to invest the idle cash in Treasury bills or a Treasury-only money fund, so much the better—but this isn't essential.

28

Bonds

Long-term bonds are essential to a Permanent Portfolio. They are the only conventional investment likely to show a big profit during a full-scale deflation.

Bonds would profit because interest rates should fall drastically—at least by the time the deflation has run its course. By then, all urgent borrowers either will have been accommodated or will have gone out of business, and a great deal of credit will be in default and wiped off the books. The reduced demand for credit, combined with the disappearance of inflation, would cause a severe fall in interest rates.

That would force bond prices upward. A newly issued $1,000 long-term Treasury bond might pay interest of only 3%, or $30 per year. And so investors would gladly pay as much as $3,000 to receive the $100 yearly interest paid by a 10% bond that had been issued only a few years before.

Bonds also provide profits during periods of gradually declining inflation, because interest rates generally fall during such periods.

This chapter examines different types of bond investments—evaluating them as prospects for the Permanent Portfolio and for the Variable Portfolio.

HOW BONDS WORK

A bond is an IOU issued by a government or corporation. The bond makes interest payments of a fixed amount to the holder of the bond every six months. On its *maturity* date, the bond pays its *face value* (the principal amount) to the bondholder.

The right to receive the semiannual interest payments is sometimes represented by coupons that can be detached from the bond. Thus the amount of interest paid by the bond each year, stated as a percentage of the bond's face value, is known as a bond's *coupon rate*.

Maturities

The more distant a bond's maturity, the more emphatically its price is affected by a change in the general level of interest rates.

A 1% change in current rates causes a change of about 1% in the price of a 1-year debt instrument—such as a 52-week Treasury bill. But the same 1% change in interest rates might move the price of a 20-year Treasury bond by as much as 10%.

By buying the longest term bonds available, you can get a great deal of volatility—which means a large potential profit—from a small investment.

Bond Prices

Most bonds come in denominations as small as $1,000. The $1,000 denomination is the face value, and refers to the amount the bond issuer will pay on the day the bond matures.

A bond's current price depends upon its coupon rate and upon the interest rates paid by bonds of comparable maturity and creditworthiness. If interest rates on similar bonds are higher than a given bond's coupon rate, the bond will sell at a discount from its face value. If prevailing interest rates are lower than the bond's coupon rate, the bond will sell at a premium to its face value. It is through changes in this discount or premium that previously issued bonds remain competitive with newly issued bonds, despite changes in the general level of interest rates.

A bond's price is quoted as a percentage of its face value. Thus a $1,000 bond selling for $950 would be quoted as "95"—since $950 is 95% of $1,000. A $1,000 bond selling for $1,045 would be quoted as "104½."

CRITERIA FOR BONDS

For the Permanent Portfolio, a bond investment should satisfy the following standards:

1. *Long maturity:* To have sufficient volatility, the bond you buy must have a very long time to maturity—at least 25 years.

2. *Call protection:* Some bonds have *call* provisions—which entitle the bond issuer to pay off the bond early, if it's to his advantage, once the call date has passed. The earlier the call date, the less volatility the bond has—since no one can be sure the bond issuer won't decide to call the bond. So unless a bond's call date is at least 25 years away, a call provision disqualifies the bond for the Permanent Portfolio.

3. *Free from credit risk:* In a Permanent Portfolio, a bond's primary function is to provide profit during a deflation. However, it is during a deflation that the greatest number of borrowers will be defaulting on their promises. To avoid having to monitor the portfolio constantly, you need to know for certain that the bond's issuer will never default.

4. *Liquidity:* The bond must be liquid. It must be easy to obtain a price quote at any time, and you should be able to buy and sell in small denominations, so that you can make the annual portfolio adjustment easily.

5. *Dollar-denominated:* The bonds should be denominated in U.S. dollars. Falling interest rates or a deflation in the U.S. don't guarantee that interest rates will fall in other currencies.

U.S. TREASURY BONDS

United States Treasury bonds are ideal for the long-term bond portion of a Permanent Portfolio.[1]

They are virtually free of credit risk, since the U.S. government, if it needs to, can print the money to pay them off. They are highly liquid. And many Treasury bond issues are completely free of call provisions.

Treasury bonds are issued with maturity dates up to 30 years away.

[1]Treasury securities are explained on page 345.

To obtain maximum volatility, I suggest that you buy the longest-maturity bond available, and then replace it when it is within 25 years of maturity.

For example, in mid-1987, the three longest Treasury bonds available were the:

$7\frac{1}{4}$% bond, maturing May 2016;
$7\frac{1}{2}$% bond, maturing November 2016;
$8\frac{3}{4}$% bond, maturing May 2017.

These bonds can't be called early, and so they will remain useful into 1991 or 1992.

Whenever two bonds appear to be similarly qualified, buy the one with the lower coupon rate. It will be slightly more volatile than the other. And slightly more of its return will be paid in the form of a capital gain (that isn't taxable until the bond is sold), as opposed to interest income (that's taxable each year).

Buying Treasury Bonds

U.S. Treasury bonds are traded through bond dealers, which include some large banks and large stockbrokerage firms. Almost any U.S. stockbroker, U.S. bank, or Swiss bank can acquire Treasury bonds for you.

As with other bonds, a Treasury-bond price is quoted as a percentage of its face value, but Treasury bonds are quoted to 1/32 of a percentage point. For instance, $85\frac{1}{2}$ would be quoted as 85 16/32. Any quotation given in print will *look* like a decimal figure, but it won't really be one. For example, 85.16 means 85 16/32—not 85 16/100. A quote of either 85.4 or 85.04 means 85 4/32.

Treasury-bond prices are listed daily in *The Wall Street Journal* and in most metropolitan newspapers. The table on page 356 explains the listings you'll find in newspapers.

The price shown in the newspaper isn't necessarily the price available to you. Bond prices fluctuate throughout the day. And there is a spread between buying and selling prices that can run as high as $1\frac{1}{2}$%, meaning that the price at which you can buy may be $1\frac{1}{2}$% higher than the price at which you can sell.

Some banks and brokers require a minimum purchase. But most will buy any amount for an established customer. Almost all Treasury bonds are available in denominations as small as $1,000.

TREASURY BOND QUOTATIONS
IN DAILY NEWSPAPERS

(1) Date	(2) Rate	(3) Bid	(4) Ask	(5) Chg	(6) Yield
Feb 95	3	92.13	93.13	– 1.2	4.00
May 94-99	8½	97.21	98.5	– 1.13	8.75
Feb 16k	9¼	102.31	103.7	– 1.31	8.94

Column 1: Maturity date of the bond — month and year. Where two years are shown, the first is the "call" year — the earliest year in which the U.S. Treasury may choose to repay ("call") the bond prematurely. "Feb 16" means February 2016. A "k" by the date indicates that interest paid by this bond to bondholders outside the U.S. is exempt from U.S. withholding tax, provided the recipient certifies that he is not a U.S. taxpayer.

Column 2: The interest paid each year, expressed as a percentage of the face value of the bond — the "coupon rate."

Column 3: The price at which dealers are willing to buy the bond in large quantities (usually $1 million or more) from their customers. The price is expressed as a percentage of the bond's face value, with digits to the right of the decimal point representing 1/32s of 1%. Thus 102.31 means 102 31/32% of a bond's face value (a price of $1,029.69 for a $1,000 bond, for example).

Column 4: Same as column 3, except that this is the price at which dealers are willing to sell the bond to their customers.

Column 5: The change in the bid price since yesterday, expressed in percent and 1/32s of 1% of the face value.

Column 6: The current interest return offered by the bond — the interest the bond will pay expressed as a percentage of the bond's bid price, compounded through the life of the bond. Digits to the right of the decimal point are 1/100s of 1%.

Some newspapers display the information in slightly different formats.

CORPORATE & MUNICIPAL BONDS

There are several problems that exclude corporate and municipal bonds from a Permanent Portfolio:

1. *Credit risk:* A Treasury bond will always be paid off—even if the U.S. government has to print the money. Neither a corporation nor a local government can print money to pay its bills, and defaults aren't unknown in these markets. Your Permanent Portfolio isn't permanent if you have to reevaluate credit risks periodically, or if you have to foresee who will and who won't default.

2. *Deflation exposure:* The credit problem will be the worst at the time you need bond profits the most—during a deflation. Most corporate or municipal bond issuers, even those that survive the deflation intact, will be under a cloud of doubt. This will prevent their bonds from matching the price gains of Treasury bonds.

3. *Call provisions:* A Treasury bond could double or triple in price if interest rates dropped to 3% or so. But most corporate and municipal bonds have call provisions that allow the issuer to pay off the bond early—which it would be eager to do once interest rates had fallen below the bond's coupon rate.

In fact, the call provision slows *any* rise in the bond's price—because investors know that the call provision imposes a ceiling beyond which the bond issuer won't allow the price to rise.

Tax Advantages

Because the interest is exempt from federal income tax, municipal bonds are attractive to many investors.

The benefit of tax exemption is already allowed for in the price and yield of a bond, however, which means that the *net* benefit to you won't be much. The yield on a tax-exempt bond is always less than the yield on a fully taxable bond of comparable liquidity, credit risk, and maturity.

Even if the yield on a municipal bond is superior to the after-tax yield on a Treasury bond, you still shouldn't forsake safety for it. You may be able to get the best of both worlds—by deferring income from Treasury bonds through a pension plan, for example. But if you can't, pay the tax and consider the slight after-tax difference to be the price of safety.

GNMAs

Another debt instrument that attracts many investors is the Government National Mortgage Association (GNMA) certificate.

A GNMA certificate represents a share in a pool of mortgages. The holder of a certificate receives monthly payments that include both interest and a partial repayment of principal on the underlying mortgages.

GNMA certificates are, like U.S. Treasury bonds, backed by the full faith and credit of the U.S. government. GNMAs usually yield about 1% to 2% more than Treasury bonds—a bonus that many investors find hard to pass up. But the bonus isn't free.

The most important drawback of GNMAs is that they provide less profit than Treasury bonds when interest rates fall, because GNMA mortgages are repayable by borrowers at any time. When interest rates drop (and bond prices rise), mortgage borrowers have an incentive to prepay their loans and refinance at a lower rate. GNMA investors receive premature repayment of portions of their principal without any capital appreciation.

Treasury bonds without call provisions can't be repaid early. Thus there's no threat that repayments will cut into the appreciation that falling interest rates bring to a bond investment.

An investment in a mutual fund that holds GNMA certificates faces the same problems as a direct investment in the certificates. In addition, you can assume that a fund will be investing in certificates with an *average* maturity of 10 years or less—which would provide far too little volatility for the Permanent Portfolio.

ZERO-COUPON BONDS

In certain cases, a zero-coupon bond might be helpful to a Permanent Portfolio or a Variable Portfolio.

A zero-coupon bond is a variation of a Treasury, corporate, or municipal bond. It earns, but doesn't pay, interest until the bond matures—at which time all the interest is paid out at once.

If a zero-coupon bond has a long time to maturity, it will sell at an extreme discount from its face value, since the stated face value represents both the repayment of the bondbuyer's original investment and the interest that will accumulate and compound over a period of many years.

For example, to provide a 10% rate of return, a $1,000, 20-year zero-coupon bond would be issued at a price of $142—a discount of 86% from its face value. At maturity, the bondholder would receive $142 as a return of principal—plus $858, which is 10% interest on $142 compounded semiannually for 20 years.

Over the bond's life, the price will rise—reaching $1,000 on its maturity date. Along the way, however, the bond's price will fluctuate upward and downward as current interest rates fluctuate.

Appendix D on page 522 provides details of the zero-coupon Treasury-bond market—how the bonds are created, the forms in which they're available, and the tax consequences. The Appendix also points out that commission rates and buy-sell price spreads were quite high in 1987.

Volatility in Zero-Coupon Bonds

Zero-coupon bonds are far more volatile than conventional bonds.

A conventional bond not only promises to pay the principal at the maturity date, it also makes interest payments along the way. But a zero-coupon bond delays all its payments until the maturity date. Thus, if two bonds mature on the same date, the time until a zero-coupon bond makes its single payment is longer than the *average* waiting time for all the payments made by a conventional bond.

Because a bondholder must wait longer to receive any money from a zero-coupon bond, the interest rate that compensates for the wait has a greater impact on the current value of the bond. So any change in the general level of market interest rates will cause a greater change in the current price of a zero-coupon bond than in the price of a conventional bond with the same time to maturity.

With interest rates at 10%, *a 10-year zero-coupon bond is nearly as volatile as a 30-year conventional bond.*

Use for Zero-Coupon Bonds

Zero-coupon bonds are roughly three times as volatile as conventional bonds of the same maturity.

That can make them attractive for the Permanent Portfolio, since the more volatile an investment is, the less money you have to risk in order to achieve a particular level of profit. However, the usefulness of zero-coupon bonds is hampered by large commissions and buy-sell spreads.

And although conventional long-term Treasury bonds don't provide as much volatility, they can provide *enough* volatility to protect against a deflation. So for a portfolio that is generally liquid, there's no advantage in reducing the Treasury-bond budget (by using a more volatile alternative), since no other portion of the portfolio needs the capital that would be saved.[2]

Zero-coupon bonds are advantageous only if you are overburdened with investments that are illiquid, leaving too little cash with which to hedge against a deflation. In that case, you would need to use the available liquid capital in the most powerful way.

BENHAM TARGET MATURITIES TRUST

If your Permanent Portfolio needs zero-coupon bonds, it probably will be more efficient to buy them through Benham Target Maturities Trust. The trust is a mutual fund that invests in zero-coupon Treasury bonds.

The trust offers some advantages over buying zero-coupon bonds directly. As discussed in the Appendix on page 524, the zero-coupon market is a rather mysterious area in which it's hard for the average investor to be sure what he's doing. The trust allows you to deal with a comfortable, familiar, mutual fund investment.

The fund avoids the large buy-sell spreads of the zero-coupon market by dealing in large lots, and by offsetting purchase and redemption orders from its own shareholders.

On the other hand, the fund involves costs that, for a long-term investment, are comparable to the spreads involved in buying zero-coupon bonds directly from a broker. The management fee and expenses come to a maximum of 0.7% per year.

For a fund that manages a stock portfolio for you, a cost of 0.7% yearly is incidental. Similarly, if a money market fund is rolling over Treasury bills for you, the fund is probably saving you more money than it's costing you.

But comparing the costs of the Benham Trust with the purchase of a buy-and-forget zero-coupon bond is a little different. If you buy a bond from a broker and keep it for 20 years, you'll pay the spread

---

[2]Putting the extra capital into Treasury bills would simply reduce the average volatility of the overall dollar position to approximately what it would be using conventional bonds.

only once. Through the fund, you pay the expense every year. And while 0.7% seems small enough, it compounds over 20 years to a cost of 14%.

It's doubtful that any broker will impose a spread that large on you. And, as this market matures, with greater trading volume, more competition, and increased public awareness of the size of the spreads, the spreads are likely to narrow.

For the Variable Portfolio

For the Variable Portfolio, however, the fund is very attractive. A management fee of 0.7% per year on a short-term investment is trivial.

In addition, the fund allows you to invest however much you want in bonds, pick the maturity you want, and even transfer the money from a money market fund account with a phone call.[3]

Fund Details

The minimum investment is $1,000 (or $100 for an IRA). You can choose among portfolios that hold zero-coupon bonds maturing in 1990, 1995, 2000, 2005, 2010, or 2015.

Using the 2010 maturity, you can invest approximately half the amount you would have invested in conventional 30-year Treasury bonds, and achieve roughly the same impact on the portfolio.

Prices for the Benham Target Maturities Trust are reported in the mutual fund listings of most daily newspapers.

CONVENTIONAL MUTUAL FUNDS

There also are a few mutual funds that invest solely in conventional Treasury bonds. These aren't a good alternative for the Permanent Portfolio, however.

For one thing, the management of a mutual fund may try to outperform its competitors by adjusting the maturities of the bonds it holds

---

[3]The trust is part of the Benham Capital Management Group, which includes Capital Preservation Fund (a money market fund that invests only in Treasury bills) and a division that sells gold coins and bullion. You can obtain information by writing to the trust at 755 Page Mill Road, Palo Alto, Calif. 94304, or calling (800) 472-3389 or (415) 858-3620.

as it believes interest rates are rising or falling. Needless to say, it has only an even chance of being right about the direction of the market.

Also, it's very unlikely that a mutual fund's holdings will have an average maturity of 25 to 30 years—even when management expects interest rates to fall. The Permanent Portfolio must have the volatility that long maturities provide.

You would need a mutual fund that is 100% invested in long maturities at all times—and no such fund exists.

Since you can obtain Treasury bonds in denominations as small as $1,000, the liquidity and divisibility of a mutual fund aren't really needed.

But if you do have a very small Permanent Portfolio and require the help a mutual fund can provide, the Benham Target Maturities Trust is the only fund available in 1987 that's appropriate. With it, you can select the maturity you want and keep it.

CHOOSING BONDS

For the Permanent Portfolio, only Treasury bonds provide full security, the assurance that you'll profit during declines in general interest rates, and absolute protection during a deflation.

If you have trouble creating a Permanent Portfolio because of large, illiquid investments that dominate your net worth, you may need more power than a simple Treasury bond provides. In that case, the greater volatility of zero-coupon bonds could allow you to get what you need with a smaller bond budget.

If that's what you require, I suggest that you invest via Benham Target Maturities Trust rather than by buying zero-coupon bonds or receipts from a broker. The zero-coupon bond market is still young. In a few years, it may have a considerably different complexion. Meanwhile, I think it's best to make your investment as liquid as possible. And for the short term, the Benham Target Maturities Trust is far more liquid than buying zero-coupon bonds directly. Its costs won't add up to much over two or three years.

Variable Portfolio

For the Variable Portfolio, any type of bond is suitable if you believe bonds are in a bull market.

If your expectation is simply that interest rates in general are going to fall, corporate bonds may be the most convenient medium because they're traded on the New York and American Stock Exchanges—where limit orders and stop-losses can be used. Brokers who offer firm limit orders and stop-losses on Treasury bonds are hard to find. If you buy corporate bonds, be sure to buy long maturities that have no call provisions.

However, Treasury bonds also have their advantages. You don't have to worry about which issues to select; just take the longest maturity available. That, in turn, means you don't need to diversify. And, usually, commissions and buy-sell spreads are very small in the Treasury-bond market.

It's also possible to buy Treasury-bond futures, which allow you to place limit orders and stop-losses in a market with small commissions and spreads.

A final alternative is the Benham Target Maturity Trust, which combines extreme volatility with the convenience of a mutual fund.

29

Real Estate

Real estate isn't an essential investment for a Permanent Portfolio. Real estate offers no profit or protection to a portfolio that can't be achieved more easily with stocks and gold.

So I'm tempted to end this chapter right here and go on to other matters. But, alas, you probably own real estate, and you will need to allow for it when planning your Permanent Portfolio.

We'll examine several aspects of real estate: how it was affected by the changes in the Internal Revenue Code enacted in 1986, how to deal with real estate in planning your portfolio, and what to do if you're over-invested in real estate.

FUNDAMENTALS

There usually is a fundamental reason for any investment boom. When stocks are in a bull market, it normally is because the prospects for the economy are improving. Gold thrives on an upsurge in U.S. inflation. Silver's big run-up in the 1970s was fueled by a worldwide shortage—the aftermath of a century of intervention in the silver market by the U.S. government.

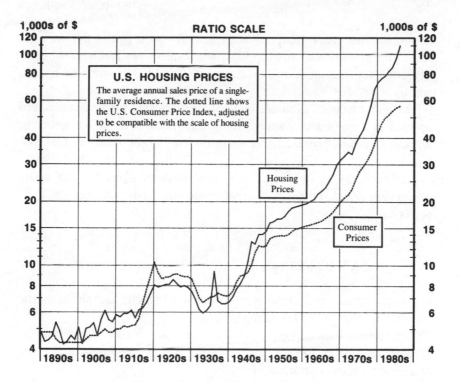

1,000s of $

1,000s of $

U.S. HOUSING PRICES

The average annual sales price of a single-family residence. The dotted line shows the U.S. Consumer Price Index, adjusted to be compatible with the scale of housing prices.

Housing Prices

Consumer Prices

1890s 1900s 1910s 1920s 1930s 1940s 1950s 1960s 1970s 1980s

The forces that move real estate prices are not quite so obvious, however.

Real estate is widely perceived as an inflation hedge, and it's believed that real estate prices shot upward in the 1970s because of inflation. But, as the graph above indicates, housing prices have been in a more-or-less steady uptrend since the start of World War II. This trend has persisted through periods of low inflation, high inflation, and no inflation.

Over the period of 1942–1986, single-family housing prices averaged an increase of 5.9% per year, while inflation averaged 4.7% per year. Housing prices outran inflation during every decade but the 1970s.

Please understand that the most carefully constructed index of housing prices is only a crude indicator of the state of the real estate market. The index doesn't consider all kinds of properties, it isn't even a wholly reliable estimate of single-family housing prices, and it certainly can't reflect your own experience with real estate.[1]

[1]There is no single index (that I'm aware of) covering the entire period in question. I pieced together the index used in the graph from several indices prepared by U.S. government agencies—including, for the period from 1963 through 1986, the average sales price of new and existing single-family homes as compiled by the Federal Home Loan Bank Board.

Because we can't analyze trends in real estate prices the way we can examine trends in stock prices, we'll never really know whether any of the legends about real estate (such as that it's an inflation hedge) are accurate.

The only evidence available indicates that housing prices have moved upward at a somewhat steady clip since World War II—whether or not inflation was present. And we don't know how accurate that evidence is.

However, even though we don't know all the reasons that real estate prices rise, one driving force in real estate obviously has been the U.S. tax code.

TAX BENEFITS

For many years, real estate was America's favorite tax shelter—the pampered child of the tax laws.

Real estate was a popular investment long before there was an income tax system to seek shelter from. But tax savings came to be real estate's most important benefit.

The changes made in the tax code in 1986 ended this, and the effect on the real estate market should be profound. Appendix E on page 528 describes those changes in detail. Here we need only summarize the main points:

1. In many cases, it no longer is possible to take tax deductions that exceed the cash you have invested in a property—which eliminates the possibility of profiting from tax savings alone.

2. In all cases, no more than $25,000 in real estate losses can be used to reduce other taxable income—salary, investments, and so on.

3. In most cases, deductions for mortgage interest on your residence are limited to debt equaling what you paid for your home plus the cost of improvements.

4. Real estate profits are now taxed at the same rate as ordinary income, instead of at lower capital-gain rates.

5. The reduction of the top tax rate to 28% from 50% reduces the need for tax shelters, thereby making real estate's remaining tax deductions less valuable.

How drastically these changes will alter the market for real estate is, of course, impossible to forecast. But it obviously would be a mistake to expect real estate's future to mirror its past.

People will continue to buy homes to live in, and investors will continue to consider tax advantages in deciding whether to buy real estate. But tax benefits should no longer dominate the real estate market.

REAL ESTATE IN A PORTFOLIO

Real estate investments create two problems for a Permanent Portfolio.

One is that so much of your net worth may be tied up in real estate that too little room is left for other investments to hold significant shares of the portfolio.

The other problem is that a large mortgage can cancel out your holdings of long-term bonds, leaving you without the profit and protection that long-term bonds are meant to provide in periods of deflation or low inflation. A mortgage is a fixed-income investment, just like a bond. For the lender, it's an asset. For you, it's a liability—one that neutralizes your bond holdings.

In fact, your mortgage might be much larger than your holdings of Treasury bills and bonds—which means you owe more dollars than you possess. That makes you vulnerable to a deflation, during which you can expect the value of your real estate to drop and the burden of your mortgage to rise.

Calculating Your Position

The first step in dealing with these problems is to determine how big they are. You need to compare the value of your real estate and the size of your mortgages with the rest of your wealth.

To do this, begin by estimating the current market value of each property you own—using the price you think it would take to get a buyer within 90 days or so. Add the estimates for all your properties to get the gross value of your real estate holdings.

Then add up all the mortgages or other debts associated with the properties.[2]

Last, make a rough estimate of your overall net worth. This is the total market value of every investment you own, minus the total of all investment debts.

---

[2]If you have a fixed-rate mortgage with an interest rate that's substantially *below* current rates for new fixed-rate mortgages, ask the lender what amount he would accept in full payment for the mortgage. Use that amount if it is less than the nominal balance.

Extent of the Problem

The results of these calculations may surprise you.

The gross value of your home may by itself equal 50%, 100%, or more of your net worth. If you own other properties in addition, the gross value of all your real estate holdings may equal several times your net worth. And your mortgage debt probably far exceeds your net worth.

In short, you're over-invested in real estate and your dollar liabilities are imprudently large. You are vulnerable to a deflation that would diminish the value of your real estate while making the debt harder to bear.

HEDGING AGAINST REAL ESTATE

If that's your situation, there are a few things you can do to reduce the risk to which you're exposed.

Variable-Rate Mortgage

If you have a fixed-rate mortgage (one for which the interest rate remains the same over the life of the mortgage), you can replace it with a variable-rate mortgage (one for which the interest rate is adjusted to current market conditions every six months or so).

This would make a deflation much less frightening, because any period of falling interest rates would reduce the size of your mortgage payments—making them less of a burden.

Of course, the payments would increase during periods of inflation and rising interest rates. But most likely you'll profit from gold during such periods.

A fixed-rate mortgage is a bet on rising inflation and higher interest rates—whether or not you think of it that way. It leaves you vulnerable to a deflation, while a variable-rate mortgage is neutral.

Zero-Coupon Bonds

If mortgage debt overwhelms your bond holdings, you can help to restore balance by using zero-coupon bonds instead of conventional Treasury bonds in your portfolio.

Zero-coupons are far more volatile; dollar for dollar, they are about three times as powerful as conventional bonds. For a portfolio with no debt problems, that's more volatility than is needed. But where real estate is involved, the extra volatility is valuable to offset the damage done by a mortgage.[3]

To make use of the volatility, the zero-coupons should have the longest maturities available.

If you have a fixed-rate mortgage, the dollar amount you invest should be the *smaller* of: (1) 25% of your liquid capital; or (2) the sum of your mortgages plus 25% of your liquid capital, divided by 3. If you have a variable-rate mortgage, cut the answer by half.[4]

As discussed on page 360, it is much easier to invest in zero-coupons through the Benham Target Maturities Trust than to buy zero-coupons directly. The trust allows you to choose the maturity you want, the units are totally liquid, and you can find their price each day in the newspaper.

Whether you should use zero-coupon bonds (either directly or through Benham Target Maturities Trust) depends on how much your mortgage scares you. If there's any chance that the mortgage could be a burden someday, conventional Treasury bonds may not provide sufficient protection.

But if your home is the only real estate you own and you feel certain that you can handle the mortgage in any circumstance, you probably can safely use conventional Treasury bonds for your bond budget.

Gold Options

One way to deal with an illiquid investment is to reduce the share of the portfolio given to any other investment that responds to economic conditions in somewhat the same way.

I'm not at all sure that the next bout of inflation will bring on a boom in real estate. But if *you* feel certain that inflation will drive real estate prices upward, the combination of gold and real estate would seem to give you more inflation protection than you need.

This suggests that you could reduce the budget for gold. You can

---

[3]Zero-coupon bonds are explained on pages 358–361 and 522–527.

[4]The formula for #2 allows you to buy enough to offset the mortgage, plus enough more to have a positive position in bonds equal to 25% of your liquid capital. Divide by 3, because zero-coupon bonds are roughly 3 times as volatile as conventional bonds.

do this without reducing too much of gold's protection by replacing some of the gold bullion or coins with call options on gold.

A call option gives you the right, for a period of time, to buy gold at a fixed price. If the market price of gold goes up substantially, a call option will profit—although the profit per ounce won't be as great as if you held gold directly. Since the options cost only a fraction of the cost of buying the same number of ounces of bullions or coins directly, you conserve cash that can be used to buy a greater quantity of bonds.

If, ideally, you would put 25% of the portfolio in gold, you could reduce that to 12%—putting 10 of the 12% directly in gold bullion or coins. The other 2% would provide a budget for the options.

The 13% taken away from the 25% gold budget should go into long-term bonds—even zero-coupon bonds, if you need that much more volatility. This would give the portfolio added protection against a deflation.

To determine how many options you should have at any time: (1) calculate how many ounces of gold bullion you could have bought with 25% of your liquid capital; (2) subtract the number of ounces you actually have in coins and bullion; (3) buy options covering the number of ounces you don't have. If any cash is left over, leave it in the cash budget until you need it.

Each year, when you make the portfolio adjustment, transfer money into or out of the option budget in order to make it roughly 2% of the portfolio.[5]

Real Estate and Gold

Having explained how to hedge this way, I have to say that I don't care much for the idea of tampering with the gold budget to accommodate real estate, because real estate isn't the reliable, powerful investment that gold is.

Despite real estate's reputation as an inflation hedge, the only evidence I've found (depicted in the graph on page 365) provides no support for the idea that real estate prices are any more affected by inflation than most retail prices are.

[5]Gold options can be purchased through stock and commodity brokers in the U.S. Swiss banks can obtain Valeurs White Weld options for you, but it's more difficult to monitor their prices.

Gold, however, tends to rise with inflation—and at a much faster rate. A 25% share in gold can protect the entire portfolio from inflation.

In addition, our only experience with real estate has been during periods when inflation rose slowly and peaked at less than 15%. At higher rates or more volatile rates, the value of real estate could be endangered by civil disorder or by government attempts to eliminate inflation with rent controls, price controls, or other attacks on property rights.

Gold is money—portable, divisible, and recognizable. As money, it can appreciate in extreme circumstances that would be bad for real estate—such as war, anarchy, or disruptively high inflation. And being money, gold enhances your sense of personal security. You know that, whatever happens, you'll always have something of value, something private and portable, to see you through. Thus gold is more versatile and powerful than real estate.

And no matter what you may believe real estate has done in the past, the new tax rules make it unlikely that real estate will be the same investment it was before. It would be a mistake to rely on real estate as your protection against inflation or any other economic environment.

As a result, I'm not eager to give any of gold's place in the Permanent Portfolio to real estate. The gold-option plan should be used only in an extreme situation—if, for example, only 10% or so of your capital is liquid.

WHERE TO PUT REAL ESTATE

I always assumed that a real estate investment should be treated as part of the Permanent Portfolio. But real estate isn't in the same world as stocks, bonds, gold, or cash—and it's foolish to pretend that they're interchangeable items on the same investment menu. Real estate differs from the others in many ways.

First, even if you buy a home because you believe that doing so is a good investment, you usually select a particular house for its features as your residence—not by any standards of investment analysis.

Second, when you plan a Permanent Portfolio, you're completely free to decide how much you should have in stocks, bonds, gold, and cash. If your decisions mean that you're currently underinvested in one area or overinvested in another, you can buy or sell whatever amounts are needed to make your holdings match the chosen percentages.

But a house is indivisible. You can't sell off the front porch to make your real estate holdings fit your investment plan. Nor can you buy an additional $8,500 worth of real estate to make an annual portfolio adjustment. The amount of real estate in your portfolio is fixed, and everything else must accommodate it. Like a freight car in the living room, you have to arrange the furniture around it.

Third, a rise in the value of your home doesn't have the same effect as a rise in gold or bond prices. When gold goes up, you profit by selling a little of it to make the annual portfolio adjustment.

But no matter how much your home appreciates, you may never take the profit. When you sell the home, you probably will replace it with another one in its new price range—changing only the location or some of the features.

Fourth, most investments have market prices that are quoted and publicized—telling you exactly what your holdings are worth. And such investments can be sold at a moment's notice. Real estate's value isn't known until you sell, and a sale requires a long, indefinite period of time.

For all these reasons, real estate—even your own home—sits in a Permanent Portfolio like an elephant at a tea party. It may be dressed correctly, but it just doesn't seem to fit in.[6]

WHAT TO DO

I have given a great deal of thought to the question of how to reconcile real estate with the Permanent Portfolio. But nothing I can think of is very satisfying.

I've reached the conclusion that the best approach is to leave both real estate and its mortgages out of the accounting for the Permanent Portfolio.

This means using your *liquid* capital to create a portfolio containing gold, stocks, bonds, cash equivalents, and any other liquid investments you want to hold. For the investor who owns no real estate except a residence, this is the easiest approach and, in many cases, the most realistic.

---

[6]Since a real estate investment is illiquid and its value can't be monitored, it is just as unsuited to be a part of a Variable Portfolio that uses a strategy resembling the one discussed in this book.

Mortgages vs. Bonds

One reason such an approach is more realistic is that long-term bonds and mortgages aren't precisely equivalent.

During a deflation, your bonds should appreciate in both nominal and purchasing-power value. And once each year, you'll realize some of that profit when you make the portfolio adjustment.

The deflation also will increase the purchasing-power value of the dollars you owe, but that may not affect you as much. All you have to worry about is keeping your monthly mortgage payments current.[7]

And if you have trouble keeping up your mortgage payments, the lender probably will be anxious to help. He would be faced with many potential foreclosures in a deflation, and he would want to avoid taking over more property than he can handle. So he might be quite willing to make concessions to keep from having to foreclose on your property.

Thus even if a deflation reduces the value of your property and increases the burden of your mortgage, the situation might not be too critical—so long as your real estate holdings are limited to your own home.

In deciding whether to leave real estate out of your Permanent Portfolio calculations, the most important question is whether you believe you can (and will want to) keep up the mortgage payments on your property in all circumstances.

GETTING LIQUID

I hope you'll recognize the burdens that real estate imposes upon you, and treat it accordingly.

Owning your home may simply be part of the way you want to live. And you may be confident that you can hang on to your home through thick and thin. If so, keep the house and leave it out of your portfolio calculations.

If you're not sure you can hang on to it in all circumstances, you're overinvested in real estate. Selling the home and renting instead is the surest way to solve the problem. If that doesn't appeal to you, at least hedge against your situation by switching to a variable-rate mortgage and/or by holding zero-coupon bonds.

---

[7]The purchasing-power value is the amount of goods and services you could buy with a given sum of dollars.

If you own properties beyond your home, the reasons to sell them are much, much stronger. You're carrying large liabilities for questionable benefits. Owning property for income or speculation is a dangerous, expensive, and obsolete idea.

Even a vacation home probably should be rented rather than owned.

And please don't make the problem worse by adding more real estate. No matter how attractive the price or terms for a given property, you're more than likely overinvested already.

REAL ESTATE

Real estate is at once the most popular investment in the U.S. and the most troublesome.

If I haven't given you a single, elegant solution to the problems created by real estate, it's because there isn't any simple cure.

If I seem unsure concerning the role real estate will play in various economic circumstances, it's because there's too little firm evidence from the past to support confident conclusions—and because the 1986 changes in the tax laws suggest that the future probably won't resemble the past anyway.

And if there seems to be a flaw in my investment strategy because it doesn't allow conveniently for property speculation, it's because property speculation isn't the convenient investment it's often represented to be.

30

Other Investments

The simple, four-investment Permanent Portfolio described in Part II is, to me, the ideal portfolio. It offers safety in all economic conditions and steady, stable growth.

You may decide that you want to include other investments in your Permanent Portfolio. Or you may be forced to accommodate certain things you already own because they're illiquid and you can't find a practical way to get rid of them. Anything you want to do with one part of the portfolio can be allowed for to some degree by the way you handle the rest of the portfolio.

But to whatever degree you stray from the basic four-investment portfolio, you complicate matters—possibly chipping away at the balance of the Permanent Portfolio, and certainly reducing the simplicity of the concept. Anything you add will make the portfolio less easy to handle.

Don't underestimate the value of simplicity. If your investment plan is going to succeed, it must be a plan that you are able to carry out, that you'll want to carry out, and that you actually will carry out.

Although a more complicated plan might be better in principle, it could be very dangerous in practice if its complexity demands more effort or attention than, year after year, you'll be willing to give.

The simple, four-investment program will give you at least 90% of the safety and balance you could achieve by devoting your entire life to supervising the Permanent Portfolio. And it will give you far more safety and balance than most investors enjoy.

In many cases, an addition to the Permanent Portfolio seems attractive only because of an optimistic analysis of the investment's prospects. An investment bought for that reason won't improve the balance and safety of the Permanent Portfolio, and should be handled through the Variable Portfolio.

In other cases, the motive for letting some long-held investment stay on as part of the Permanent Portfolio is just the convenience of not having to reevaluate old choices and undo old habits.

This isn't to say that all other investments should be rejected out of hand. But they should be approached very skeptically.

This chapter will examine some additional investments that you might own now, or that you might be considering for your Permanent Portfolio. We'll cover foreign currencies, foreign stocks, collectibles, and a privately owned business.[1]

FOREIGN CURRENCIES

In previous books, I've suggested Swiss francs as a diversification from gold. The Swiss franc is the most volatile of the major currencies, and it tends to appreciate during periods of U.S. inflation, because the Swiss monetary authorities are more cautious than American authorities about creating new money.

The franc has done well. Its price tripled during the inflationary 1970s. But I don't believe it is essential to the Permanent Portfolio.

The franc is the most volatile of the strong currencies, but it's not nearly so volatile as gold. While the franc tripled in price, gold rose 20 times over. In fact, the franc's rise against the U.S. dollar was only a little greater than the extent of U.S. inflation. Consequently, I've decided against keeping the franc in my Permanent Portfolio.

However, you might decide you want the extra diversification— since gold and francs sometimes respond to U.S. inflation on different schedules. If you decide to include Swiss francs in the Permanent

---

[1]Annuities and life insurance are discussed on pages 390–394.

Portfolio, buy the francs with part of the gold budget. But I hope you don't devote more than 5% or so of the entire portfolio to the franc.

Because the Swiss franc is the most volatile of the strong foreign currencies, and because Switzerland enjoys the benefits of international neutrality, the franc is more appropriate for the Permanent Portfolio than the German mark, the Japanese yen, or any other currency that might occasionally make headlines.

Buying Francs

The easiest and safest method for holding francs is to buy Swiss federal government bonds through a Swiss bank account.

As in choosing U.S. Treasury bonds for the long-term dollar portion of your portfolio, you should stick to a bond issuer that has a license to print the money to pay its debts. Other Swiss franc bonds, issued by corporations or by other governments, pay higher rates of interest than bonds issued by the Swiss government, but you shouldn't expose yourself to the credit risk.

Swiss government bonds come in denominations as small as 1,000 francs (worth $650 in mid-1987). If you buy bonds that mature in five years or so, the investment won't be affected much by changes in Swiss interest rates, while you'll have the convenience of not having to replace the bonds for five years.

You can ask a Swiss bank to purchase bonds worth whatever number of dollars you want to invest; the bank will figure out how many bonds to buy. Ask the bank to buy Eidgenossenschaft (Swiss federal government) bonds maturing in around five years.[2]

FOREIGN STOCKS

Foreign stock markets did well during 1985–1987, and foreign stocks have become very popular in the United States.

However, most foreign stock markets—measured in their own currencies—performed no better than the U.S. stock market during this period. The foreign markets produced extra profits for U.S. investors because foreign currencies were rising against the U.S. dollar.

Many of the foreign markets began their uptrends in 1982—just as

---

[2] The process of acquiring a Swiss bank account is described in Chapter 32.

the U.S. stock market did. But because the local currencies were *falling* against the dollar until 1985, foreign markets weren't nearly so profitable for Americans as U.S. stocks. And in some cases, the dollar's rise during 1982–1984 turned foreign market gains into net losses for U.S. investors.

At all times, the results of an investment in foreign stocks will depend as much on the trends in currency prices as on the trends in foreign stock prices.

The major stock markets of the world tend to rise and fall more or less as a group. You would achieve a small degree of additional diversification by including foreign stocks; but, for most investors, the benefit is too modest to justify the added complication.

Foreign Stocks in the Variable Portfolio

Investing in foreign stocks might be something to consider for the Variable Portfolio from time to time. But realize that *two* questions are involved: Do you think stocks are in a worldwide bull market? And do you think the U.S. dollar will fall against other currencies?

If at some time you answer "yes" to both questions, you might hope to make more profit speculating in foreign stock markets than in either U.S. stock markets or currency speculation alone. But you would pull out of foreign stocks as soon as your answer to *either* question changed to "no."

The easiest way to invest in foreign stocks is to buy U.S. mutual funds that specialize in them. This will save you the trouble of having to familiarize yourself with the particulars of exotic foreign markets.

If you decide to use such a fund, you can consult some of the sources listed on pages 441–443 to find the fund that fits your investing plans.

COLLECTIBLES

Collectibles include paintings, stamps, diamonds, other precious stones, numismatic coins, rare books, and so forth.

If one of these areas gives you pleasure, I trust you'll indulge your hobby and have a good time. But don't tell yourself you're making an investment. Collectibles aren't an investment; they're merchandise. Dealing in them is a business.

An investment normally has a markup (or spread) between its buying and selling prices of 1% or 2% or less—and rarely more than 5%. Collectibles, being merchandise, routinely have markups of 20% to 50% or even 100%.

Investments are interchangeable; one share of IBM common stock has the same value as every other share. Collectibles are all different; they must be identified, graded, and displayed in showcases.

Information about investments is public, or at least easily communicated. What is known to some investors about gold, stocks, interest rates, and the economy can be known by most investors. Dealing in collectibles, however, requires the expertise to evaluate each particular specimen.

Most investments are traded in public markets; anyone can learn the value of gold by looking in the morning paper. Collectibles must be appraised one piece at a time, by an expert.

In the 1970s, a great many people thought they were investing when they bought collectibles. For a while, it seemed that everyone was getting rich. As inflation raged and a collector read in the newspaper about record auction prices, he had good reason to believe that his wealth was growing.

But the auction prices applied to other people's collectibles. An investor never knew what his own treasure was worth, and he had no way to know when to sell. So, even if big profits were earned in the 1970s, very few people pocketed any money before the markets fell.

If you want to be a collector, more power to you. I collect many things—art, books, even phonograph records, rare videotapes, and a good deal of moss. But I keep them on shelves, not in my portfolio.

A BUSINESS

It's ironic that many of the most successful businessmen have the most unbalanced portfolios.

One day an entrepreneur wakes up to find that he's worth $10 million. However, $8 million or so of that is the value of his business.

Chances are that a good part of the rest of his wealth is in real estate—his own home, perhaps a vacation home, and maybe a real estate project he bought as a tax shelter. If anything is left, it's probably in the stock market.

Unfortunately, that $10 million could turn into $5 million within a few years—if there's an outbreak of 1970s-style inflation. And most of it could be lost if there's a 1929-style crash.

Such a lopsided portfolio isn't unusual among businessmen, but it is very dangerous. The portfolio has no protection to speak of against either inflation or deflation. While it thrives on the prosperity of the mid-1980s, it is vulnerable to everything else.

If this is the position you're in, there are a few remedies to consider.

1. Since you know you live in an uncertain world—and you can't guarantee the continued success of your business through intelligence, effort, or heroism alone—perhaps you should consider selling part of the business. You don't need to relinquish control, just sell enough shares to free up some liquid capital with which to protect yourself.

2. You can institute a permanent program of holding put options on a stock index. Put options profit when stock prices go down. If there's a crash, a deflation, or simply a long period of poor economic conditions, the put options should show a substantial profit—a profit that may offset the losses incurred by your business.[3]

3. If the profitability of your business tends to move upward or downward with general economic conditions, you can treat your business as part of your budget for stock-market investments. However, I believe you should have some stock-market investments apart from your own business—so that you're sure to profit fully from a big bull market in stocks, and so that you can take profits through the annual portfolio adjustment.

4. If only a small part of your net worth is liquid, cut the budget for long-term bonds to about one third of what it would have been, and use zero-coupon bonds with maturities at least 20 years away. Don't alter the gold budget.[4]

If none of these remedies is workable for you, disregard your business in planning the Permanent Portfolio. Use all the liquid capital available to you to create a balanced Permanent Portfolio, as though you didn't own the business.

If you can't use the capital tied up in your business, and if you can't be sure it will always have the value it apparently has now, it might be more realistic to think of the business primarily as a source of income rather than as a part of your wealth. Doing so may inspire you to treat whatever liquid capital you have with greater care.

---

[3]*Inflation-Proofing Your Investments* (described on page 447) provides a detailed description of such a program. That program suggested using put options on individual stocks, but options on stock indices are now available—simplifying the program considerably.

[4]Zero-coupon bonds are described on pages 358–361 and 522–527. You can use the same formula as that given on page 369 to hedge against real estate.

OTHER INVESTMENTS

If my world seems to consist of gold, stocks, Treasury bonds, and Treasury bills—and nothing else—it isn't because no other investments are desirable or worth considering. It is because no other investments are essential to a Permanent Portfolio.

If you believe an investment such as foreign stocks or foreign currencies will add safety and balance, I won't argue against including it in the Permanent Portfolio. But I do hope you'll limit your position to a small percentage—say, 10% or so.

Coping with Illiquidity

When too much of your Permanent Portfolio is illiquid, the problem isn't a simple matter of deciding which other investments to include and which to leave out. The task is to decide how best to use your liquid capital to hedge against the dangers created by one illiquid asset dominating the portfolio.

In that situation, no hedging strategy will be fully satisfactory. But if you can't balance your portfolio perfectly, because of some asset you can't or won't part with, please don't forget about safety and balance. Even if only 10% of your net worth is liquid, deploying that 10% wisely can greatly reduce your overall risk.

Using the liquid assets available to you to get the portfolio even partly balanced will leave you far safer than if you had neglected the job altogether. If bad luck should strike, the effort you've made could mean the difference between damage and disaster.

PART IV

Making
Investment Decisions

31

Tax Considerations

The 1986 changes in the Internal Revenue Code eliminated many tax-planning methods for investors. Fortunately, the changes were accompanied by lower tax rates that reduced the need for tax planning.

The investor who's willing to make the effort still can find means and methods to reduce his tax bill substantially. But the subject is complex, and a full treatment would take us too far from our purposes in this book.

Most investors can start their tax planning—and possibly even complete it—by considering the three simple tools discussed in this chapter. They are pension plans, annuities and life insurance, and the formal identification of items to be sold.

PENSION PLANS

The phrase "pension plan" as used here refers to an Individual Retirement Account (IRA), a Keogh plan for the self-employed, a corporate profit-sharing or defined-benefit plan, a deferred-compensation

385

plan, or any other program for which the Internal Revenue Code permits the tax-free accumulation of investment income.

Our concern here is with pension plans for which you can choose the investments.

A pension plan isn't itself an investment. It is a legal arrangement for holding investments (the same investments you might hold otherwise) that provides certain tax advantages.

All pension plans have five things in common:

1. Up to specified legal limits and subject to certain qualifications, money put into the plan can be deducted from the taxable income of the person putting it in—whether he is an employer, employee, or both. Additional, non-deductible contributions may be permitted in some cases, but not in unlimited amounts.

2. The plan pays no taxes. Interest, dividends, and capital gains accumulate and compound tax-free so long as they stay inside the plan.

3. Money coming out of the plan is taxed—except for the return of contributions to the plan that weren't tax-deductible when they were made.

4. There is a penalty for withdrawing money from the plan "prematurely"—which generally means withdrawing money before you reach age 59½.

5. There must be a formal, written document covering the plan, and it must satisfy the requirements of the Internal Revenue Code applicable to that type of plan.

Through the legal mechanism of a pension plan, you can hold Permanent Portfolio or Variable Portfolio investments in a way that allows the income and profits from them to accumulate tax-free for many years.

Where to Get a Plan

Setting up a pension plan is easy in most cases. Almost any bank, savings and loan association, mutual fund, stockbroker, or insurance company will sponsor or provide a variety of ready-made plans that require only your signature and your check.

Generally, a plan sponsored by a financial institution allows you to invest only in the investments the sponsor handles. Thus a plan provided by a bank typically will permit you to choose among different kinds of savings accounts—but not among stocks, Treasury bills, bonds, gold, or other investments.

However, many stockbrokers offer pension plans with lengthy menus of investments—including stocks, bonds, Treasury bills, even gold coins in some cases. You can choose from among these investments, and switch from one to another.

In addition, some families of mutual funds offer pension plans that allow you to switch among funds invested in common stocks, foreign stocks, bonds, gold stocks, Treasury bills, and so on.

It's possible to have more than one of each type of pension plan for which you're eligible, so long as your yearly contributions to the plans, taken together, don't exceed the legal limits. Each plan can be kept at a different institution.

It isn't possible to set up a pension plan outside the U.S.—such as at a Swiss bank.

How Much to Put into the Plan

A pension plan provides two benefits: (1) tax deductions for some or all of the money contributed to the plan; and (2) tax-free accumulation of everything the plan's investments earn. The first benefit is immediate, but in the long run the second benefit is more important.

Both are extremely valuable, and they can be achieved while investing in almost anything you want. Thus it makes sense to put into a pension plan as much as you can afford—up to the limits set by the rules of the plan.

For privacy and liquidity, some money should be kept out of pension plans. After satisfying those needs, most investors have every reason to fill a pension plan to capacity.

What to Keep in the Plan

Your investments fall into two categories:

1. Those that produce dividends or interest—taxable income—each year.

2. Those that don't produce dividends or interest—and incur taxes only when they're sold.

A pension plan can reinvest 100% of its earnings without losing anything to taxes. You'll waste this benefit if you fill the plan with Permanent Portfolio investments that generate no current earnings, while continuing to pay tax yearly on income-producing investments sitting outside the plan.

To put a pension plan to best use, choose investments for it in the following order:

1. Variable Portfolio investments, if you have a Variable Portfolio;

2. Permanent Portfolio Treasury bills and bonds;

3. Permanent Portfolio stock-market investments that pay dividends;

4. Permanent Portfolio investments that produce no current income—including gold and warrants.

In other words, use your pension plan exclusively for the Variable Portfolio until the plan's size exceeds your Variable Portfolio budget. Then use the pension plan for investments in Treasury bills and bonds—until your pension plan has the Treasury bills and bonds needed by your Permanent Portfolio. After that, use any additional room in the pension plans for investments first from category #3, and then from category #4.

We'll look at each of the four investment categories.

1. Variable Portfolio

The Variable Portfolio's investments generate taxable income when they're sold at a profit. If the portfolio is successful, that might mean a good deal of taxable income from time to time.

In addition, money in the Variable Portfolio, when not invested, should be in Treasury bills or a money market fund—drawing interest that would be taxable outside a pension plan. And investments in stocks or bonds can generate income even while you're holding them.

Thus a considerable amount of tax might be saved by operating the Variable Portfolio from within the "tax-free zone" of a pension plan.

For this purpose, the pension plan should be kept with a stockbroker or a family of mutual funds that provides a wide range of investment alternatives—including common stocks, bonds, gold coins or gold stocks, a money market fund for keeping idle cash, and so on. This will make it easy to switch from one investment to another.

Gold is the one major investment that isn't handled easily inside a pension plan. An IRA can invest in American Eagle gold coins, and some stockbrokers have arranged to acquire them for customer IRAs. However, any other variety of pension plan whose investments are directed by the investor may not invest in any form of gold.

Very few mutual funds hold gold bullion or coins. So you might have to settle for a gold-stock mutual fund if you keep the pension plan with a family of funds and you want the Variable Portfolio to invest in gold.

Needless to say, if you don't make a profit with the Variable Portfolio, you may wish you had sheltered Permanent Portfolio items instead. And if the Variable Portfolio operates at a loss, you can't use the loss to offset capital gains earned outside the pension plan.

2. Treasury Bills & Bonds

Since T bills and bonds produce the greatest taxable income every year, they are the Permanent Portfolio items that most need the tax-saving power of the pension plan.

So these are next in line after you've found a place in your pension plan for the Variable Portfolio. If you don't have a Variable Portfolio, Treasury bills and bonds are the first items to buy for the pension plan.

3. Dividend-Paying Investments

Stocks and stock-market mutual funds can use the tax sheltering of a pension plan, if there's room for them. But they need the shelter less urgently than Treasury bills and bonds do.

The dividend yield on stocks generally is lower than the interest yield on Treasury securities. Yields on highly volatile stocks are lower yet; such stocks become volatile usually by reinvesting most of what they earn.

Volatile mutual funds also are unlikely to generate sizable dividends, because they achieve their volatility by investing in low-yielding, volatile stocks.

All these investments can benefit from sheltering, but they are near the back of the line to get into a pension plan.

4. Other Investments

Gold bullion, coins, and stock warrants produce no current income to be sheltered.

However, any investment might bring a taxable profit when a portfolio adjustment is made. The tax will be relatively small (in comparison to the size of the portfolio), because the sale normally will involve a very small percentage of your portfolio.

But avoiding any tax is a blessing. So if your pension plan is large enough to accommodate more than the first three categories, there's no reason not to add non-income investments.

Gold Investments

Investments in gold bullion or gold coins are not allowed in most pension plans directed by the owner. However, American Eagle gold coins may be kept in an IRA.

Annual Adjustments

If your pension plan is big enough to include some of each type of Permanent Portfolio investment, you can make annual adjustments without being taxed on the items sold at a profit.

For example, if gold outperforms the other investments, some gold would be sold to restore its designated percentage. If all your gold were outside the pension plan, you would have to pay tax on the profit (unless you could offset the gain with capital losses from another investment). But if some gold were inside the pension plan, you could sell it without the profit being taxed.

Pension Plans

A pension plan provides the simplest, most readily available method for deferring taxation on investment earnings.

For many investors, nothing more involved is needed than to make full use of the tax sheltering that pension plans provide.

ANNUITIES & LIFE INSURANCE

Most deferred annuities and many whole-life insurance policies accumulate interest at rates that rise and fall with open-market rates. In that respect, they are similar to an investment in Treasury bills.

They are not a perfect substitute, however, because of their credit risk. An insurance company might default on its policies during a deflation—or at any time because of mismanagement. An even more likely hazard is that an insurance company short of cash might drag its feet in honoring requests for withdrawals or policy loans. Using deferred annuities as a complete replacement for Treasury bills would be as unwise as using bank CDs or other money market instruments for that purpose.

However, annuities and life insurance also offer tax advantages. If your portfolio is badly in need of tax relief, they may be worth considering.

Insurance companies operate more cautiously than banks do. So, within limits, I don't object to using dollar-denominated policies to fill part of the cash budget in the Permanent Portfolio. These are the limits I suggest:

1. Hold contracts issued only by companies that have *Best's* ratings of A or A+, so that the risk of default is minimal.[1]

2. Limit any one company's annuities and life insurance policies (measured by the cash value) to no more than 5% of your Permanent Portfolio.

3. Limit all the annuities and life insurance together to no more than 15% of your Permanent Portfolio.

If you need life insurance coverage, a term insurance policy will provide that coverage without tying up additional capital in a savings program. The life insurance and annuities discussed here should be considered only if you are in the top tax bracket, can't shelter the investments any other way, and are willing to tie up the money for at least 10 years. Even in that case, please remember the drawbacks of these investments and take seriously the limits I've suggested.

Tax Advantages

The 1986 tax act made only a few changes in the rules concerning annuities and life insurance. The tax benefits of such investments have always been significant, and they've been made comparatively more attractive by the elimination of other tax-planning techniques.

[1]The A. M. Best Company rates the ability of insurance companies to remain liquid and solvent. You can order the *Best Agents Guide to Life Insurance Companies* (an annual publication) for $45 by writing to A. M. Best Company, Ambest Road, Oldwick, N.J. 08858, or by calling (201) 439-2200.

Annuities and life insurance—like pension plans—enable you to accumulate investment earnings without current taxation. And you can borrow against the policies—which allows you to withdraw some of the earnings without paying tax on them. You don't get a tax deduction for the amount you invest in annuities or life insurance, but there are no limits to the amount you can invest.

Annuities and life insurance are available from life insurance agents and brokers. We'll consider here those types of policies that might be relevant to a Permanent Portfolio or Variable Portfolio.

Deferred Annuities

A deferred annuity is a contract issued to an investor by an insurance company—usually in exchange for a single payment.

The annuity's formal purpose is to provide lifetime income payments to the investor, beginning sometime in the future. Until then, the annuity earns and accumulates investment income without being taxed.

The investor can elect to close out the annuity at any time—taking a lump-sum payment of the capital and accumulated income. At that point, he must pay tax on the accumulated income.

Most deferred annuities are dollar-type investments. They earn interest—at a rate that fluctuates along with market interest rates. Although the insurance company can set any rate it chooses, it is motivated to pay an attractive rate so that investors won't close out their annuities and turn to the company's competitors.

If you expect to hold a deferred annuity for at least 10 years, the after-tax results can be much better than for Treasury bills that are held outside a pension plan. However, please don't let that fact inspire you to go beyond the limits given on page 391.

Each company's annuities include their own idiosyncrasies, and some of those features make it hard to evaluate the investments. So you need to study a policy carefully before buying.

Variable Annuities

A variable annuity is a special kind of deferred annuity. As with other annuities, the earnings of a variable annuity accumulate tax-free.

But a variable annuity isn't necessarily a dollar-type investment. Its value depends on the value of a pool of investments owned by the insurance company that issues the annuity.

The investment pool might be comprised of stocks, or of bonds, or of something else—depending on the particular contract you select. The Permanent Portfolio could contain one variable annuity tied to Treasury bonds and another tied to stocks.

Some variable annuities allow you to switch back and forth among several different investment pools. Any trading profits, like other annuity earnings, accumulate tax-free until withdrawn. Thus you could use the annuity for a tax-sheltered Variable Portfolio.

The idea of having a tax-free Permanent or Variable Portfolio is very attractive. However, there are at least two drawbacks:

1. The investment pools generally won't contain the specific stocks or bonds that you would choose, or the ones I'm suggesting in this book. Normally, the stocks are average-volatility blue chips, and the bonds are corporate bonds.

2. Variable annuities have fees and charges that may more than offset the tax benefits. In effect, they are like an expensive mutual fund—with an initial load of 4% to 6%, plus continuing yearly expenses that are about double those of a mutual fund.

In addition, the most urgent tax problem for the Permanent Portfolio is to shelter the interest income, which you probably can do with pension plans or simple deferred annuities.

Life Insurance

Some life insurance policies can serve as investments while reducing your tax bill.

"Investment Life" is a type of policy for which you prepay a lifetime of insurance premiums. The money paid to the company is invested, and the investment earnings increase the insurance coverage and the cash value (the amount you can claim at any time by cashing in the policy). The growth in cash value is tax-free until you withdraw it.

In addition, if the eventual payoff is made to a beneficiary rather than to you, there is no income tax at all on the earnings. The tax is eliminated—not just deferred.

However, for an insurance policy to qualify for this tax treatment, a portion of the investment income must be used to cover the risk that you'll die prematurely. This expense reduces the yearly increase in the policy's cash value.

So "investment life" makes sense only if you want life insurance coverage. In other words, if you need life insurance, an investment life policy is a way to get it while reducing the tax bill on your Permanent Portfolio.

No matter what the tax benefits, however, please stay within the guidelines given on page 391, limiting the total of deferred annuities and cash-value life insurance to no more than 15% of the Permanent Portfolio.

Variable Life Insurance

Like variable annuities, variable life insurance allows you to switch from one investment pool to another tax-free. But the drawbacks for variable annuities apply here as well.

IDENTIFYING SALE ITEMS

By observing certain formalities, it's possible to reduce or avoid the tax on sales (such as those you'll make for annual portfolio adjustments) of investments purchased at two or more different prices.

Suppose that you own 300 shares of a particular stock—100 of which were bought at $35 per share, and 200 of which were bought at $60 per share. And suppose that 30 shares are now to be sold at a price of $70 in order to make an annual adjustment. You can designate that the 30 shares to be sold are part of those bought at $60—thereby minimizing the taxable profit on the sale.

You can do this even though you don't have stock certificates for the shares. Simply issue the sell instruction in a letter that reads:

> Please sell 30 (thirty) shares of XYZ stock from those that were purchased at $60 on [date of purchase]. Please confirm to me in writing that you have sold these particular shares.

Insist that the broker's confirmation identify the shares, and keep the confirmation for your tax records.

This technique can be used for gold coins, ounces of gold bullion, shares of stock, warrants, mutual fund shares, and bonds. (It serves no purpose for Treasury bills or shares in a money market fund.)

For sales of mutual fund shares, it isn't even necessary to request or receive a confirmation that identifies the shares. You need only identify the shares in your written instruction to the fund.

TAX CONSIDERATIONS

Even after the 1986 changes in the tax code, many fancy plans for reducing taxes are sure to come to your attention.

Some of them may in fact be worthwhile. But I hope you'll evaluate all of them skeptically.

Most red-hot schemes for reducing taxes require that you sacrifice some of the safety and balance a Permanent Portfolio is supposed to provide. It may be preferable—or even cheaper—to pay a bigger tax bill than to risk the capital you've worked so long to accumulate.

The tax bill on a Permanent Portfolio shouldn't be a burden—even if you can't use a pension plan to shelter the income. If interest yields are around 10%, Treasury bills and bonds (if they comprise half the portfolio) will lead to a maximum yearly tax equal to only about 1½% of the total value of the portfolio.

And even if gold or stocks were to double in value in one year, the sale generated by the annual adjustment would lead to a tax of no more than 2½% of the value of the portfolio—even though the portfolio would have appreciated by 25% or more. The champagne might cost more than the tax.

Avoiding such a small tax isn't a sensible reason for taking risks with the Permanent Portfolio.

32

A
Swiss Bank Account

For your Permanent Portfolio to be safe enough to walk away from and forget, it will have to allow for more than just the problems and hazards that are obvious to you today. It will have to allow for all the unforeseeable events of the next 5, 10, 15, or 20 years.

We don't know what the next 20 years will be like. They may be so dull that future historians will refer to them as the Era of Awful Boredom—when absolutely nothing exciting happened. Or perhaps the years will be known as the Era of Great Progress—a period of peace, prosperity, and advancement in science and industry.

Or maybe the next 20 years will be remembered for crises of inflation, depression, civil disorder, war, government confiscations, or political turmoil.

Only time will tell us, so we need to be prepared now for every kind of surprise—including surprises we know we wouldn't enjoy.

One part of the preparation is to place some of your investments outside the United States. Doing so offers several benefits:

1. It will preserve your ownership even if war or civil disorder should disrupt record keeping in the United States.

2. It will give you the time and opportunity to respond to any

extraordinary policies adopted by the U.S. government. No one knows how the President or Congress elected in 1996 might choose to solve the economic problems they'll face. Expropriating your property for some urgent public purpose might strike them as the ideal solution.

3. It will reduce what you might lose to mismanagement, a weakening of law enforcement, or a physical catastrophe in the United States.

These hazards may seem remote. And they are—in the sense that I don't expect any of them to happen tomorrow morning. But they are real hazards, and now and then you feel the reality—when a politician urges something especially dangerous or foolish, or it's revealed that the Internal Revenue Service has acted in a particularly heavy-handed way, or an international conflict threatens to erupt into something big.

Someday a remote hazard will grow into an immediate threat. And geographic diversification is the final step in making sure the Permanent Portfolio can handle whatever hazard materializes.

WHY SWITZERLAND?

If you agree that geographic diversification is important, the next step is to choose a country. I believe Switzerland is the obvious first choice—for its stability, its freedom, its respect for privacy, and its facilities.

Stability

What Switzerland is today, you can expect it to be ten years from now.

The stability that prevails in Switzerland is truly amazing to a North American. We can find it hard to understand that Swiss policies and laws don't change every time there's an election or a politician gets a bright idea.

I have a Swiss Almanac that shows the results of the last 18 federal elections, going back to 1919. In every election during those 67 years, the Christian Social Party has won between 21% and 25% of the seats in the Swiss parliament; the Radical Democratic Party has always won between 24% and 33%; the Social Democrats between 21% and 29%; and so on with the rest of the parties.

The parties are genuinely independent, they compete actively, and the votes are all counted. But in election after election, the results are always pretty much the same. A coalition of what we might call conservative parties has shared power for half a century. On election night, no one stays up late to hear the results, because everyone knows what they will be.

Part of the reason for this political consistency is that politicians have less power to change the lives of citizens than they do in America. So there is much less reason for people to worry about politics.

Another source of Switzerland's stability is its 200-year-old policy of international neutrality. The Swiss in general don't seem to believe that wars or alliances serve much purpose. Switzerland hasn't joined the United Nations, NATO, the International Monetary Fund, or any collective security arrangement. Consequently, the Swiss don't represent a threat to anyone—nor do the Swiss feel threatened by anyone.

Another element is the use of the referendum. Before taking effect, many laws passed by the legislature have to be ratified by a vote of the people, who typically veto any radical changes. In recent years, the Swiss people have rejected proposals to join the United Nations, reduce the official work week, weaken bank secrecy laws, and introduce a value added tax.

Because the rules in Switzerland don't change significantly from year to year, you can use Swiss institutions without fear that everything might change suddenly because of a change in the political atmosphere.

Freedom

Another Swiss advantage is the degree of financial freedom, and the prosperity this freedom has produced.

It has enabled people to get on about their business, import raw materials, produce products and services that are wanted, and deliver them to Swiss and foreigners alike.

In annual surveys of the wealth of nations, Switzerland usually finishes first or second. And yet the country has little in the way of natural resources—much less than most African or South American countries, for example.

Swiss citizens are habitual savers, with a savings rate well above the rates in other countries of Europe or the United States. Swiss people tend to think of themselves as capitalists, and they don't tolerate plans to take away what someone has earned.

Accordingly, the Swiss government is exceptionally respectful of property. It has never confiscated anyone's gold or silver holdings, nor prohibited trading in metals or foreign currencies—even during world wars and other crises.

Please understand that Switzerland isn't a free enterprise Utopia. There are laws, regulations, and taxes. But the degree of government intervention today is roughly what it was in the U.S. or Canada a few decades back.

Respect for Privacy

An important part of the Swiss mentality is the respect a Swiss person has for his neighbor's freedom, property, and privacy.

The Swiss concern for privacy has been widely noted, but very little understood, by foreigners. I lived in Switzerland for six years, and I noticed that a Swiss seemed to worry more that he might invade *your* privacy (or appear to be doing so) than that you might intrude upon his.

This facet of the Swiss personality helps to explain a great deal— such as Switzerland's neutrality, its privacy laws, and the widespread respect for property.

If you understand how deeply these things pervade the Swiss character, you'll be very skeptical of reports that bank privacy in Switzerland is dying. A free and prosperous nation like Switzerland isn't likely to discard its traditions simply because the U.S. government believes it has found a new way to catch tax evaders or drug dealers.

Facilities

In Switzerland, a bank is legally permitted to handle almost every type of financial transaction—the placing of money, the purchase of investments, and so on. By dealing with a single bank, you receive the services of a commercial bank, a savings and loan association, a stockbroker, a commodity broker, a gold dealer, and a currency exchange.

Advantages of Switzerland

Switzerland's stability is valuable to a Permanent Portfolio because it means that you won't have to reevaluate your use of Switzerland constantly. Its free markets mean that you aren't likely to run into rules that prevent you from carrying out your portfolio plan.

The respect for privacy and property suggest the care with which your investments will be treated. And the facilities allow you to accomplish many things in one place.

Over the years, I've become acquainted with the banking opportunities available in several countries, and I've studied the banking systems of several more. But so far, I've found no country as attractive as Switzerland.

TYPES OF ACCOUNTS

Swiss banking is a big topic. Here we'll focus only on the information needed to use a Swiss account for a Permanent Portfolio or Variable Portfolio.[1]

Two types of accounts at a Swiss bank are of concern to us here.

The first is a *current* account, which is like a checking account at a U.S. bank. It is a demand deposit—meaning that you can withdraw your money from it whenever you choose.

The second is a *safekeeping* account (also called a *custodial* account or *safe custody* account). For this account, the bank serves as your storehouse—a place in which to keep the investments the bank acquires for you. The investments are separate from the bank's own assets.

Current Account

If you use the four-investment Permanent Portfolio I've suggested, your current account at the bank will be somewhat incidental.

Its principal functions will be to receive the interest and dividends earned by investments kept at the bank, and to pay custodial charges for the safekeeping account.

A Swiss bank will denominate your current account in U.S. dollars or in Swiss francs—whichever you choose. Some banks will maintain a current account in almost any major currency you request. For the sake of familiarity and convenient accounting, I suggest keeping the account in U.S. dollars.

---

[1]This should be sufficient for most readers. If you need more, my book *The Complete Guide to Swiss Banks* (described on page 453) provides detailed coverage of the subject.

Safekeeping Account

A safekeeping account holds the stocks, gold, U.S. Treasury bonds, U.S. Treasury bills, or other investments the bank has acquired for you.

A Swiss bank can buy stocks or bonds for you from any exchange or over-the-counter market in the world and hold them in a safekeeping account. As a rule of thumb, commissions for transactions in non-Swiss markets are about half-again greater than if you acquired the investments yourself.

The bank also can purchase American mutual funds for you, but foreign banks have always had a great deal of trouble dealing with U.S. mutual funds.

A Swiss bank can purchase U.S. Treasury bills or shares in a U.S. money market fund for you. However, you may prefer to handle these in the United States.

Many Swiss banks do a big business in gold and silver bullion and gold coins. The Zürich gold market is a very large, liquid market—and most trading by Swiss banks is done there. The normal commission for gold is ½% to 1% for each purchase or sale. Gold owned by the bank's customers is stored in the bank's own storage facilities or with another bank that has larger facilities.

Normally, your gold is mixed with that of other customers. However, some banks will hold your gold in "segregated storage." This means that your gold is tagged and distinguished from all other gold held by the bank, whether for itself or for its customers. Although this may cost more, it enhances the safety of the investment.

Some banks sell "claims" against gold, rather than the gold itself. This creates what is called a "claim account" or a "metals account," rather than a safekeeping account. It is a somewhat less safe way to handle gold, because you don't actually own the gold; instead, it is owed to you. So it's important to specify that you want the gold kept in a safekeeping account.

Minimum Accounts

The minimum amount required to open an account varies from bank to bank—ranging, in general, from $5,000 to $50,000. Some banks require less and some even more.

In addition to a basic minimum for opening an account, a bank may have minimum purchase amounts for particular types of transactions.

VARIABLE PORTFOLIO

Because a Swiss bank can handle so many different investments, it is a practical location for the Variable Portfolio. Although transaction costs for U.S. stocks and bonds will be higher than in the U.S., the costs usually won't be enough to reduce an investment's reward-risk ratio substantially.

Uninvested funds can be kept in U.S. Treasury bills, or in a simple, non–interest-bearing, U.S. dollar current account if the balance is less than $10,000 (the minimum for a T-bill).

As you direct it, the bank will invest for you in stocks, bonds, or mutual funds anywhere in the world—or in gold, silver, platinum, foreign currencies, U.S. futures contracts for commodities or financial instruments, and so on.[2]

U.S. TAXES & LAWS

The U.S. government taxes income earned by its citizens and residents anywhere in the world. So investments you keep in Switzerland are subject to U.S. taxation—just as they would be if kept in the United States. Interest, dividends, and capital gains must be reported on your tax return.

Reporting Accounts

U.S. law also requires that you report your foreign holdings to the U.S. government yearly on your income tax return if the total of all your foreign accounts is more than $10,000. This refers to the total value of all kinds of financial accounts—covering commodities, securities, and so on. There are no special taxes, limits, or regulations to meet; the government simply wants you to confide in it.[3]

This requirement doesn't eliminate the protection afforded by a Swiss bank account. Even if the U.S. government were to confiscate assets within its reach, it couldn't reach yours. You probably could

[2] A non-U.S. bank can't qualify as a custodian for an Individual Retirement Account (IRA) or a Keogh plan.

[3] The $10,000 cutoff point for reporting applies to persons filing tax returns. If you and your spouse file separate returns, you could each have $10,000 in unreported foreign accounts, provided you didn't have signature authority for each other's accounts. In any case, all income from the accounts must be reported.

delay your compliance with the government's whims without getting into legal difficulty—giving you time to dispose of the taboo assets profitably and without getting into trouble.

Reporting Money Transfers

Finally, if you carry or mail $10,000 or more in cash or other bearer instruments (such as bearer bonds) across the U.S. border (in either direction), you are required to report the fact to the U.S. government.

You do *not* have to report the sending of checks or money orders payable to a specific bank, company, or person; the sending of registered securities, or the sending of money by bank wire. In other words, you probably won't have to file any reports concerning money transmittal, so long as you don't physically carry more than $10,000 in cash across the border.

WITHHOLDING TAX

Most national governments withhold tax on interest or dividends. The U.S. and Swiss governments are no exceptions.

If you buy Swiss government bonds, the Swiss bank will collect the interest for you. But it must withhold from you a tax equal to 35% of the interest paid by the bonds. It will forward that money to the Swiss government. Since you're not a Swiss taxpayer, you can apply to the Swiss government for a refund of 30 of the 35 percent that was withheld. The other 5% can be applied as a credit on your U.S. tax return. The same procedure applies to interest earned on a Swiss bank account.

Through a combination of withholdings by the U.S. and Swiss governments, 30% of the dividends and interest earned on U.S. investments held in Switzerland is withheld. Half the withholding on dividends and ⅚ of the withholding on interest will be refunded by the Swiss government if you ask for it. The portion that isn't refundable can be used as a credit on your U.S. tax return.

For several reasons, the withholding shouldn't create any problems for a Permanent Portfolio:

1. Any money withheld can be recaptured through refunds or tax credits.

2. There is no Swiss or U.S. withholding on capital gains. And

stock warrants produce no dividends, while volatile stocks and volatile mutual funds focus on capital gains rather than dividends.[4]

3. Gold produces no interest or dividends, so there is no withholding.

4. There is no withholding on U.S. Treasury bills.

Interest paid to foreign holders of Treasury bonds and notes issued after July 18, 1984, is exempt from U.S. withholding. However, this exemption requires any foreign broker (such as a Swiss bank) to certify that the buyer of the bond isn't a U.S. taxpayer. Most Swiss banks prefer not to become involved in that procedure—and so they won't buy the Treasury bonds that are potentially exempt, and some banks won't buy any Treasury bonds at all.

If you want to buy a U.S. Treasury bond through a Swiss bank, I suggest that you acquire the 13¼% bond of May 2009–2014. That is the longest maturity available for a bond that *isn't* exempt from withholding. The bank will give you a confirmation of any interest withheld, and you can use that as a credit on your income tax return (just as you would for tax withheld by an employer).

OPENING AN ACCOUNT

You can handle a Swiss bank account entirely by mail.

Begin by writing a letter of inquiry to the bank. Explain what you want to do—listing the amounts you want to invest in each item. This gives the bank a chance to identify anything it can't handle, so that it won't disappoint you later.

The bank will send you a packet of information, including brochures that describe the types of accounts the bank offers, and possibly a personal letter that answers any unusual questions you may have posed. Also included will be an application form and signature card.

To open the account, fill out the forms, sign them, and return them to the bank, together with a letter of instructions. Enclose a cashier's check (which you can buy at your local bank) for your initial investment. Or, if you wish, you can wire money from your local bank to the Swiss bank—indicating in the letter that you've done so.[5]

If you send a personal check to open the account, the bank may

---

[4]Real estate profits earned by foreign investors in the U.S. are subject to U.S. tax.

[5]When you want to bring back money, the bank will send you a cashier's check or wire the money to your U.S. bank—whichever you prefer.

delay making purchases for you until the check clears, which could take a couple of weeks.

If at all possible, type the letter—even if doing so is inconvenient. This will make it easier for the bank to handle your requests, make the bank more willing to do so, and reduce considerably the possibility of a misunderstanding.

Some banks require that your signature be witnessed by a U.S. banker or notary public. But the form used for this purpose makes no reference to a Swiss bank.

On pages 406 and 407, you'll find sample letters for making an inquiry and for opening an account.

CHOOSING A BANK

There are about 450 commercial banks in Switzerland, and over 1,000 mutual credit banks. Of these, only a few dozen are suitable for our purposes.

Swiss banks fall into six legal classifications. Of these, three groups —Cantonal Banks, Regional and Savings Banks, and Mutual Credit Banks—are not investment specialists. A fourth group, Private Banks, may be appropriate for some investors with large portfolios, but such a bank should be used only after a personal visit.

The fifth group is the Big Banks. Three of them—the Union Bank of Switzerland, the Swiss Bank Corporation, and the Swiss Credit Bank—are referred to as the Big Three, and are by far the largest banks in Switzerland. There are two other Big Banks—Bank Leu and the Swiss Volksbank (known also as Banque Populaire Suisse).

The Big Banks concentrate mainly on commercial loans, international loans, mortgages, and the typical services of an American commercial bank. In general, a big Swiss bank can't provide the kind of service that a smaller bank offers to a non-Swiss investor handling his account by mail.

The sixth and last group is called, appropriately enough, the Other Banks. It includes the 200 banks that don't fit any of the first five categories.

This group includes some banks that were formed for very narrow purposes by foreign governments or investment groups. It also includes a few commercial banks that resemble banks in the United States.

Most of the Other Banks are similar to investment brokers or dealers —in that their primary business is to acquire and store investments

LETTER OF INQUIRY TO A SWISS BANK

John Smith
222 Smith Avenue
Smithville, Indiana 68825
Telephone: (308) 555-4231

January 22, 1988

Mr. Gustav Mahler
Swiss Friendly Bank
Inderstrasse 23
CH-8078 Zurich, Switzerland

Dear Mr. Mahler:

I am interested in opening an account at your
bank in order to purchase the following
investments:

    1. $10,000 worth of Canadian Maple Leaf
gold coins, to be stored in a safekeeping
account;

    2. $5,000 worth of U.S. Treasury bonds.

Please send me whatever information and forms
I need in order to open an account.

Thank you for your attention to this matter.

                Sincerely yours,

                John Smith

                John Smith

LETTER TO OPEN A SWISS BANK ACCOUNT

John Smith
222 Smith Avenue
Smithville, Indiana 68825
Telephone: (308) 555-4231

February 3, 1988

Mr. Charles Gounod
Swiss Security Bank
23, Avenue d'etoiles
CH-1245 Geneva, Switzerland

Dear Mr. Gounod:

Enclosed is a cashier's check for $15,000.
Please open an account for me and use the
funds as follows:

    1. With $10,000, purchase 1-ounce
Canadian Maple Leaf gold coins, and store
them in a safekeeping account;

    2. With $5,000, purchase U.S. Treasury
bonds, using the 7 1/4% issue of May 2016;

    3. With any remaining funds, open a
current account in U.S. dollars.

Enclosed also are the account forms previously
sent to me.

Thank you for your attention to this matter.

Sincerely yours,

John Smith

John Smith

for customers. They are in business to serve investors like you and me, and they are the best banks for our purposes.

Among the Other Banks, there are considerable differences in services offered, the type of clientele, and investment specialties. So the fact that a particular bank is in the Other Banks category doesn't assure that it will be useful for you.

Standards for Choosing a Bank

A Swiss bank can be evaluated using four qualifications.

The first is the range of services the bank offers. If a bank doesn't provide what you need, or if its minimums are too high, there's nothing else to evaluate.

The second concern is the quality of service. Does the bank execute instructions promptly and correctly? Does it answer questions quickly, courteously, and articulately? You can't be sure about these things until after you have an account, but you can get a good indication from the way the bank handles your initial letter of inquiry.

The third question is how articulately the bank's employees communicate in English. Some banks specialize in dealing with Americans; others have employees who seem to be speaking English, but never say anything you can understand.

Safety & Liquidity

The fourth standard is financial safety.

It isn't true that all Swiss banks are safer than all American banks. However, the capital requirements imposed on a Swiss bank by law are extremely high—probably the highest in the world.

Even so, safety standards enforced by governments usually provide very little real protection. So it's up to you to protect yourself by choosing a bank carefully—no matter what the country.

In the United States, individual banks rarely use claims of safety as a drawing card, since the government's deposit insurance is supposed to provide perfect safety. Unfortunately, because of deposit insurance, a banker assumes that nothing will ever provoke a run on his bank, and so he sees no need to keep most of the bank's assets liquid.

There is no deposit insurance in Switzerland. As a result, bank financial statements are more widely circulated and examined. No one mistakenly believes that banks can't fail, and so some banks employ policies whose safety can be seen and measured—which is one reason that Swiss banks rarely fail, and that so little is lost when they do.

Difficulty in Finding Safety

Unfortunately, safety is difficult for the average investor to evaluate.

It's easy to say, "Investigate a Swiss bank before doing business with it," but much harder to act on the advice. How do you do it? Where do you investigate? Whom do you ask? How do you evaluate the answers you get?

Reputations aren't assurances of safety. The ranks of business failures include large companies, famous companies, and honored companies. In America, companies like Penn Central and Franklin National Bank weren't considered fly-by-night outfits before they went under.

Swiss Bank Failures

The failure of a Swiss bank usually is much like the failure of any business. The owners and general creditors suffer losses, but not the customers. Only rarely does a depositor suffer from a bank failure.

The stocks, bonds, gold, and other assets a customer holds in a safekeeping or custodial account belong to him, and can't be used to satisfy the creditors of the bank.

The assets in jeopardy are those in a current account, savings account, certificate of deposit, or a claim account. They're the only holdings that aren't the depositor's property; they are debts that the bank owes to him. Even these usually aren't lost in a Swiss bank failure.

Liquidity

Despite these reassurances, caution is warranted.

The situation could be quite different if a worldwide banking panic caused large numbers of depositors to demand their money all at once. Such a crisis would be a problem for banks in any country.

To survive the crisis, a bank must be highly liquid—able to raise enough cash to meet every withdrawal request it receives. This means having an abundance of assets it can sell at a moment's notice without having to sell at bargain prices.

Liquidity is the ability to meet financial obligations on demand. It is measured against the liabilities a bank might be forced to satisfy suddenly. A bank that is 100% liquid has enough liquid assets to pay every potential claim—even if every depositor wants to withdraw his money from the bank at once.

The appearance of 100% liquidity isn't a guarantee that a bank can't fail. But it's a strong indication that you won't lose anything if it does fail.

Since 1974, my newsletter has made a yearly study of the liquidity status of a number of Swiss banks. The results for the 1987 study are shown in the table on page 411. The list includes 38 banks that subscribers have asked about. It isn't a list of recommended banks.[6]

BANK SUGGESTIONS

The four important standards to apply in evaluating a Swiss bank are:
1. Does the bank provide the services you need?
2. Does it provide good service?
3. Do the officers speak and write understandable English?
4. Is the bank liquid?

The table on page 412 provides information on three banks with which I've had dealings for many years. All three satisfy the requirements.

There may be many other banks in Switzerland that meet my standards. These three happen to be the banks with which I've had firsthand experience, and have found to be suitable for American investors.

If you want to explore Swiss banks on your own, most libraries have international banking directories that include the names and addresses of many Swiss banks.

Not a Life Sentence

Switzerland is a free country, so opening an account doesn't commit you for life. It's easy to change banks if your initial choice turns out to be a disappointment.

---

[6]Appendix H on page 543 explains how the liquidity rating is computed.

SWISS BANK LIQUIDITY

	Assets	Liquidity
Algemene Bank Nederland (Schweiz), Zurich	960	45.4%
Banca Commerciale Lugano[12.86]	119	86.2%
Banca del Ceresio, Lugano[9.86]	44	95.7%
Banca della Svizzera Italiana[12.86]	6,509	42.2%
Bank Cantrade, Zurich	1,188	67.9%
Bank Hofmann, Zurich	867	51.8%
Bank J. Vontobel & Co, Zurich	1,290	61.0%
Bank Julius Bar & Co., Zurich	3,320	50.3%
Bank Leu, Zurich	14,411	33.2%
Bank Neumunster, Zurich	457	60.4%
Bank von Ernst & Cie, Bern[9.86]	151	64.8%
Bankinstitut Zurich[12.85]	72	46.0%
Banque Ankerfina, Lausanne[12.86]	80	82.5%
Banque Pasche, Geneva	229	103.6%
Banque Romande, Geneva	629	61.8%
Barclays Bank (Swiss), Geneva[9.86]	540	63.7%
British Bank of the Middle East, Geneva[6.86]	98	64.8%
Cambio + Valorenbank, Zurich[12.86]	91	163.4%
Clariden Bank, Zurich	528	59.9%
Dreyfus Sohne & Cie, Basel	713	79.1%
Finter Bank, Zurich	585	89.3%
Foreign Commerce Bank, Zurich[12.86]	313	91.9%
Guyerzeller Bank, Zurich	346	53.4%
Habib Bank, Zurich[9.86]	750	72.7%
Handelsbank Lugano[12.86]	119	86.2%
Handelsbank N.W., Zurich	3,397	56.3%
Handelskredit-Bank, Zurich[12.86]	104	86.2%
Interpopolare Bank, Zurich	263	50.3%
Migros Bank, Zurich	4,767	49.0%
Nederlandsche Middenstandsbank (Schweiz), Zurich	542	26.8%
Private Bank & Trust Company, Zurich[12.86]	512	85.6%
Rothschild Bank, Zurich[12.86]	1,078	42.9%
Swiss Bank Corporation, Basel	137,701	32.9%
Swiss Credit Bank, Zurich	105,272	36.2%
Swiss Volksbank, Bern[9.86]	28,229	47.6%
Ueberseebank, Zurich[12.86]	194	83.1%
Union Bank of Switzerland, Zurich	153,329	27.0%
United Overseas Bank, Geneva	3,211	61.3%

Data as of March 1987 unless footnoted otherwise.

Assets shown are millions of Swiss francs, and do not include assets in safekeeping or fiduciary accounts.

[6.86] As of June 1986   [12.85] As of December 1985

[9.86] As of September 1986   [12.86] As of December 1986

Liquidity ratings are computed from data on financial statements supplied by the banks or published in the *Schweizerisches Handelsamtsblatt*, Bern. The formula for computing liquidity is given in Appendix H.

THREE SWISS BANKS SUITABLE
FOR THE TWO-PORTFOLIO STRATEGY

Banque Ankerfina SA[1]
50 Avenue de la Gare
P.O. Box 159
CH-1001 Lausanne, Switzerland
Telephone: (21) 20-4741
Contact: Mrs. Francine Misrahi, Mr. Jean Gander
Minimum to open account: $5,000
Assets: 80 million Swiss francs; Liquidity: 82.5%

Cambio + Valorenbank
Utoquai 55, P.O. Box 535
CH-8021 Zurich, Switzerland
Telephone: (1) 252-2000
Contact: Mr. Werner W. Schwarz, Mr. Hans Bachmann
Minimum to open account: $50,000
Assets: 91 million Swiss francs; Liquidity: 163.4%

Foreign Commerce Bank (Focobank)
Bellariastrasse 82
CH-8038 Zurich, Switzerland
Telephone: (1) 482-6688
Contact: Mr. Bruno Brodbeck, Mr. Peter Weber, Mr. Roger Badet
Minimum to open account: $10,000
Assets: 313 million Swiss francs; Liquidity: 91.9%

> Representative office in North America:
> P.O. Box 91717
> West Vancouver, British Columbia, Canada V7V 3P2
> Telephone: (604) 925-3551
> Contact: Mr. Adrian Hartmann

Asset figures and liquidity ratings are as of December 1986. Asset figures do not include safekeeping accounts and managed accounts.

[1]Formerly Banque Indiana.

If you ever want to switch banks, simply instruct the old bank by mail to transfer all the accounts to the new bank—sending a copy of the letter to the new bank. With the exception of Treasury bills, options, and forward contracts, your investments can be transferred intact—without having to sell them and then repurchase them.

GETTING STARTED

The thought of sending your money to a bank far across the sea may produce a strange sensation in your stomach. If so, I can understand it.

But I'm not suggesting that you send everything you have to Switzerland—nor even a major part of your wealth. Only a small part. And having that small part in another country increases your safety, by lessening your vulnerability to what happens at home.

But we can make it easier on you if you like. When you plan your Permanent Portfolio, determine the amount of money that, in principle, would be appropriate to keep in a Swiss bank. If that amount makes you nervous, begin on a smaller scale. Open an account no larger than the minimum required by the bank you select.

Get the feel of having a Swiss bank account. Receive statements from the bank. Make a withdrawal and bring some of the money home—to reassure yourself that the bank really will send your money back when you want it.

You'll see that it isn't much different from handling a bank account by mail in the United States. And you may notice that you read the daily newspaper with a little less uneasiness—simply because a small portion of your capital is out of reach of the problems the newspaper describes.

At that point, it might be much easier to transfer to Switzerland the amount you originally decided would be appropriate. And then your safety program will be complete.

33

Storing
Investments
Safely

Your investments are only as secure as the places where they're stored
and the manner in which they're kept.

A winning investment won't help you if it's lost to theft, fraud,
confiscation, institutional bankruptcy, or other catastrophe. To protect
yourself against such dangers, you need to hold or store each investment properly.

Most of the dangers are remote, but from time to time the remote
suddenly shows up on your doorstep. By facing these possibilities
now, you can protect yourself against them for years to come. You'll
be free to turn your attention away from your portfolio, and you won't
have to be concerned every time you read of some new hazard.

Convenience vs. Safety

Some measures that add safety are inconvenient. How much convenience you're willing to give up depends on how seriously you take the

414

threats you're aware of and how genuinely you believe there are dangers you're not aware of.

Absolute safety isn't available in any area of life. If you refused to cross city streets on foot, or drive a car, or fly in airplanes, or take baths, you would avoid certain risks—but your life would be very awkward and your safety still wouldn't be absolute. The same is true for your investments.

So it isn't a question of what you must do to be completely safe. It's more a matter of how much safety you feel is necessary and how high a price you'll pay for it.

As you read the suggestions in this chapter, note those that seem most practical—those for which the added safety seems to outweigh any added inconvenience. Then review what you've decided to do. Ask yourself if those measures are sufficient for your Permanent Portfolio to weather anything that might happen.

You can't arrange to withstand every conceivable economic disaster with no loss at all. The point is to survive the very worst that might happen—by retaining more than enough to go on from there. Thus a key objective is to assure that only a small part of what you own is exposed to any single danger.

We'll begin by examining the principal storage arrangements, and then we'll apply this information to each investment in the portfolio.

STORAGE WITH BROKERS

For most investments, the most convenient storage is with a broker in the United States. This allows you to sell or add investments with a phone call. The principal concern in leaving investments with a broker is what would happen if the broker went bankrupt.

Ordinarily, when a broker acquires a security for you (a stock, bond, or Treasury bill), he registers it in his own name—making him the nominal owner. In turn, he gives you a confirmation showing that you are the true owner. In effect, the broker is merely storing your property for you.

If he goes bankrupt, the security remains your property. It can't be sold with his other assets to satisfy his creditors. You could lose the investment only if the broker had been grossly negligent or an incompetent record keeper—or if he had committed fraud or theft.

It would be fraud for a broker to fail to buy an investment for you and instead use the money for himself. And it would be theft for him to take your security without your permission—either to sell it or to use it to secure a loan for himself.[1]

Such things happen rarely, but they do happen. And they are most likely to happen at the time you're concerned about your investments the most—during a financial panic or banking crisis. That's when a broker might see his business crumbling, feel that he'll survive if he can hang on for just a few more days, and borrow your investment—expecting to return it next week.

The Securities Investor Protection Corporation (SIPC) provides some protection against this risk. Every brokerage account is insured against loss due to the misdeeds or bankruptcy of the broker. The maximum coverage is $100,000 for cash in a brokerage account, and $500,000 for the combination of cash and securities. Precious metals aren't covered.

SIPC insurance does for brokerage accounts what FDIC insurance does for bank accounts. It protects the investor against isolated problems—problems of one particular company. But in a general financial crisis, when many brokerage firms might be failing, SIPC's limited resources might not be sufficient to pay all the claims that would be presented to it; nor would its administrative staff be large enough to deal with the "boom" in the bankruptcy business.

So misdeeds by a broker are a risk that shouldn't be ignored.

STORAGE WITH A U.S. BANK

It is possible to purchase Treasury bills and bonds through a U.S. bank, and to store them with the bank. Almost everything I've said about storing securities with a broker applies equally to storing securities with a bank.

The one exception is that banks aren't covered by SIPC insurance. And Federal Deposit Insurance Corporation (FDIC) coverage applies only to bank deposits—not to securities the bank stores for you.

---

[1]If you pledge securities as collateral for a margin loan, the broker has the right to pledge the securities to obtain a bank loan, and he may sell them for you, without your permission, if the equity in your margin account becomes too small.

STORAGE WITH A SWISS BANK

A Swiss bank normally will buy gold or silver in Zürich. It will store it for you as a claim account, in safekeeping, or in segregated safekeeping. These three arrangements are described on page 401. Segregated safekeeping is the safest, with safekeeping only slightly less so. Claim accounts should not be used for the Permanent Portfolio.

If the bank buys Swiss securities for you, it can take delivery of them and keep the certificates in the bank. It can even register them in your name, if you so desire, although Swiss securities normally are kept in bearer form.

A checking or savings account in Swiss francs at a Swiss bank is just like a U.S. bank deposit in dollars. The bank isn't storing your property for you; it owes you the money. If the bank fails, you must wait in line for that money with other creditors.

A bank deposit in any other currency at a Swiss bank is a little different. The bank normally places the money for you in a bank account in another country—in America, for example, if you want U.S. dollars. Your Swiss bank doesn't owe you this sum, the other bank does. It is as though the Swiss bank had purchased stocks for you somewhere. It is merely a go-between.

When a Swiss bank purchases securities, it normally buys through a U.S. broker. The securities will be registered in the broker's name, so two middlemen will stand between you and the investment. Thus every hazard of leaving stocks and bonds with a U.S. broker applies to leaving stocks and bonds with a Swiss bank.

In practice, there is no meaningful geographic diversification achieved by keeping U.S. securities for the Permanent Portfolio in a Swiss bank. Gold is the most appropriate investment for a Swiss bank account.

STORAGE WITH U.S. GOLD DEALERS

Some U.S. gold dealers offer programs that might seem attractive on the surface.

For example, some dealers allow you to buy gold at a price below the market price if the delivery of the gold can be delayed for a few months. This is a tipoff that your gold won't be purchased and stored for you, and that the dealer intends to use your money for other purposes between now and the delivery date.

With such a program, you haven't acquired gold; you've acquired nothing but an IOU for gold. If the gold price rises drastically (the circumstance in which the gold will be most precious), the dealer may not be able to afford to acquire the gold to meet his obligations.

A number of U.S. gold dealers offering special plans or "insured storage" have failed during the past five years or so—leaving investors without the gold they had paid for. So U.S. dealers in general are at the bottom of the list of places to store gold.

For storage in the U.S. I prefer to use a facility of the kind described on page 322, and I prefer to minimize my risk by having only part of my gold so stored.

PRIVATE SAFE DEPOSIT COMPANIES

There are private safe deposit companies in the U.S. that aren't affiliated with a bank or savings and loan association.

The industry has had a checkered past—with companies going into and out of business, and some strange burglaries.

The advantage of using a non-bank depository is that it places part of your wealth completely outside the banking system—providing greater privacy, as well as protection against problems your bank might have. It makes a good place to store some gold coins, bearer securities, and the like.

If you consider using one, observe a cardinal rule: *Obtain your own insurance covering the property you put in the box.* The storage company's insurance is of no reliable value to you, because the insurance could be canceled or dropped without your knowing it.

STOCK-MARKET INVESTMENTS

Stocks (and warrants) can be registered in your name, and you can receive certificates of ownership directly from the companies involved.

Since the stocks you might have in the Permanent Portfolio probably will be kept for a long time, it makes sense to acquire physical certificates for some of them—so that they can be stored in a private or bank safe deposit box and avoid any troubles that might beset a broker.

A registered certificate for a security must be endorsed and returned to the issuer when you want to sell. This means inconvenience and delay, since you'll have to take the certificate to a broker. But by leaving some of each security with the broker, you can make quick, convenient sales for annual portfolio adjustments or to raise cash in a hurry.

Mutual fund shares are registered in your name when you buy directly from a fund. The fund will send you a certificate if you request it. However, I can't think of any benefit in having a certificate, since you're not dependent upon a broker or bank as a middleman. And certificates must be returned to the fund when you want to sell your shares.

TREASURY BONDS

Each Treasury bond is available in one or more of four forms.

One is as a credit in the Federal Reserve Book-Entry System. In practice, this means ownership is recorded in a computer system operated by the Federal Reserve. If you buy directly from the Treasury, your name is in the computer as the owner.

The second method is to purchase the bonds through a broker or bank, and allow its name to be in the Federal Reserve computer as the owner.

The third and fourth forms involve certificates—pieces of paper that show your ownership of the bonds. These certificates can be either "registered" or "bearer."

If the certificate is registered, your name is on file at the U.S. Treasury as the owner. You can sell the bond only by endorsing it over to your broker (or to the buyer).

A bearer bond is a certificate with no name on it. Like cash, it's the property of the bearer—whoever holds it.

A certificate, whether registered or bearer, can be lost or stolen. A registered certificate is less attractive to a thief, since it's harder to resell without proper identification. If a registered certificate is lost or stolen, you can get a replacement upon posting a surety bond—the cost of which is 5% or so of the value of the bond. If a bearer bond is lost or stolen, you have no recourse.

The safest form of Treasury bond is a registered certificate that's stored in a place you consider to be safe. The registration allows the certificate to be replaced, at some cost, if it's lost. And the certificate assures that even a computer foul-up can't cloud your ownership.

Next in order of safety is a bond purchased in your own name directly from the Federal Reserve System, but without a certificate.

Then comes a bearer certificate stored in a place you consider to be safe. If no place seems safe, this alternative should be ignored.

The least safe is a bond registered in the name of a U.S. bank or broker. A bond held by a Swiss bank in its name with a U.S. bank or broker would be one step further removed from absolute safety, since the bond would actually be registered in the name of the bank's broker in the United States.

As with other investments, the ideal arrangement would include some bonds stored with a broker—for easy handling of portfolio adjustments—and some bonds stored on your own.

TREASURY BILLS

U.S. Treasury bills do not come in physical certificates. They are issued by the government only in "Book-Entry" form.

Since the U.S. Treasury is the issuer of the bills and you are the owner, the safest form of storage is to have your ownership recorded directly with the Federal Reserve, which is the Treasury's transfer agent.

You can do this by buying the T-bills directly at a Treasury auction. You can make your purchase by mail, buying through the Federal Reserve System—which conducts the auctions.

You don't have to place a competitive bid to buy at the Treasury auction. You merely agree to pay whatever turns out to be the average price paid by all successful bidders. When you enter your order, you also can arrange to have the T-bills replaced with new ones automatically when they mature.

The entire procedure is described in the form "Tender for Treasury Bills," which you can obtain by calling the nearest Federal Reserve Bank branch, or by writing to:

The Board of Governors
Federal Reserve System
Washington, D.C. 20551

You also can buy Treasury bills through a U.S. bank or broker. The T-bill will be registered in the name of the bank or broker, or in the name of a correspondent who makes the purchase for him.

A Swiss bank usually buys through an American broker, with the T-bill registered in the broker's name.

It is convenient to have some of your cash budget in a money market fund—to facilitate portfolio adjustments and emergency withdrawals from the portfolio.

Treasury Notes

If, for any reason, you would prefer to have a paper certificate, you can buy Treasury notes or bonds that mature within a year, instead of Treasury bills.

You can buy through a broker, and then request delivery of the certificates. Your broker probably won't welcome the request, and he may charge an extra fee.

Most daily newspapers list prices of Treasury notes and bonds. You can look there to find an issue that matures in about a year. Otherwise, simply ask your broker to buy one that has about a year to maturity.

Treasury notes and bonds come in denominations as small as $1,000.

MONEY MARKET FUNDS

As explained on pages 349–350, a money market fund for the Permanent Portfolio should invest only in Treasury bills.

Some money market funds use repurchase agreements ("repos") covering Treasury bills to increase their yields slightly, but these arrangements aren't quite as safe as simply owning Treasury bills. So I suggest using a money market fund that limits its investments to owning T-bills themselves. Three such funds are listed on pages 445–446.

GOLD

In addition to the threats to safety that apply to other investments, plans for gold storage have to allow for the possibility of government confiscation. Because gold is money, governments have often been tempted to solve their financial problems by confiscating gold or prohibiting private ownership of it.

However, when a government isn't on the gold standard (and no government of the world is on a gold standard today), the government's financial activities aren't hampered by private holdings of gold.

So today the danger of confiscation is remote—although it isn't non-existent.

If the U.S. government did decide to round up all the gold in the hands of the public, gold dealers and other customary gold depositories would be the first places visited by the official vacuum cleaner.

So the two safest places I can think of for gold are a Swiss bank and your own possession. For gold in a Swiss bank, I think it's best to pay whatever slight extra cost might be charged for segregated storage (described on page 401). And I think it's wise to have a few small-size gold coins in your own hands (as discussed on page 326).

For diversification, you might want also to have some gold in a U.S. storage facility of the type described on page 322.

For convenience, keep some gold in a place that allows you to make relatively small purchases or sales for the annual portfolio adjustment by telephone. This could be a Swiss bank or a U.S. dealer.

The Variable Portfolio doesn't require the same extreme caution for gold holdings that the Permanent Portfolio does. Since convenience is much more important for the Variable Portfolio, I think it's acceptable to store Variable Portfolio gold with a U.S. dealer from whom you buy the gold.

My preferences for storage locations in the U.S. are given on page 323. U.S. and Canadian coin dealers are listed on pages 443–444.

PENSION PLANS

As discussed on pages 387–390, some investments are more appropriate than others for Individual Retirement Accounts (IRAs), Keogh plans, and other pension plans.

Investments stored in a pension plan forsake privacy, and there's usually a middleman between you and the investments. Thus it's best not to keep everything in a pension plan—even if the plan is large enough to accommodate everything.

DIVERSIFYING STORAGE

Whenever possible, and especially when you're using less than the safest means, you can reduce the risk of a total loss by dividing your holdings between two locations.

For example, if you store gold only in the U.S., try to use two depositories. If you keep stocks and bonds with a broker, use two brokers. And use two Swiss banks if there are enough assets in Switzerland to warrant diversification.

RELAXATION

Once you've made your plan, try to imagine how it would survive any financial disaster you can think of. For each disaster, consider which assets are likely to be lost and which should be safe, and estimate how the portfolio's total value would be affected. If the results are gloomy, tighten your storage plan and review the possibilities again.

The effort you make to store an investment safely needs to be made only once. And having made it, you can relax and forget about it for good. If you read about a scandal at a bank or brokerage company, you won't have to wonder what your broker is doing tonight—or who will have to pay for it.

When the world is calm, the extra cost of safety may seem excessive. But once the need for safety has become obvious, it's usually too late to acquire it at any price.

For example, I've always suggested using Treasury bills for the cash budget of the Permanent Portfolio—insisting that the greater safety of Treasury bills is more important than the higher yield of less secure instruments such as certificates of deposit and commercial paper. More than once I received objections from subscribers to my newsletter who felt such caution was unreasonable. But in 1984, I received this letter:

. . . Over many years in the past I have kept my uninvested cash in CDs with Deak & Co., and enjoyed high interest returns.

Since I began subscribing to your Special Reports, I have switched to T-bills as you recommended, despite slightly lower returns.

Last week Deak filed bankruptcy.

I saved my nest egg while several of my friends lost theirs with Deak. . . .

34

Using an
Investment Advisor

In Chapter 4, I discussed some of the tricks an advisor might use to demonstrate his superhuman abilities.

While I was hoping to throw cold water on the unreasonable claims that some advisors make, I wasn't trying to convince you that all investment advisors are useless or dishonest. In fact, there are competent advisors—and a good one can be worth far more than you pay him.

However, it is also true that if you accept the Permanent Portfolio concept, you'll have a good deal less need for an advisor than you would otherwise.

In this chapter, I'll cover some of the ways an advisor can help you or hurt you.

TYPES OF ADVISORS

There are five basic types of investment advisors, each of whom provides a different service:

1. *Personal consultant:* You deal with this advisor personally—

usually face-to-face. He evaluates your situation and recommends a portfolio, or helps you carry out the portfolio plan you've worked out yourself.

2. *Institutional money manager:* You use this advisor's services when you invest in a pool of investments of a particular type—as when you buy a stock-market mutual fund.

3. *Personal money manager:* This advisor takes control of your money and manages it according to his understanding of your goals, but without consulting you about each transaction.

4. *Trader:* He takes as much of your money as you're willing to give him, and tries to make it grow rapidly. He makes no attempt to understand or allow for your circumstances.

5. *Financial writer:* This is someone who writes about investing— in books, newsletters, magazines, or newspapers.

We'll look at each of the five to see what he has to offer.

PERSONAL CONSULTANTS

Personal consultants include financial planners, investment advisors, and some brokers.

The consulting service may come free of separate charge—as with the advice given by a stockbroker. Or a consultant might be hired on a continuing basis. But in most cases, a consultant is visited only as needed—for help in planning a portfolio or handling a thorny financial problem.

There are several benefits a personal consultant can offer:

1. Unlike a writer or impersonal advisor, he will deal with *your* circumstances and nothing else.

2. You can make him sit still while you ask every question you have—something you can't do with a book or a mutual fund.

3. If there's some procedure or idea you don't understand, he can explain it over and over—in as many ways as necessary—until it's clear to you.

4. His aptitude and experience allow him to comprehend all the details of your financial life and keep them in proper perspective— while you might have trouble comprehending one small part of them, or be too concerned about one thing to notice something else.

5. He can review the decisions you've already made—possibly pointing out considerations you've overlooked, or identifying steps that aren't really needed, or confirming that your plan is realistic.

6. He may be able to show you how to do something that's complicated, such as a way to hedge against an illiquid position—or very simple, but unfamiliar to you, like writing a letter to a Swiss bank.

7. He knows where to go to acquire the things you need to put your program into place.

8. He can even do some of the actual work for you—contacting brokers, writing letters, and so on—if you want him to.

Using a Consultant

If you accept the Permanent Portfolio concept, you most likely would hire a personal consultant to do one or more of these things:

1. Explain ideas presented in this book that have left you with unanswered questions.

2. Integrate a business, trust, or illiquid asset into a Permanent Portfolio.

3. Adapt the Permanent Portfolio concept to emphasize certain goals or opportunities that may be especially important to you—such as privacy, tax planning, estate planning, protection from lawsuits or other threats of seizure, or international diversification.

4. Render an opinion as to whether your plan actually lives up to the standards of a Permanent Portfolio.

5. Help you move from decisions about generalities to a step-by-step, concrete plan of action.

6. Help you carry out the plan.

If you find a consultant you like, you might even want to see him once a year—to review your investment program to make sure it is what you intended it to be, and to help with the annual portfolio adjustment.

Finding a Consultant

Personal investment consultants normally are listed in two places in the phone company's Yellow Pages—under "Financial Planners" and under "Investment Advisory Services." Some of the firms listed in either section might be companies that sell investment products, but that's usually obvious from the listing.

No one can tell you how to size up a consultant to determine when you meet him whether you'll be happy with him. You will evaluate him subjectively—just as you do other people you meet.

But feel free to contact several advisors, go in for exploratory interviews, explain what you want, see what each has to say, and then decide which one seems best for you.

You must make it clear what you want, and insist upon the program you've chosen for yourself. If you do, the odds favor your getting what you want, and at a modest cost. If you don't make it clear, the odds favor your winding up with something far more complicated—and less safe—than you had hoped for.

If you like the Permanent Portfolio concept, present that to the consultant as a fact of life—something you want him to help you implement. If he's not familiar with it, lend him this book. Ask him to read Chapters 17–20, 24–30, 31–33, and 36.

If your situation isn't too complicated, your accountant probably knows everything necessary to help you implement the program. And he ought to be happy to do so if you offer to pay him for it.

You have to make the big decisions. A consultant is there to help you *get* what you want—not to *tell* you what to want.

MONEY MANAGERS

A money manager is someone who invests your money for you, without getting your approval for each transaction. We'll look at each of three types.

Institutional Money Manager

An institutional money manager is the advisor who manages a mutual fund or some other "packaged" investment. For example, you choose how much you want to have in the stock market, and the mutual fund selects the particular stocks.

This kind of money manager provides a convenient—and sometimes more economical—way to handle one part of the Permanent Portfolio.

Personal Money Manager

Of more concern here is the personal money manager.

He examines your situation (as a personal consultant would) and then takes over the job of managing your capital. He makes overall planning decisions—deciding what investments you should own and in what amounts.

You usually don't call for a personal money manager unless finance baffles you, or your affairs are especially tangled, or both. So he can seem like a man on a white horse when he arrives on the scene.

But, at best, he's a reasonable and conscientious—but fallible—human being. At worst, he may be no smarter than the horse.

He can't work wonders, and he can't fully appreciate your goals or how you feel about different risks. He will do what seems best, based on what he knows about you and on his own attitudes about investing. And he will be operating with incomplete orders—since it will be very difficult for you to define precisely which investments are permissible and which are off limits.

There undoubtedly are many honest, conscientious, and effective personal money managers. There also are office buildings full of money managers who are none of those things. And there's no way to tell one group from the other at first glance.

Rich people have become poor with the help of personal money managers. Their money was lost by managers who became carried away with tax shelters, or fell for attractive schemes promoted by cronies, or bet too much on well-laid plans that went awry.

One goal of this book is to eliminate the need for a personal money manager. With a minimum of effort and attention, a Permanent Portfolio can be handled by almost anyone. If you have trouble with any part of it, a financial planner or accountant can show you how to take care of that part—provided you insist that this is all you want him to do.

If your affairs seem to be too tangled for you to handle yourself, even with the aid of an arm's-length consultant, the solution is to move to a simpler program that you *can* handle—rather than to put your fate into the hands of someone who promises to "take care of everything." Liquidate the things you can't handle, and use the proceeds to set up a balanced portfolio you can understand.

There is no virtue in complexity. You don't have to tie your finances into knots in order to make profits and keep them. And that's especially the case now that tax rates are so much lower than they were.

When a money manager handles things that are too complicated for you to do, he does things that are too complicated for you to monitor. By handing him your checkbook, you merely replace one problem with another.

The answer is to eliminate the need for a manager.

Trader

A trader invests your money for you, in search of high profits, but he doesn't tailor the investments to your circumstances. Like a hired gun, he's paid to get the job done—any way he chooses.

He may be a firm or an individual, an investment advisor or a stockbroker. He may invest your money in securities, commodities, currencies, Australian greasy wool futures, or any other liquid investment.

Sooner or later, you'll hear about a whiz whose managed accounts gained 125% last year, or the commodity genius who makes investors rich overnight. All you have to do is give him a little money and soon it will become a lot of money.

The odds against your getting rich that way are similar to the odds against winning the state lottery. The whiz operates in the same world as the coin flipper; he comes to your attention because he was recently blessed by chance. And his recent success may make him bolder—so that when the inevitable losing streak arrives, it will be more spectacular than the triumphs that made him a star.

However, I doubt that anything I say will dissuade you from giving him a try. And I won't belabor the point—if you'll promise to give him money only from your Variable Portfolio.

FINANCIAL WRITERS

Books, newsletters, and financial articles can explain concepts you don't understand. They can call your attention to financial products that might help you achieve your objectives. And they can present new ideas that might enhance your investment strategy.

Often a book or newsletter writer, even though saying something you don't agree with, will stimulate your thinking so that you uncover a new idea on your own.

If you like investing, you probably enjoy reading about investing. So newsletters and books can be a source of entertainment as well.

Help with the Permanent Portfolio

If you don't agree with the Permanent Portfolio concept, you will need to develop your own strategy. You aren't likely to get one from newsletters—because a newsletter doesn't usually lay out a strategy from beginning to end. Instead, your best bet is to read books on financial planning until you come across one that offers a plan with which you're comfortable.

If you do agree with the Permanent Portfolio concept (or if you develop another strategy), books and newsletters can help you refine your plans.

Newsletters & the Variable Portfolio

Most newsletters also offer trading suggestions—which can be grist for the Variable Portfolio.

Most of the time, a fantastic track record will be dangled in front of you—to encourage you to take the writer's suggestions seriously. And since it has been 364 pages since I've said anything about track records, let me give you one more anecdote.

In September 1986, *The Hulbert Financial Digest* (which tracks the performance of newsletters' model portfolios) reported that one news-letter's recommendations had produced a gain of 204% after the first 8 months of 1986. Wow! And this was after a gain of 99% for 1985. Here was a track record too wonderful and too consistent to be pure chance.

You might have felt confident staking your future on the newsletter genius who earned that record. But if you began acting on his advice at the end of August 1986, *you would have lost 49% of your capital in the next four months*.

That nosedive was bad enough for long-time readers, who had begun to believe they were on a one-way street to San Simeon. They saw their magnificent profits fall through a trap door.

But it would have been much worse for you, walking in cold. You had no profits to cushion the jolt. Just 49% sliced off the top of your capital.

This example points up the fact that an advisor who has achieved spectacular results probably is taking spectacular risks. So when *his* cold streak arrives, it's going to be a blizzard.

Still, there's nothing inherently wrong with acting on a newsletter's trading suggestions—so long as only the Variable Portfolio is involved.

SIZE

If you consider hiring a consultant or a trader, you might be impressed by a firm's size.

A large firm may be able to provide more research, facilities, and other services than a solo advisor can. But bigness has disadvantages as well.

You won't be dealing with a single mind, with a consistent point of view. Decisions at a large firm are often made by committee; and the decisions don't reflect a single, coherent philosophy of investing.

The person you deal with probably didn't create the advice he offers, and he may not be equipped or authorized to alter it for your benefit. With a solo advisor, you can ask questions directly of the person doing the thinking.

A large firm may have extensive research facilities. But profitable ideas seldom come from amassing huge amounts of information. They usually come from independent thinking about the information that's available to everyone.

If you consider hiring a large company, the most important consideration is the person you'll be dealing with.

BEWARE

With any advisor, there are a few things to watch out for.

Knowledge & Research

A lot of what passes for knowledge and research in the investment world is just gossip.

As with practitioners in any field, very few advisors are original thinkers. Many of them simply run with the pack and repeat what they read or hear. In this way, ideas that may never have been useful, or even correct, manage to live on as tribal wisdom.

Some advisors will dish out advice on anything—how to cut taxes, increase an investment's yield, hedge a risk, save transaction costs, or circumvent government restrictions—with no firsthand knowledge of whether, or at what cost, the ideas work.

It's not uncommon for an advisor to recommend an investment he's never bought—especially now, when so many new types of investments (such as zero-coupon bonds, marketable partnership units, fancy life insurance products, and options on indices) are flooding the market.

I don't mean to suggest that an advisor should buy for himself everything that might be helpful to his customers. But before offering advice, he should be aware of the trading peculiarities, all the transaction costs, the pitfalls, and the potential liquidity problems of any market he asks you to dive into.

Objectivity

One thing you hope for when you consult a professional is the objectivity that you can't give to your own affairs.

But, unfortunately, an advisor often has less objectivity than you do. You might wind up trading your own emotions for the advisor's desperation.

Once you've bought an investment, your objectivity about it fades because you want it to succeed. But if the investment goes sour, your only difficulty is to convince your spouse of the value of the tax loss you've found.

An advisor, on the other hand, has far more to fear from an investment going bad. He faces the difficult job of telling all his customers that he was wrong, or of explaining how the spaceships from Mars threw the market off its track, or of showing somehow that the latest disaster represents another triumph to be added to his "uncanny track record."

It's much easier to continue to believe that the investment will work out. So he has an emotional interest in denying the counter-evidence and postponing the day of surrender.

He may be very conscientious and objective when he's considering an investment. But once he's completed his study and pronounced "bull market" or "good investment," he has an awful lot at stake in the outcome. To reverse his opinion and turn back would raise doubts about his competence.

So, after a recommendation has been made, you shouldn't be surprised that the advisor finds support for his viewpoint in everything that happens—no matter how strained the interpretation.

Substitutions

Another problem is that many brokers and financial planners have products to sell you.

"Why buy Treasury bills when we have a special Treasury security mutual fund that will do the same job for you more easily?" The answer is that Treasury bills have minuscule commissions, while the mutual fund may involve a very large commission—and the fund won't provide the safety and coverage a Permanent Portfolio expects from Treasury bills.

"Why buy Treasury bonds [or stocks] when I can get you a variable annuity that will accomplish the same thing?" Again, the costs undoubtedly will be much greater, while the contribution to the balance of a Permanent Portfolio will be much smaller.

You might not be able, on the spot, to recognize why a product offered isn't appropriate for a Permanent Portfolio. But it's safe to assume that I would have mentioned such a product in this book if I'd thought it would help. You don't need to explain your reasons; just say, "No, thanks."

One way to discourage an advisor from inundating you with inappropriate products is to make it plain at the outset that you intend to pay for his help. Then he shouldn't feel the need to sell you high-commission products in order to justify his time.

WHAT TO DO

It isn't possible to draw up a list of guidelines for evaluating an advisor. Sizing up anyone, for any purpose, is a subjective matter.

That doesn't leave you helpless, however. There are many ways you can make sure you use an advisor's strengths without becoming vulnerable to his weaknesses.

If an advisor proposes something that seems hazardous to you, get a second opinion before you act.

And when an advisor starts talking about his track record, his sure-fire system, the events that are certain to happen next year, or anything else that reminds you of Part I of this book, you know it's time to reach for the saltshaker.

The strongest safeguard in dealing with an advisor is to remain the boss. Don't ever forget that the discussion is about *your* money, and that no one but you should decide what to do with it. Others can make suggestions, offer programs, urge action—but don't ever let them make decisions for you.

No matter how authoritative or reassuring the advisor may be, don't do anything you don't understand. Don't get involved in a plan that's too sophisticated or complicated for you. The only information and advice to accept are information and advice you understand well enough to evaluate.

The responsibility is always yours, because the profit or loss will be yours. An advisor can speak with great conviction about the shape of the future and the confidence you can have in investing accordingly, but he isn't talking about *his* money, he's talking about *yours*.

If he's wrong, he may fudge enough on his recollection of what he said and on his performance record to protect his reputation—as many of them do. *But there's nothing you can do to retrieve the money you have lost.*

Hired Help

Actually, all I'm saying is that you should treat an advisor as you would any other professional you might engage.

You rely on a medical doctor to treat sickness and care for wounds. But you don't expect him to prescribe a magic elixir that will give you eternal life.

You ask an auto mechanic to service or fix your car. But you don't ask him to decide what kind of car you should own or how much you should spend to have one.

It's the same with any professional service. You decide for yourself what you want, and you hire the help needed to get it—if it is obtainable and if you need help. You don't allow others to make choices for you, or expect them to accomplish the impossible.

Nor do you expect anyone to disregard his own interests and put yours first. You know that you have to examine and evaluate the service you receive, so that you can replace anyone who isn't providing what you want.

Dealing with an investment advisor is no different. You will profit from his service only if you approach him realistically—reserving the final decisions to yourself, and recognizing that he has his own goals and purposes. You'll have to monitor his work to be sure it's pointed in the direction you want to go, and you have to realize that the performance of miracles is the province of a different calling.

And if it turns out that someone has failed you or cheated you, lay the blame upon yourself. You gave him the power to do what he did; he didn't snatch it away from you.

Deflating Urgency

One way to reduce the pressure that may be put upon you by advisors is to be sure that you're exposed—through newsletters or personal contact—to advisors with differing views.

If one advisor is pressuring you with bullish arguments about an investment, it helps to hear the views of an advisor who's bearish. Whenever *you* get a strong feeling about something, it's a good idea to search for contrary arguments.

At investment seminars featuring many speakers, I often hear someone say, "I came here to find out what to do about my investments, but now I'm more confused than ever."

Good. If you're confused, you won't do anything dangerous or silly. It's when you've found a sure thing, when you're certain that something is inevitable, that you're in trouble.

If one advisor can demonstrate that inflation is dead while another advisor can prove that inflation is lurking in the shadows, you won't bet everything you have on either contention. Instead, you'll try to prepare for both possibilities.

The best protection of all is to rely on a balanced Permanent Portfolio for your financial salvation, so that no one has the power to lead you astray. The worst that can happen is that you'll incur a loss in the Variable Portfolio—the capital you had decided you could afford to lose.

BILLIONAIRES & JUST FOLKS

An investment advisor is often confronted with the assertion that if he knows all the secrets of investing, he should be so rich that he doesn't need to sell his services as an advisor, newsletter writer, book author, or promoter of a trading system.

The question is very appropriate for any advisor who claims to know how to beat the markets. If his claim were true, he would be making too much money to have the need or the motivation to be out hustling books or newsletters.

If he truly knew all the secrets, he could get very rich very fast—even if he started with very little capital. If he could double his money every year, he could turn $10,000 into $10 million in only 10 years—or into $327 million in 15 years—or into $10 *billion* in 20 years. Who needs to peddle books, subscriptions, or trading systems? Who would have the time?

But, of course, he can't double his money every year. His system, his methods, his insights, his strategy are *not* infallible.

For advisors who *don't* claim to be able to beat the market, "If you're so smart, why aren't you rich?" isn't a relevant question. They don't claim to be able to make anyone rich. They claim only to help investors improve their chances, and to give investors the benefit of the knowledge a specialist has at his fingertips.

They acknowledge that they're working with imperfect theory and limited knowledge in a world of uncertainty. They devote themselves to *dealing* with uncertainty—not denying it.

However, it's also true that some advisors *are* rich and continue to advise others. Someone who is good at something usually enjoys doing it. If he builds a business—any kind of business—into an enterprise worth millions of dollars, that doesn't mean he wants to retire. He'll continue doing what he likes to do.

The same—and more—is true for many an investment advisor. He probably enjoys his work—and enjoys counting the money that demonstrates that he's doing a good job. And he may be too much of a show-off to want to stop.

35

Finding Help

This chapter describes some products, services, and companies you may find helpful in designing and carrying out a plan for your Permanent Portfolio or your Variable Portfolio. Included here are investment dealers and brokers, investment companies, books, periodicals, data sources, and computer programs.

Obviously, you don't need all the services you'll find here. You may not even need any of them. I've included this material in case you don't know where to find something you need.

I suggest that you read through the chapter once quickly—to get an idea of what's here. Mark any item that catches your eye, and come back to the chapter later to decide which sources to pursue further.

I've listed only firms with which I've had some favorable personal experience or for which I've received good reports from customers. There undoubtedly are many useful sources that I'm not aware of.

To make it easier for investors who agree with the ideas in this book, I have tried to further the development of appropriate products —either by encouraging the work of others or by becoming directly involved myself. So, I am associated with some of the products listed in this chapter, and I hope you won't find that irritating. Where I haven't indicated that I'm directly involved, I have no financial interest—except perhaps as a customer.

Guarantees

I am neither endorsing nor recommending any of these sources—only pointing to them as possibilities for you to consider. I can't know what their policies will be next year, or how you'll react to what they provide or the way they provide it.

And, needless to say, I can't guarantee the future solvency of any firm. I'm often amazed at how ready a writer or advisor is to put his own reputation on the line, as he does when he assures you that some investment or firm can't fail. After it *does* fail, the advisor's excuse is, "Well, I exercised 'due diligence'—that's all anyone can do."

No, that isn't all anyone can do. One can learn to keep his mouth shut, and refrain from giving guarantees he can't deliver on.

No advisor can force a firm run by someone else to operate efficiently or to remain solvent. Nor can an advisor monitor a firm closely enough to know that something has gone awry. And, even if he could know when something is amiss, how would he get in touch with all the people he had reassured about the company?

For the same reason, I don't appear on boards of directors or as an editorial advisor to publications. If the post is meant to carry real responsibility, I don't want it; I don't have the time or energy to make sure everything is done as I believe it should be. And if my participation is meant to be mere window-dressing, I'd be a fool to let myself appear responsible for something I can't control.

I'm a consultant to the Permanent Portfolio Fund (described on page 446) and its affiliated companies because I believe the fund answers a need for many investors, and so I want it to continue to succeed and operate correctly. I think I can contribute to making these things happen, because the fund's president is a close colleague and friend—which makes it easy for me to keep in touch with the fund and provide real help. And I've reserved the right to communicate directly with the fund's shareholders. But here, too, my participation is no guarantee of anything.

Reputations

As he sends you off into the world to carry out your investment plan, an advisor may give you the cliché warning: "Remember, deal only with a reputable firm."

That seems simple enough. But what does "reputable" mean in practice? How do you know who deserves his reputation and who doesn't?

This kind of advice protects the person giving the advice—but it doesn't protect you. When the firm you do business with cheats, blunders, or goes bankrupt, the advisor can remind you that he warned against dealing with shady people. But he didn't tell you how to spot them.

Everyone's reputation is sterling until it's time to run off with the money, and everyone's performance record is outstanding until he goes broke.

So with these disclaimers, I offer the firms listed in this chapter as possibilities for you to consider. But remember, deal only with a reputabmdcxscwrvscxap[fsr.

COMMON STOCKS

If you decide to use individual volatile stocks for the stock-market budget of the Permanent Portfolio, or if you want to buy individual stocks for the Variable Portfolio, you might want to refer to the list of volatile stocks on page 336.

Also, many stockbrokers will provide a list of "high-beta" stocks —stocks that are unusually volatile and tend to move in concert with the general market.[1]

If you want to make your own choices, you'll need to do some research.

A multitude of companies publish stock-market graphs and statistics. Their services may help you find undervalued or volatile stocks. Here I'll mention the only two I've used extensively—one that provides graphs and one that publishes statistical information in tabular form.

---

[1]"Beta" is explained in the Glossary on page 493.

Securities Research Company

Securities Research Company publishes three periodicals devoted to stock graphs.

Security Charts, a monthly publication, has graphs showing the weekly high-to-low price ranges of 1,100 stocks for the latest 21 months. *Cycli-Graphs*, a quarterly publication, provides monthly high-low price charts covering the last 12 years for the same stocks. And *35-Year Charts*, an annual, has monthly high-low graphs of 400 stocks covering 35 years.[2]

In addition to the stocks, each publication covers market indices, stock groups, market indicators, and economic indicators. Each stock graph is annotated to show earnings, dividends, capitalization, liquid assets, book value, and other pertinent data.

Every graph is plotted to the same ratio scale—making it easy for the eye to compare a stock's performance and volatility with that of other stocks, stock groups, and market indices.

The monthly *Security Trends* is valuable for selecting stocks for the Variable Portfolio. The quarterly *Cycli-Graphs* and yearly *35-Year Charts* would be more useful for verifying the volatility of stocks over long periods for the Permanent Portfolio.

The cost of *Security Charts* is $83 per year ($10 for a sample copy); *Cycli-Graphs* is $65 per year ($19 for a sample copy); and *35-Year Charts* is $69 per copy. A combined subscription to *Security Charts* and *Cycli-Graphs* is $118 per year.

Securities Research Company, 208 Newbury Street, Boston, Mass. 02116; (617) 267-8860.

The Value Line Investment Survey

This is a weekly service that monitors approximately 1,700 stocks. It gives a great deal of statistical data on each stock every week. In addition, every stock gets a full page of its own every 13 weeks—including a graph, income and balance sheet data, and background information about the company. A beta rating (defined in the Glossary on page 493) is always shown for each stock, to help you spot the most volatile.

---

[2]These graphs are "bar charts"—as are the graphs of most chart services. Bar charts are explained in the Glossary on page 493.

The Value Line Investment Survey is published by Value Line, Inc., 711 Third Avenue, New York, N.Y. 10017; $425 per year; 10-week trial subscription, $55.

WARRANTS

A list of warrants appropriate for the Permanent Portfolio is on page 335. If you decide to use warrants for the stock-market budget, I can suggest two other sources of information—one to explain warrants and another to let you know what's available.

Using Warrants, by Terry Coxon, is a 36-page booklet that explains warrants and dual-purpose investment funds. It was written in 1976, so the few statistics it contains are out of date, but the explanation of how these instruments work is the best I know of. It's available free of charge from the office of my newsletter: *Harry Browne's Special Reports*, Box 5586, Austin, Texas 78763; (512) 453-7313.

Value Line Convertibles is a weekly publication that reports on warrants, convertible bonds, and preferred stocks. It provides all the specifications for every warrant except those for which there's very little trading. It is published 48 times per year, and is available from Value Line, Inc., 711 Third Avenue, New York, N.Y. 10017; $350 per year; 8-week trial subscription for $30.

MUTUAL FUNDS

If you use mutual funds for the Permanent Portfolio, you can contact the funds I've suggested (on page 340) or choose some for yourself.

Here I'll suggest some services that can help you if you want to select mutual funds on your own—whether for the Permanent or Variable Portfolio.

Mutual Fund Chartist

Mutual Fund Chartist, a monthly newsletter, is a graph service that follows about 165, mostly volatile, no-load mutual funds. Each graph shows the high-to-low price range for each week over the last two to three years. All graphs are drawn to the same ratio scale, making comparisons easy.

Mutual Fund Chartist is available from P.O. Box 6600, Rapid City, South Dakota 57709; $170 per year; sample issue, $17.

Growth Fund Guide

This monthly newsletter—a sister publication to the *Mutual Fund Chartist*—deals exclusively with aggressive, volatile mutual funds.

In addition to buy and sell recommendations, the newsletter provides statistical data that are very helpful. Tables are published from time to time that show the performance records of volatile no-load funds over different periods—usually periods coinciding with bull and bear phases of the market.

There normally are graphs of 25 or 30 funds in each issue—showing monthly high-low price ranges for the past three years or so, as well as some information about each fund's policies. Every graph is drawn to the same ratio scale.

Growth Fund Guide is available from P.O. Box 6600, Rapid City, South Dakota 57709; $85 per year; sample issue for $2.

Wiesenberger Investment Companies Service

This service comes in three parts.

The first is a yearly, oversized, 900-page, hardcover book that contains information on virtually every U.S. mutual fund (both load and no-load funds) and closed-end investment company. Performance records are shown for the past 25 years. And, except for the smallest funds, there is a description of each fund's history, policies, annual yields, size, and so on. Of particular interest are tables comparing the volatility of funds. The book also includes chapters explaining how mutual fund investments work. Nothing published about mutual funds is more extensive.

The second part of the service is a monthly newsletter that updates the book. The heart of the monthly letter is a statistical section showing each fund's performance over the past 12 months—dividends and other distributions, change in net asset value, and so forth.

The third part is a *Mutual Funds Investment Report*, an 8-page monthly report on mutual fund investing.

The Wiesenberger Service is expensive, but it is by far the most thorough coverage of the industry. If you need to consult it only once, you might find it in a large library.

Wiesenberger Investment Companies Service, 210 South Street, Boston, Massachusetts 02111; $345 per year.

The No-Load Fund Investor

This monthly, 12-page newsletter shows recent performance, cash positions, and yields for about 400 stock and bond funds. The service recommends specific funds, and advises when to enter and exit the market.

The No-Load Fund Investor, P.O. Box 283, Hastings-on-Hudson, New York 10706; $82 per year; $10 for 3 issues.

The Handbook for No-Load Fund Investors

This is an annual, cardcover, letter-sized, 400-page directory of no-load and low-load mutual funds—with performance records going back ten years, as well as information concerning the funds' investment policies, their betas (volatility), and the like. Also included are valuable articles explaining methods for investing in mutual funds.

The Handbook for No-Load Fund Investors, P.O. Box 283, Hastings-on-Hudson, New York 10706; $38, or $100 combined with *The No-Load Fund Investor* (described above).

GOLD AND SILVER

Under "Coins" in the Yellow Pages, you can find coin dealers that sell low-premium gold coins such as Canadian Maple Leafs, Krugerrands, and American Eagles, as well as "junk" silver coins minted by the U.S. government before 1965. In addition, many stockbrokers now sell gold coins.

The companies listed here sell nationwide by mail or telephone.

Benham Certified Metals
755 Page Mill Road
Palo Alto, Calif. 94304
(800) 447-4653
(415) 858-3609

World Money Securities, Inc.
207 Jefferson Square
Austin, Texas 78731
(800) 531-5142
(512) 453-7558

Investment Rarities
One Appletree Square
Minneapolis, Minn. 55420
(800) 328-1860
(612) 853-0700

Monex International Ltd.
4910 Birch St.
Newport Beach, Calif.
  92660
(800) 854-3361
(714) 752-1400

Camino Coin Co.
851 Burlway Road, #105
Burlingame, Calif. 94010
(800) 348-8001
(415) 348-3000

Numisco Rare Coins, Ltd.
1423 West Fullerton
Chicago, Illinois 60614
(800) 621-1339
(312) 528-8800

Guardian Trust Company
International Dept., 3rd Floor
74 Victoria Street
Toronto, Ontario M5C 2A5
Canada
(416) 863-1240

Blanchard & Co., Inc.
2400 Jefferson Highway
Jefferson, Louisiana 70121
(800) 535-7633
(504) 837-3010

All the dealers are appropriate for coin purchases for the Permanent Portfolio—provided the coins are shipped to you or to a storage facility you designate.

All but World Money Securities sell bags of U.S. silver coins as well.

When making a purchase, it's wise to call several dealers for quotes. When you find what appears to be the best bet, you usually can tie up the purchase on the telephone by agreeing to mail your check the same day.

A list of potential storage places for gold appears on page 323.

World Money Securities isn't a gold dealer. It is the primary distributor for units in the United States Gold Trust—a mutual fund whose sole activity is to hold gold bullion and coins. The units are redeemable for cash or, at the investor's option, for physical gold owned by the trust. Since the units are a "paper gold" investment, they shouldn't be relied upon for the lion's share of the Permanent Portfolio gold budget.[3]

---

[3] I am a limited partner in, and a consultant to, the management company that owns World Money Securities and the trust's sponsor.

U.S. TREASURY SECURITIES

To find what maturities of Treasury bills, notes, or bonds are currently available, you need only to look in a daily newspaper under "Treasury Securities" or a similar heading. The table on page 356 of this book shows how to read the listings.

You can buy Treasury bills or bonds from stockbrokers, Swiss banks, and most U.S. banks.

If, for any reason, you want to understand these instruments better, here are two books that do a good job of explaining the government securities markets.

The Money Market: Myth, Reality, and Practice, by Marcia Stigum, tells you virtually everything you could ever want to know about the buying and selling of short-term dollar instruments—Treasury bills, CDs, commercial paper, Eurodollars, banker's acceptances, repurchase agreements ("repos"), and on and on and on. It even includes detailed explanations of the futures markets for these instruments.

Although some of the topics aren't easy to grasp on a first reading, the author does the best job possible to make the material understandable. Published in 1978 by Dow Jones-Irwin, Homewood, Illinois 60430; $39.95.

The Complete Bond Book, by David M. Darst, is an attempt, largely successful, to explain interest, yields, bonds, and the works right from the beginning. It assumes much less knowledge on the part of the reader than the book by Marcia Stigum (above) does. And yet Mr. Darst's book introduces a great many advanced concepts as well. It covers both short-term and long-term fixed-interest securities. Published in 1975 by McGraw-Hill, Inc., 1221 Avenue of the Americas, New York, N.Y. 10020; $41.95.

MONEY MARKET FUNDS

Here are three money market funds that invest only in Treasury bills. These funds are suitable for the cash budget of the Permanent Portfolio.

Capital Preservation Fund
755 Page Mill Road
Palo Alto, Calif. 94304
(415) 858-3609
(800) 227-8380

Neuberger & Berman
  Government Money Fund
342 Madison Avenue
New York, New York 10173
(212) 850-8300
(800) 367-0776

Permanent Portfolio Fund—
   Treasury Bill Portfolio[4]
Box 5847
Austin, Texas 78763
(512) 453-7558
(800) 531-5142

HELP IN CREATING
A PERMANENT PORTFOLIO

The services in this section are designed to provide help in creating a
Permanent Portfolio. Three of them involve myself or my colleague
Terry Coxon.

Permanent Portfolio Fund

The Permanent Portfolio Fund is a no-load mutual fund established
explicitly to carry out the Permanent Portfolio concept described in
this book and in *Inflation-Proofing Your Investments*. I am a consultant
to the fund, as well as a limited partner in the company that manages
the fund.

Because the Permanent Portfolio Fund is able to achieve greater
diversification than the average investor could achieve on his own, it
includes more investments than those I have suggested in this book.
The fund maintains designated percentages for those investments, never
attempting to outguess the markets.

The fund was created in 1982 by Terry Coxon, who has been my
associate since 1974. During its first few years of operation, the fund
has performed as you would expect a Permanent Portfolio to perform.
(A graph of its performance is on page 256.)

The fund is an attractive alternative if you dread the chore of operating your own Permanent Portfolio. Even if you plan to construct
your own Permanent Portfolio, you may want to consider putting part
of your budget into the fund for additional diversification, to have a
convenient way to add or withdraw money from your own Permanent
Portfolio without disturbing its balance, or simply so that you can

---

[4]I am a limited partner in, and a consultant to, the management company that owns the
Permanent Portfolio Fund.

receive shareholder communications that discuss the Permanent Portfolio concept.

You can obtain a prospectus and brochure from the Investor's Information Office, P.O. Box 5847, Austin, Texas 78763; (800) 531-5142, (512) 453-7558.

Personal Consulting

Terry Coxon, president of the Permanent Portfolio Fund, also provides an individual advisory service to help investors design, establish, and maintain a Permanent Portfolio.

He is well versed in a wide range of financial matters—including tax planning, the use of foreign banks and other foreign institutions, and the creation of hedges to offset illiquid investments. Some of the ideas in this book were developed by him in the course of assisting clients and in establishing the Permanent Portfolio Fund. He edited this book and edits every issue of my newsletter.

You can contact him at Private Investors, 7 Fourth Street, Suite 14, Petaluma, California 94952; (707) 762-5336.

Inflation-Proofing Your Investments

Inflation-Proofing Your Investments is a 500-page book, written by Terry Coxon and me, and published in 1981. It deals wholly with the creation of the Permanent Portfolio.

Parts of it have been superseded by this book, and much of its tax-planning section has been made obsolete by the tax reform of 1986.

But it provides a good deal of material that isn't in this book, and it might be especially useful for an investor with special problems.

The hardcover edition is now out of print, but the paperback edition of *Inflation-Proofing Your Investments* can be ordered through a bookstore or directly from the publisher: Warner Books, 75 Rockefeller Plaza, New York, N.Y. 10019; $3.95.

Computer Programs

Two computer programs have been designed specifically for the Permanent Portfolio concept. I wasn't involved in developing them, but I'm glad that they're available.

The Dual Portfolio Manager was designed to implement the program presented in this book. It allows you to use my 4-essential-investments approach, or to expand upon it with additional investments—including real estate and mortgages, or anything else you might own. The program identifies the purchases and sales needed for annual portfolio adjustments, calculates reward-risk ratios for the Variable Portfolio, identifies the tax consequences of investment sales, and tells you just about anything you need to know about either portfolio. The program comes with detailed, step-by-step instructions—and makes all the bookkeeping chores relatively easy.

A second program, *The Permanent Portfolio Analyzer*, handles the more complicated strategy that was outlined in *Inflation-Proofing Your Investments* (described on the preceding page).

The programs run on any IBM-compatible personal computer. Both are available from C. R. Hunter & Associates, Inc., 1176 Inner Circle, Cincinnati, Ohio 45240; (513) 825-8669; $99 for either program.

GENERAL NEWSLETTERS

Investment newsletters allow you to keep up with new developments in the investment world, receive new ideas that might enhance your strategy, get trading suggestions for the Variable Portfolio, or—if you enjoy investing—simply be entertained. Of course, you may not need a newsletter at all.

Many investment newsletters are merely exercises in self-congratulation. But a number of them offer interesting observations about the state of the investment markets and the world.

As you may have detected in Part I, I read dozens of them every month. Some of the specialized letters are mentioned elsewhere in this chapter. Here, I'll mention three that are more general—beginning with the one I read most often.

Harry Browne's Special Reports

My newsletter discusses the Permanent Portfolio strategy—describing techniques and new investment products that can make it more effective or easier to apply.

The newsletter also makes concrete suggestions for short-term investments—maintaining and tracking a model Variable Portfolio. I make comments on the investment markets, the economy, and current events—and discuss ideas about investing that I believe are particularly useful or particularly foolish.

A typical issue runs 20 to 30 pages—including market comments, a dozen graphs of major investments, feature articles on investment strategy, and answers to questions from subscribers.

The letter isn't published on a calendar schedule. Instead, an issue is sent whenever I feel I have something useful to say—which usually turns out to be every 4 to 6 weeks. A subscription is for the next 10 issues and costs $225. You can purchase the current issue (one time only, as a sample) for $5.

Harry Browne's Special Reports, Box 5586, Austin, Texas 78763, (512) 453-7313.

Dow Theory Letters

Richard Russell, the publisher, is an elegant and interesting writer— a rare find in the newsletter business. In fact, Mark Hulbert of *The Hulbert Financial Digest* (discussed next), who must read over 100 newsletters each month, recently referred to *Dow Theory Letters* as one of the two most interesting newsletters to read.[5]

A 6-page issue is published every two weeks. It focuses on stocks, bonds, and gold—and occasionally the author offers comments on other markets. In addition, he has interesting things to say on non-investment subjects. The newsletter is so good that you'll probably be happy to overlook the occasional dabbling with Fibonacci numbers.

A subscription is $225 for one year (26 issues), or $1 for the next three issues (one time only). *Dow Theory Letters*, P.O. Box 1759, La Jolla, Calif. 92038; (619) 454-0482.

The Hulbert Financial Digest

The formal purpose of this newsletter is to measure the investment results an investor would achieve (or suffer) by following to the letter the suggestions made by newsletters. The editor, Mark Hulbert, constructs a model portfolio for each of over 100 newsletters, and reports on the results—going back, in some cases, to 1980.

---

[5]*USA Today*, December 22, 1986, page 7B.

A newsletter can be very useful even if it doesn't spell out its recommendations clearly enough for *Hulbert* to construct a model portfolio. But many newsletters *claim* to have provided clearcut recommendations that produced amazing profits for their readers. *The Hulbert Financial Digest* allows you to discover which claims are true, and to put those claims into the context of a complete record.

Portfolio results are presented in summary every month, and in detail every three months. In addition, each issue explains and analyzes the ideas and strategies of newsletter writers, and attempts to help readers make the best use of the newsletters they subscribe to. Mr. Hulbert makes no investment suggestions of his own.

His newsletter is published monthly. A one-year subscription is $135; a 5-issue trial subscription is $37.50. *The Hulbert Financial Digest*, 643 South Carolina Avenue, S.E., Washington, D.C. 20003; (202) 546-2164.

Select Information Exchange

Select Information Exchange is a subscription clearinghouse for newsletters. The company sells various packages of trial subscriptions—each package providing a short-term look at 15 or 20 different newsletters. If you would like to receive some newsletters but don't know which ones you'd like, this is an inexpensive way to sample what's available.

A free, 56-page catalog describes the various packages available from among several hundred newsletters offered. The catalog can be obtained from Select Information Exchange, 2095 Broadway, New York, N.Y. 10023; (212) 874-6408.

VARIABLE PORTFOLIO LOCATIONS & PENSION PLAN LOCATIONS

It is convenient to have a pension plan located with a firm that handles a wide variety of investments. The same is true for the Variable Portfolio. Particularly valuable is the ability to switch among investments with a phone call—or at least without having to transfer money from firm to firm.

Many of the large, national stockbrokerage companies can handle common stocks, Treasury bonds, Treasury bills, and American Eagle gold coins. Most medium-size and regional brokerage firms provide a similar range of services.

Charles Schwab, the discount broker, handles stocks, bonds, and Treasury bills—and also handles a long list of no-load mutual funds for a small fee. However, his company doesn't handle gold bullion or coins (in mid-1987), only gold stocks.[6]

A Swiss bank can handle every investment you might want for the Variable Portfolio. But it can't handle a pension plan.

You can check the local telephone book for local phone numbers for these firms. Or you can write or call the home office for information. All these firms do business by telephone and mail, in addition to having local offices throughout the United States.

E. F. Hutton & Co., Inc.	Merrill Lynch, Pierce, Fenner
31 West 52nd Street	& Smith, Inc.
New York, N.Y. 10019	One Liberty Plaza
(212) 969-5300	New York, N.Y. 10006
	(212) 637-7455
PaineWebber Group, Inc.	Prudential Bache Securities
1285 Avenue of the Americas	One Seaport Plaza
New York, N.Y. 10019	199 Water Street
(212) 713-2000	New York, N.Y. 10292
	(212) 791-1000
Charles Schwab & Co.	Shearson/American Express,
101 Montgomery Street	Inc.
San Francisco, Calif. 94104	2 World Trade Center
(415) 398-1000	New York, N.Y. 10048
(800) 227-4444	(212) 321-6000

VARIABLE PORTFOLIO MANAGEMENT

For investors who like the idea of having a Variable Portfolio but who don't want to manage it themselves, I advise on managed accounts operated by two Swiss banks.

The procedure is fairly simple: the investor deposits the funds at one of the banks, authorizing the bank to invest the money as I advise—subject to any restrictions the investor imposes. The invest-

---

[6]Of the mutual funds listed on page 340, Charles Schwab handles all *except* Evergreen, Tudor, and Twentieth Century.

ments might be in stocks, gold, bonds, silver, currencies, or anything else that looks good to me. The annual fee is 2% of the value of the account.

The banks that offer the service are two of the three liquid banks suggested on page 412. You can obtain information by writing to either bank and asking for information about Managed Variable Portfolio Accounts. The minimums shown apply to this type of account only.

Cambio + Valorenbank	Foreign Commerce Bank
Utoquai 55	Postfach 5022
CH-8021 Zürich, Switzerland	CH-8022 Zürich, Switzerland
Minimum: $50,000	Minimum: $25,000

SWISS BANKS

Information on three Swiss banks appears in the table on page 412. Each bank is highly liquid, well prepared to do business with Americans, and provides the kinds of services that are needed to carry out the investment strategy given in this book.

What follows are some additional services that might help you to employ a Swiss bank account profitably.

Multicapital Services Inc.

This Swiss company helps North Americans establish Swiss bank accounts and foreign corporations. The firm maintains an office in Vancouver, Canada, to serve North American clients.

The company will help you to open a Swiss account, assist you if any problems arise, and familiarize you with the practices of Swiss banking.

Multicapital Services Inc., P.O. Box 91515, West Vancouver, B.C., Canada V7V 3P2; (604) 926-5811.

The Privacy Tapes

Multicapital Services has produced a three-hour program of audio cassettes describing foreign banking, investment and tax planning, and privacy in investment transactions. I wrote the program and acted as the host—interviewing Swiss bankers and other specialists in the field.

The program costs $39.95 and can be ordered from Multicapital Services Inc., P.O. Box 91515, West Vancouver, B.C., Canada V7V 3P2.

The Complete Guide to Swiss Banks

This is a 532-page, hardcover book that I wrote in 1976—describing how Swiss bank accounts operate. It includes explanations of everything I could think of that you might run into when dealing with a Swiss bank—from choosing the bank to reading your bank statements.

A new edition is scheduled for publication in 1987. You can order *The Complete Guide to Swiss Banks* for $24.95 from Harry Browne's Special Reports, Box 5586, Austin, Texas 78763; (512) 453-7313.

ECONOMIC DATA

The Permanent Portfolio concept eliminates the need to be aware of everything that goes on in the world. If you're going to have a Variable Portfolio, however, you might want to have a convenient source of general economic data. The three publications mentioned here provide the economic statistics that are usually of the most interest to investors.

Economic Indicators

This 38-page booklet, published monthly by the U.S. government, provides statistics and graphs for major economic indicators—such as gross national product, employment, prices, money supply, government finance, interest rates, and so forth. Most tables show monthly data for the past 12 months and yearly data for the past 8 years. The graphs cover 5 to 8 years.

Economic Indicators, Superintendent of Documents, Government Printing Office, Washington, D.C. 20402; $27 per year, $2.50 for one issue.

Federal Reserve Bulletin

This monthly publication is more detailed than *Economic Indicators*. Each issue includes about 75 pages of tables on the U.S. economy and financial markets. Most tables show monthly data for the latest 6 months and annual data for the last 3 years.

Federal Reserve Bulletin, Publications Services, Board of Governors of the Federal Reserve System, Washington, D.C. 20551; $20 per year, $2 per copy.

International Financial Statistics

This monthly, 500-page, statistical summary, published by the International Monetary Fund, is the best source I've found for data on foreign countries.

For each of more than 100 countries, the most important economic indicators—including money supply, exchange rates, gold holdings, prices, interest rates, and many others—are provided. Figures are shown for the latest 7 to 10 months, 13 to 16 quarters, and 7 years. A yearbook (included in the subscription) provides annual data going back 30 years or so.

International Financial Statistics, International Monetary Fund, Washington, D.C. 20431; $100 per year, $10 for a single issue, or $25 for the yearbook alone.

EDUCATION IN INVESTING

Here are some books that can advance your financial education.

Dow Jones-Irwin Business & Investment Almanac

This is a yearly cardcover publication, running about 600 pages. It contains an amazing amount of information—statistics about the investment world, articles explaining how markets operate, instruction in understanding financial statements, and so on. Also included is an extensive glossary of investment terms. It is an education in the practices and procedures of the investment world.

The Dow Jones-Irwin Business and Investment Almanac, edited by

Sumner N. Levine, can be ordered through a bookstore or directly from the publisher: Dow Jones-Irwin, Homewood, Illinois 60430; $19.95.

Understanding Wall Street

This 200-page, cardcover book provides a helpful introduction to the world of investing—explaining how things work, what the listings on the financial pages of the newspaper mean, and so on. Even the rudiments of fundamental analysis and technical analysis are explained.

Understanding Wall Street, by Jeffrey B. Little and Lucien Rhodes, is available from Tab Books, Inc., Blue Ridge Summit, Pennsylvania 17214; $9.95.

ECONOMIC UNDERSTANDING

I have read a number of outstanding books on economics. Here I'll mention just two.

Economics in One Lesson, by Henry Hazlitt, is the best introduction to economics I've come across. It concentrates on the "art" of economics—which is to look beyond the obvious. Published by Crown Publishers, Inc., 34 Engelhard Ave., Avenel, N.J. 07001; $6.95, cardcover.

Human Action, by Ludwig von Mises, is the supreme challenge for any student of economics. It isn't easy reading, but it is fascinating. Published by Contemporary Books, 180 Michigan Ave., Chicago, Illinois 60601; $49.95.

You can obtain these or other books by phone or by mail from Laissez Faire Books, a large mail-order dealer. You can ask for a free copy of its monthly catalog—which contains several pages of books on investing and on economics approached from a free-market orientation. Laissez Faire Books, 532 Broadway, 7th floor, New York, N.Y. 10012; (800) 238-2200, (212) 925-8992.

36

Getting Started

When we looked at the steps for designing and starting a Permanent Portfolio in Chapter 20, we hadn't yet discussed the particular investments that might go into each of the portfolio's four main categories. Nor had we discussed real estate or other investments in which you may have an interest. And so the narrative was necessarily very general.

Now that we've examined all aspects of both the Permanent Portfolio and the Variable Portfolio, we can walk through the process of setting up both. I hope this review will clarify any details that may have been hazy up to now.

Setting up the portfolios will involve a series of decisions. We'll look at them one at a time.

1. HOW TO CALCULATE YOUR NET WORTH

To make concrete decisions, in dollars and cents, you need to know how much you have to work with. That means determining your net worth—the sum of your assets, minus all your liabilities.

So decision #1 is the question of which assets and liabilities to include in your calculation.

You should include all liquid investments you own—stocks, bonds, gold, other commodities, mutual funds, and the like. Also include all cash and cash equivalents—such as savings accounts and other deposits, Treasury bills and other money-market instruments, and so forth.

Include anything you're holding in a pension plan. But don't include property you keep for personal use—such as furniture and automobiles.

If you own collectibles or other illiquid assets, you have three choices: (1) treat them as personal-use property that you derive pleasure from; (2) sell them, but not in haste, and use the cash for liquid investments; or (3) keep them and include them in your investment planning. If you're going to sell them or make them part of your planning, include a conservative estimate of what you can get for them in your net worth.

If you own a business or a non-marketable limited partnership interest, you have to decide whether to include its value as part of your Permanent Portfolio. Even if it's an important source of income, you may want to exclude it from your wealth for the purpose of planning your Permanent Portfolio.[1]

Real Estate

For most people, real estate is the asset most likely to require an important decision concerning inclusion or exclusion when calculating one's net worth and in planning a Permanent Portfolio.

On pages 371–373, I explained why you might want to leave your home and its mortgage out of your calculations.

Property other than your own residence should be included in the calculation, however. Doing so will more accurately reflect the extent to which your wealth depends upon the ups and downs of the real estate market.

Debts

Any debt associated with an item you're counting in your net worth must be deducted from the net worth. That applies to margin debt on

[1] This is discussed in more detail on pages 379–380.

investments, mortgage debt on any real estate you include in the portfolio, any other debt that's associated with an asset in the portfolio, and any debt that you would pay off if you sold an investment.

Computing Your Net Worth

Your net worth is the sum of all your investment assets minus the total of all debts related to those assets. That is your investment wealth—the capital available to you for investing and speculating.

2. HOW MUCH FOR THE VARIABLE PORTFOLIO

The next decision to be made is whether you will have a Variable Portfolio—a portion of your capital set aside for speculating on investment trends.

As I've indicated, having a Variable Portfolio isn't essential. You should have one only if you have capital you're willing to lose—and if you want to try to increase your wealth quickly or you enjoy the adventure of speculating.

If you've decided not to have a Variable Portfolio, feel free to skip over to page 461—where we will continue with the Permanent Portfolio.

A Cushion

If you're going to have a Variable Portfolio, you need to decide how big it will be.

Start by deciding how much of your capital must be devoted to the Permanent Portfolio. How much of your wealth is precious to you and must be retained under all circumstances? Your Permanent Portfolio should have that amount, plus another 20% of that amount as a cushion.

For example, suppose your wealth amounted to $100 and you considered half of it to be precious. You would reserve at least $60 for the Permanent Portfolio ($50, + 20% of $50 = $60). If you considered $75 as precious, you would reserve $90 for the Permanent Portfolio ($75, + 20% of $75 = $90).

The cushion allows for periods (such as the one that may start tomorrow morning) when the portfolio declines in value. As the graph on page 253 shows, such periods occurred in mid-1973, in early 1974, in early 1980, from late 1980 through mid-1982, and from early 1983 through mid-1984.

The portfolio will resume its growth after the period of decline, but you don't want its value to dip—even temporarily—below the amount you consider essential.

Even if you had started the Permanent Portfolio on the first day of one of those declines, your temporary loss wouldn't have exceeded the cushion. You would still have at least the amount you had decided was precious to you.

There's no guarantee that the portfolio's value won't ever decline by more than the cushion. But the chances are very good that the portfolio will grow before you encounter any significant decline— increasing the cushion before it's needed. And under the worst possible circumstances, you probably always would have at least 90% or 95% of the amount you decided was precious.

Variable Portfolio Amount

Having set aside the portion of your wealth you consider precious, plus a cushion, the remainder is available for the Variable Portfolio.

However, you may decide that this remainder exceeds what you want to put into the Variable Portfolio. If you don't feel very confident about your ability to use the money profitably, start slowly—giving the Variable Portfolio only a small part of what's available. Even if it's money you're willing to lose, you don't have to waste it.

Having decided how much to devote to the Variable Portfolio, the next step is to put that money somewhere.

Making Variable Portfolio Investments

Variable Portfolio investments are chosen as the investment winds seem to change. Unlike the Permanent Portfolio, you don't know now what will be in the Variable Portfolio next year.

But, to help you visualize how it operates, here are some examples of what the Variable Portfolio might look like at different times:

1. The portfolio is completely in cash equivalents (such as a money

market fund) because no investment currently satisfies your criteria for a Variable Portfolio speculation.

2. The portfolio is invested 100% in the stock market—perhaps through mutual funds or in individual stocks you've selected.

3. The portfolio is invested 50% in stock-market investments and 50% in bonds.

4. The portfolio is invested 50% in stocks (or bonds or gold) and 50% in cash.

5. The portfolio is invested 33% in gold, 33% in silver, and the balance in cash.

And so on. The possibilities are unlimited. What the Variable Portfolio should hold depends simply on what looks good to you at the moment. Investments are chosen in accordance with your appraisal of their reward-risk ratios.

How much of the Variable Portfolio to invest in any one speculation depends on:

1. The investment's volatility (the more volatile the investment, the less you need to risk in order to have a significant stake in the outcome);

2. The number of attractive investments you see at any time; and

3. The degree of confidence you have in the speculation.

3. WHERE TO KEEP
THE VARIABLE PORTFOLIO

Understanding what you might be doing with the Variable Portfolio helps you decide where to keep it.

The choice of a central location is controlled by the range of investments (stocks, bonds, gold, currencies, commodities, or whatever) you would consider buying. Ideally, the portfolio should be kept with a broker, Swiss bank, mutual fund family, or other firm that happens to handle all the investments you're ever likely to want for the portfolio.

If you later want to buy an investment that isn't available at the central location, you'll have to transfer money out to another institution. Choosing the most versatile location for the portfolio in the first place will help you avoid this inconvenience.

It might turn out that the Variable Portfolio is located with the same firm that keeps part of your Permanent Portfolio. If so, it isn't essential to separate investments for the two portfolios into two accounts. But it is important that your own bookkeeping and thinking be clear about what belongs to each portfolio.

Some companies that might be used as the central location for the Variable Portfolio are listed on page 451.

4. TRANSFERS BETWEEN PORTFOLIOS

After the Variable Portfolio is established, new capital for it should come only from one of these sources:

1. Profits made on the Variable Portfolio's own investments;
2. Income from outside your investments;
3. Profits in the Permanent Portfolio that take its value beyond the amount that's precious to you (plus a cushion).

If the Variable Portfolio loses money, don't replenish it by taking money from the Permanent Portfolio—unless the Permanent Portfolio's growth has made money available for such a transfer. One standard applies always: How much of your wealth is precious and must be kept in the Permanent Portfolio?

On the other hand, if the Variable Portfolio is successful, you may want to "bank" some of its profits by transferring them to the Permanent Portfolio. If you do so, add to each Permanent Portfolio investment in accordance with its designated percentage. However, if it's near time for the annual portfolio adjustment, you may prefer to leave the new money in cash until then, or make the adjustment early.

You also might choose occasionally to withdraw some of the Variable Portfolio profits to spend on yourself.

This completes our look at the Variable Portfolio. The rest of the chapter will concern only the Permanent Portfolio.

5. CHOOSING THE PERMANENT PORTFOLIO

The next decision is the choice of what to have in the Permanent Portfolio.

This isn't the only decision that's important, but it is by far the most important decision you have to make. It should determine your investment position for many years.

As you know, I'm very partial to the basic, four-investment portfolio—divided equally among stocks, bonds, gold, and cash. If you decide to change the proportions or include other investments, I hope you won't devote more than 35% to any one investment, and I hope that each of the four essential investments will get at least 20% of the portfolio.

If there are illiquid investments to contend with, you'll have to plan around them. Some techniques for doing so are described on pages 368–371 and 379–381.

Imagining the Ideal Portfolio

But before you build your portfolio around what you have now, explore another possibility. Sit in an easy chair, put your feet up, and use your imagination.

Imagine that you've sold all the investments you own now—the good, the bad, and the ugly—for whatever you could get for them. Assume that even the illiquid investments are gone.

As a result, you don't own any investments at all. You have only a pile of cash that's equal to your present net worth—cash that can be invested in whatever seems best to you. You are free to create the ideal portfolio—unhampered by any restrictions that have affected you.

How would you invest the money? What would you do if you weren't constrained by your present investments? What would the ideal portfolio contain?

By approaching the matter this way, you keep your present investments from clouding the picture. By contrast, when you start your plans by asking which of them you should sell, the answer often turns out to be "Nothing." There's generally a persuasive reason for holding on to each thing you have—even an investment that's dead weight in your portfolio.

You may decide against selling one thing because it has fallen below the price at which you bought it, against selling something else because it's rising in price, against selling another investment because it's illiquid and the selling costs are steep, against getting rid of another because you have a profit on which you don't want to pay tax. Almost any investment, when you look at it individually, will have a compelling reason that it should be kept.

But if you start by imagining that everything has been converted to cash, you may find that you wouldn't want to buy back some of those investments. You get a fresh look at a whole world of possibilities; your evaluation is more open-minded than if you try to build around what you already have.

In making this fresh start, don't be concerned about tax planning, where you will store investments, or which mutual funds or brokers you will use. Focus your attention on what, in general, you want your portfolio to be—what percentage will be devoted to each kind of investment.

You may want to spend a day, two days, or several days thinking about the ideal portfolio. Make notes as you go. After you have an idea of what you want, think about it for a day or two longer—in case you've overlooked something.

Returning to Reality

Once you've identified the ideal Permanent Portfolio, you can begin to adapt it to your actual circumstances.

But if you start with the ideal, you might not be willing to settle for anything less. Picturing yourself owning the portfolio you consider most sensible might inspire you to do something about the holdings that stand in your way.

Once you've decided what the portfolio should be, you'll need to make decisions of a more specific nature—identifying how you'll fill the budget for each of the investment categories.

6. USING THE PERMANENT PORTFOLIO FUND

You might decide to use the Permanent Portfolio Fund (described on page 446) for a large or small portion of your own Permanent Portfolio.

The fund provides balance and diversification in a single package, and so can be a convenient way to carry out the general Permanent Portfolio strategy described in this book. However, you should not leave your entire Permanent Portfolio with *any* one institution. So, even if you decide to use the fund as the main ingredient of your portfolio, you should keep *at least* 15% of your net worth in gold coins stored under your own control, and at least 15% in cash and cash equivalents.

If you want to use the fund for a small portion of your Permanent Portfolio, you will need to make room for the fund shares by reducing your own budget for each of the investments you buy directly. For example, with a $10,000 Permanent Portfolio, you might decide to put $2,000 in the fund, and then allot $2,000 to each of the four essential investments—which you would hold directly.

7. CHOOSING THE STOCK-MARKET INVESTMENTS

The next decision concerns the investments to be used for the stock-market portion of the Permanent Portfolio.

As explained in Chapter 26, my three choices are aggressive mutual funds, volatile stocks, and warrants. Owning three to five mutual funds will be the most convenient method for most investors. Volatile stocks can be used by those who prefer to choose stocks for themselves. And warrants might be attractive to someone who enjoys doing a good deal of work to uncover bargains.

Of course, it's possible to use more than one medium. And you probably should have at least part of the budget in mutual funds—for convenience in making annual portfolio adjustments.

Mutual Funds

If you use mutual funds, the first step is to get a prospectus from each fund that interests you. Write to the funds I've listed on page 340 or to funds you choose on your own.

Divide your stock-market budget by the number of funds you intend to use—giving each fund an equal share. If any fund requires a minimum investment that's bigger than its share, use a fund with a smaller minimum instead. Don't accommodate any fund by enlarging its share. No matter how various mutual funds have performed in the past, you don't know which one will be the leader next year.

Once you've chosen the funds, send a check and a completed application form to each one.

The application form will ask whether you want dividends and other distributions reinvested automatically. If you so specify, the fund will pay you its dividends by buying additional shares of the fund for you—rather than sending you the money.

Volatile Stocks

A list of volatile stocks appears on page 336. In addition, *The Value Line Investment Survey* (described on page 440) identifies stocks that have high betas—meaning that they are highly volatile. If you decide to use volatile stocks, you can refer to these or other lists to make your selections.

Don't give any one stock more than 1% of the total portfolio. Choose stocks that represent many different areas of the economy—with no more than two stocks from any one industry group. You wouldn't want the Permanent Portfolio to miss out on a bull market by being over-invested in a single group that failed to rise with the overall market.

In reviewing the stock choices later, delete a stock from the portfolio only if the company it represents has changed in some fundamental way—so that the stock has become less volatile or less likely to move in the same direction as the general market. Don't drop a stock just because you don't care for its current prospects.

Once you've chosen the stocks, split the budget as evenly among them as possible. Don't worry too much about round lots; the extra commission for an odd-lot purchase won't be much of a burden on an investment you'll probably hold for many years.

The final step is to give a stockbroker (or Swiss bank) the money to purchase the stocks for you.

Warrants

If you prefer to use warrants for the stock-market budget, consult the list of warrants on page 335 or the source of current information on warrants that's discussed on page 441.

Pick warrants that don't expire for at least three years, so that they won't have to be replaced frequently. Warrants whose exercise prices are above their current stock prices have the maximum volatility.

Because very few major companies are represented by warrants, it's easy for any one warrant to be left behind by a bull market in stocks. Thus you shouldn't devote more than ½ of 1% of the entire Permanent Portfolio to any one company's warrants. Since there aren't a great many warrants available, you will need another medium, such as mutual funds, to fill up the stock-market budget.

The purchases can be made through any stockbroker. Leave the warrants with the stockbroker, and tell him to make sure that each warrant is sold just prior to its expiration date.

8. CHOOSING THE BONDS

The next step is to choose bonds for the Permanent Portfolio.

This should be easy enough. As I explained on pages 250 and 354, I believe you should use only U.S. Treasury bonds. Choose a bond whose maturity is as far away as possible, so that it will provide maximum volatility.

In early 1987, the three longest Treasury issues available were the 7¼% bond of May 2016, the 7½% bond of November 2016, and the 8¾% bond of May 2017. Each had almost 30 years to go before maturity, and none could be called in ahead of time by the U.S. Treasury.

As a general rule, the Treasury issues at least one new 30-year bond each year. So new maturity dates should be available by the time you read this.

The table on page 356 shows how to read the bond tables published in newspapers, to determine what's available. From the half-dozen or so bonds that mature the latest, eliminate any that have call provisions, and then choose the one with the lowest coupon interest rate.

A bond with a lower coupon rate will be a bit more volatile. And a little larger part of its return will come in the form of its rising value, rather than from coupon interest payments. This means that there will be slightly less taxable interest generated each year, while your overall return will be as great.

Conventional Treasury bonds can be purchased through a stock-broker, U.S. bank, or Swiss bank.

Zero-Coupon Bonds

There are two situations in which you might want to use zero-coupon Treasury bonds instead of conventional Treasury bonds. If you're in one of these situations, it is easier to use Benham Target Maturities Trust (a mutual fund) than to invest directly in zero-coupons.

If your portfolio is burdened with illiquid investments, zero-coupon bonds provide greater volatility for your undersize bond budget. In that case, use the trust that matures in 2015 in order to get the most volatility.

Zero-coupon bonds also should be considered if your bond budget is $10,000 or less. That amount makes it difficult to handle annual adjustments with conventional bonds (whose prices may be at least $900 each). With the trust, you can buy or sell any dollar amount needed for an annual adjustment. Use a maturity about 10 years away, so its volatility will equal that for 30-year conventional bonds.

Zero-coupon bonds are explained on pages 358–361 and in Appendix D on page 522.

9. CHOOSING BETWEEN
GOLD BULLION AND COINS

Whether to buy gold bullion or to buy only coins depends chiefly on the size of your gold budget.

The smallest standard size bar of gold bullion is 1 kilogram (32.15 ounces); at $500 per ounce, that's $16,075 per unit. A 1-ounce gold coin (at $500 per ounce for gold) would cost about $530 per unit.

The gold coins most suitable for the Permanent Portfolio are American Eagles (which are acceptable for IRAs), Canadian Maple Leafs, and South African Krugerrands. Each contains exactly 1 troy ounce of fine gold. In lots of 20 or more, each should sell for no more than about 6% over the gold bullion price (after allowing for premium, commission, and bid-ask spread). Coins purchased in smaller quantities might cost 2% or 3% more.

Small gold budgets can use smaller-sized coins—½ ounce, ¼ ounce, even ⅒ ounce—which have premiums up to 15%.

Very large gold budgets can include 100-ounce and 400-ounce bars. But no matter what the size of the budget, it should allow for enough coins to make annual adjustments easily.

It's also a good idea to include some of the smaller, ¼-ounce or ½-ounce coins. They facilitate annual adjustments for small portfolios. And in the very worst circumstances, they might become spending money—so they are best kept in your own possession.

10. CHOOSING WHERE TO KEEP THE GOLD

The question of where to store gold is discussed on pages 322 and 421. Where you'll store it influences where you choose to buy it.

I prefer holding a substantial portion of the gold outside the U.S., and my first choice is at a Swiss bank. Since the bank also will buy the gold for you, you need only issue an instruction to buy a dollar amount of gold coins (specifying the particular coin you want) and to store the coins in a safekeeping account. You can make portfolio adjustments by instructing the bank to buy or sell from your account a specified number of coins.

If the idea of a Swiss bank account is too exotic for you at this point, open a minimum-sized account at a Swiss bank and buy a few gold coins. If and when you begin to feel comfortable about the account, add to it.

If you decide to keep the bulk of the gold in the U.S., check the dealers on pages 443–444. You can buy from one of them, with instructions for the dealer to ship the coins to one of the storage facilities listed on page 323. Before buying the coins, set up an account at the storage facility. If the dealer from whom you buy the gold offers to store it for you at an acceptable storage facility, accept the offer only if you will have your own account at the storage facility.

You also need to decide how you can safely keep a few coins in your own possession. If nothing else seems safe to you, put the coins in a bank safe deposit box.

11. CHOOSING THE CASH EQUIVALENTS

The next decision involves cash equivalents—which should be in one-year Treasury bills or in a money market fund that invests only in Treasury securities.

Even if you choose to invest directly in Treasury bills, some of the cash budget should go into a money market fund. The fund can keep odd amounts that are too small for a Treasury bill—and it can be a temporary holding place, where dividends and interest you've earned on all your investments can await the next portfolio adjustment. Using a money market fund also makes it easy to conform to the cash budget's designated percentage precisely when you make an adjustment.

Since the minimum-size Treasury bill is $10,000 face value (costing around $9,400 when interest rates are at 6%), a budget of less than $10,000 should be kept entirely in a money market fund.

Breaking Up T-Bills

A Treasury bill can be of any face value that's divisible by $5,000—but not less than $10,000. If your cash budget is over $20,000, you could buy a single bill for the full amount, but I suggest you break the budget into at least two T-bills with different maturity dates.

If you are buying in November, for example, you might buy one bill that matures in May and another that matures next November. When the May bill matures, replace it with one that matures the following May. When the November bill matures, replace it with one that matures the following November.

Doing this may add slightly to commission costs. But it allows you to diversify in one more way against the unthinkable—against the possibility that a bank or broker could go broke the day it receives the proceeds from your maturing Treasury bill.

If you purchase the bills through the Treasury's auctions, with your ownership kept in the Federal Reserve's computer, staggered maturities provide no additional safety, but they do provide added liquidity.

If you don't purchase the T-bills directly from the Treasury, you can buy them through a stockbroker, U.S. bank, or Swiss bank. You can issue an instruction to have any maturing bill replaced automatically with a new one-year (52-week) bill.

Money Market Funds

Although money market funds operate in a much safer world than banks do, it still makes sense to diversify. Unless your cash budget is too small to meet the minimums of two money market funds, I think you should split the budget between two funds. The minimums vary from fund to fund, with the smallest $1,000—less for an IRA.

Once the money is in the funds, there's nothing to be done until you make an annual portfolio adjustment.

Three money market funds that invest only in Treasury bills are listed on pages 445–446. Each one is a little different from the others, so I suggest you get information from all three.

12. HANDLING OTHER INVESTMENTS

If you've decided to include other investments in the Permanent Portfolio, there undoubtedly will be decisions to be made concerning them. Since I can't know what those investments will be, I can't comment on them here.

I assume that, between anything I might have said about such an investment in this book and what you know already, you'll be able to determine the best way to handle it.

13. CHOOSING LOCATIONS

No one location is best for every investment.

A key question is whether you'll use a Swiss bank as part of your program. If so, gold is the first choice to store there, because gold would profit the most from almost any kind of serious problem in the United States. The bank will buy the gold in Zürich—where transaction costs are small—and store it in a safekeeping account, where it remains your property.

There is less to be gained by keeping other investments in Switzerland. The bank will store U.S. stocks, bonds, or T-bills with the U.S. brokers with whom the bank does business. So buying in Switzerland merely adds an extra step to what you could do yourself.

Wherever you do business, I think it's wise to take delivery of some physical stock certificates (if you buy common stocks directly) and certificates for some of the Treasury bonds. These can be purchased through a broker in the U.S., who will deliver them to you.

Warrants should be left with a stockbroker who agrees to be sure that no valuable warrant expires without being sold or exercised. Nothing is to be gained by taking delivery of mutual fund certificates.

I also prefer to have some gold coins and cash in banknotes (currency) in my own possession—for protection against a period of war or civil disorder, or one during which the U.S. government forces all banks to close or fails to keep yours open.

Pension Plan

The choice of location for a pension plan will be dictated partly by what you want to put into it. My thoughts regarding the most effective ways to use the pension plan are given on pages 387–390, and some potential locations are listed on page 451.

SALES & PURCHASES

On page 275, you'll find the format for a table you can construct for your own portfolio. It will help you calculate how much of each thing you need to sell, and how much of each investment to buy, in order to arrive at the portfolio you've chosen for yourself.

ANNUAL ADJUSTMENTS

Once the portfolio is in place, you can ignore it until it's time to make an annual portfolio adjustment.

The best time to calculate the adjustment is in December, so that you can make the necessary sales in the current year or in January of the next year—whichever provides the best tax result.

If you set up the portfolio sometime between October and December, feel free to leave the first adjustment to December of the following year.

But don't neglect the adjustment process. As the graph on page 265 demonstrates, a portfolio adjusted once each year is more profitable and more stable than one that's never adjusted. Only through the adjustment process do you actually realize and "lock in" profits from rising investments.

DIVIDENDS & INTEREST

During the year, you'll receive some interest payments, and you might receive dividends.

Interest earned by most money market funds is paid to you each day as a tiny dividend, which is automatically reinvested for you in additional shares. Most stock and bond mutual funds will let you specify, when you open your account, that all dividends are to be reinvested automatically in additional shares of the fund. So these forms of income require no handling on your part.

Treasury bonds make coupon payments twice each year. If you register the bonds in your own name, each interest payment will come directly to you as a check in the mail; the check can be deposited in a money market fund. If a broker keeps the bonds, you can instruct him to send the interest payments directly to the money market fund for deposit in your account.

When Treasury bills are rolled over, the difference between the face value of the maturing bill and the price of the new one will be paid to you—either as a check in the mail or as a credit to your brokerage account. This interest also should be forwarded to the money market fund.

If you use common stocks for the stock-market budget, the dividends will be credited to your cash account at the brokerage company. If the broker won't transfer the dividends automatically to your money market fund as they're received, you can send him a specific instruction, every three months or so, to make the transfer. The dividends will be relatively small.

When it's time for the annual adjustment, the cash budget may

$100,000 PERMANENT PORTFOLIO
(At inauguration on March 27, 1987)

510.899 shares, Fund A @ $14.68 [1]	$ 7,500.00
317.259 shares, Fund B @ $23.64 [1]	7,500.00
400.855 shares, Fund C @ $18.71 [1]	7,500.00
185.185 shares, Fund D @ $13.50 [2]	2,500.00

Total stock-market investments: $ 25,000.00

11 T-Bonds, 7¼%, May 2016 @ $950.625 [3]	10,456.88
10 T-Bonds, 7¼%, May 2016 @ $950.625 [4]	9,506.25
2 T-Bonds, 7¼%, May 2016 @ $950.625 [5]	1,901.25
3 T-Bonds, 7¼%, May 2016 @ $950.625 [6]	2,851.88

Total bond investments: 24,716.26

40 American Eagle 1-oz coins @ $437.50 [7]	17,500.00
6 American Eagle 1-oz coins @ $437.50 [5]	2,625.00
16 American Eagle 1/4-oz coins @ $116.25 [5]	1,860.00
6 American Eagle 1-oz coins @ $437.50 [6]	2,625.00

Total gold investments: 24,610.00

1 $10,000 T-bill due 3/17/88 @ 97.2450% [3]	9,724.50
1 $10,000 T-bill due 9/17/88 @ 94.3262% [4]	9,432.62
Shares in Money Market Fund A [1]	2,664.06
Shares in Money Market Fund B [2]	2,664.06
Cash in currency [5]	500.00

Total cash & equivalents: 24,985.24

TOTAL PORTFOLIO: $ 99,311.50

LOCATIONS

[1] = Held directly at the fund
[2] = In a pension plan with the fund
[3] = Held with stockbroker A
[4] = Held with stockbroker B

[5] = Held in your own possession
[6] = Pension plan at stockbroker A
[7] = At a Swiss bank

Figures may not agree because of rounding.

The value of the portfolio is less than $100,000 because of commissions and bid/ask spreads incurred in buying investments.

$10,000 PERMANENT PORTFOLIO
(At inauguration on March 27, 1987)

68.120 shares, Fund A @ $14.68 [1]	$ 1,000.00	
42.301 shares, Fund B @ $23.64 [1]	1,000.00	
37.037 shares, Fund C @ $13.50 [2]	500.00	
Total stock-market investments:		$ 2,500.00
60.606 units, Bnhm Target Trust 2000 @ $33.00 [1]	2,000.00	
15.152 units, Bnhm Target Trust 2000 @ $33.00 [2]	500.00	
Total bond investments:		2,500.00
4 American Eagle 1-oz coins @ $437.50 [7]	1,750.00	
2 American Eagle 1/4-oz coins @ $116.25 [5]	232.50	
1 American Eagle 1-oz coin @ $437.50 [6]	437.50	
Total gold investments:		2,420.00
Shares in Money Market Fund A [1]	1,809.46	
Shares in Money Market Fund B [2]	500.00	
Cash in currency [5]	250.00	
Total cash & equivalents:		2,559.46

TOTAL PORTFOLIO: $ 9,979.46

LOCATIONS

[1] = Held directly at the fund   [5] = Held in your own possession
[2] = In a pension plan with the fund [6] = Pension plan with a stockbroker
[3] = Held with stockbroker A   [7] = At a Swiss bank
[4] = Held with stockbroker B

Figures may not agree because of rounding.

The value of the portfolio is less than $10,000 because of commissions and bid/ask spreads incurred in buying investments.

The cash budget holds more than 25% because it contains odd amounts not used in purchasing the other investments.

exceed its designated percentage because of the income the money market fund has accumulated during the past year. The adjustment will distribute the excess to the other sections of the portfolio.

GETTING STARTED

Pages 472 and 473 show examples of a Permanent Portfolio worth $100,000 and one worth $10,000—each just after its inception or an annual adjustment. Each portfolio uses the four-investment strategy I've suggested.

Notice that the smaller portfolio is constrained only slightly by its size. There is little problem dealing in small units.

These two examples should provide sufficient guidance to enable you to create a portfolio of any size.

All that remains is for you to get started.

Epilogue

37

Safety & Profit in an Uncertain World

At the start of this book, I said the best-kept secret in the investment world is that *almost nothing turns out as expected.*

What may seem to be the best-laid plans usually go wrong, because they're usually the worst-laid plans in disguise. Plans that depend on an advisor who boasts of his fabulous performance, or a forecaster who pretends that he isn't surprised by anything that happens, or a trading system with a track record concocted solely from what might have been, aren't plans at all. They're fantasies.

The real world is a world of uncertainty—a world in which we have to be prepared for the unexpected. Outside of the investment markets—in our careers, family life, friendships—we accept surprises as a way of life, and we're so prepared for them that they don't seem remarkable when they happen. Yet, in the investment world, we're continually reassured that we can know everything before it happens. And because it's so comforting to believe that, we're constantly disappointed.

The secret will remain a secret so long as thousands of experts continue to promote the gospel—the good news that you can get rich, quickly, by acting on their uncanny abilities to divine the course of the investment markets.

The most inventive minds in the investment business devote themselves to developing sophisticated new techniques—not techniques for achieving investing success, but techniques for persuading you that you can achieve investing success by following their well-laid plans.

As I was writing this chapter, I came across a magazine ad that offered professional management for investment portfolios worth $250,000 or more.

The ad is dominated by a graph covering the years 1977 through 1986. It shows that the Standard & Poor's Index of 500 stocks rose 266% during those ten years. But the gain in the S & P is dwarfed by an investment that seems to be ascending to the heavens. The headline in the graph says:

2,806% (IN TEN YEARS)

Very professional management.

There is, however, a footnote. If I can read the small print, this is what it says:

> Based upon an initial investment of $100,000 on January 1, 1977, utilizing an equally weighted investment portfolio of 10 of the top-performing no-load mutual funds as determined on a year-to-year basis including reinvestment of dividends. The graph is intended solely to illustrate the exceptional performance which theoretically could be obtained by carefully selecting top-performing mutual funds for an investment portfolio as opposed to the S & P 500. This graph is not intended to imply that the above performance has been or will be achieved in the [*name withheld to protect the guilty*] program and past performance is not necessarily indicative of future results.

In other words, the advisor didn't produce a gain of 2,806% over 10 years. He doesn't even claim he *would* have produced such a result using his current system—or any other system.

The graph merely shows what would have happened if, each year, you somehow could have known in advance which 10 mutual funds would be the best performers for the year and had bet your money on them.

Yes, and if only my aunt had whiskers, she could be my uncle. And if wishes had wings, we all could fly.

I eagerly await the appearance of an ad with the headline:

Do You Sincerely Want to Have $3,012,110,000,000?

A footnote will explain:

Based upon the value of all shares on the New York Stock Exchange, the American Stock Exchange, and the over-the-counter market. This hypothetical wealth figure is intended solely to illustrate the exceptional potential in investments. It is not intended to imply that you could acquire every share of stock of every company in the United States using the Foley Foolproof Fluctuation Formula, or that anyone has become rich using the Formula, or that anyone has ever used the Formula, or that we have figured out what the Formula is.

The creativity and daring of the investment world is truly amazing. There is no end to the ideas that the world's hottest hands will place in your mailbox.

TRACK RECORDS & LUCK

It isn't that no advisor has an impressive track record. There are some truly remarkable records around.

But luck plays a much greater part in such records than most people are prepared to accept. If there are thousands of advisors, mere chance assures that a few of them will have amazing records.

I know that *I've* been blessed with good luck. Many people have told me that they made a great deal of money in gold and silver as a result of my advice. But they probably don't realize how much luck affected the outcome.

I happened into hard-money investments (gold, silver, and Swiss francs) because of my beliefs about what governments should and should not do—not because I had dispassionately analyzed the prospects for those investments. As a result of government mismanagement of the economy, it seemed inevitable to me in the late 1960s that hard-money investments would rise fairly soon. They didn't—but, fortunately, not many people heard me talk about them then.

It was lucky that my first book (*How You Can Profit from the Coming Devaluation*) wasn't published until 1970—about 20 months before the first devaluation of the U.S. dollar. The timing, though unplanned, was fortuitous. Gold started rising in price from $35 in 1970, followed by silver (from $1.29) and the Swiss franc (from $.23) in 1971.

I was lucky to have, without any attempt at timing, my first two investment books published in 1970 and 1974—years in which stocks were in severe bear markets. Thus my message of salvation through gold and silver couldn't have caught its audience in a more receptive mood. The timing undoubtedly had a great deal to do with the sale of those books, with the number of people who acted on what I said, and with my subsequent reputation.

It was very lucky that in 1974 I met Terry Coxon, who has edited every word of my newsletter and every book of mine since then, and who has had a profound effect upon my thinking, my writing, and the investment advice I've given.

The first tangible benefit of his help came in 1975. He showed me how stock warrants could, by using only a small portion of one's portfolio, provide a hedge against the hard-money investments (gold, silver, and francs) I had been recommending for the bulk of one's portfolio.

Again, I was very lucky. With no attempt at timing, I introduced the concept in my newsletter in April 1975—only 3 months after the 1975–1976 bull market in stocks had begun. Needless to say, I didn't know the 3-month-old rally was the start of a 2-year bull market—but I didn't complain when that turned out to be the case and the warrants rose 30% in 4 months.

Selling

I was just as lucky getting out of investments at the right time as I had been getting into them.

Common sense, not luck, told me that hard-money investments would have to be sold someday, since there was no point in buying unless we would sell eventually. But, again, luck took care of the timing.

The first of a series of lucky breaks occurred in 1978. My book *New Profits from the Monetary Crisis* said that the big run-up in the Swiss franc was over, and that we had to learn to treat the U.S. dollar with respect after seven years of decline. Although the book was written many months beforehand, it happened to be published in October 1978—the very month the franc hit its high point, at $.67, a price not reached again until 1987.

When silver skyrocketed during 1979, I knew we would have to sell at *some* point. But who could know when the top had been reached? Terry Coxon's urging to sell silver in January 1980, when the price was $40, made me realize that there was no reason to hang on longer in the hope of further gain.

I didn't know whether the price would continue upward to $100 (as some advisors were announcing) or was about to crash. But, having seen the price of silver go up 25 times over since I first publicly recommended silver in 1970, and with the market so wild that the price sometimes rose or fell 20% in a single day, it seemed to make sense to get silver out of the Permanent Portfolio while the getting was good. So, even if silver had continued upward, the decision to sell would have been a correct one—and I would have been satisfied with it.

But, once again, the timing was remarkable, and *that* was luck. The newsletter article "Farewell to Silver" appeared with the price at $38—within two weeks of the all-time high of $48. Two months later, the price had crashed to $10, and it later fell to $5. It hasn't come anywhere close to $38 since then.

Throughout 1978 and 1979, the newsletter's Variable Portfolio was invested in gold, starting at a price of $165. The investment was always covered by trailing stop-losses that were set in the manner I described in Chapter 21. In early 1980, I suggested two stop-losses, each covering half the gold. They were triggered in January and March 1980, and the gold was sold at an average price of $582.50.

Using trailing stop-losses wasn't a matter of luck; it was a matter of strategy, a technique available to anyone who isn't addicted to fortune-telling. But it was lucky that the decline that triggered the stop-losses didn't turn out to be a false alarm.

The End of Inflation

The concept of two portfolios was introduced in my newsletter in December 1977. A more polished version appeared in my October 1978 book—which used the terms *Permanent Portfolio* and *Variable Portfolio* for the first time.

These early versions of the Permanent Portfolio were heavily weighted toward precious metals. I then began to move toward more balance—not because there was any way to know that the long bull market in precious metals was almost over, but because it didn't make sense to be so dependent on investments that had already gone so far.

Fortunately, my good luck wasn't quite ready to abandon me. Terry Coxon and I wrote *Inflation-Proofing Your Investments*, and it was published in February 1981. Despite its title, the book urged the reader to realize that inflation would come to an end (although we didn't know when), and that one should be ready before it did. The book argued strenuously for a balanced Permanent Portfolio.

As we know now but couldn't see then, inflation was in the first year of a 7-year remission (that may have ended in January 1987). The timing fairy had struck again.

Track Records

Among all the publicly known investment advisors who were recommending gold and silver throughout the 1970s, I'm not aware of anyone else who actually told his customers to sell when the long bull market ended in 1980. The strange thing was that I was the only one who didn't presume to know what the future would bring.[1]

With such a track record, it would be easy to claim that I have an "uncanny" knack for seeing the turning points. But, as I've tried to make clear, that just isn't so.

Common sense kept me from getting carried away with an investment and allowing big profits to slip away. But it was luck that made the timing of the sales seem so perceptive. And there's no reason to assume my luck will be as good the next time.

You may have noticed, too, that I've discussed only the recommendations that worked out. I didn't mention that I wasn't convinced a new bull market in stocks had begun in 1982—and that I delayed recommending Variable Portfolio purchases until the second leg of the bull market was under way in 1984.

And I didn't mention that . . . Well, never mind, one example is enough.

When you see the track record of a brilliant market timer, remember that it's probably the product of good luck and a selective memory.

Other Kinds of Luck

I've been fortunate in other ways as well. Often, the incidents in which luck *didn't* bless me provided valuable lessons.

---

[1]Six months after "Farewell to Silver," with the silver price down to $15, I had a public debate with a silver expert who still hadn't sold his silver. The principal issue was whether it's possible to spot major turns in the investment markets. Ironically, he argued that you can, and I said that you can't.

In 1968, I was helping customers buy silver through Swiss bank accounts. Many of the investors had bought their silver on margin—in some cases, margin as thin as 33%. As the price rose, some customers used their increased equity to buy more silver, so that the equity was never much more than 33%.

After rising from $1.29 up to $2.54, the price fell to $1.84—and investors were receiving margin calls they hadn't expected to be a part of the game.

One of my customers was a middle-aged man whom I knew fairly well. His wife hadn't wanted him to make the investment, since he was risking a large part of their savings, and he didn't have the cash to meet his margin call. He called me on the phone a few days later. He was crying as he said, "Harry, they sold me out. I lost everything."

Although I wish the incident hadn't happened, I was fortunate to have been so close to it—and so early in my career. I know I'll never forget that moment. I can still hear his voice; it has been my conscience ever since. His words remind me constantly that what I say can affect people's lives and savings—and not necessarily for the better.

Without that experience, I might be oblivious to what should be obvious—that lives can be damaged by investment advice that serves the advisor more than the investor.

Having faced investors who lost money because of my advice, I could never ask anyone to put his faith in me, to let me play with capital that is precious to him.

APOLOGIES

As this long book draws to a close, let me make a few apologies.

If I have overstated my case anywhere, just attribute it to the normal ravings of a newsletter writer.

If there has been too much repetition, please excuse it as the price to be paid for clarity and detail. Realize, too, that others who read this book may not be as familiar as you are with the ins and outs of the investment world.

If any detail is incorrect, please forgive the oversight. I have checked and rechecked every point about which I thought there could be any question—and, indeed, I have removed some "facts" that turned out to be unverifiable. But some false notion may still be stowed away in a book this large.

If I seem to effect an air of superiority toward others in my business, blame my clumsy writing and not my attitude. I have found many people to admire in the investment business. And many of those who pretend to be fortune-tellers are very good investment advisors. Although I chide them for claiming to be soothsayers, I don't hold it against them that they're not.

If I failed to justify some premise on which I later relied for a conclusion, please don't think I was trying to slip something by you. Sometimes I feared I was beating a dead horse back to life by criticizing an idea too long and too hard—and this concern might have led me to rush through some other matter too quickly.

If I haven't explained an apparent contradiction between something said in this book and what I said in an earlier book, please assume that this book reflects my present attitude. In some cases, I've called attention to a change of opinion; in others, I've decided to leave the past alone.

If I seem to be pressing you to take some action that isn't comfortable for you, that isn't my intention—and please don't do it. I feel very strongly that you should have a balanced Permanent Portfolio. But that's how *I* feel.

Don't do anything that overreaches the limits of your present understanding, or starts something you might not finish, or adds to your worries rather than alleviates them.

Even though I've often used the word "should," please believe that I have no desire to make your decisions for you. It's *your* money that's at risk—not mine.

If I've written as though only four investments (stocks, bonds, gold, and T-bills) are worth thinking about, I'm sorry for the misunderstanding. I haven't been trying to banish all other investments—only to demonstrate that you can get along without them.

And if, somehow, I seem to have guaranteed a healthy profit or absolute safety through a Permanent Portfolio, forgive my boyish enthusiasm. Nothing is certain in the real world. I believe that the strategy I've presented here achieves far greater safety than most investors have now—and with the added bonus that it should provide an attractive profit. But nothing in this book comes with a guarantee except the spellin.

IT HAPPENS TO ALL OF US

And now, before we part, let me tell you one more story.

In February 1984, I had the chance to meet for the first time a well-known gold analyst, a man whose work I had read and respected for several years.

At the time, gold had been in a bear market for almost four years. In our conversation, I said, "Isn't it funny how many times during the past few years various advisors have announced the beginning of a new bull market in gold?"

He said, "Yes, many people have jumped the gun."

And then he added, "But, you know, the bull market did begin today."

At first I thought he was kidding. But then I realized he was serious, and I stopped giggling. "Today?" I asked, "Why do you think that?"

"Well, the London gold fixing finally exceeded $390, the 5-week moving average rose above the 13-week moving average . . ." and so on.

If you've read the past 484 pages, you've figured out that I'm the world's #1 skeptic. For 40 years, I've been a card-carrying member of the National Organization of Wary & Agnostic Youth (NOWAY). I'm skeptical of *everything*.

But I must admit that, as I sat there listening to him, I thought to myself, "Am I missing out on something? Should I run home, call my Swiss bank, load up on gold, send a special bulletin to my newsletter subscribers?"

But, lucky me, I sobered up before doing anything foolish. No bull market in gold started that day or that month or even that year. In fact, it was exactly one year later that gold finally shook itself awake and began climbing upward from $285.

Obviously, if *I* can be unnerved by confidence and authority, I well understand how *you* can be stampeded by plausible, compelling claims. There always will be someone who knows without question what's coming next, and who wants to make you feel that you'll lose out if you don't act now.

I hope this book has helped to arm you against such pressure. I hope it allows you to reduce your vulnerability to the unforeseen, to be less dependent on the best-laid plans, to find safety and profit in an uncertain world, and to forget about your investments whenever you want to.

Thank you for spending this time with me.

I wish you the very best.

California; September 1, 1987   Harry Browne

Appendices

A

—

Acknowledgments

This book took almost two years to write. And Terry Coxon suffered through all of it with me. He edited, re-edited, made suggestions, and challenged assumptions—making the book much better than I could have fashioned on my own. The only reason his name isn't on the book with mine is that I had the last word—so that everything said represents my opinion, and not always his.

Since 1974, I've been fortunate to be able to write a newsletter that is published by John Chandler and Charles Smith—two successful businessmen who persuaded me to write the letter. By seeing to all the details, they made it easy for me to do so. Without them, my first newsletter issue would have been the last. And without the newsletter, I would not have developed the ideas that evolved into this book.

Part of the credit for this book goes also to Richard Barbarick (who compiled the very extensive index), Alan Sergy (who checked many of the facts), Howard Cady (who chose the book for William Morrow & Co.), my wife Pamela (who read the manuscript chapter by chapter and kept me understandable and honest), and Oscar Collier (who must be the best literary agent in the world).

A number of people have contributed to my economic education over the years, but probably the three most important influences were Ludwig von Mises, Murray Rothbard, and Henry Hazlitt.

The book was written using a word-processing program in a Hewlett Packard 9845C computer—one that is nine years old but very fast and very efficient. The graphs were prepared with the same computer system.

Futura Press in Austin, Texas, under the direction of Novella Carnline, put the graphs into presentable form and composed the tables.

And, as always, I am sincerely grateful to Mr. Webster and Mr. Roget—without whom I can't seem to string together a coherent sentence.

B

Glossary

Here are definitions of many of the terms used in this book, as well as other terms you might come across when dealing with the investments we've discussed

A definition isn't authoritative; its purpose is to make communication more intelligible. In most cases, I've defined a word in the way it's generally understood in the investment and economic worlds, or as I've used it in the text.

A term appearing in **boldface** within a definition is itself defined elsewhere in the Glossary. Where a more detailed explanation of a term appears elsewhere in this book, the page number is shown here.

ADR (American Depository Receipt): A redeemable receipt issued by an American bank for shares of stock in a foreign company. The underlying stock certificates are deposited in a bank (usually a foreign affiliate of the U.S. bank), and the ADRs are traded in the U.S. in place of the stock itself.

Advisor: Someone who provides advice regarding investments. He may do so as a personal consultant or financial writer, or as a manager of money—such as through a managed account or a mutual fund.

Agency security: A **bond** or other **debt instrument** issued by an agency of the U.S. government other than the U.S. Treasury Department.

Annuity: A contract, usually with an insurance company, that promises to pay someone a fixed amount periodically (such as monthly or yearly) over a given period of time—usually for the rest of the person's life. (See page 392.)

Arbitrage: The purchase of an **asset** in one market accompanied by a simultaneous sale of the same (or a similar) asset in a different market, to take advantage of a difference in price. The arbitrage principle can be applied to simultaneous buying and selling of related **currencies**, commodities, or **securities**; or the same asset for different delivery dates. An arbitrager (or arbitrageur) makes such pairs of trades if he believes that one price is likely to change in relation to the other.

Ask price: The price at which a **dealer** is willing to sell to his customers.

Asset: Anything owned on which a value can be placed.

At the bank's risk: In describing an investment acquired for you by a bank, this means that the bank—not you—assumes most of the risk.

At your risk: In describing an investment acquired for you by a bank, this means that you will bear any loss—whether from government confiscation, **exchange controls**, **default**, price decline, or other cause.

Austrian school of economics: An approach to **economics** based on the theory of **human action**; it places special emphasis on the actions of individuals in studying aggregate economic activity, and generally concludes that government intrusions into the economy will produce results different from those intended.

Bag: In **junk silver coin** investments, the basic unit of trading. It is composed of 10,000 dimes, 4,000 quarters, or 2,000 half-dollars—in other words, coins whose **face value** totals $1,000.

Bail-out point: A predetermined price at which you'll sell an investment, rather than allow the loss to become larger. (See page 282.)

Balance: Diversification of investments to prevent being vulnerable to the fortunes of any one.

Balance sheet: A financial statement that lists a firm's or individual's **assets**, **liabilities**, and **capital**.

Bank discount basis: A convention for stating **yields** on, and for pricing, Treasury bills, **banker's acceptances**, and certain other short-term **money market instruments**. It does not represent the true yield the investment provides. (See page 346.) The formula for determining the actual yield from the quoted T-bill rate is:

$$Y = \left(\cfrac{1}{1 - \left(\cfrac{R \times D}{36,000} \right)} \right)^{\frac{365}{D}} - 1 \times 100$$

where Y = the true yield (as a percentage), R = quoted rate (as a percentage), and D = the number of days until **maturity**.

Bank holiday: A period during which banks are legally permitted to deny, or forced by the government to deny, withdrawal requests from depositors.

Bank run: An epidemic of withdrawal requests motivated by doubts about a bank's solvency.

Banker's acceptance: A post-dated business check, usually for $1 million or more, that has been "accepted" (guaranteed) by a bank and sold to an investor at a discount from its **face value**.

Banknote: Currency in paper form, as opposed to a bank deposit.

Bankruptcy: The inability to pay debts or other obligations. Also, a formal recognition of that inability.

Bar chart: For an investment, a price graph in which vertical lines (bars) are drawn between the highest and lowest price reached during each period. Depending on the graph, each bar might show the range of prices reached during a day, week, month, or year. A small line may be drawn horizontally from the right side of each bar to show the last price of the period.

Bear market: A period during which a price is moving generally downward.

Bearer instrument: Any certificate of ownership (**stock, bond**, note, etc.) that isn't **registered** or made payable to a specific name—and thus is effectively owned by whoever possesses it (the "bearer" of the certificate).

Beneficiary: The individual entitled to receive the benefits of a **trust**, **annuity**, or insurance policy.

Beta: A measure of a **stock**'s **volatility** and its tendency to move in harmony with stocks in general. A beta of 1.0 indicates (a) a stock that always moves in the same direction, and to the same extent, as the general stock market; or (b) a stock that merely tends to move in the same direction as the general market but also tends to be more volatile. A beta higher than 1.0 indicates that the stock tends to move in the same direction as the market and is more volatile than the average. A beta lower than 1.0 (but greater than 0) means the direction of the stock's movement corresponds to some degree with the general market, but may be less volatile. A negative beta means the stock tends to move in the opposite direction from the general market.

Bid price: The price at which a **dealer** is willing to buy from you.

Big Three: The three largest Swiss banks: Swiss Bank Corporation, Swiss Credit Bank, and the Union Bank of Switzerland. (The "Big Five" includes Bank Leu and Swiss Volksbank as well.)

Bill: A short-term debt, usually of no more than 12 months' duration, paying no interest until **maturity**. (See also **Treasury securities**.)

Blue-chip stock: The **stock** of a large, well-known, financially sound company.

Bond: A **debt instrument** issued by a corporation or government, on which periodic interest payments are made (usually twice yearly), and whose **face value** is payable in full on the **maturity** date.

Book value: A measure of a firm's net worth derived from its **balance sheet**; the difference between stated **assets** and stated **liabilities**.

Borrowing short, lending long: Usually in reference to a bank, the practice of making long-term loans with money provided to the bank by short-term deposits. (See page 348.)

Bottom: A price level below any reached during some period of time following.

Broker: One who acts only as a middleman between buyers and sellers; unlike a **dealer**, he doesn't buy and sell for his own account. (Some firms act both as brokers and as dealers.)

Bull market: A period during which the price trend is upward.

Bullion: Bars of refined gold, silver, or other precious metals.

Bullion coin: A gold or silver coin that normally sells at a price close to the value of the metal in the coin. (See pages 324–326.)

Business cycle: The alternation of prosperous and recessionary periods, sometimes called the "boom-bust cycle." (See page 140, and see also **Monetary cycles** and **Cycle**.)

Call loan: A loan for which the **creditor** can demand repayment at any time, or can demand repayment by giving notice of a specified number of days.

Call option: The right to purchase a specified **investment** at a specified price on a specified date or, in some cases, any time prior to a specified date. (See pages 330 and 331.)

Call privilege: The right of a **bond** issuer to pay off his debt before its **maturity** date. (See page 354.)

Capital: [1] The sum of money paid into a company by its shareholders. [2] The **net assets** of a person or firm.

Capital appreciation or **capital gain:** A profit made from a change in the price of an **investment**.

Capital good: A product that is used to produce other products or services.

Carrying charges or **carrying cost:** The interest and storage costs of owning an investment.

Cash: [1] In investment terms, money in coin, **banknotes**, checking accounts, or other **liquid** forms. (See page 344.) [2] Coins or paper banknotes alone. [3] Paid for without credit.

Cash equivalent: A liquid investment with a nearly constant dollar value (such as a Treasury bill, savings account, certificate of deposit, and so on) that is held in place of **cash**. (See page 344.)

Cash flow: The payments received during a given period.

Cash value life insurance: Life insurance that, in addition to paying benefits in the event of death, accumulates value that the owner can borrow against or can receive by terminating the policy.

CD: Certificate of deposit.

Central bank: A bank, usually created by a government, that's licensed to issue legal tender money, and which usually supervises and lends to the country's commercial banks.

Certificate of deposit: A bank deposit represented by a certificate that is transferable.

CH: The international postal abbreviation for Switzerland (the Confederation of Helvetia); it appears in a Swiss address just before the postal zone number.

Chart: A graph that plots an investment price or economic indicator over a period of time.

Claim account: A financial account representing the right to receive a commodity—as opposed to ownership of the commodity itself. (See page 401.)

Closed-end investment company: A company that invests its stockholders' money in **securities**, and that does not continually issue new shares or **redeem** (buy back) existing shares (as a **mutual fund** does). Its shares are traded in the open market. It is also called a *publicly traded investment fund*.

Collateral: An **asset** that is pledged for a loan, to be sold for the benefit of the lender if repayment is not made.

Collectible: An article valued for its artistic merit, natural beauty, or historical associations. (See page 378.)

Commercial paper: A **marketable**, short-term **debt instrument**, usually for $100,000 or more, of a well-known corporation.

Compound annual gain/return/profit: The average yearly percentage gain achieved by an investment during a specified period of time. This is *not* computed by dividing the total gain by the number of years; the compound annual gain is always smaller than that. The gain "compounds" because it is added each year to the balance—allowing the next year's percentage gain to affect a larger amount. For example, a 20% gain turns $100 into $120 after one year; the next year's 20% gain is applied to $120, making a gain of $24, for a total of $144; and so on. The formula for determining the compound annual return is:

$$R = \left(\frac{E}{B}\right)^{\frac{1}{Y}} - 1 \times 100$$

where R = the annual return (as a percentage), E = the ending value, B = the beginning value, and Y = the number of years involved.

Compounding: The process of reinvesting **interest**, **dividends**, or profits at the same rate of return as they earned—allowing them to multiply, rather than simply add to the result.

Consumer Price Index (CPI): An index constructed from the prices of several hundred products and services sold in the U.S., meant to give an indication of the general level of U.S. consumer prices. The **inflation** rate is derived by measuring changes in the CPI. For example, if inflation is said to be 5.0%, it means that the CPI has risen by 5% from its level 12 months earlier.

Consumption: [1] The use or enjoyment of a product or service as an end in itself, rather than as a means to a further end. [2] The using up of something.

Content: The precious metal in a coin, medallion, or token—usually expressed as a number of troy ounces—and disregarding any other metals contained in the coin.

Contrary Opinion Theory: The belief that investments tend to move in the opposite direction from that expected by public opinion. (See page 199.)

Convertible security: Any **security** that can be exchanged for another security, on fixed terms, upon demand by its holder.

Coupon equivalent yield: The **yield** of a **Treasury bill** expressed as the yield that a **bond** would have to pay in order to provide the same return. If the bond will make a coupon interest payment before the **maturity** of the T-bill, the interest can be compounded to increase the return; thus a bond requires a lower nominal yield than a T-bill in order to provide the same return.

Coupon rate: The annual rate of interest, expressed as a percentage of the **face value**, paid by a **bond**. (See page 353.)

Credit: [1] Borrowed money. [2] On a bank statement, an amount that adds to your balance (as opposed to a **debit**, which is subtracted from your balance).

Creditor: Someone to whom money is owed.

Currency: [1] A brand of **money**, usually created by a government or a **central bank**. [2] **Banknotes** and coins, as opposed to bank deposits.

Current account: [1] A bank account allowing the depositor to withdraw any or all of the funds at any time. (See page 400.) [2] A nation's exports of goods and services minus its.

Custodial account: A **safekeeping account**.

Custodian: An agent, usually a bank, that stores investments.

Custody account: A **safekeeping account**.

Cycle: A pattern of swings and reversals in a trend that recur on a regular time schedule. (See page 136, and see also **Monetary cycles** and **Wave**.)

Dealer: One who is available to buy or sell a given investment, as the customer wishes, usually at quoted prices; unlike a **broker**, he owns the investments he offers to sell.

Debit: On a bank statement, an amount that is subtracted from your balance (as opposed to a **credit**, which adds to your balance).

Debt instrument: A **bill**, note, **mortgage**, debenture, **bond**, or other promise to repay a debt.

Deductive reasoning: Arriving at a conclusion from stated principles, rather than through direct observation.

Default: Failure to keep a promise.

Deferral: See **Tax deferral**.

Deferred annuity: An **annuity** that promises to begin making payments at a future time. (See page 392.)

Defined-benefit plan: A **pension plan** that specifies the size of the pension the beneficiary will receive or a rule for determining it; contributions to the plan are determined by estimates of what is necessary to produce the benefit. (See also **Defined-contribution plan**; neither is applicable to an **IRA**.)

Defined-contribution plan: A **pension plan** that specifies the size of the yearly contributions that must or may be made. (See also **Defined-benefit plan**.)

Deflation: A fall in the general price level—caused by a growth in the **demand for money** that isn't offset by a comparable growth in the **money supply**, or caused by a decline in the supply of money that isn't offset by a decline in the demand for money. Deflations, especially those occurring abruptly, have sometimes been accompanied by stock-market crashes and **depressionary** business conditions. (See also **Inflation**, **Disinflation**, and **Consumer Price Index**.)

Demand deposit: A bank deposit that can be withdrawn without penalty at any time (on demand); money held in a **current account**.

Demand for money: The portion of a person's wealth that he wants to hold in the form of **money**. Or the aggregate of the individual demands for money for an entire population.

Demand loan or **demand note:** A loan or note that is payable whenever the **creditor** demands it. A **call loan**.

Deposit account: A bank account for which there are withdrawal restrictions. Normally, it earns a higher rate of interest than a **current account**.

Depreciation: [1] A loss of value. [2] A system for estimating loss of value over time according to a fixed schedule. [3] A reserve fund that facilitates the replacement of an **asset** when it wears out.

Depression: A prolonged period of declining standards of living.

Designated percentage: The share of a **Permanent Portfolio** assigned to an investment. The annual **portfolio adjustment** will cause some of the investment to be bought or sold in order to restore the investment to this share of the overall portfolio.

Devaluation: A government's dishonoring of its promise to **redeem** its **currency** at a stated rate of exchange, lowering the currency's value in relationship to gold or other currencies. (A devaluation can't occur during a time of **floating exchange rates**, because there is no promise to dishonor when rates are floating.)

Discount: [1] The amount by which an **asset** is priced under its **face value** or **book value**, or under the price of another asset that is comparable in some way. [2] The amount by which a **forward price** is below the **spot price**. [3] The amount by which a coin is priced under the value of its metallic **content**. (See also **Premium**.) [4] (verb) To allow for anticipated events when valuing an investment. It is assumed that the present price of an investment already allows for the possibility of future events that are widely anticipated; thus the market is said to "discount" the future. (See pages 107–108.)

Discount rate: The interest rate charged by a **Federal Reserve Bank** on a loan to a commercial bank.

Discretionary account: An account for which the owner empowers a bank, **broker**, or **advisor** to make the investment decisions.

Disinflation: A slowdown in the rate of **inflation**, without turning into **deflation**. (See also **Consumer Price Index**.)

Diversification: Combining investments that respond differently to economic conditions. (See pages 247–248.)

Dividend: Money or other assets distributed by a company to its **shareholders**, usually out of profits.

Divisibility: The capability of being divided into smaller parts. For example, 100 shares of stock are divisible because the owner can sell 60 shares and keep 40; a gold coin is not divisible because the owner cannot break the coin without changing its character.

Dow-Jones Industrial Average: An index reflecting the prices of 30 **blue-chip stocks**; its changes indicate the direction of the market for stocks of large companies.

Dow Theory: A school of stock-market analysis based on the assumption that the stock market moves in **waves**. (See page 137.)

Dual-purpose investment company: A **closed-end investment company** that issues both (a) income shares, whose owners receive all the net interest and **dividends** earned by the fund, and (b) capital shares, whose owners realize all the net long-term profit from the fund's investments.

Economics: The study of how people use limited **resources** to achieve maximum well-being (whether on a personal, commercial, national, or international scale); the art of making decisions. (See page 74.)

Efficient entry point: For a **speculation**, a buying price just above a level at which there's a logical reason to place a **stop loss**. (See pages 292 and 296–297.)

Elliott Wave Principle: A school of investment analysis that assumes that every investment trend will divide and subdivide into a fixed pattern of **waves**. (See page 138.)

Equity: The current market value of an **investment**, minus all claims against it (from creditors or option holders).

Equity investment: An **investment** that does not promise to pay a specific number of dollars to the investor.

Eurocurrency: A deposit in a bank located outside the country in which the **currency** of the account was issued (such as a U.S. dollar account in a Swiss bank or a Swiss franc account in an English bank).

Exchange control: A government regulation restricting or prohibiting the exporting or importing of **banknotes**, bank deposits, or other monetary instruments.

Exchange rate: The price of one country's **currency** expressed in units of another country's currency.

Exercise price: Striking price.

Exercise value: For a **warrant** or a **call option**, the amount by which the price of the **underlying investment** exceeds the **striking price**. For a **put option**, the amount by which the striking price exceeds the price of the underlying investment.

Face value: [1] The amount promised to a lender at the **maturity** of a **bond**, note, or **bill**. (See page 353.) [2] The **legal tender** value of a coin, **banknote**, or other token.

Family of funds: A group of **mutual funds** under the same general management, usually allowing easy switching by telephone from one fund in the family to another fund in the family.

Fed: The **Federal Reserve System**.

Federal Reserve System: A system of 12 Federal Reserve Banks, supervised by a Board of Governors, that acts as a **central bank** in the U.S., and that sets **reserve** requirements and other regulations for commercial banks.

Fibonacci numbers: Numbers that are in the sequence 1, 1, 2, 3, 5, 8, 13, and so on—in which each number (after the first two) is the sum of the two numbers preceding it. Some investors believe that numbers appearing in this series have special significance for the investment markets. (See page 92.)

Fiduciary account: [1] A **safekeeping** account. [2] At Swiss banks, an account owned by a non-Swiss for which all the investments are made outside of Switzerland.

Fineness: The degree of purity of a bar of **bullion** or a coin, expressed as a decimal fraction. Gold bullion of .995 fineness means that 99.5% of the total weight is pure gold. The stated gold weight of a coin or bar of bullion includes only the weight of the gold or silver, disregarding any base metal (such as copper) and impurities, and thus it isn't usually necessary to know the fineness.

First in, first out: The accounting practice by which the particular units of an investment sold are deemed to be the units bought at the earliest date—so that, for determining taxable gain, the cost of the first unit sold is the price paid for the first unit purchased. (See page 394 for a way to circumvent this assumption, for tax purposes, when selling investments.)

Fixed deposit account: A **time deposit**.

Fixed-rate mortgage: A **mortgage** whose interest rate doesn't change.

Floating exchange rate: An **exchange rate** that is allowed to fluctuate, not influenced by government purchases and sales. A *dirty float* occurs when the government influences the exchange rate through purchases and sales, but does not announce an official, fixed exchange rate; the dirty float has been the exchange rate system used by most governments since 1973.

Foreign exchange rate: See **Exchange rate**.

Forward contract: A contract for delivery of an **asset** in the future at a price determined in the present.

Forward price: The price of an **asset** to be delivered and paid for on a given date in the future. (See also **Spot price**.)

Free market: Any arrangement for voluntary transactions; an absence of government regulation.

Full-recourse mortgage: A **mortgage** agreement making the borrower **liable** for any unpaid balance in the event that a foreclosure sale fails to repay the mortgage in full. (See page 531, and see also **Non-recourse mortgage**.)

Fundamental analysis: A method of investment analysis that considers only those sources of supply and demand that are independent of investment opinions. (See page 98, and see also **Technical analysis**.)

Fundamental value: The value an investment appears to have that's separate from what investors may think of it. (See page 98.)

Fungible: Interchangeable. For example, shares of stock in General Motors are fungible because any one share is a perfect substitute for any other. Fungible storage of, for instance, gold coins is storage in which no distinction is made as to which owner owns which coins. In non-fungible storage (or **segregated storage**), each coin is attributed to a specific owner.

Futures contract: A **forward contract** with standardized specifications, traded on an organized exchange.

Gap: A sudden, drastic change in an investment price, with no transactions at prices in between. A gap most often occurs between one day's closing and the next day's opening. (See page 290.)

Gold content: See **Content**.

Gold exchange standard: A **gold standard** under which only foreign governments and central banks may convert a **currency** into gold.

Gold-silver ratio: The price of gold divided by the price of silver. (See page 185.)

Gold standard: A policy by which a government ties its currency in some way to a fixed quantity of gold. Under the classical gold standard, the government promised to convert every unit of its **currency** into a fixed quantity of gold on demand. (See also **Gold exchange standard**.)

Gram: The basic unit of weight in the metric system. There are 31.1035 grams to a **troy ounce**; 1 gram equals .03215 troy ounce. A kilogram is 1,000 grams or 32.15 troy ounces. A metric ton is 1,000 kilograms, 1,000,000 grams, or 32,151 troy ounces.

Gross national product (GNP): The estimated value of all goods and services produced in a country during a given period of time.

Hard-money investments: Gold and silver, because these metals have served as money that isn't dependent upon the actions of a government. The designation sometimes includes **currencies**, such as the Swiss franc, that have been subjected to less than average **monetary inflation**.

Hedge: An **investment** purchased to offset possible loss in another investment.

High-grade: Involving a minimum of risk.

Human action, theory of: The proposition that every human action is motivated by an individual's desire to increase his well-being, to prevent a decrease in well-being, or to eliminate uneasiness. It is the underlying theory of the **Austrian school of economics.**

Hyperinflation: Runaway inflation.

Ideal portfolio: The **portfolio** an individual would select if all his wealth were in **cash**. (See page 462.)

Illiquidity: For an **investment**, the absence of a market in which the investment can be resold easily without paying a penalty for haste.

In the money: The status of a **call option** or **warrant** when the price of the **underlying investment** is greater than the option's **striking price**. The status of a **put option** when the price of the underlying investment is below the option's striking price.

Income (investment): Dividends or **interest** received from an **investment**.

Indicator (investment): A statistic that is meant to describe the state of an investment or an investment market, or to reveal the future direction of either, or a formula for computing such a statistic.

Individual Retirement Account (IRA): A type of tax-sheltered **pension plan**, not sponsored by an employer, funded by an employee's voluntary contributions.

Inflation: A rise in the general level of consumer prices—caused by a depreciation of the value of **money**, resulting from an increase in the **money supply** that isn't offset by a corresponding increase in the **demand for money.**

Interest: Payments made to compensate a lender for the use of his **capital**.

Intuition: The unconscious processing of information and ideas. (See page 162.)

Investing: The attempt to earn **income** or profit by making your capital available to an investment market. (See pages 169 and 239–240, and see also **Speculating**.)

Investment: An **asset** that is purchased in order to profit from the **income** it provides or from an increase in the asset's price.

Investment analysis: A systematic application of principles and rules in an attempt to derive opinions about investments from information available. (See also **Fundamental analysis** and **Technical analysis**.)

Investment company: A company that places its stockholders' money in other investments (usually in **securities**).

IRA: Individual Retirement Account.

Junk silver coins: U.S. coins (dimes, quarters, and half-dollars) minted prior to 1965 and containing 90% silver, or half-dollars minted 1965 through 1970 and containing 40% silver, and having no **numismatic** value. (See also **Bag**.)

Kaffir: Any South African gold mining company.

Keogh plan: A tax-sheltered **pension plan** for self-employed individuals and partnerships.

Kilogram: See **Gram**.

Kondratieff Wave: A **cycle** of general business conditions in a capitalist economy lasting 47 to 60 years (from one low point to the next low, and from one high point to the next high), as hypothesized by Nikolai Kondratieff. Also called the *Long Wave*. (See page 142.)

Leverage: Any arrangement (such as a **margin** purchase or an **option** contract) that exaggerates the effect of any change in the price of the **underlying investment**. By analogy, **volatility**.

Liability: A financial obligation.

Limit order: An instruction to a **broker** or **dealer** to buy at or below a specified price, or to sell at or above a specified price. It states the maximum price you are willing to pay or the minimum price you are willing to receive. (See page 293.)

Limited partnership: A partnership in which some of the partners (the "limited partners") are not **liable** for the partnership's obligations beyond the amount they have invested.

Liquid asset: An **asset** that can be sold quickly without paying a penalty for haste.

Liquidation: [1] The sale of an **asset**. [2] The closing out or winding down of a company, **annuity**, **pension plan**, or other **investment** or enterprise.

Liquidity: [1] The ability to turn an **asset** into **cash** quickly without a penalty for haste. [2] The relationship of a firm's **liquid assets** to the **liabilities** that might have to be paid in the near future.

Listed option: A **call option** or **put option** that is traded (listed) on an organized exchange.

Load: A sales charge imposed on the purchase of **shares** of a **mutual fund**. (See page 337, and see **Low-load** and **No-load**.)

Long Wave: Kondratieff Wave.

Low-load: A small buying commission, usually 1% or 2%, for a **mutual fund**. (See also **Load**.)

Managed account: Discretionary account.

Margin: [1] The net worth of a **margin account**, sometimes expressed as a percentage of the current **market value** of the **investment**. [2] In a **forward contract** or a **futures contract**, the value of the investor's deposit, sometimes expressed as a percentage of the current **market value** of the investment.

Margin account: An investment account whose **assets** are used as **collateral** to secure a loan. An investor might borrow money against his investments in order to purchase a greater quantity than would be possible on a cash basis, or to raise cash without selling investments.

Margin call: A demand by the lender of a **margin loan** that the borrower repay all or a portion of the loan. A margin call ordinarily is made to reduce the loan balance to no more than a certain fraction of the value of the assets in the **margin account**.

Margin loan: A **call loan** for which an investment is used as **collateral**.

Margin sale: A sale of **assets** to satisfy a **margin call**.

Market: [1] A place where (or an arrangement whereby) investors meet to buy and sell a particular investment. [2] An opportunity to exchange.

Market value The price at which an **asset** can be sold.

Market-maker: A **dealer** in a particular investment who stands ready to buy or sell the investment, as requested by customers.

Maturity: The date on which a contractual obligation (such as repayment of a **bond**) falls due.

Metals account: At a Swiss bank, a **claim account.**

Metric ton: See **Gram.**

Monetary cycles: Periods of rapid growth in an economy's money supply alternating with periods of very slow growth. Monetary cycles may result in alternating periods of inflation and recession. The "**cycles**" do not have a fixed length.

Monetary inflation: An increase in the **money supply.**

Money: Any instrument that is immediately acceptable as a medium of exchange.

Money market fund: A **mutual fund** that invests only in **money market instruments.**

Money market instrument: An easily **marketable** short-term note or **bill** carrying little risk of **default.**

Money supply: All of the money (by whatever definition) held by the public. In practice, several definitions of the money supply (known as M_1, M_2, and so on) are referred to in calculating monetary statistics.

Moratorium: A period during which a debtor (such as a bank, company, or individual) is legally permitted to delay payment of his obligations.

Mortgage: A loan that uses real estate as **collateral.** (See also **Full-recourse mortgage** and **Non-recourse mortgage.**)

Moving average: An investment's average price over a specified period of time. For example, a 5-day moving average is the average price of the investment over the latest 5 market days. An exponential moving average gives greater weight to the more recent prices in the period covered. (See pages 175–176.)

Municipal bond: A **bond** issued by a state or city government, or by an agency of a state or city government.

Mutual fund: A company that invests its shareholders' money in other **investments** (usually **securities**) and agrees to **redeem** (buy back) its shares at **net asset value** upon request of the shareholder. (See pages 334–337.)

Negotiable instrument: A certificate of ownership that can be transferred to a buyer without **registration** with the issuer.

Net assets: Total **assets** minus total **liabilities**.

Net asset value: **Net assets** of an **investment company** divided by the number of shares outstanding.

Net worth: Total **assets** minus total **liabilities**.

Newsletter: A periodical, available through mail subscription only, designed to provide news and advice regarding a specific subject— such as investments.

No-load: With no commission imposed when purchasing a **mutual fund**. (See page 337, and see also **Load** and **Low-load**.)

Non-recourse mortgage: A mortgage for which the borrower bears no further **liability** in the event of a foreclosure. (See page 531, and see also **Full-recourse mortgage**.)

Numismatic coin: A coin that has substantial value in excess of its metallic **content**.

Odd lot: An investment transaction that is smaller than the customary minimum transaction. An odd-lot transaction may be subject to additional charges.

On the money: The condition of a **warrant** or an option (**put** or **call**) when the price of the **underlying investment** is equal to the **striking price**.

Option: See **Call option** and **Put option**.

Ordinary income: Interest, dividends, rents, royalties, income from annuities, and income from employment or a business.

Out of the money: The condition of a **call option** or **warrant** when the price of the **underlying investment** is lower than the **striking price**. The condition of a **put option** when the striking price is lower than the price of the underlying investment.

Over-the-counter market: An investment **market** in which the transactions take place between **dealers** and customers, rather than on an organized exchange.

Paper promise: An **investment**, such as a **security**, that relies for its value on the promise of its issuer to make payments in the future.

Paper money: **Money** in the form of **banknotes** or bank deposits. Normally, the expression refers to money that isn't convertible into gold.

Par: [1] See **Par value**. [2] Equal in value.

Par value: The nominal or **face value** of a **security** or **currency**.

Peak: A price level above any reached during some period of time following.

Pension plan: A legal arrangement for holding investments that allows the income and profits from investments to accumulate tax-free until money is withdrawn from the plan. (See pages 385–386.)

Permanent Portfolio: A **balanced** collection of investments whose structure is meant to remain unchanged from year to year. (See pages 241–242, and see also **Variable Portfolio.**)

Portfolio: A collection of **investments**.

Portfolio adjustment: For a **Permanent Portfolio**, sales and purchases of investments made in order to restore each investment's share of the portfolio to its **designated percentage**. (See page 260.)

Power of attorney: For a bank account, **signature authority**.

Precious metals: For investment purposes, gold, silver, platinum, and palladium.

Premium: [1] The amount by which a **security** is priced above its **face value**, **book value**, or the value of its component parts. [2] The amount by which a **forward price** exceeds the **spot price**. [3] The amount by which the price of a coin exceeds the value of the coin's metallic **content**. [4] The amount by which the price of an **option** exceeds its **exercise value** (colloquially, "premium" often means the entire price of the option). [5] The payment required to keep an insurance policy in force.

Price inflation: An increase in the general price level.

Public market: An investment **market** in which most relevant information is publicly available, and to which any investor has access. (See also **Specialist market.**)

Publicly traded investment fund: A **closed-end investment company**.

Purchasing power: The value of a unit of **money** or other **asset** measured by the goods and services it can purchase. The purchasing power value of an investment normally is calculated by adjusting the investment's price in accordance with changes in the U.S. **Consumer Price Index**.

Purchasing power parity: The **exchange rate** between two **currencies** that causes the general level of merchandise prices to be the same in both countries.

Put option: The right to sell a specified **investment** at a specified price on a specified date or, in some cases, any time prior to a specified date.

Ratio scale: A graphic scale in which any given percentage difference between prices will cover the same vertical distance, no matter at what level it occurs. For example, the physical distance on the graph between 40 and 60 will be the same as between 100 and 150, because both intervals represent an increase of 50%. On a *linear scale*, the physical distance between 100 and 150 (the difference between which is 50) will be $2\frac{1}{2}$ times as great as that between 40 and 60 (the difference between which is 20).

Recession: A period during which the level of economic activity declines.

Recourse mortgage: Full-recourse mortgage.

Redemption: [1] The repurchase of a **security** by its issuer—usually the repurchase of its shares by a **mutual fund** upon request of the shareholder. [2] The conversion of a **currency** into gold or silver by the currency's issuer.

Registered security: A **security** whose ownership is recorded with the issuer.

Repo: Repurchase agreement.

Repurchase agreement: A contract under which an **investment** is sold by one party to another with the stipulation that it be repurchased on a specified date at a specified (higher) price. It is, in effect, a loan of money using the investment as **collateral**, with the difference in the two prices representing the interest.

Reserve: [1] An allocation of **capital** for possible losses or to meet a legal requirement. [2] For a bank, the money available to meet withdrawal requests.

Reserve Bank: One of twelve banks comprising the **Federal Reserve System.**

Resistance level: A price range at which a rising investment should encounter an increased amount of selling—which would likely cause the price rise to slow or halt. (See pages 113–114.)

Resource: Anything—natural, human, or fabricated—that has a value in use or exchange. (See page 73.)

Restrike: A coin that was actually minted after the date marked on the coin, but in every other way is genuine.

Reversal: A change in the direction of a price movement.

Reward-risk ratio: The potential gain for a speculation, divided by the potential loss. (See page 286.)

Risk: The possibility of loss and the extent of the potential loss.

Round lot: The customary minimum size of an investment transaction—100 shares of stock, for example—that incurs no special charges.

Runaway inflation: A rapid increase in prices aggravated by a widespread drop in the **demand for money.**

Safekeeping account: An account by which a bank stores property belonging to the customer. (See pages 400 and 401.)

Secured loan: A loan for which **collateral** is pledged.

Securities and Exchange Commission (SEC): An agency of the U.S. government that regulates issuers of **stocks**, **bonds**, and other **securities**, as well as individuals and companies that sell, manage, or provide advice on securities.

Security: [1] A **stock**, **bond**, or investment contract. [2] **Collateral**. [3] Safety.

Segregated storage: Storage of an asset in such a way that it can be identified as belonging solely to a particular person. (See page 401.)

Selling short: See **Short sale**.

Semi-log scale: Ratio scale.

Short sale: [1] The sale of a **security** or other **asset** an investor has borrowed. The short-seller will have to purchase the asset eventually in order to repay what he has borrowed; thus he profits from a fall in the asset's price. [2] The sale of an asset for future delivery. If the seller does not own the asset now, he is betting that he will be able to buy the asset before the delivery date at a lower price than that at which he has sold it.[1]

Signature authority: The authority given by the owner of a bank account or financial account to another person to transact business for the account.

Soft landing: An end to **price inflation** accompanied by neither a **depression** nor **runaway inflation**.

Specialist market: An investment market in which most relevant information is available only through dealers or other specialists. (See also **Public market**.)

Speculating: An attempt to exceed the gains achievable through **investing**—by careful timing of investments, by selection of individual stocks, or by attempting to outwit the market in any other way. (See pages 169 and 239–240, and see also **Investing**.)

Speculative: In conventional usage, involving more than a minimum of **risk**. (See also **Speculating**.)

Spot price: The price for immediate delivery of an **asset**. (See also **Forward price**.)

Spread: [1] The difference between the **bid price** and the **ask price**.

---

[1]Daniel Drew is reported to have said:
He who sells what isn't his'n
Must make good or go to prison.

[2] A type of **hedge** or **arbitrage** involving the purchase of an **asset** for delivery on one date and the sale of the same asset for delivery on a different date. [3] The simultaneous buying of one commodity or financial instrument and the selling of another, in order to profit from an expected change in the price relationship between the two. Also called a *straddle*. (See page 184.)

Stability: An absence of fluctuations. The opposite of **volatility**.

Stock: An interest in the net income and **net assets** of a corporation.

Stockpile: An existing inventory.

Stop-loss order: An instruction given to a bank or **broker** to sell an investment if the price drops to a stated level. (See page 289.)

Strategy: A plan or program that provides guidelines for achieving a given objective.

Striking price: The price at which the holder of a **call option** or **warrant** may buy an **asset**; also, the price at which the holder of a **put option** may sell an asset. Also known as the *exercise price*.

Superstition: A belief that hasn't been verified, and for which there is no reasonable explanation. (See pages 87–88.)

Supply of money: See **money supply**.

Support level: A price range at which a falling investment should encounter an increased amount of buying—which would likely cause the price decline to slow or halt. (See pages 113–114.)

System (investment): A trading program that generates buy and sell instructions automatically, usually by reading one or more **indicators**. (See page 174.)

Talent: A natural ability—one not acquired through learning or practice. (See page 160.)

Tax credit: A reduction in one's net tax (as contrasted with a *tax deduction*, which reduces one's taxable income).

Tax deferral: The delaying of the date when income will be recognized for tax purposes.

Tax-exempt: Free of taxation. The interest on a **municipal bond** is exempt from federal income tax, while the interest on **Treasury securities** is exempt from state and local taxation.

Tax shelter: An **investment** or arrangement that legally provides **tax deferral** or tax reduction.

T-bills: U.S. Treasury bills. (See **Treasury securities**.)

Technical analysis: A system of investment analysis that considers factors relating to supply and demand only within the investment market without regard for **fundamental values**. (See page 112, and see also **Fundamental analysis**.)

TED spread: An acronym for Treasury-Euro-Dollar spread, it is the difference between yields on 91-day Treasury bills and 91-day Eurodollar deposits. (See page 185.)

Theory of Contrary Opinion: See **Contrary Opinion Theory.**

Time Cycle: See **Cycle.**

Time deposit: A non-transferable bank deposit that is not withdrawable until a fixed date.

Ton, metric: 1,000,000 **grams** or 1,000 kilograms.

Top: Peak.

Track record: Record of performance. For an **advisor**, the gains or losses achieved by actual or hypothetical accounts for which he has chosen the investments.

Transaction costs: Commissions, **spreads** (definition #1), or other costs incurred in buying and selling **investments.**

Treasury securities: Debts that are direct obligations of the U.S. government. They include Treasury **bills** (maturing within one year after they are issued), Treasury notes (maturing between 1 and 10 years after issue), and Treasury **bonds** (maturing more than 10 years after issue). (See page 345.)

Trendline: On a graph, a straight line drawn through two plot points that are believed to be significant (usually **peaks** or **bottoms**); the line is then extended further on the graph. Some practitioners of **technical analysis** believe that the price and time intersections created by this line will have special significance. (See page 127.)

Troy ounce: The unit of weight used to measure gold and silver. One troy ounce equals 1.097 avoirdupois ounces—the weight used in the U.S. for commercial and household purposes.

Trust: An entity created and financed by one person (the grantor) for the benefit, usually, of another person (the **beneficiary**), and controlled by a third person (the **trustee**).

Trustee: The entity, often a bank, who controls a **trust** and is usually empowered to buy and sell investments for the trust.

Underlying investment: The **investment** that can be purchased or sold on specified terms by the holder of an **option, warrant,** or other **convertible security.**

Variable annuity: An **annuity** whose value depends upon the performance of a pool of investments. (See pages 392–393.)

Variable life insurance: An insurance policy, the cash value of which depends upon the performance of a pool of investments. (See page 394.)

Variable Portfolio: A collection of investments that is altered as investment prospects change. It should be funded only with money you can afford to lose. (See pages 241–243, and see also **Permanent Portfolio**.)

Variable-rate mortgage: A **mortgage** whose interest rate is adjusted to current market conditions every 6 months or so.

Volatility: The tendency of an investment's price to fluctuate. The opposite of **stability**.

Volume: The quantity of transactions for an investment or an investment market, usually stated in shares of stock or other investment units.

Walk-away mortgage: Non-recourse mortgage.

Warrant: An option to purchase a share of **stock** at a specified price until a specified date. A warrant differs from a **call option** in that a warrant is issued by the company whose stock is involved. (See page 332.)

Waves: A recurring pattern of swings and reversals in a trend—but which do not occur at regular intervals of time. (See page 136, and see also **Cycle**.)

Yield: An investment's **interest** or **dividend** stated as a percentage of the investment's current **market value**. For example, a bond paying $90 per year interest and selling for $900 has a yield of 10%.

Zero-coupon bond: A **bond** that earns **interest** but does not pay it until **maturity**. A zero-coupon bond accumulates and **compounds** interest, so that all interest earnings are reinvested at the same interest rate that prevailed when the bond was bought. (See pages 358–359.)

C

Permanent Portfolios Suggested Previously

This appendix reviews the Permanent Portfolio suggestions I've made in past writings, summarizes the results flowing from those suggestions, and explains the graph on the top of page 256 (which shows a composite result of the suggestions).

Each portfolio is assumed to have been established eight weeks after the publication date of the book or the newsletter article that announced it.

NEWSLETTER, 1977

The two-portfolio concept was introduced in my newsletter *Harry Browne's Special Reports* in an article dated December 13, 1977.

I didn't use the terms *Permanent Portfolio* and *Variable Portfolio* then. Instead, I suggested that a particular group of investments be held through thick and thin (that is, the Permanent Portfolio), while a specified percentage of the investor's capital be available for short-term trading (that is, the Variable Portfolio).

The performance shown on page 520 doesn't allow for annual portfolio adjustments, because none was suggested in this early presentation.

The newsletter article presented sample allocations for three types of investors. One was for aggressive investors, who might want a large short-term trading budget (Portfolio A below); another for "conservative" investors, who would do less short-term trading (B); and one for "long-term" investors, who would do little or no short-term trading (C). The percentages shown below are the shares allocated to each investment from the "permanent" part of the portfolio.

There are practically no differences among the allocations of investments—since the differences had to do mostly with how much the investor diverted to short-term trading (which isn't relevant here). So I have used the average of the three as a single portfolio in calculating the results shown on page 520.

The figures shown are percentages of the share of the total capital that was to be devoted to the permanent investments.

	A	B	C	Average
Gold	27.3%	28.6%	29.4%	28.4%
Silver	27.3%	28.6%	23.5%	26.5%
Swiss francs	27.3%	28.6%	29.4%	28.4%
Stock market	18.1%	14.2%	17.7%	16.7%
Total	**100.0%**	**100.0%**	**100.0%**	**100.0%**

The portfolios are assumed to have been established on February 10, 1978.

1978 BOOK

The two-portfolio concept had been refined considerably by the time of publication of my book *New Profits from the Monetary Crisis* in October 1978. There the terms *Permanent Portfolio* and *Variable Portfolio* were used much the way they're used in this book.

A "Sample Program" was offered for the Permanent Portfolio (page 335 of the hardcover edition). It devoted a hypothetical $40 to the Permanent Portfolio, including $5 in an "Income Account"—cash holdings from which living expenses could be drawn for the following year. The $40 were allocated as follows:

Gold bullion or coins	30.00%
Swiss francs	22.50%
Stock market	7.50%
Cash	13.75%
Silver bullion or coins	13.75%
Home (equity)	12.50%
Total	100.00%

The Swiss franc budget includes half the Income Account (which was to be split between Swiss francs and U.S. dollars). The Cash budget includes the categories "T-bills or money market fund," "Cash (U.S. banknotes)," "Life insurance (cash value)," and half the Income Account.

The result for this portfolio on page 520 treats the home equity as if it were the total value of the home. This removes the leverage from the calculation, making the real estate gain less dramatic than it might have been in practice.

The result reflects an annual portfolio adjustment, made on the last Friday of each year, to restore the portfolio to its designated percentages—as suggested on page 323 of the hardcover edition of the book.

The portfolio is assumed to have been established on December 1, 1978.

1981 BOOK

Inflation-Proofing Your Investments (written with Terry Coxon) was published in March 1981. It provided a very detailed treatment of the Permanent Portfolio, and it stressed the importance of balance.

However, it did encourage the investor to weight a Permanent Portfolio toward the type of future he expected to see. Six sample portfolios were offered, each one oriented toward an expectation for inflation for the next ten years or so.

On page 516, I've reprinted the table from *Inflation-Proofing* that displays the six sample portfolios and a summary explanation. Figures for long-term dollars are negative if an investor's mortgage outweighs his holdings of long-term Treasury bonds.

In the table's explanation, it is suggested that the silver allocations

SAMPLE PORTFOLIOS FROM "INFLATION-PROOFING YOUR INVESTMENTS"

Item	Level Inflation	Rising Inflation	Runaway Inflation	Soft Landing	Deflation	Uncertain
Gold coins & bullion	25%	35%	50%	20%	20%	30%
Silver bullion	15%	12%	0%	15%	0%	8%
Silver coins	1%	3%	10%	1%	1%	2%
Swiss francs	10%	15%	20%	9%	4%	15%
Stock market investments	15%	10%	5%	25%	5%	15%
Real estate	15%	20%	20%	5%	5%	10%
Cash[1]	—	—	—	—	—	—
Short-term dollars[1]	14%	15%	10%	15%	25%	15%
Long-term dollars	5%	(10%)	(15%)	10%	40%	5%
Miscellaneous[2]	0%	0%	0%	0%	0%	0%
Total	100%	100%	100%	100%	100%	100%

Each of the first 5 portfolios emphasizes an expectation concerning inflation for the next 10 years: *Level inflation*, that inflation will level off at some rate; *Rising inflation*, that inflation will continue to rise in waves as it has for the past 20 years; *Runaway inflation*, that inflation rates will reach 100% or more; *Soft landing*, that inflation will ease gradually down to 0% without an economic crash; and *Deflation*, that there will be a 1929-type deflationary crash. Each of these portfolios emphasizes its expectation but still hedges against other possibilities. The *Uncertain* portfolio assumes no particular expectation regarding inflation.

Silver bullion percentages assume a silver price of $10 per ounce or less. The figures shown should be reduced by 1/3 if the price is between $10 and $15, by 2/3 if the price is between $15 and $20, and eliminated if the price is over $20. If the budget is reduced, the difference should be spread evenly among the other items.

Silver coins are U.S. pre-1965 90% silver coins or 1965-1970 Kennedy half-dollars.

If other foreign currencies are desired, they should be part of the Swiss franc budget.

The stock-market budget is for warrants, dual-purpose investment funds, leveraged stocks, equity in your own business, or interests in business partnerships other than real estate. For the runaway inflation portfolio, only warrants are suggested.

Collectibles and real estate partnerships, if any, should be allocated from the real estate budget.

Long-term dollars include long-term Treasury bonds *minus* long-term fixed-rate debts (such as mortgages). Figures in parentheses are negative (more owed than owned).

[1]Short-term dollars include cash, checking accounts, Treasury bills, money market funds, and floating-rate dollar assets *minus* short-term debts and floating-rate debts. A separate budget should be assigned to cash (including checking accounts and money market funds), but the amount to assign is a consideration of the size of the total portfolio, personal preference, and whether money will be drawn from the portfolio for living expenses.

[2]The miscellaneous budget is for items not otherwise listed—such as gold stocks, foreign stocks, Social Security, etc. While we are not suggesting any of these items, a budget of up to 10% will not distort the emphasis in any of the portfolios.

should be reduced by one third if the price is between $10 and $15. Since the portfolio is assumed to have been created on May 8, 1981, when the price of silver was $11.33, the silver budget is reduced by one third for each portfolio—with the savings distributed equally among the other investments.

The following is an average of the six portfolios on page 516 (after the adjustment in silver holdings just described):

Gold	30.46%
Silver	8.56%
Swiss francs	12.63%
Stocks	12.96%
Real estate	12.06%
Short-term dollars (T-bills)	16.13%
Long-term dollars (T-bonds)	6.30%
Total	100.00%

The results for the portfolios on page 520 assume that the long-term debt incurred interest at the average rate prevailing for conventional mortgages each year. Each portfolio was adjusted on the last Friday of each year, with special adjustments made whenever any investment's Friday price was 30% above or below its level at the time of the preceding adjustment. This procedure was suggested on page 434 of the hardcover edition of *Inflation-Proofing*.

The portfolios are assumed to have been established on May 8, 1981.

NEWSLETTER, 1981

In an article dated September 23, 1981, my newsletter updated and clarified some of the concepts of the Permanent Portfolio that had appeared in the *Inflation-Proofing* book.

As in the book, six sample portfolios were offered—each one corresponding to a particular expectation for inflation. From the rate of inflation prevailing at the time (11%), the investor could choose to weight his portfolio in accordance with an expectation that:

A. Inflation would remain somewhat the same indefinitely (portfolio A on the next page); or

B. Inflation would continue to rise upward in waves, as in the 1970s; or

C. There would be a runaway inflation, with prices rising 100% or more each year; or

D. There would be a soft landing, in which the inflation rate would descend slowly to around 0% without a crash (the actual course inflation took for the following five years); or

E. We would have a deflation—a crash and falling prices; or

F. He could choose an "Uncertain" portfolio that wasn't weighted in any direction.

Here are the sample portfolios given:

	A	B	C	D	E	F
Gold	18%	35%	40%	20%	25%	30%
Silver bullion	16%	15%	6%	16%	9%	10%
Silver coins	2%	2%	11%	2%	6%	2%
Swiss francs	7%	10%	17%	9%	12%	15%
Stocks	25%	5%	3%	21%	5%	10%
Real estate	10%	15%	10%	5%	5%	10%
Cash	1%	0.5%	0.5%	0.5%	1.5%	1%
Treasury bills	10%	14%	9.5%	12%	15%	15%
Treasury bonds	18%	14%	10%	18%	25%	14%
Long-term debts	(7%)	(10.5%)	(7%)	(3.5%)	(3.5%)	(7%)
Totals	100%	100%	100%	100%	100%	100%

The following is an average of the six portfolios:

Gold bullion & coins	28.00%
Silver bullion & coins	16.17%
Swiss francs	11.67%
Stock-market items	11.50%
Real estate	9.17%
Treasury bills & cash	13.42%
Treasury bonds (less debts)	10.08%
Total	100.00%

The results on page 520 are based on the same assumptions I've given for the portfolios drawn from the *Inflation-Proofing* book.

The portfolios are assumed to have been established on November 20, 1981.

ALL PORTFOLIOS

Certain assumptions apply to the computation of results for all the portfolios previously suggested. Where applicable, they also apply to the hypothetical, four-investment portfolios shown in the graphs on pages 253 and 265.

For stock-market investments, I've suggested the use of warrants or dual-purpose funds in every case; the 1981 suggestions included volatile stocks as well. To simplify the calculation of the results for so many different stock and warrant possibilities, the results use the New York Stock Exchange Composite Index as a proxy for all stock-market investments.

Because the NYSE Index generally isn't as volatile as warrants, dual-purpose funds, and volatile stocks, this change gives the portfolio slightly better results during periods when stocks are weak (such as in 1981 and the first half of 1982), and slightly poorer results for periods when stocks were strong (such as from mid-1982 to early 1987).

Since there is no dividend yield published for the NYSE Index, I have arbitrarily assumed a dividend of 4% per year. Although this is a low figure, it is in keeping with the concept of using volatile securities, which traditionally are low-yielding.

The results use the London afternoon fixing for the gold price; an index based on 20-year Treasury bond yields reported by the Federal Reserve for bonds; and daily Handy & Harman prices for silver. The Bank of America daily closing rates are used for the Swiss franc— and, since all sample portfolios suggested using Swiss government bonds for the Swiss franc investment, the results include interest earned on the bonds.

Real estate investments are measured using the Federal Home Loan Bank's price index for single-family homes. Although this result won't match the performance of *your* real estate, this is the only way I know to calculate the effect of real estate prices in general on a portfolio.

For portfolios that include Treasury bills, it's assumed that 1-year bills are purchased on the first day of the calendar year, so that the yield prevailing on the first day of the year is earned throughout the year. Portfolios that include Treasury bonds earn coupon interest rates on their holdings.

Transaction costs of 2% to buy and 2% to sell are assumed for all purchases and sales.

PORTFOLIO RESULTS

Using the foregoing assumptions, I've calculated for each portfolio its average (compound) annual return from the time of its inception through August 28, 1987.

Portfolio Source (and starting date)		Annual Return
1977 Newsletter (2/10/78)		17.5%
1978 Book (12/1/78)		10.9%
1981 Book (5/8/81)		
Level inflation portfolio	7.6%	
Rising inflation portfolio	5.0%	
Runaway inflation portfolio	2.9%	
Soft landing portfolio	9.8%	
Deflation portfolio	11.2%	
Uncertain portfolio	7.7%	
Average portfolio		7.2%
1981 Newsletter (11/20/81)		
Level inflation portfolio	10.9%	
Rising inflation portfolio	6.2%	
Runaway inflation portfolio	5.4%	
Soft landing portfolio	10.6%	
Deflation portfolio	8.8%	
Uncertain portfolio	8.0%	
Average portfolio		8.3%
Composite portfolio		**14.3%**

The composite portfolio provides the results obtained if the latest Permanent Portfolio suggestions from the above sources are used at any given time. Thus it starts with the portfolio from the 1977 newsletter article, switches to the 1978 book portfolio in December 1978, and then switches in May 1981 to the average portfolio from the 1981 book. (The 1981 newsletter portfolio would have produced substantially the same results as the 1981 book portfolio did.)

Because the composite portfolio is derived from all Permanent Portfolio suggestions made in my books or my newsletter, silver's share of the portfolio was reduced from 13.75% to 5.00% at $39.00 on February 6, 1980, in accordance with the suggestions made in my newsletter article "Farewell to Silver," two weeks earlier. The proceeds were divided evenly among all other investments in the portfolio except real estate. (The 1977 newsletter portfolio includes the same silver sale—with repurchases, as suggested in the newsletter, in June and December 1981.)

The composite portfolio benefited by being heavily in precious metals in the late 1970s, and then switching to a more balanced portfolio in 1981. Thus it performed better than the individual portfolios.

The graph on the top of page 256 is derived from the composite portfolio.

Purchasing Power Results

By adjusting the nominal results for the change in the Consumer Price Index during the period in which the portfolio was in effect, we can see how well each portfolio stood up to inflation.

Portfolio Source (and starting date)		Annual Gain in Purchasing Power
1977 Newsletter (2/10/78)		10.4%
1978 Book (12/1/78)		4.4%
1981 Book (5/8/81)		
Level inflation portfolio	3.6%	
Rising inflation portfolio	1.1%	
Runaway inflation portfolio	− 1.0%	
Soft landing portfolio	5.7%	
Deflation portfolio	7.1%	
Uncertain portfolio	3.6%	
Average portfolio		3.2%
1981 Newsletter (11/20/81)		
Level inflation portfolio	7.2%	
Rising inflation portfolio	2.7%	
Runaway inflation portfolio	1.9%	
Soft landing portfolio	6.9%	
Deflation portfolio	5.2%	
Uncertain portfolio	4.4%	
Average portfolio		4.7%
Composite portfolio		**7.4%**

D

Zero-Coupon Treasury Bonds

This appendix explains how zero-coupon Treasury bonds are created, what costs are involved, and how they're treated for tax purposes.

The U.S. Treasury doesn't issue zero-coupon bonds, even though there's a demand for them. To satisfy that demand, brokerage firms have created zero-coupon bonds by buying U.S. Treasury bonds and separating the coupons from the bond certificates.

For example, suppose a broker buys a Treasury bond with a face value of $1,000, paying 10% interest and maturing in 20 years. The bond will include 40 interest coupons—one for each half-year between now and the maturity date. Each interest coupon will be worth $50 (one half of 10% of $1,000) on its payment date.

If its coupons are taken away, the body of the bond becomes a zero-coupon bond, entitling its owner to a single payment of $1,000 in 20 years. If the interest yield on long-term Treasury bonds is, say, 10%, the market price of the stripped bond today will be about $142.05.[1]

In addition to the body of the bond, the broker also can sell each

---

[1]Appendix F on page 534 explains the concept of *present value*, which creates a market price for the bond of $142.05.

of the 40 semiannual coupons. When separated from the bond, each coupon becomes a mini-zero-coupon bond with a face value (or single-payment principal amount) of $50.

A given coupon's market price will depend on how far away its payment date is. With a current interest rate of 10%, a $50 coupon due in one year would sell today for about $45.35. A $50 coupon due in 20 years would sell for about $7.10.

If the broker buys 20 $1,000 bonds, he can sell:

1. Twenty $1,000 zero-coupon bonds payable in 20 years; plus

2. A single $1,000 zero-coupon bond maturing in each 6-month period during the next 20 years. These bonds are created by combining the 20 coupons worth $50 each that are due on each coupon date.

Many stockbrokers have done this—purchasing Treasury bonds, stripping the coupons from the bonds, and selling each of the bonds and each of the coupons as separate single-payment zero-coupon bonds.

Some brokers have created investment trusts that purchase Treasury bonds. They then sell trust certificates, or *receipts*, to their customers—each certificate representing a share in the principal or interest payment to be received from the U.S. Treasury for a given date. As far as the customer is concerned, he's buying a single-payment zero-coupon bond.

Most well-known retail stockbrokers have created their own brands of zero-coupon Treasury bonds. In each case, the broker acts as a dealer—selling his own products and standing ready to rebuy them from you. However, no quoted buying and selling prices are published anywhere, so it's difficult to judge the prices being offered to you or to estimate the market value of your holdings.

STRIPS

The Federal Reserve's "book-entry" system serves as a registrar and transfer agent for Treasury securities, so that a bond owner can receive his payments directly from the government without any concern for a middleman.

In January 1985, the U.S. Treasury and the Federal Reserve System began a service, called Separate Trading of Registered Interest and Principal of Securities (STRIPS), which expands the book-entry system. Now a bond's principal and each of its coupons can have a separate registered owner. Thus each coupon, as well as the body of the bond, can be a single-payment, zero-coupon bond.

So, with STRIPS, you can buy an individual coupon (in effect, a zero-coupon bond) and have your ownership registered with the Federal Reserve System—which allows you to invest in zero-coupon bonds without relying on any broker's promise to pay.

Most brokers will handle STRIPS. However, when this service began, the normal trading unit was $1 million maturity value. For 30-year bonds at 9% (the rate prevailing in mid-1987), that meant a market value of about $71,300. For 10-year bonds, the market value would be about $415,000. But the market apparently is becoming more liquid and the "round lot" size is dropping.

If you're interested in buying zero-coupon bonds and you want to use the STRIPS system, you can ask a broker whether he's willing to register the bond in the STRIPS system in your name. Don't expect an enthusiastic reply.

TAX CONSEQUENCES

There are no tax advantages for an investor in zero-coupon bonds.

Even though you receive no money until the bond matures, you're liable each year for income tax on the interest being accumulated. Thus, as with conventional bonds, zero-coupons are best kept in an IRA, Keogh plan, or other tax-deferred account.

TRANSACTION COSTS

Most sales material for zero-coupon bonds concentrates on the small investment required to tie down a large payment far off in the future. Very little mention is made of transaction costs.

If transaction costs are discussed at all, only commissions are mentioned. And, with zero-coupon bonds, commission rates can be misleading.

A broker may suggest that the commission on a zero-coupon bond is small, by quoting it as a percentage of the *face value* of the bond. But the commission for any other bond would be expressed as a percentage of the sales price. And for a zero-coupon bond with a large discount, the difference can be considerable. A commission that's only 1% or less of the face value might be over 8% of the bond's market price—which is extraordinary for a bond transaction.

Spreads

Some brokers sell zero-coupon bonds "net" (meaning with no commissions), but there is a *spread*—the difference between the price at which you can buy and the price at which you can sell the same bond.

The spread is probably the most overlooked cost in any investment. Very rarely does a published analysis of investment costs even refer to it; usually, commissions are treated as if they were the only transaction costs.

When you buy an investment through a stock or commodity exchange, there generally is no spread. Your broker gives your order to a floor trader—someone working on the floor of the exchange—who finds a floor trader representing a seller, and a deal is struck. The cost of the floor trader's service is included in the commission you pay your broker.

When the market is quiet, there may not be a supply of ready buyers and sellers. In that case, a floor trader who is also trading for his own account will act as a "market-maker" by offering to sell at a price a little above the price of the last actual trade; and he or another floor trader will offer to buy at a price a little below the price of the last actual trade.

The difference between this "bid" price (the price at which someone offers to buy from you) and the "ask" price (the price at which someone offers to sell to you) is the spread. Even then, spreads generally are very small for investments traded on an exchange.

In dealer markets, however, the spread is all-important. A dealer market is one in which individual investors do not trade with each other—not even through floor traders acting as representatives. The investors buy from dealers and sell to dealers. The dealer maintains an inventory of the investment, offering to buy and to sell at two different prices. He makes his living from the spread between the two prices.

When you buy, you're normally interested only in the price at which you can buy, so you don't notice the spread. But if you resold the investment an hour later, you would become very aware of the spread.

The spread can be small—$1\frac{1}{2}\%$ or less in the case of conventional U.S. Treasury bonds, which trade in high volume and at fairly stable prices. Or the spread can be substantial—5% to 10% in the case of over-the-counter stocks that are traded infrequently. Or the spread can be gigantic—25% to 50%, as is the case with many collectibles.

Zero-Coupon Spreads

Many brokers don't charge commissions on zero-coupon bonds. They act as dealers and try to profit from the spread between the bid and ask price. Even if a commission is quoted, there still will be a spread of some size.

How big is the spread with zero-coupon Treasury bonds? Unfortunately, very few people have any idea.

Most zero-coupon bonds are bought for retirement accounts and are meant to be kept for many years. Although the brokers make markets in these products, the market is almost entirely one-way. Investors buy and the dealers sell; rarely does an investor sell to a dealer.

Consequently, the question of the spread seldom arises. Your broker can quickly provide a price at which you can buy. But to get a price at which you can sell, he'll have to call the home office. He may even have to make several calls before he finds someone who can quote a price.

So no one can tell you offhand how big the spread is. When I investigated the matter by pushing for the necessary information at several brokerage firms, I came to the conclusion that the spreads for most zeros are in the area of 4% to 7%—which is substantial.

The principal reason for the large spread on zero-coupon bonds is their volatility. The greater the volatility of an investment, the greater the chance that a dealer would have to sell a bond at a price below the price at which he bought it. The only safeguard against that possibility is to enlarge the spread.

In the same way, spreads in other markets become larger during times when the price is very volatile.

The size of the spread also results, in part, from lack of awareness by a zero-coupon investor that the spread exists at all. He doesn't consider the spread until he tries to sell—and, even then, he may not be aware that the price at which he's told he can sell is considerably below the price at which he could buy on that day.

Even if he *is* aware of the spread then, he has no choice but to sell to the broker from whom he bought the bond. So the broker has no incentive to reduce the spread.

BUYING ZEROS

If you want to buy zero-coupon Treasury bonds, ask a broker to provide buying and selling prices for the maturity and investment amount you want. Ask whether there are any other costs—commissions, annual fees, etc. Ask for similar figures for conventional Treasury bonds of similar maturity and investment size.

Compare the two. Most likely, you'll find that any increased volatility provided by zero-coupon bonds is offset by expensive transaction costs.

E

Changes in the
Tax Code Affecting
Real Estate

This appendix summarizes the 1986 changes in the Internal Revenue Service Code that affect real estate as an investment.

We'll begin by looking at the special benefits real estate enjoyed *before* the tax law changes were enacted in 1986.

1. Depreciation Expense

For the owner of any kind of building that could produce income, the most valuable feature of the tax code was the depreciation expense he could deduct yearly from his taxable income.

With almost any other investment, the purchase price has no tax significance until you sell. But the tax rules allow you to start deducting the purchase price of a building as soon as you buy it.

Under the depreciation rules, you can deduct a portion of the purchase price each year, according to a fixed schedule, until those deductions add up to your original cost (unless you sell the property first).

The original purpose of the depreciation deduction was to take into account the gradual physical deterioration that afflicts any building. The gradual wearing out of a building is a cost borne by a landlord, and must be recognized each year to measure *net* rental income accurately.

The particulars of the depreciation rules have been changed frequently. At times it has been possible to deduct as much as 9% of the cost of a building in the first year of ownership, and to deduct the entire cost within 18 years. During all recent years, the depreciation recognized by the tax rules was far more rapid than the actual rate of deterioration for most buildings.

Rapid depreciation deductions are an important tax advantage for real estate. And the benefit could be enhanced by buying with a mortgage.

Under the old tax rules, no matter how small the actual cash investment in the property, the full depreciation allowance was available. Thus, within a few years after buying the property, you might be able to deduct depreciation expenses equal to twice your down payment. If you were in the 50% tax bracket, the tax savings alone could return your cash investment to you.

Because the depreciation deduction allows you to recover some of your investment (through tax savings) even before you sell the property, it probably has been real estate's most significant advantage over other investments.

2. Ordinary Expense vs. Capital Gain

When a building is sold, the purchase price for tax purposes (the "cost basis") is reduced by the amount of the depreciation deductions that have been taken. Lowering the cost basis increases the size of the profit upon which you pay tax.

But under the old tax rules, the depreciation deductions reduced your ordinary taxable income on a dollar-for-dollar basis—while, in most cases, each dollar of profit, being treated as a capital gain, added only 40 cents to your taxable income.

Thus depreciation expenses could reduce your taxable income $2\frac{1}{2}$ times more powerfully than it added to taxable income at the time of the sale.[1]

---

[1]To qualify as a long-term capital gain, a property must be held longer than 6 months. There have been times during the last couple of decades when the qualifying period has been one year, and the taxable profit has been 50 cents per dollar rather than 40 cents.

3. Interest Payments During Inflation

Real estate prices—like all prices—are usually pushed upward by inflation. Interest rates also rise, as a general rule, during an inflationary period.

Of course, the relationship isn't precise. But if inflation is running at, say, 10% per year, there will be pressure on real estate prices to rise, and mortgage interest rates aren't likely to be less than 10% for very long.

If you buy real estate with a mortgage, the high interest costs and the price appreciation seem to offset one another. But the price appreciation of the property won't be taxed until the property is sold, while the interest payment is a deduction from this year's taxable income.

In addition, under the old rules, the interest could be deducted dollar-for-dollar, while each dollar of profit might add only 40 cents to the investor's taxable income.[2]

4. High Tax Rates

The value of any tax shelter depends on the severity of the tax rates. The higher the rates, the more valuable the deductions generated by the shelter.

The maximum tax rate on personal income was 70% until 1981, when it was lowered to 50%. From then on, every dollar of real estate deductions was worth 50 cents in after-tax income.

It's not surprising that many investors found real estate more attractive than stocks, bonds, or gold—which generated no current tax deductions.

5. Leverage in an Inflation

Even when real estate appreciates no faster than prices in general, the return to an investor can be better than the overall inflation rate suggests.

When a property is bought with a mortgage, any increase in price

---

[2]The other side of the coin is that the interest payments have to be made each year, while the price appreciation isn't collected until the property is sold.

will represent a larger percentage of the actual cash investment than of the total purchase price. If you buy a $100,000 house with a $20,000 down payment, a 10% (or $10,000) increase in price is a 50% gain on the money invested.

Of course, you also can buy other investments with borrowed money (margin buying), but there are two significant differences.

The interest rate on a margin loan rises if inflation (or any other factor) forces market interest rates upward. But the interest cost of a fixed-rate mortgage never changes, no matter what happens to market rates.

And while a margin lender can demand repayment at any time, a mortgage lender can't demand immediate payment (or even ask for more margin), so long as you keep up the monthly payments.

Thus many investors who would never dream of buying stocks or gold on margin felt quite comfortable buying real estate with a mortgage.

However, buying with a mortgage during inflation doesn't assure you of a profit. If you buy after inflation has become obvious to lenders, the interest rate may be high enough to eat up the property's price appreciation. The best results occur when you finance a purchase with a fixed-rate mortgage *before* the inflation rate rises.

6. Limited Risk

In many cases, the benefits of real estate could be obtained without incurring comparable risks.

If you purchase a property with a "full-recourse" mortgage, you are risking the entire purchase price—not just the down payment. If there's a foreclosure, and the lender can't collect the full loan balance by selling the property in the open market, you owe the difference.

With a "non-recourse" mortgage, if the price obtained at a foreclosure sale is less than the unpaid mortgage balance, the lender loses the difference. You owe nothing.

In some states, such as California and Florida, non-recourse mortgages are the only residential mortgages legally enforceable. In other states, a lender and a borrower might negotiate a non-recourse provision.

With a non-recourse mortgage, it was possible to claim depreciation write-offs that exceeded the amount of money you had at risk. Although many people wouldn't walk away from a mortgage unless they were on the verge of bankruptcy, knowing there was an emergency exit decreased the sense of risk and made a large debt seem acceptable.[3]

TAX CHANGES

The 1986 changes in the tax code eliminated most of real estate's value as a tax shelter. Here is how the six advantages were affected:

1. *Depreciation deductions:* The two most significant changes occurred in this area.

First, tax deductions now are limited to what you have actually spent plus any debts for which you're personally liable.

If you buy with a non-recourse mortgage, you have no further liability, so you can deduct only what you've actually paid out. That generally includes just the down payment, the cost of any improvements, and any net cash paid to operate the property. Deductions no longer can outrun your outlay—which eliminates the possibility of profiting from tax savings alone.

If you buy with a full-recourse mortgage, this change in the tax law won't prevent you from deducting expenses you haven't actually paid.

But the second major change affects you in any case. It limits the net real estate loss that can be applied to offset current taxable income.

If your total real estate deductions (depreciation, interest, maintenance, and so on) exceed the income (if any) from your property, you have a net loss. The old rules allowed you to deduct this loss, no matter how great, from your other taxable income—salary, investments, and so forth.

Now there is a ceiling of $25,000 per year on the use of real estate losses to offset other income. The limit embraces all your investment properties; it isn't $25,000 per property.

Worse yet, if your losses exceed the $25,000 limit, you can't use the excess to reduce next year's taxable income. The excess is useless for tax purposes until you finally sell a property. At that point, any undeducted losses pertaining to that property are considered to be part of the cost when computing your gain or loss on the property.

These two changes put an end to real estate's most potent tax-shelter advantages.

(Interest paid on mortgages on your residence and one vacation home are exempt from this provision.)

---

[3]In a foreclosure, you would have to add back into your taxable income the depreciation expenses you had deducted.

2. *Ordinary vs. capital gain rates:* The 1986 tax law changed the special treatment for capital gains. Now every dollar of profit adds one dollar to your taxable income.

A capital gain's only remaining distinction is that, unlike ordinary income, you can use capital losses from other investments to reduce or nullify a capital gain, with no limits.

3. *Interest payments:* You now can deduct interest payments without limit only for the mortgages on your residence and one vacation home. On other properties, interest deductions are restricted by the $25,000-per-year limit on deductions described under point #1 on the preceding page.

And, with some modest exceptions, the new rules limit interest deductions on your residence to debt equaling what you paid for your home and the improvements you put into it.

4. *High tax rates:* The reduction of the top rate to 28% from 50% will have a profound effect on real estate and on other tax shelters. The lower tax rates reduce the need for a tax shelter, thereby making real estate's remaining tax deductions less valuable.[4]

5. *Leverage:* It is still possible to leverage your profit by buying with a mortgage.

6. *Small risk:* A non-recourse mortgage still limits the risk. But now, as described for point #1, such a mortgage limits the tax advantages as well.

---

[4]There is a 33% bracket, but it applies to only a limited portion of one's income—adding only $4,959.50 in tax to a joint return, no matter how large the income.

F

The Methodology of Fundamental Analysis

This appendix explains the concept of *fundamental value*—the value an investment appears to have that's separate from what investors may think of it.

In the simplest cases, determining fundamental value is merely a matter of arithmetic. But other cases depend heavily on the personal judgment of the investment analyst.

PRESENT VALUE

We'll begin by looking at the mathematical element—which involves the calculation of *present value*.

The present value of money you will receive in the future is the amount that would have to be invested today—at today's interest rates—to grow to the sum to be paid on the delivery date.

For example, if the current market interest rate is 10%, an IOU that will pay $275 in one year has a present value of $250—because $250 invested at 10% will earn $25 interest, and thus grow to $275 in one year.

If a fundamental analyst came across an IOU selling for $900—one that would pay $1,000 one year from today with no chance of default—he'd decide whether it was a good investment by determining the present value of $1 to be paid one year from now.

He'd identify the present value by looking at the prices being paid for other 1-year, guaranteed IOUs. If he found that they could be bought now at a 20% discount from face value, he'd say that the present value of $1 to be paid one year from now is $.80—and that the $1,000 IOU is worth only $800.

But if he found that 1-year, first-class IOUs were trading at a discount of only 5%, he'd say that the present value of $1 to be paid one year from now is $.95, and that the $1,000 IOU has a fundamental value of $950—making it a bargain at $900.

The fundamental analyst is aware that investor sentiment might push the market price of the IOU higher or lower during the next 12 months, but he treats those possibilities as random events that are impossible to forecast.

He also would consider them unimportant, because in 12 months the fundamental value will assert itself, and the investment will be redeemed for $1,000—no matter what anyone thinks about IOUs, no matter what "trendlines" show up on a graph of IOUs, and even though 900 isn't a Fibonacci number.

BOND VALUES

A bond provides an easy example of the use of the present value concept to evaluate an investment.

A bond's fundamental value comes from the payments a bondholder expects to receive. The value is the sum of the present values of each coupon interest payment the bond has yet to pay, plus the present value of the bond's face amount—which will be paid on the maturity date.

Each of those present values depends upon the current interest rate —the yield—that can be earned on bonds of similar risk and similar periods to maturity. With that interest rate, you can calculate the present values of the interest payments and of the face value—and determine the present value of the bond.

Default Risk

So far, fundamental analysis seems to require only a calculator and a copy of *The Wall Street Journal*. But there's more to it than just arithmetic.

A U.S. Treasury security is assumed to be free of any risk of default, and thus is what I earlier called a guaranteed or first-class IOU. So a fundamental analyst can determine the value of a Treasury security by reference to the current interest yield on Treasury securities of similar maturities. With that, he can calculate the security's fundamental value.

But bonds of municipal governments, foreign governments, and corporations are more difficult to handle. The estimate of fundamental value must allow for the risk that the payments promised by the bond won't actually be made, or won't be made on time.

The greater the risk that a payment won't be made, the lower the payment's present value—which is another way of saying that the interest rates on bonds believed to be risky generally are higher.

So, to evaluate a bond, the fundamental analyst must first judge the risk of default, and then determine the interest rate that can be earned on bonds with similar risk. Then he can use that interest rate to calculate the present value of the payments the bond promises.

Value Will Out

If a fundamental analyst identifies a bond that's priced below his opinion of its fundamental value, he'll purchase it. After the purchase, he may hope that others in the market will soon come to share his appraisal—since that would push the price up and provide a quick capital gain.

But he doesn't base his decision to buy on that hope, and he won't hold his breath waiting for others to come around to his way of thinking. Even if no one ever agrees with his judgment, he'll be rewarded for being right by earning an unusually high yield on his bargain-priced bond.

VARIABLE INVESTMENTS

Appraising a bond's risk is the beginning of the element of judgment in a fundamental analyst's work.

The analysis of equity securities, commodities, and currencies—because they don't involve regular, fixed payments—is more complicated and more subjective.

We'll take a brief look at what fundamental value means for each of these investments, and at how analysts attempt to estimate it.

Common Stocks

A common stock's fundamental value comes from the dividends that an analyst expects it to pay in the near or distant future. So the first step in determining a stock's fundamental value is to forecast its dividends.

Next, the analyst must decide on the interest rate that properly reflects the uncertainty of his forecast, and then use that interest rate to calculate the present value of the anticipated dividend payments. The result is the stock's fundamental value—as one analyst sees it.

Even a stock that isn't paying a dividend has some fundamental value—because of the possibility that someday it will pay one.

(If it seems that dividends aren't everything, imagine a company whose management announced that all earnings would be reinvested in the company *forever*, no dividends would ever be paid, and the company would never be sold to another company. Since no stockholder would ever receive any income from his stock, the stock would have almost no value—only the value that represents the possibility that the management might someday change its mind.)

Although a stock's fundamental value depends on prospective dividends, in practice the analyst will focus on other things—especially the company's anticipated earnings (profits). Earnings are an indication of the dividends that eventually will be paid, since each dollar of earnings will be paid out soon as dividends, or will be reinvested in the company's business to enhance the prospects for future earnings and dividends.

To estimate future earnings, an analyst might judge—among other things—past rates of earnings growth, comparisons of earnings with sales, various ratios of costs to revenues and revenues to capital, the future demand for the company's products, the strength of the competition, and the ability of the company's management. Needless to say, many of these judgments are conjecture.

An analyst may also look at the company's assets. Its net assets (after subtracting its debts) are an indication of the resources available for generating profits, and of the amount the stockholders would receive if the company were liquidated or sold to another company.

Every analyst lights upon his own favorite formulas for appraising a company's long-term profitability and dividend-paying power.

As with the bond analyst, the stock analyst doesn't rely on the hope that the rest of the world will come around to his way of thinking. If his judgment is correct, he'll earn exceptionally large dividends on his investment eventually—no matter how others value the stock.

But, as a bonus, the larger and larger dividends will cause yield-conscious investors to pay higher and higher stock prices just to obtain the dividends—producing a capital gain in the stock.

Commodities

A commodity generates a payment only when the owner sells it. So an analyst considers its fundamental value to be the discounted present value of the price at which he believes he'll be able to sell it in the future.

This means he has to make a forecast of its price. But the fundamental analyst doesn't try to anticipate the actions of other investors in making his forecast. Instead, he bases his forecast on the supply he expects to come from producers of the commodity and the demand he expects from users of the commodity.

Neither supply nor demand is easy to estimate. The supply might come from anywhere in the world or be disrupted by events anywhere in the world. And the plans of producers will be affected by expectations of future prices. Consumption will be affected by changes in consumers' income and tastes, by changes in technology, and by changes in the prices of substitute commodities.

As with an analyst of stocks and bonds, a fundamental analyst in the commodities market isn't banking on other investors eventually getting excited about the commodity he's bought. He's counting on the users and producers of the commodity to cause the price to change.

If he expects the price to rise, it's because he judges that consumption is outrunning production—or that it soon will. When the resulting shortage appears, users of the commodity can be counted on to bid the price up.

If he expects the price to fall, it's because consumption is below production—or he believes it soon will be. So he anticipates a time when all the customary stockpilers of the commodity will be out of cash or out of warehouse space, and producers will have to dispose of the surplus by trying to undersell one another.

It doesn't matter whether the analyst trades in the cash market or the futures market; the actions of producers and consumers will be felt in both markets.

A commodity differs from stocks and bonds in that it doesn't pay interest or dividends. So there's no income to console the analyst while he waits. This means that time is of the essence, and his forecast of a commodity's price has to include an estimate of the time when the price will be reached.

A time estimate also is required in order to determine the discounted present value of the expected price. Only by calculating the present value can the analyst decide whether the anticipated price rise is worth betting on.

Gold

Gold represents a special case. Gold's fundamental function is as money. The "consumers" of gold are people who hold it in place of currencies as a store of value (not necessarily because they expect it to rise in price).

The demand for gold as money depends on many factors, but the most important is the degree to which currencies—especially the U.S. dollar—appear to be losing value to inflation.

So a forecast for gold is preceded by a forecast for inflation. But, even with an inflation forecast in hand, there's no reliable ratio between a given inflation rate and a price for gold.

So an analyst can only guess at a future gold price. He then needs to decide on an interest rate that reflects the uncertainty of his forecast, so as to calculate a present value for gold. With this, he can decide whether gold is a bargain fundamentally at today's prices.[1]

Currencies

The fundamental value of a foreign currency, like that of a commodity, is the discounted present value of what the analyst expects its price to

---

[1] The relationship between gold and inflation is discussed further on pages 314–317.

be in the future. If a currency investment generates interest, the analyst will add the present value of those future payments.

The analyst isn't concerned with what investors will think of the currency. His concern is with the supply generated by the government that issues it, and the demand by foreign users who will need the currency in order to buy the country's products.

There are numerous fundamental systems for forecasting currency prices, but the most popular revolve around the Purchasing Power Parity (PPP) theory. That theory maintains that the exchange rate between two countries will gravitate toward the level at which the products traded between them will have roughly the same price in each country (as translated by the exchange rate).

However, there's no unequivocal way of calculating that level. So every currency analyst has a favorite method.

COMPONENTS OF VALUE

The fundamental value of any investment has three components:

1. Payments to be received in the future (whether interest, dividends, repayment of principal, or the proceeds of a sale).

2. The basic interest rate that can be earned without risk of default (the yield the invested capital could be earning elsewhere).

3. A premium added to the basic interest rate—reflecting the risk that the payment will be less than expected or won't be made at all (the uncertainty of the future price or the possibility of default).

If you thought the price of silver would be $10.00 one year from now, $10.00 would be component #1. If you could earn 7% safely on your money elsewhere, 7% would be component #2.

These two components seem to imply a present value of $9.35. You wouldn't pay more than $9.35 per ounce, because $9.35 would grow to $10.00 in one year if left in Treasury bills or in a bank account.

But although you expect the price of silver to be $10.00 in one year, you can't be certain of it. It could turn out to be much less. So component #3 adds a premium of, say, 10% to the interest rate to reflect the degree of uncertainty that surrounds the price of silver. This produces a 17% interest rate, according to which silver would have a present value of $8.55.

Please understand that this is a hypothetical example.

G

Permanent Portfolio Alterations for Non-Americans

The suggestions in this book are made with American readers in mind. If you live outside the United States, some of the suggestions I've made for the Permanent Portfolio can be changed. Whether you should use U.S. investments or use investments of the country in which you live depends on how stable and useful you consider the investment markets in the country where you live.

If you are an American living abroad and you expect to return to the U.S. to live within the next few years, it isn't necessary to make any changes from the suggestions I've made. If you don't know when or whether you will return to the U.S., consider making the changes.

The purpose of Treasury bills in the portfolio is to provide stable purchasing power through a default-proof investment in the currency you rely on. So, for U.S. Treasury bills, you can substitute the equivalent investment in the country in which you live. That can be bills, notes, or bonds issued by the government and maturing within one year.

The long-term bonds can be bonds of the government of the country in which you live, so that you will have protection if there's a deflation in your country. Use the longest maturity available.

Stock-market investments are meant to provide profit when your country is prosperous and inflation is low. So, in general, you should buy stocks of companies in your country.

However, you might prefer to use American stock-market investments instead. Usually, the stock markets of the world move upward or downward together. And the U.S. securities markets offer a greater number of alternatives—including such things as warrants and specialized mutual funds.

The decision may depend upon how adequately you believe you can cover yourself with stock investments of your own country. One possibility is to split the stock-market budget between investments of your country and the United States.

There is no reason to alter the suggestions I've made for gold, no matter where you live.

H

Swiss Bank Liquidity Rating Formula

On page 411, the liquidity status of 38 banks is shown.

A bank's liquidity percentage is computed by comparing its liquid assets (assets that can be turned to cash immediately) with its current liabilities (liabilities that might have to be paid on short notice).

The assets I count as liquid are: cash on hand; demand deposits at other banks; bills of exchange; money market paper; and current (demand) loans that are secured by collateral held within the bank (such as margin loans on securities or precious metals). Securities owned by the bank are included as liquid assets, but only to the extent of 50% of their value.

The liabilities I count as current are: amounts owed to other banks or depositors on demand; time deposits due to banks or customers within 30 days; 15% of savings and deposit accounts; acceptances and promissory notes; and "miscellaneous liabilities."

A rating of 100% indicates that the bank has liquid assets equal to all liabilities that might require quick payment. A rating of over 100% indicates that the bank has more than enough liquid assets to cover all potential requests for payment. And a rating of less than 100% indicates that the bank would have to draw on non-liquid assets to cover a portion of its current liabilities.

JUDGING A BANK

A high liquidity rating isn't an absolute guarantee against bank failure. A bank with dishonest management can fail even when its balance sheet shows high liquidity.

Nor is the liquidity percentage the only standard by which you should judge whether to deal with a bank. Other considerations are the types of investments the bank will handle and the quality of service the bank can give you (including the bank's ability to communicate with you in your native language).

Unfortunately, it's difficult to measure most of these factors. A bank may express a willingness to handle the types of transactions you're interested in, but you won't know whether the service is satisfactory until you've dealt with the bank for a while. And, unless there's a public scandal, there's no way you'll ever know how honest the officers are.

Liquidity is the one consideration that can be measured, and it is very important. A bank may survive very well during normal times. But during a deflation or other panic, the bank may not have the liquid resources with which to pay all the customers who are trying to withdraw their funds. In such a situation, a bank can be brought down even if it's solvent. You might then have to wait weeks or years for your money.

As I've said elsewhere in this book, I wouldn't deal with a bank simply because I was told it had a "good reputation." It is the weakest banks that will go to the most trouble to protect their reputations—since reputation is the only thing that keeps them going.

If you want to know that you'll get your money back when you ask for it, visible liquidity is a greater assurance than a 300-year record of financial soundness.

INDEX

The Author

Harry Browne is an investment advisor, the author of seven books, a newsletter writer, and a public speaker.

He was born in New York City in 1933, but grew up in Los Angeles. He has since lived in Vancouver, Canada, and Zürich, Switzerland. He now resides in Northern California with his wife, Pamela.

His first book was *How You Can Profit from the Coming Devaluation* (1970). His most popular books have been *You Can Profit from a Monetary Crisis* (1974), which was #1 on the *New York Times* best-seller list, and *How I Found Freedom in an Unfree World* (1973), a non-investment book that continues to be in demand today.

In addition, he has written *The Complete Guide to Swiss Banks* (1976), *New Profits from the Monetary Crisis* (1978), *Inflation-Proofing Your Investments* (1981, with Terry Coxon), and *Investment Rule #1* (1985).

Since 1974, he has been writing *Harry Browne's Special Reports*, a financial newsletter published eight to ten times yearly.

Among his other interests are classical music, opera, German operetta, good food, wine, sports, television, fiction, and his 14-year-old dog, Tobi.